Preface

In a leafy glade in Kensington Gardens, Long Water, there is a delicate bronze statue of a boy playing a pipe. Erected by James Matthew Barrie, the statue marks the spot where the seven-day-old Peter Pan landed after he first flew out of his bedroom window and "escaped from being a human." This moment, described in the author's novel "The Little White Bird" published in 1902, introduced Peter Pan as the boy who never grew up. There was another boy called Peter who never grew up and I have dedicated this book to his memory.

Conceived in the decade that followed World War II, Peter and I were born into what should have been a time of hope. In fact, it was an era overshadowed by the chilling possibilities of the Cold War and countless outbreaks of discord across the globe. British troops had been fighting in Malaya, the Middle East and in Africa. Reports of casualties haunted the front pages and a nation had begun to realise that once again, the end of a great war had not led to peace.

My mother in particular had resigned herself to the prospect of her sons being called up to fight for Queen and Country and calculated that it was unlikely that we would all survive the battles that lay in our path.

She had already seen how the loss of her youngest son had ravaged my American grandmother, leaving her psychologically damaged for the rest of her life. Harry had been killed in Burma by Indian troops fighting with the Japanese during World War II. At first, he was posted as being *missing in action* and eventually *killed in action*. His body was never recovered.

When Harry died, he left a boy-sized hole in my grandmother's heart that she took to her grave. After she died, the shadow of Harry's premature death hung over my parents like a shroud.

This account of a journey made in 1987 would have remained untold, were it not for a question that caught me by surprise nearly twenty-five years later. The young man who set out on that journey was then middle-aged and had become accustomed to life as a father, husband and householder. The carefree days of youth were long gone and almost forgotten. That question set in motion the train of thought that led to me writing these words.

In a Victorian mansion, built to meet the needs of a wealthy family, long since converted into a corporate training centre, all nine of us listened as our tutor spoke. As time slipped past, marked by our beating hearts and the gentle tick-tock seeping from the grandfather clock in the hall, a question skipped across the room with a lightness that caught me by surprise.

Instead of paying attention to the course tutor, I had let my mind wander beyond the confines of meeting room and had been watching a blackbird with a bright yellow beak pulling a worm out of the carefully manicured lawn. In my moment of fancy, I had not noticed that rain seeping out of a leaden sky had formed a fine mist that flattened the morning light and created a world within a world, a singular world in which secrets could find their way into the light.

A secret that had never been shared lay waiting for this moment, shivering with anticipation on the threshold of release as the shackles of fifty years slipped away.

We were sitting in a semi-circle around the tutor who was asking each of us the same question, although I cannot remember why. He leaned forward, embracing us with his presence and the intimacy of his words.

"If you could meet anyone who has ever lived in the next five minutes, who would you most like to meet?"

My mind went blank and could not think of an answer. I listened to the others as they each gave their answer. Their responses revealed the quality of their education and depth of their learning. They wanted to meet ancient philosophers; poets who had shown them hidden worlds; the sportsmen who had inspired them; and the men and women who had changed the world with their words. As my turn to speak approached, my mind remained blank.

All too soon, it was my turn and out of the emptiness that cloaked my thinking, I heard myself speaking.

"Of all of the people who have ever lived, the person I would most like to have met is my twin brother, Peter."

The words had escaped from a corner of my mind that had lain undisturbed for many years, stirring up memories that shimmered like particles of dust caught in a beam of sunlight. In an instant, I found myself shocked by my public statement of what had been an unspoken secret for so many years.

Peter had died shortly after a difficult delivery, leaving behind a new-born twin brother and two grieving parents. I had lived and he had died. The difference between living and dying had been no more than the junior doctor's lack of experience. He had hesitated in the delivery room and my brother's life had slipped away.

For nine months, we had developed in our mother's womb, lying against each other as our cells multiplied and formed our tiny bodies. Our pulses pattered in unison, synchronised with the slower rhythm of our mother's comforting heartbeat.

I do not remember not knowing about Peter. I can imagine that there must have been a day when my parents told that I had had a twin brother, but it is long gone and forgotten. Learning to live with the sense of loss that comes from losing someone you have never met, but has been at your side for nine long months, is an experience that is hard to explain.

Peter Pan once tried to cut away his shadow, but I have never once felt the need to rid myself of the shadow within me, which is all that is left of a boy who never grew up.

I came into the world in the middle of winter and spent the first few months of my life in a tiny half-timbered cottage, deep in the heart of rural Gloucestershire, without central heating or running water, but it was home and it was my world. I knew nothing of the wider world outside and as long as the milk kept coming, I did not really care. As spring came, my mother decided that fresh air would be good for me and moved me out into the garden. As my young eyes began to focus, images of mottled English skies and leafy branches bobbing in the breeze appeared and deep within me, my wandering spirit began to stir.

As soon as I could move without help, I began to explore the boundaries of my world. At first, I travelled by rolling lengthways and soon found myself trapped under beds and cupboards, until my mother or father found me by following the sound of my frustrated yells and pulled me out.

One day, my parents loaded all our possessions on to a borrowed handcart and we moved to the newly-built house, which had been designed by my father. There we had little or no furniture, but we did have central heating and running water.

According to my long-suffering parents, I set out on my first proper solo journey when I was eighteen months old. It was a warm summer's afternoon in June and my mother put me to bed for an afternoon nap. As a precaution, she put a safety net over the cot to stop me climbing out and left me to sleep.

Hearing the birds singing outside, I stood up and through the bars of my cot watched the leaves on the elm trees at the end of the garden tossing in the wind and clouds scudding past the spire of the distant parish church.

Urged on by a need to explore, I released the childproof safety catches; lowered the side of the cot and climbed out. It was easy enough for me to move a chair so that I could climb on to the windowsill and even easier to tumble out into a flowerbed below. Fortunately, my nursery was on the ground floor, so I fell without damaging the flowerbed or myself.

Lying on my back on the soft earth, I looked up at the sky and felt the warmth of the sun on my face. For the first time, I faced the world on my own and experienced the thrill of setting out on a journey. I picked myself up, toddled to the end of the garden, clambered over the rotting stump of a long dead elm and landed in a vast ploughed field. Undaunted, I clambered over the clay-heavy furrows and made a beeline for the distant spire of the Church of the Holy Innocents.

It was not long before my mother discovered my escape. After searching the house and the garden in vain, she spotted my diminutive figure in the middle of the field, heading away from the house.

I know now that I was heading directly towards my twin brother's final resting place, in the shade of the great lime trees that marked the edge of the graveyard. This was perhaps my first journey in search of Peter, but it would not be the last.

Almost thirty years later, I found myself at the end of a journey that had taken me from my birthplace to a bridge in the foothills of the Himalayas in the same way that a river flowing down from the mountains to the sea finds its natural course.

Part 1 - First steps

"This man is freed from servile bands, of hope to rise, or fear to fall; Lord of himself, though not of lands and leaving nothing, yet hath all".
Lord **Byron**

Chapter 1

As the deep forests of Luxembourg embraced the first chill winds of winter towards the end of 1986, I wrote the letter of resignation that ended my career as a NATO civil servant.

After a great deal of thought, I had concluded that NATO would function better without me. After all, the defence of the Western world relied on NATO operating effectively and I needed to do my bit for world peace. All that remained for me to do was deliver the letter to my boss.

Bob Smart, an exiled Californian in his late fifties with silver hair and piercing eyes, saw me approaching and called me in to see him. Word of my planned resignation had reached him and he did not look happy.

He led me into his office, lit a cigarette and leaned back in his leather-bound chair. Half hidden in a cloud of smoke, his blue eyes bore into me and I was still not sure if I was about to face the start of the lecture that I had been secretly dreading.

"Chris, I think that you are crazy to leave."

As trails of blue smoke curled like demons around his eyes, he paused for an instant and added.

"But, I wish that I had been as crazy as you were when I was your age."

As the demons swirled away, a grin spread across his face. He shook my hand and in that moment forgave me for leaving him with a recruitment problem. Whether I could ever have explained to him why I had chosen that moment in my life to leave was another matter. I was not even sure myself.

Perhaps the soft whispers of a song carried by a westerly wind that had blown all the way from the plains of Wisconsin had breathed life into a long dormant dream of a journey. For a year, the Zephyr and I had travelled across Europe, from the frozen forests of the Ardennes, to the most southerly, westerly tip of Portugal and across the deep waters of the Danube. When the Zephyr moved on, I knew that it was time for me to go, but still did not really know why.

In the weeks that followed, I sold off my possessions. As each day passed, I shed a little more of the cocoon of urban life that kept me safe from the outside world. All too soon, it was all gone, leaving nothing to hold me back. It was as if I had to undergo a cleansing process that was now complete. The last few days vanished into a whirl of farewells, embraces and tears. This was my way of reaching out to my own Never-Never Land, where I could avoid growing up and escape the world of grownups.

A few months later, in a flea-bitten Cairo hotel where nothing seemed quite real, I found myself trying to decide how to get to India to search for traces of my father's colonial past. All through my childhood, I dreamed of experiencing the world in which he started his life and to put flesh on the stories he told me when I was growing up.

Thinking about my father in that Cairo hotel opened a door into a childhood world filled with fleeting memories. In the instant of remembering, fragments of long forgotten moments of sharing appeared as a butterfly's wings caught in a shaft of light in a leafy glade. As a bedtime treat, he would turn down the lights and make coloured patterns in the darkness with the glowing tip of his cigarette. Then he would tell me about his life as a boy in India.

Sitting in a room filled with the sounds of the largest city in the Middle East, I remembered his tales of the cobra that lived in the roots of a tree at the bottom of his garden; the ceremonial processions with painted elephants; and the unimaginable power of the monsoon rains. Standing in the darkness at the foot of my bed, he filled my young mind with images of an exotic world that lay beyond the bounds of the sleepy village in Gloucestershire that was my world.

I could still remember him teasing my mother whenever she tried to explain what it was like to be a child growing up with food rationing in World War II.

"None of us saw a banana until the war was over", my mother would explain with a wistful expression across her face, having never really forgiven Adolf Hitler for his part in blocking imports of exotic fruits into wartime England.

Invariably, my father reacted to such tales of woe by launching into one of his wartime reminiscences. Tales of hardship and shortages gave way to stories about breakfast tables piled high with pineapples, bananas and sweet mangoes. He told us about waking up to the roar of a dawn chorus in the Burmese jungle, with songbirds competing with families of gibbons hooting at the rising sun. All of these tales burst into my imagination and filled me with a lust to experience all of these experiences for myself.

As I grew up, I paid regular visits to my grandparents in Sheffield and had some sense of the world that had shaped my mother's early years. On the other hand, the world from which my father emerged was a mystery. Apart from a very small number of many times repeated stories, I knew almost nothing about my father's early years in Poona or his wartime experiences in India, Burma and Indochina.

The strange thing was that although he was happy to share some of these tales with us, he never really seemed to enjoy talking about his life in India or his experiences as a soldier in South East Asia during World War II. As he approached the twilight years of his life, I felt that it was time for me to try to gain some personal knowledge of the world in which he spent so many of his early years. Perhaps the experience would help me to get to know him a little better.

Chapter 2

India seemed a good place to start. The only remaining question was how to get there. One option was to take a train south to Khartoum in the Sudan and then travel east by road to the coast. According to a Sudanese engineer I met in a café in Alexandria, it should have been easy for me to get a berth on a freighter or even on a *dhow* heading for Bombay.

Nothing was that easy. The Sudanese Embassy in Cairo refused me a visa just because the newness of my passport hinted at a recent trip to Israel. The embassy clerk who turned down my application informed me that I would not be passing through Sudan in the near future. I left the Embassy feeling very despondent and frustrated.

Undeterred, I took the train to Port Said in the hope of finding a berth on a cargo ship bound for India. After a few visits to shipping agents, I soon discovered that commercial shipping companies did not want to take on passengers, especially those without contacts with shipping company owners.

One balding shipping agent scratched his spreading belly and explained wearily why it was so hard.

"It is the insurance companies that do not want passengers on commercial ships. They do not want to have to pay compensation if a ship is lost. In the old days, I used to arrange for many people to travel by freighter. It is just too difficult these days. Why don't you fly? It is much quicker."

Of course, he was right. The easiest option would have been to take a direct flight from Cairo to Bombay. From there, the long haul up the Western Ghats would have taken me to Poona in a matter of hours.

My father's first home was a bungalow in a tree-lined street in the Poona cantonment. Even the address, inscribed in copper plate on his birth certificate, seemed to take me back to another age: No 16, Right Flank Lines.

The bungalow was so near that I felt that I could have reached out and touched its walls. Half a day in a plane, a few hours in a taxi and I would have been there. What had seemed like a good idea, no longer seemed like the right thing to do. The problem was that a Zephyr from Wisconsin had slipped some ideas into my head that just would not go away. Carried by the westerly wind, her words buzzed in my ears.

"Relax, let go and let the journey carry you forwards. Trust that your journey will be your guide and for once, let it take you where it wants to go."

The Zephyr was right of course, but I was struggling to give up the idea that I should plan and structure everything in my life.

As the wind blew harder, tears ran from my eyes and guided me to a chance meeting with a young German from Hamburg that changed everything. As his girlfriend rolled him a joint, the German turned to me and held my arm.

"Did you know that the Karakoram Highway, which was once part of the Silk Road and links Pakistan with China, is now open? You should go there. That is where I would go. You never know if it will close again. You could go to India anytime you like. While you are in Pakistan, you should go to Chitral and find the pagans living on the Afghan border."

China? Why not? The idea of travelling to a country that had only just started to emerge from the vice-like grip of Chairman Mao's Communist Party was strangely attractive to me. The idea of travelling along a highway that formed part of the ancient Silk Road and linked western and eastern philosophies was even more compelling.

The construction of the Karakoram Highway was the result of a joint venture between Pakistan and China and one of the most challenging engineering projects of the twentieth century. Following one of the key trading routes of the ancient Silk Road, the Highway climbs up into the Karakoram Mountains, reaching an altitude of 14,500 feet at the Khunjerab Pass. Beyond the Pass, the Highway sweeps down into the desolate wastelands of western China. Built to encourage trade between Pakistan and China, the construction of the Highway was a clear sign that a key section of the ancient Silk Road was undergoing a process of regeneration.

I also realised that this would also make it possible for me to follow in the footsteps of Sir Francis Younghusband, one of my childhood heroes. He had first entered Chitral, a town in Pakistan's North West Frontier Province, in 1893 and was appointed Acting British Political Officer. Shortly afterwards, the British government decided against having a presence in the territory and pulled him out of Chitral, much to his frustration.

In 1895, he returned to Chitral in a very different capacity. While on leave from the British Army, he was employed as a special correspondent for the Times newspaper and attached to a 15,000 strong force, led by Major-General Sir Robert Low, sent to relieve British and Indian troops who had been besieged in Chitral fort for a month and a half. Younghusband had ridden into Chitral ahead of the main force and discovered that the besiegers had withdrawn as they were outnumbered by the massive size of Low's force.

Younghusband had also travelled across China from Beijing, crossed through what was then Turkestan and made his way through the mountains into India, having discovered a route through the Muztagh Pass.

In 1903, he also led an invasion of Tibet, which led to the massacre of hundreds of Tibetan soldiers and transformed his perspective on life. On his way back to India in 1904, he experienced a spiritual enlightenment that filled him with "love for the whole world" and convinced him that "men at heart are divine".

With the opening of the Karakoram Highway, I now had the opportunity to follow his route all the way to Beijing. The prospect of being able to follow in his footsteps all the way to Lhasa was even more intriguing.

There was now no question in my mind. India would have to wait.

On reflection, this was perhaps a choice between setting out on a journey and travelling to a destination. The latter I could do any time, but to be able to set out on a journey with no clear idea of where I would be going was a prospect that filled me with a growing sense of anticipation. This was indeed a singular moment. For the first time in my life, I was able to afford the luxury of travelling for no particular reason, other than to seek out new worlds, meet new people and boldly go where I had never been before. The wind that blew had taught me well.

My imagination was also fuelled by a desire to rediscover an almost forgotten world that I invented as a child. Enthralled by Victorian adventure yarns and my father's stories, I imagined a faraway world in which strong-winged eagles soared over vast valleys and snow-capped peaks glistened under a deep blue sky. The Karakoram Mountains might very well have been those dreamland peaks.

Having made up my mind to abandon my plans to look for my family's colonial roots, I wandered back to the hotel to rest, recuperate and read. The only English book in the lobby library was a battered copy of Conrad's Heart of Darkness. I was soon engrossed in this classic tale of a long journey into the heart of the

Dark Continent in search of Kurtz, a man who had tumbled deep into his own black heart.

As I read, I wondered how far my own journey would take me away from the supporting pillars of home and friends towards the bounds of my own limitations. Time alone would tell.

Buried deep in the heart of Cairo, the dusty hotel lobby was an island of peace tucked away from the heat and noise of the city. The air was warm and musty, perfumed with a cloying combination of cat piss, stale tobacco smoke and leaking drains. Piles of broken furniture, rubble and masonry littered the hallways. It was clear that this once gracious structure had given up hope and was quietly crumbling into dust.

Around me, was a deathly stillness broken only when the hotel manager appeared out of the gloom of his office and greeted me with a polite 'Salaam?'

"Good afternoon sir, please may I introduce myself? I am Muhammad Orman and I am at your service."

He held out his hand and smiled. His English was almost perfect, with only a trace of an accent. A balding man in his fifties with coffee-coloured skin, dark sad eyes and a slight paunch, Mr Orman reminded me of a kindly grandfather. At the same time, the combination of his faded and much repaired tweed suit, portly stature and ancient brown leather brogues gave him the look of a gentleman farmer fallen on hard times.

Seeing that I was reading, he moved over to the battered front desk and carefully unfolded a newspaper and buried himself in the headlines. We read together in a shared silence with only the regular ticking of an ancient clock disturbing the still air.

Our reverie was shattered when a furious female cat on heat, closely followed by a moth-eaten tomcat, skidded down the stairs. As they vanished out of sight, there was the sound of a struggle, followed by a sudden screech of sexual anguish that echoed up the stairwell. We both looked up and our eyes met. Mr Orman carefully folded his newspaper and settled back in his chair to face me. I nodded and smiled as pleasantly as I could, expecting yet another invitation to visit a long lost brother or cousin who just happened to own a perfume shop or a carpet emporium. However, happily I was wrong.

"You are English?"

As he had already seen my passport, I knew that was a rhetorical question and nodded.

He looked at me thoughtfully, leant forward and asked:

"You have seen the pyramids?"

I shook my head, trying not to feel too guilty. After all, I had been in Egypt for some time and had not taken the time to visit the pyramids. They were only a short distance to the west on a low plateau in sight of the ever-expanding conurbation of Greater Cairo. How could I have been in Cairo for so long and not gazed in awe at their glory? How could I have ignored five thousand years of history? With a puzzled smile, he shook his head disapprovingly and tried again.

"You will see the Sphinx?"

I had not seen the Sphinx either. According to at least one theory, the Sphinx was already ancient when Pharaohs built the Great Pyramids. They had all been there a long time and would be there long after I had gone. At that moment, I felt that there was no need to rush. There would be plenty of time to see these monuments to the Third and Fourth Dynasties. In the meanwhile, there was time to reflect on the people who believed that the living could prepare them for a life after death and used their beliefs to capture the hearts and minds of the farmers and artisans who lived along the banks of the Nile.

"You must have visited the Museum of Antiquities?"

At least I had done that. The museum was only a short walk from the hotel and was a mausoleum in its own right, filled with so many exhibits that the conservationists could not keep up with the damage caused by Cairo's polluted air; the humid traces left behind by each visitor; and the sulphurous gases seeping out of their digestive systems. Each breath added moisture to the air that combined with airborne pollutants to form an invisible mist that was rotting artefacts that had lain preserved for thousands of years in the arid sands of the desert.

His questions left me feeling guilty and he insisted that I made more of an effort.

"Promise me that you will go to the Pyramids tomorrow."

With a grin, I agreed to take a bus there in the morning.

Despite his gentle nagging, I knew it was good to have had some company. Mr Orman was keen to get me to describe my visits to Luxor and to Alexandria, where my grandfather had been posted by the British Army after the Great War. He listened with interest for a while and then stood up so he could see me better, before settling back to slide his polished rear up on the front desk.

With his shoes swinging slowly from side to side, he asked, "Tell me, what do you think of Cairo? Is it like London?"

Muhammad Orman was an educated Arab, with an air of wisdom and peace befitting a man of his age. Twisting his prayer beads between his fingers, he leant forward and stared intently at me, waiting patiently for my response.

Compared with London, or any other major Western city, Cairo was a shambles. In fact, there was every indication that Cairo was slowly crumbling back into the desert. There was dereliction on every corner and air pollution bad enough to kill trees and rot buildings. The roads that formed the arteries of the city were furred up with potholes and traffic jams were commonplace.

There were signs of great poverty wherever I looked and the overcrowded streets served as testimony to the fact that an exodus of Egypt's rural populace had tripled Cairo's population over the previous thirty years. With a population of some eighteen million, Cairo had an infrastructure barely able to cope with half that number. Despite the shadows of past glories that humbled those of the modern world, Cairo was still the largest city in Africa and was by any standards, a great metropolis.

I tried to answer truthfully without appearing rude.

"Cairo is very different from London, but in some ways they are the same. The roads in London are better, but we still have traffic problems and the air is also polluted."

My answer was partly true, but missed the real point of Cairo. It was humbling to consider that when London was little more than a small village on the banks of the Thames, the conurbation that is Cairo had already seen three thousand years of history. Some historians have suggested that modern Cairo was founded towards the end of the tenth century, but it is probably much older than that. The pyramids were already ancient in what we today consider ancient times. When Herodotus gazed up at the pyramids as a tourist in the fifth century BC, he was looking at structures that had been built two thousand years before.

The land at the base of the Nile's delta has been of great importance to Egypt for more than five thousand years. The young prince Menes, who unified Egypt's northern and southern territories about five thousand years ago, built the first real capital of Egypt. He became Egypt's first Pharaoh and chose the site of Memphis as his capital along the North-South border and about fifteen miles south from the centre of what is Cairo today. For the next eight centuries, Memphis prospered under the rule of more than thirty dynasties: Zoser, Cheops, Chephren, Mycerinus, Unas and others, each lasting many times longer than the British Empire. We know their names today because they developed a written language and recorded their history in stone. By contrast, the names of the builders of Stonehenge on the Wiltshire Plains, who lived four and a half thousand years ago, have long since been lost.

Mr Orman leant forward and began to speak with a calm, gentle voice that flowed like water into the chasm of my ignorance.

"The Great Pyramid of Cheops was constructed on the Giza plateau, a necropolis of the city of Memphis on the Nile's West Bank. The economics of pyramid building suggest that the builders lived in prosperous times. The land supported the ruling classes, the military and the workers who built the pyramids as well as the peasants who toiled in the fields to feed them. Egypt was a prosperous country in those days."

He spoke with a quiet authority that was captivating. I settled down to listen to his impromptu lecture.

"The Pharaohs who built the pyramids controlled both religious and political power and exerted almost absolute control over the lives of the people they ruled. They demonstrated how the combination of religious and political power in the hands of a divine Ruler could be used to great effect. In the world that they created, the Ruler was God and his word was the word of God. Life was very simple in some ways. When the Ruler wanted a Great Pyramid, the people built him one. And it had to be bigger and better than any that had been built before."

Ironically, the completion of the Great Pyramid coincided with two major changes in the political landscape of Egypt. Firstly, no more great pyramids were built and secondly, the first Ancient Egyptian priests emerged from historical obscurity. As the power of the priests grew, the power of the Pharaohs in Giza declined. This was the beginning of a segregation of political and religious power and the dawn of a new era.

The priests established a new city on the east bank, Heliopolis where Ra, the Sun God was worshipped. While the Pharaohs to the south sought to consolidate both their position and their political powers, the priests sought to extend their knowledge of the world of the living and the world of the dead. With knowledge came power and influence. In life, they supported their political leaders. In death, they served as the gatekeepers to the After World. In return, they won the freedom to establish great centres of learning and to live like kings in their own right.

The Persians destroyed Heliopolis when they invaded Egypt in 525 BC. Babylon-in-Egypt arose at the junction of the re-opened canal linking the Nile to the Red Sea. In 30 BC, Octavian finally overcame Anthony, his old enemy and Cleopatra killed herself with an asp. In the political vacuum that followed, Egypt became another Roman province, with Alexandria as its capital.

As Christianity began to surface, the Greek and Roman pagans at first confronted the Egyptian Copts. When the Romans adopted Christianity, even Babylon became a Christian stronghold.

Mr Orman had realised that my ignorance of Egypt's history was boundless and was keen to remedy this gap in my education. His passion for the tangled web of his county's history was exhausting, but what he really wanted to teach me had its roots in Egypt's more recent past.

"I will also tell you about the coming of Islam to Egypt. Let's go back to 640 AD when Amr Ibn-el-Aas led a victorious army of Moslem horsemen into Egypt and besieged the impregnable fortress of Babylon."

The story of Egypt's first encounters with Islam was compelling. Defeat came quickly and Cyrun, the Viceroy of Egypt surrendered, making Amr the first Arab ruler of Egypt. These Arab invaders chose to build a new city, Al-Fusat outside the fortress, on the east bank of the Nile.

Mr Orman's knowledge of Egypt's Islamic history was expansive and I soon realised that he had not always been a hotel manager.

"Twenty-one years later, Amr decided to back the powerful Umayyads, who ruled in Damascus, in a power struggle over the Islamic caliphate. The Umayyad Empire stretched from China in the east to Spain in the west. The Egyptians were unable to stem the expansion of the Islamic Empire and Cairo eventually became the Islamic capital of Egypt. For the next three hundred years, the fortunes of Egypt mirrored the ebbs and flows in the struggle for supreme control of the Islamic world."

As he paused to take a breath, I realised how little I knew about the origins of Islam.

"The Abbasids started as a Shi'ite movement loyal to Muhammad bin Ali, the great grandson of Muhammad's uncle, Abbas. Ibrahim, his son, rebelled against the Umayyad caliphate. Eventually, the Umayyads captured and killed him, but the rebellion he started continued after his death. The Abbasids continued to move west until they reached Iraq in 749 AD and declared Ibrahim's brother, Abu al-Abbas, to be the new caliph with the title al-Suffah. When this last Umayyad caliph was killed in 750 AD, the seat of power shifted from Syria to Baghdad.

Under Al Mansur (754-775 AD), there was a major period of change and the Arabs lost the political and social superiority that they had under the Umayyads. Al Mansur also renounced the Shi'ite origins of the movement, became a champion of Sunni orthodoxy and helped unify the growingly cosmopolitan Muslim empire. The apex of Abbasid power came in the reign of al-Rashid (786-809 AD), which also marked the beginning of their decline."

His voice was authoritative and I began to suspect that he had lectured to better students in his past. As a student, I had not always paid as much attention to my lecturers as I should, but Mr Orman held me in his spell.

"In 905 AD, Egypt having fallen into anarchy was once again invaded by the Abbasids who destroyed the palace, devastated the gardens of Al-Qatai and moved the capital back to Al-Fustat. Egypt's status was briefly restored to that of a province, which was ruled this time by governors sent from Baghdad.

Just sixty-four years later, Egypt was captured by Al Gawar, a Shi'ite general under the command of Al-Muez Ledin-Ellah, who was supported by his claim of being a direct descendent of the Prophet Muhammad's daughter, Fatima.

The last Fatimid Caliph was only eighteen when the Seljuks captured Cairo. The Seljuks who came originally from Central Asia had already conquered Syria and Palestine and established their capital in Damascus."

A police siren wailed in the distance. Voices locked in argument clattered up the stairwell. A cat stalked past, leaving behind a trail of disdain. Mr Orman paused to watch this display of unconstrained arrogance and then continued.

"By 1168 AD, Egypt had become a battleground on which the Seljuks and the Crusaders fought, with the Fatimids having virtually little or no control, although they sided mostly with the Crusaders. When Noor el Din, the governor of Egypt appointed by the Sultan of Damascus died a year later, his nephew was immediately appointed as the next governor. A young man in his early thirties, he was to become one of the most famous figures in medieval history. His name was Salah-el-Din the Ayyubid, better known to you, I think, as Saladin.

In 1516 AD, the Mamelouk Sultan Kansuh Al-Ghoury was defeated and killed in a battle against the Ottomans. A few months later, the Turkish army commanded by Ottoman Sultan Selim entered Cairo and the life of the last Mamelouk Sultan, Tooman Bey, came to a brutal end."

This often-brutal interplay between politics and religion set the scene for the continued conflict within the Muslim community and between the community and the rest of the world.

A dilapidated hotel lobby was a fitting place to learn about the long and bloody route taken by the Egyptians from the days of the Pharaohs to the present day. Mr Orman had not finished and leant even further forward with his comfortable backside balancing precariously on the edge of his perch.

"Egypt's glory is in its past. Ever since the 1952 Revolution, Egypt has become a very rundown and dirty place. Before the revolution, each town and each city had a municipal authority. The streetlights worked and the municipal authorities collected the rubbish from the houses. In those days, the people that lived in them cleaned the pavements and streets. There was a pride in being clean and tidy. Now, the government controls everything and nothing happens."

He stared into the gloom of the stairwell.

"The hallway of this building used to be always spotlessly clean. Now it is filthy and the smell of cats is everywhere. The 1952 Revolution took the building from the family that owned it and now a government insurance company runs it. The government pays a man to clean the stairs and hallways, but he does nothing but sell cigarettes on the pavement by the front door. For doing nothing, he gets a cheque from the government every month. This is typical of Egypt today."

He pointed at the piles of rubble in the stairwell and shrugged his shoulders.

"Even the British came here. Do you know how your country came to play a part in the creation of this mess?"

I did not.

"It all started when Tawfik, the Khedive, asked the British to help him regain control following an attempted military coup that had started because of all the foreigners trying to gain influence in Egypt. They arrived in 1892 and set about establishing control."

His predecessor was Ismail, grandson of Muhammad Ali, an Albanian appointed by an Ottoman Sultan as Pasha of Egypt in 1806. Ismail was a man of vision. He ordered the construction of the Suez Canal and commissioned the composition of the opera Aida by Verdi. The burden of foreign debt soon became too crippling to Egypt's economy and Ismail was forced to abdicate.

The British Consul, Lord Cromer, effectively ruled Egypt and it was under his tenure that electricity was introduced to Cairo in 1889, at least for the colonial powers and the elite. After the Great War, Britain declared Egypt a British Protectorate. Imperial Britain's reason for wanting control of Egypt was strategic, as the Suez Canal provided the means to maintain Britain's influence over India and the Far East.

In 1922, the British established Fouad I of the Muhammad Ali dynasty as king and declared Egypt a sovereign country. Significantly, British troops did not withdraw, leaving most people with the view that Fouad I was little more than a puppet king.

Amhed, son of Fouad I was deposed in the 1952 Revolution, which ended the British involvement in Egypt and established General Muhammad Naguib as president. The last British soldiers left Egypt two long years later.

Naguib fought to return Egypt to its people but needed cash to fund the radical change programs needed to modernise the economy. The Soviet Union was quick to offer assistance and hoped to gain influence in both Northern Africa and the Arab world by investing in the Egyptian economy. Like all other colonial powers of the twentieth century, they failed and the Aswan Dam remains today as a monument to socialist ideals that failed in Egypt just as they failed in the Soviet Union.

"But now we are at peace with Israel and we can start to put our country back into the state it was before the revolution. The wars with Israel took away all our money and made us a very poor country. What was worse was that we were fighting for the Palestinians, not for Egypt."

He paused and took a deep breath.

"Did you know that when the Jews began to settle in Palestine, they bought land from the Palestinians? Later, the Palestinians wanted us to go to war against Israel to get back the land they sold. To fight a war for your own country is one thing, but to fight a war for the stupid Palestinians is another?"

His long fingers came together and he almost looked as though he was praying.

"Before this time of peace, families used to be very frightened when their sons were called away to the army. In the wars, many, many young men were killed and many more were wounded. Now, we have peace we do not fear for our sons when they join the army."

The tomcat returned with a grin on its face and its tail in the air, pausing on the landing for a moment to stare at us with contempt before vanishing up the stairs for a well-earned sleep.

"All these wars and the Revolution have been very bad for Egypt. In private business, we used to be able to throw out those men who did not work well. Now we have to keep them and pay them. No-one cares whether they work hard or not."

He pulled at his shirt, testing the quality of the fabric between his fingers.

"Egyptian cotton used to be world famous, but after the revolution the quality became so poor that the industry was nearly destroyed. The same thing happened with Egyptian sugar. There was a time when sugar was made in the privately owned refineries that stood in lines along the banks of the Nile. After the revolution, the government took over the refineries and the quality of the sugar became so poor that we lost nearly all our customers. Sadat began to change all this and tried to give control back to private industry, but religious fanatics killed him five years ago. The only good news now is that the changes that he began continue and now Egypt has a chance to be a better place to live."

Somewhere in the building, a heavy door slammed shut, sending echoes up the stairwell.

"Do you not think it is ironic that today, Sadat is not remembered for his political and economic reforms as well as he is remembered for winning a Nobel Peace prize for signing a peace treaty with Israel in 1979?"

"There have been many changes in the past ten years, but progress takes a long time. Here, everything moves very slowly. Perhaps it is already too late to repair the damage, but the people have good health and we have Allah to help us."

"You seem proud to be a Muslim?"

"I am very proud."

"How can you still be proud to a Muslim when so many bad things have been done to your country in the name of Islam by religious fanatics?"

On reflection, it was a ridiculous question considering the atrocities carried out in the name of Christianity over the centuries.

"This is a problem for you Europeans. You can never understand Islam because you cannot read the Qur'an. This is why so many Europeans think such bad things about Islam. Islam is a very good religion for Arab people. The Qur'an teaches us to obey Allah and teaches us how to live. The Qur'an tells us to pray five times a day. It tells us to obey Allah and it tells us when to fast."

He tilted even further forward and once more nearly slipped off the desk.

"But the people who think we fast just because the Qur'an tells us do not understand why the Qur'an instructs us to fast during

Ramadan. You see, when we fast, we are not allowed to drink or eat anything for a month, except after sunset and before sunrise. We get to know hunger and thirst and we think about the poor people who are hungry and thirsty. If you are sick or if you are travelling, then you do not have to fast. This is what the Qur'an teaches us."

He paused to savour a sip of tea and then continued.

"You have to understand that every rule and regulation is there for a reason and is there to be obeyed. The Qur'an teaches us that the will of Allah is absolute and that we must learn to obey him and follow his regulations as they are written in the Qur'an."

I listened carefully and with genuine interest.

"Don't you think that there are religious fanatics who have given Islam a bad name? Many people in Europe see Islam as a violent religion that threatens their Christian way of life. How could you believe in a religion that seems to encourage so much violence?"

With great patience, Mr Orman explained, "Islam does not threaten anyone. In Islam, all religions are respected. All peoples are respected. It is a very good and a very kind religion. It is all here in the Qur'an."

With a smile, Mr Orman reached into his desk and produced his Qur'an, which he opened and read aloud in Arabic. The words flowed easily, filling the silence with their music. When he finished, he caught my eye and smiled.

"This is a very beautiful book."

His voice took on a new tone as he remembered the words of an old teacher.

"The soul of ecstasy and mysticism is in the Qur'an. It is the world's most beautiful book. I will show you."

With great tenderness, he placed his Qur'an on the desk and opened it for me to see.

He then explained how the flowing Arabic script and coloured symbols told the reader how the words of Allah as revealed to Muhammad the Prophet should be spoken. He was a good teacher and explained how the Qur'an was organised.

"These characters are letters and these symbols tell you how the words should be read. They tell you both rhythm and tone. The Qur'an is divided into 114 chapters called *suras* arranged more or less in order of length. The longest chapters are at the beginning and some contain over two hundred verses. The shorter chapters are at the end and have only three or five short verses. Let me show you."

"The first *sura* starts with an invocation that is used widely and held by many Believers to represent the essentials of Muslim belief:

"In the name of God, Most Gracious, Most Merciful.

Praise be to God, the Cherisher and Sustainer of the Worlds;

Master of the day of Judgement;

Thee we do worship and Thine aide we seek."

The other 113 *suras* are a collection of passages of revelation, as uttered by Muhammad at different times and on different occasions, compiled some thirty years after his death from oral and written records. The Qur'an describes the role of God and man's relationship with him and the way in which man is expected to live with his fellow men. In many ways, the Qur'an is comprehensive and covers everything from the religious obligations of prayer, alms, fasting and pilgrimage to basic institutions such as marriage, divorce, inheritance and the basic structure of law.

The Qur'an sets out a code of living that reflects the values prevalent in the Middle Ages. For many non-Muslims, these values and social mores are outdated and at odds with the values of the modern world. In an attempt to turn the clock back, some of the more fundamentalist Muslims seem to be seeking a way of escaping the decadence of the twentieth century to a long distant Golden Age that probably never existed.

The Qur'an is not just a code for living. It also carries a powerful message in which its followers are invested with a duty and power of expansion, universal in aim. Followers are urged to "strive in the path of God, until allegiance to God is victorious over all other allegiance."

As my lesson ended, he found a page almost at the end of the Qur'an and showed me a *sura* with just six lines.

"I will read you *sura* one hundred and nine, which tells us how to deal with people who are not of the Faith."

The way he read the *sura* sounded beautiful, almost musical, but I did not understand a single word. He then remembered that I did not speak Arabic and corrected himself.

"I will translate for you."

With painstaking care, he wrote out a translation of the *Sura* in my notebook:

"Say: O ye that reject Faith

I worship not that which ye worship

Nor will ye worship that which I worship

And I will not worship that which ye had been wont to worship

Nor will ye worship that which I worship

To you be your way and to me mine."

He finished and turned to me with a broad smile on his face.

"Now do you see? Islam tells Muslims to tolerate other peoples' religions. It is all in here."

Later, I discovered that the Qur'an also states that Christians, Zoroastrians and Jews should be tolerated as long as they acknowledged the supremacy of the Muslim state and pay a stipulated tribute. Idolaters on the other hand were not to be tolerated.

"Perhaps I should read the Qur'an."

"Yes, but first, you must learn to read Arabic."

For someone with my limited ability to learn languages, this would be a challenge.

"I think that would take a long time. I'd better start with a translation in English first."

Mr Orman shook his head and waved a finger at me.

"That would not be the Qur'an. It would only be a translation of the *meaning* of the Qur'an. The Qur'an can never be translated into another language. I was only a small boy when I learned to read the Qur'an and first experienced its meaning in rhythm and music.

These could never be translated. The Qur'an can only be read and understood properly in Arabic."

He paused and was silent for a moment.

"When I completed my first recital of the Qur'an, we celebrated my *Khatm al-Qur'an* with a prayer. I remember that day as if it was yesterday. For me, it was a very special day."

He smiled at the memory and left me to attend to his prayers. I dined out and returned for a good sleep. In my dreams, I walked with Mr Orman along the banks of the Nile in the shadows of the Pyramids, chanting the words of the Holy Qur'an in unison with him.

Chapter 3

Morning arrived all too quickly and I left Mr Orman praying beside the river. After breakfast, my first priority was to get a visa for Pakistan. Rashly, I decided to put my trust in a taxi driver who barely spoke English and did not know his way around Cairo.

An hour passed and it was clear that he was lost. There was no sign of the Pakistan Embassy and I was not convinced that we were even in the right part of the city. My driver had already asked most of his taxi driver friends for help, but they all seemed equally lost. Taxi driving in Cairo seemed to be a matter of driving aimlessly around the city until the passenger got bored or by sheer chance, the driver blundered into the right street. A second hour passed and I began to feel uneasy, as the Embassy was about to close. Fifteen minutes before closing time, we picked up two passengers who just happened to know how to get to the Pakistan Embassy. With their help, I arrived just two minutes before the official closing time. Many other embassies would have asked me to come back later, but instead the Embassy staff invited me inside. They accepted my application and told me to come back the next day to collect my visa.

The next day, I returned to find my passport waiting for me and left the Embassy with a good impression of the efficiency of Pakistani bureaucracy. Feeling suitably relaxed, I kept my promise to Mr Orman and visited the Pyramids.

Following his instructions, I took a bus and soon found myself on the outskirts of Cairo, at the point where the city and desert stand facing each other. The sheer presence of the Pyramids seemed to be enough to hold back the urban sprawl. For reasons that I did not understand, there were very few other tourists and I was lucky enough to be able to climb up into the heart of the Great Pyramid on my own. In the still of the final chamber, I was alone and paused for a moment to share a moment with the men who toiled for years to build a structure capable of standing as a silent witness to the passing of the Millennia.

As I had a few days to kill before I flew to Karachi, one of Muhammad Orman's suggestions took me by train to Al Minya, a small town four hours upstream from Cairo. He told me that I would find some paintings in the Palace Hotel that would make my visit worth the effort.

The central railway station in Cairo was vast and filled with people running in every direction. Never before had I felt so much empathy for the humble ant. The act of buying a ticket was a battle against an administrative system that seemed to defy logic. Like so many other people, I joined queue after queue only to find each time that I was in the wrong queue. No one seemed to know where to go, but eventually and after using up most of my patience, I found myself on the right train with a return ticket to Al Minya.

The train was grimy, solid and packed. Leaving the squalor of the industrial suburbs of Cairo behind, the train steamed southwards between sugar cane fields and scattered villages caught somewhere between the eleventh and twentieth centuries. The train crawled slowly but surely upstream and eventually came to screeching halt in Al Minya station.

The streets of Al Minya were mostly unpaved and delicately perfumed with a rich mixture of animal dung, horse urine and dust. The Palace Hotel stood on the town's main square, overlooking a dilapidated public garden with a few ragged shrubs and a lawn that had seen better days. The Palace was a perfectly preserved colonial hotel that had survived untouched by the passage of time and remained as a reminder of long gone days when Europeans ruled in Egypt. From the outside, the hotel was unremarkable, but on the inside, it was an architectural masterpiece.

The front door opened into a rectangular atrium with galleries on each floor. The walls of the atrium had been decorated with hand painted murals showing scenes of daily life in rural Egypt painted in a strange mix of modern European and ancient Egyptian styles.

The building appeared deserted and it seemed that I was the only guest. The air was cool and kept in motion by great fans toiling in the gloom of the high ceiling. When the manager appeared, he told me that a Frenchman had painted the murals towards the end of the nineteenth century.

The French first arrived in Egypt in 1797, when Napoleon's army landed in Alexandria and advanced to take Cairo. They only stayed three years in Egypt, but left behind strong ties that would bring them back to construct the centre of Cairo to European standards under the rule of Muhammad Ali in the nineteenth century. French scholars started the science now known as Egyptology. A Frenchman finally deciphered hieroglyphics, much to the chagrin of early British scholars. It was a shame, by contrast, that the French had had so little influence on Egyptian cooking.

In the morning, I took the local bus to Abukoran, where I hitched a ride in a covered truck to Beni Hassan, a small town on the banks of the Nile. Squeezed in with twenty villagers and their assorted baggage, there was little room for my legs. Two scrawny chickens glared at me with baleful eyes and a goat with exotic eyes sat nervously between two vast women. The seats were hard and the roads unmetalled. Near to the front of the truck was a small mentally retarded boy with a running nose, rheumy eyes and food dribbling out of his sad, drooping mouth. Large black flies settled on his eyes, nostrils and mouth, but he made no to attempt to fend them off. It was a pitiful sight and one that no one else seemed to have noticed.

The truck finally stopped in Beni Hassan by a faded sign hanging outside the shanty-built teashop that proclaimed:

"WELCOME! SMILE! YOU'RE IN Bane HASSAN!"

Beni Hassan was not much of a place as far as I could see, but it did have a jetty and a sagging teashop. There was even a deserted ferry waiting at the jetty. In vain, I searched for a timetable to try to find out when it would leave. Eventually, the owner of the teashop told me that I would have to wait for a tourist group to arrive before the captain of the ferry would even think of waking up or starting his engines. No one could tell me when or even if a tourist group would arrive. The sun climbed ever higher into a cloudless sky and the temperature rose steadily. There was nothing to do but take a glass of sweet dark tea and settle down to read in the shade of a tree.

As the minutes crawled by, more travellers arrived and waited patiently on the benches provided. There was a thin dark faced salesman with a battered travelling bag; a fat, cheerful woman with intense dark eyes and gold teeth; and two male students with dark manes of shining hair. A band of children from the village came to play in the sand and stare at the strangers in their midst.

The quay was both a focus for village life and a hive of slumberous activity. I could imagine the French painter who had decorated the Palace Hotel coming here for inspiration. He must have seen the grandparents of these people and captured them in his murals. I wondered if any of these people had seen his work.

Beyond the quay was the Nile, a broad expanse of slow moving, brown water disturbed only by rusting sugar-cane barges gliding slowly downstream to unload their cargo at one of the many riverside sugar refineries. There, the raw cane would be processed into the low-grade sugar that no one but the Egyptians would buy.

We waited patiently with no sense of urgency. What could be better than having the time to sit beside the Nile and watch boats sailing past under an azure sky? As I settled down to wait, a felucca skitted downstream with two turbaned men on board, a white lateen sail billowing in the gentle breeze and a muddy wake folding into the deep waters of the Nile. Stretching along the far bank was a thin line of irrigated land that looked green and cool and beyond that, was an endless tract of sun baked rock and sand.

Beside my feet, five ants struggled to carry a dying wasp to their nest. As they worked together, the wasp turned in a slow dance of death, its yellow bands flashing in the light of the sun. Soon more ants arrived and the wasp was bundled away to be dismembered and eaten.

Time crawled by until a truck pulled up, bringing an eerie calm that settled on the waiting villagers like a chill blanket and for an instant time stood still. Hushed men clambered out of the back of the truck and unloaded a coffin supported on long poles. The box was open and the corpse wrapped in a white cotton shroud was just visible.

The pallbearers hoisted the coffin high on their shoulders and walked in silence, coming to a halt in front of the teashop. With great care, the pallbearers set the coffin down in the shade. A small delegation of the mourners set off to rouse the ferryman and agree the price of a ferry crossing.

When the price had been agreed, the pallbearers bundled the coffin onto the ferry, where it vanished into the throng of turbaned men in white robes. Chaos erupted as the pallbearers screamed and shouted at each other until they finally managed to secure the coffin on the boat. With the dead man safely aboard, they fell silent again and the ferry pulled away. As they moved upstream, the passengers waiting in teashop returned to a slumberous state of inactivity.

The sight of a body of men crossing the Nile in silence with a wrapped corpse was a sombre reminder of Egypt's long and complex obsession with death and the afterlife.

The ferry returned an hour or so later with a high-ranking official, his entourage of fawning minions and two heavily armed guards. As His Excellency clambered on to the jetty, no mean feat for a man of his size, a large black Mercedes appeared as if from nowhere. The waiting villagers gathered around to watch the great man squeeze his vast bulk into the car. The car moved off to a shotgun and machine pistol salute. As the dust settled, young children scrambled to retrieve the empty cartridge cases.

An hour later, a tour bus arrived with a party of tourists. The ferryman ushered us on to the ferry and we crossed over to the east bank. A steep climb brought me to the thirty-nine tombs built for feudal lords of the Middle Kingdom. The tombs were mostly simple, with two rooms and a niche at the back as a burial chamber. The frescos in some of the tombs showed scenes of everyday life with paintings of wrestlers, gazelles and harvests of grapes and papyrus. There were also scenes that showed musicians and dancers entertaining their feudal masters. These ancient tombs overlooked the new city of the dead on the east bank of the Nile with its fresh grave and the throng of silent mourners. The ferry took me back to the land of the living and an evening in the bustling streets of Al Minya.

The night slipped past unseen and I rose early to greet the new day on the bank of the Nile. In the chill greyness of an early dawn, the river was inky black, turning slowly to the colour of burnished silver as the sky lightened. There was no sense of motion on the surface of the water as it cut like a blade through the desert. Overhead, a flitting bat span after an insect. In the river, a fish rose in a flurry of ripples. The grey sky warmed and changed to a soft salmon pink. The birds began to sing in anticipation of the rebirth of Ra, the Sun God of ancient times.

A breeze chilled by the icy waters came off the river and I shivered violently in my shirtsleeves, but the moment was too perfect to waste worrying about the cold. A solitary swallow skimmed along the icy waters, swooping briefly to drink. Moving steadily upstream, gliding effortlessly against the wind, seven egrets brushed the surface of the water with perfect wings. As the sky lightened, grey hills on the far bank loomed out of the darkness.

Three Arab boys joined me in my vigil. Having left my coat in Cairo, I watched their grimy, but warm, quilts with undiluted envy. We sat on the quayside without speaking until the sun had escaped the confines of the night and after exchanging quick glances, we parted to start our separate days.

All too soon, it was time to leave the dust and noise of Egypt and despite everything, I was sorry to go. I had grown to like the Egyptian people and their stoic attitude to a landscape that continues to both feed them and make their lives so hard.

With some reluctance, I took the train back to Cairo. As I was checking out of the hotel, Mr Orman shook my hand and wished me a safe journey.

"When you come back to Cairo, you must come and tell me about your journeys. You are always welcome here."

He waved as I stepped over the wreckage of this once proud building and clambered into a taxi that I hoped would get me to the airport in time for my flight to Karachi. As the driver worked his way through Cairo's traffic, I realised that Mr Orman had taught me that Cairo's biggest asset is the humanity of its people.

The departures lounge reeked of stale tobacco smoke and sweating bodies. The waiting passengers greeted the news of a delay with a wave of indifference. There was nothing to do but join the other stranded travellers and try to sleep on the airport floor. The hours passed and there was no news. The indicator board was no help and Pakistan International Airlines officials placated the passengers with the hope that the flight would take off "*soon*."

After a delay of eleven hours, a flight attendant finally sealed the cabin door ready for take-off. With a sudden surge of power, the 747 rumbled down the runway, before climbing slowly into the darkness, turning away from the crumbling tenements of Cairo. The pilot made a sweeping turn over the Pyramids, before heading east towards the Red Sea. Behind us, the city continued its inexorable collapse into the sands of the Sahara. I was exhausted, but relieved to be in the air.

The flight was dry and instead of the beer that I hoped for, the steward offered me a plastic glass of orange juice that left a sour aftertaste in my mouth. The cabin crew were friendly enough and took care to make sure that I was comfortable. Who needs beer anyway?

Later, as my evening meal arrived, the man in the seat in front of me turned and introduced himself.

"My name is Aziz Khan."

Aziz was thickset, with close-cropped hair and a broken nose. Perhaps he had been a boxer or a wrestler in his youth. Despite his thuggish appearance, he was very amiable and his eyes sparkled with good humour and open friendliness.

"What is your name?"

Mumbling through a mouthful of stale chapatti, I told him. He leant back towards me, the cords of his neck bulging with the effort, He was keen to find out who I was and why I was on his flight.

"What is your country? What is the purpose of your journey?"

"Britain." I felt a twinge of post-colonial embarrassment. After all, I was the son of a Sahib and came from a country where there were people who thought that "Paki-bashing" was good for society.

He did not seem to mind and beamed at me anyway.

"Are you married?"

Almost guiltily, I confessed that I was not married. At first, he laughed and winked conspiratorially at me. He then grabbed my hand and crushed my fingers in the friendly sort of way that one might expect from a heavy weight boxer.

"You should get married and have many childrens."

He shook his head and scolded me with a smile. I asked him where he was going.

"I am going home to my wife in Lahore."

"Do you have children?" I asked. His frown suggested that this was not the best of questions and shook his head slowly. A dark mood clouded his face as he grasped the seat back with his slab of a fist.

"I was thinking that I will have to find a new wife. I have been married for fifteen years now and she has not given me a son."

He twisted the gold ring on his middle finger.

"Anyway, she is getting too old now."

Aziz was a truck driver, living a nomadic life hauling spare parts across the deserts of North Africa and Arabia. In a month, he made more than he could make in a year in Pakistan.

"How often do you get home?"

I was curious to know more about his marital sex life. It occurred to me that his poor wife's fertility problems probably had a great deal to with their lifestyle.

"Once a year. Then I visit my home for ten days. I do not really like going home. It is a bloody mad house, full of women fighting, screaming and complaining."

His face darkened and his voice dropped to a whisper.

"Bloody crazy. Too bloody crazy." He laughed but closed the subject with another frown.

"Anyway, tell me, where are *you* going?"

I would have enjoyed finding out more about his family problems, but I could tell from the look on his face that a change of subject was needed, but I avoided answering anyway and we fell into silence. His words stayed with me as I finished off the remains of the then cold lamb biryani. It was a good question. I decided that I had to get a map and start planning how I was going to get to Chitral.

The plane was only half-full and I slept dreamlessly across three empty seats, as did most of the other passengers. We flew out into the darkness wrapped in our blankets like mummies in the solitude of the night. In front of me, my friend from Lahore stirred to clear his nasal passages, before drifting back into sleep.

As dawn approached, the huddled corpses stirred and small children ran past me, a mess of giggles and squeals as they played between the aisles. They ignored me and scurried back down the plane trailing shrill screams of joy. Shivering in the air-conditioned chill, I wrapped myself in a blanket and found an empty window seat. Below me, the clouds gave way to blue waters specked with fishing boats, dhows and container ships set like jewels in a sheet of burnished steel.

Finally, in the stillness of dawn, I caught my first glimpse of land through the porthole, as the coastline appeared abruptly, its smooth line shattered by the many mouths of the Indus delta. It was a magnificent sight. Here, the snows that once fell in the mountains of the Hindu Kush spilled out into the clear blue waters of the Arabian Sea in a harmony of light and colour. Vast trails of suspended sediment drifted out to sea creating coloured milky swirls of marbled icing. In time, these sediments would settle and form new rocks that one day would rise out of the sea as mountains.

As we flew inland, the landscape changed dramatically; the scenery becoming vast and alien. It was overwhelming and terrifying. There was no sign of vegetation and as far as the eye could see, there was nothing but emptiness. A feeling of apprehension started working its way into my stomach, but it was too late to turn back.

Part 2 - Land of the Pure

پاکِستان

Chapter 1

The plane turned to make its approach and Karachi appeared out of the haze. From a distance, the city was a dark stain seeping into the purity of a salmon-pink desert. As our descent continued, symmetrical lines etched into the desert appeared. As the undercarriage rumbled into position, the lines thickened and became roads, houses, factories and shantytowns.

As we turned to make our final approach, I could even see trucks and buses jostling in the streets and dark columns of smoke from rising chimneystacks across the sprawling city. This was Pakistan, the Land of the Pure.

The remaining flaps slid into place and the aircraft rumbled awkwardly down towards the runway, buffeted by currents of rising warm air. As the ground rose up to meet us, I realised that this was my first sight of a continent that had fascinated me for as long as I could remember.

Like many colonial families, our links with India spanned several generations. My Irish paternal grandfather first came to Bombay at the turn of the twentieth century and his earliest sight of India would have been from the decks of a steamer.

He died before I was born so I will never know how he felt as he approached India for the first time. Instead, I have to rely on the description of an Englishman's first sight of India. Hallam Murray arrived in India at the turn of the century and described his first impressions of India in his book, "High roads of the Empire" published in 1905. I think he captured the moment nicely:

"The first sight of India for the travellers lucky enough to sail by P & O to Bombay, was the wondrous panorama of the Western Ghats,

with their fine rugged outline broken by isolated, precipitous and almost inaccessible peaks, silhouetted against the sunrise. That great barrier range runs south for eight hundred miles following the line of the coast. It rises sometimes in splendid precipices, sheer out of the water, sometime abruptly in terraces, beyond to a strip of flat green and low-lying land, to an extreme height of nearly seven thousand feet.

After days of empty seas, the coastline becomes gradually clearer and two days afterwards, numbers of small brown lateen sails appear and clumps of fishermens' stakes, like Venetian pali, standing out of the sea. At last, Bombay emerges misty above the horizon and two hours later, you sail into the harbour.

The beautiful bay studded with green islands and jutting precipices, unfolds itself, with its backcloth of strange, almost quaintly shaped hills, among which the Bawa-Melang catches the eye with its peculiar cylindrical and bottle-shaped peak crowned with a ruined fort."

Born in 1878, my grandfather was brought up in a staunchly Catholic family in a village near the market town of Newmarket-on-Fergus, County Clare. His parents made sure that he had a good education and eventually sent him to Dublin to study medicine at Trinity College. Like his brother, he chose to join the British Army and soon found himself in India as a doctor in the Royal Indian Army Medical Corps.

Most of his career was spent serving overseas. Over the length of his career, he spent time in Egypt; Mesopotamia; India; China and Hong Kong. He spent three months touring Japan in 1907 while on leave from the army. In a pile of his old photographs, I came across a faded picture of him on horseback with two local guides hired to carry his luggage as he explored the foothills of Mount Fuji.

His bachelor life ended when he married Adele Dillon, a feisty young Irish-American woman from Rhode Island. They met in Dublin in 1911, when she was eighteen and he was on study leave at the Trinity College Medical School. She happened to have been staying as a guest of the family with whom he lodged.

On the face of it, they did not seem ideally suited. There was a fifteen-year age gap between them and I suspect that his formal, military manner may have clashed with her ancestral fiery Irish temperament. To cap it all, she was American. I do not know quite how it happened, perhaps a combination of his Irish charm and her beautiful dark eyes, but he asked for her hand in marriage and she accepted.

Their union was to trigger a family rift that was to last more than sixty years. The problem was that Adele was not a Roman Catholic and to make matters worse still, she was a Protestant.

Given the circumstances of the marriage, a family wedding in Dublin was out of the question. Instead, they travelled to India and in November 1915, married in Bombay. Not long afterwards, the Army posted my grandfather to the Poona Cantonment, where they found some relief from Bombay's heat and humidity. Ironically perhaps, Poona's name is derived from the Sanskrit, Punya Nagari, meaning "City of Virtue."

In those days, Poona was a sedate hill station to the east of Bombay, surrounded by green forests that flowed endlessly over the jagged peaks of the Ghats, with a kind climate that was almost temperate. In those halcyon days of the British Raj, life for the families of Army officers in India was very comfortable. Supported by a host of servants, they lived in a style unheard of in rural Ireland by anyone except the wealthiest landowners.

Adele fell pregnant immediately and my father was born in Poona just nine months after their wedding.

In Europe, the Great War was already two years old as my father took his first breath. As he gurgled and played through the first two years of his life, millions of soldiers were dying in the bloody fields of Flanders and the Somme. As the Great War neared its end, his brother Harry was born. The brothers had escaped the First World War. They could not have known that the Second World War lay like a shadow across their futures.

While they were still both very young, they lived under the watchful eyes of their Indian Ayah. She was a tall, thin-faced woman, immortalised by my grandfather in a sepia print taken just after my father's birth. Her eyes stare back at the camera with a look of detached disinterest. She had the look of a woman who had lost too much sleep looking after a crying baby, but she cared for the two boys and kept them safe in a difficult world.

When the two boys were old enough and big enough to make her life a complete misery, my grandmother replaced her with a fierce looking Sikh with a turban and a wild moustache. He was more than a match for the two boys and kept them out of serious trouble. In 1921, the family returned to England and Tom was packed off to preparatory school in Eastbourne.

After a brief spell in England, my grandfather was posted to Egypt, which was only few days from England by steamer, so the boys could travel to Alexandria to be with their parents over the summer break. Before long, the boys were as home there as most of their friends were in Dublin or Eastbourne.

After prep school, the brothers were packed off to Rossall School, a boarding school on the windswept Lancashire coast. All too often, freezing, horizontal rain carried by storm winds from the Irish Sea made them long for the warmth and power of the monsoon rains.

Their earliest memories were of India. They remembered the dry scent of sun-baked, earth, the fury of the monsoon rains and the sight of elephants bathing in the glow of the setting sun. They both dreamed of escaping the misery of English winters and returning to the warmth and bustle of India.

The years passed and in 1933, my grandfather returned to England. After a sojourn in Blackheath, he moved to Berkshire to run a military hospital in Reading. He built a house and began to settle down to life in pre-war England. My father began his training to be an architect and his brother won a scholarship to Cambridge. In Germany, Adolf Hitler was making plans to invade Poland. As they watched events unfold in Germany, both brothers came to the conclusion that war was inevitable.

In 1939, they decided to enlist and were soon commissioned into the Royal Berkshire Regiment. After a period of basic training, the Army posted both brothers to India. Harry was transferred immediately to Burma and was killed there in 1943. Tom spent a year at Landi Kotal on the Khyber Pass with the Royal Gawahal Rifles and then transferred to the Intelligence Corps. He and his band of brothers were attached to 3 Special Service Brigade, a combined army/navy commando unit. For several months, they practiced for a sea borne assault of Burma. In 1944, they boarded HMS Keren and set sail for Burma. In the end, the planned seaborne assault was abandoned and instead, the force landed at Cox's Bazaar. My father's Field Security Section was then posted to a small village on the river Naf, which then marked the India-Burma border. Their duties included trips into Japanese-held Burma to gather intelligence and manage double agents that they had recruited.

They were eventually attached to XXXIII Corps Head Quarters in Burma. With the XIVth Army, XXXIII Corps moved down through Burma, chasing the retreating Japanese forces. My father ended his war in Burma in 1945, but his time in the Army continued. The Army sent him to French Indochina in September 1945, where he became embroiled in the early days of what was to become the Vietnam

War. It was a particularly strange period of history. The British found themselves re-arming their Japanese prisoners and using them against nationalist guerrillas led by Ho Chi Minh, who had been funded and armed by the American government.

In February 1946, he flew to the Dutch Celebes to help quell a mutiny of Dutch troops. Two months later, he received orders to go home. He returned to Karachi to wait for transport back to Britain. Whiling away his last few days in India playing squash and horse-riding, he had time to reflect on the prospect of a return to war-torn Europe and a family still mourning the death of his brother. Finally, in April 1946, after a wait of a couple of weeks, he managed to hitch a ride on a RAF Lancaster bomber flying to Tel Aviv. He spent much of the flight asleep on the escape hatch. He never went back to India.

Many years later, I returned from a honeymoon in Kashmir with my new wife, who told my father how much we had enjoyed ourselves.

He smiled and in his wonderful soft voice said, "I am so glad you liked my country."

I was sure that in one corner of his heart, he always felt that India was his home. As I arrived in Karachi forty years after his departure, I experienced the oddest feeling that I too was coming home.

Chapter 2

As a small boy, I was fascinated by the mysterious East and devoured the works of Kipling, Conrad, Ballantine, Masters and the rest with an almost consummate fervour. The books that I read in primary school were full of ripping yarns about the British Empire that today would be considered politically incorrect.

The globe that stood in the corner of my classroom marked out the countries of the British Empire in pink. The very idea of the British Empire filled my mind with possibilities that extended beyond the confines of my West Country home in rural Gloucestershire. The fact that the dismantlement of the British Empire was then well under way was one that seemed to have bypassed my school.

India was also a place that I knew because of my father's bedtime tales of his childhood in Poona. As a child, I had dreamed of steaming to India on a P & O steamer. In my fantasy, I wore a pith helmet hat, a linen suit and had a sun-burnished face. I dreamed of my first experience of India, imagining the heady scent of pungent, spice-laden air, a cacophony of noise, overwhelming heat and a chaotic maelstrom of people pushing and shoving each other.

As I shuffled towards the exit door, it occurred to me that this was one fantasy that was about to become real. Pakistan was no longer a part of India, but as far as my fantasy was concerned that was nothing more than a political inconvenience. For me, this was India, at least for the moment.

The reality was not as I had expected. Karachi Airport was clean and modern and through no fault of its own, a disappointment. Perhaps it was its newness, but there was something missing. I was not sure what. Perhaps it lacked the chaos and confusion that reigned in the India of my childhood dreams?

As I pondered over this puzzle, I followed my fellow travellers in a procession through the spotless immigration and customs halls where uniformed officials watched us with indifference. Only when I stepped into the Arrivals hall, did I start to get a sense of the India that I had imagined. Groups of men dressed in long shirts worn over baggy pyjama-like trousers waited patiently for their baggage to arrive. Sitting on the floor was a wild-looking man with orange hair, his face half-hidden behind a flowing beard. As I passed, he stared at me with polite disinterest. Children of all ages slumbered in loose-limbed bliss on plastic chairs, watched over by women hiding their shadowy faces behind coloured muslin shawls.

Amidst the confusion, skeletal porters struggled to control trolleys piled high with plastic suitcases; travelling trunks; bales tied with rope; and wooden crates filled with engineering parts.

I looked around and noticed that no one else was wearing Western clothes. I began to suspect that I was the only one who had not travelled with a change of clothes, but no one was really paying any attention to my attire or me.

Ignoring the clasping hands of the taxi drivers prowling around the Arrivals hall, I stepped out into the oven-like heat of an Indian day for the first time.

Thomas Stevens was one of the first Englishmen to reach India. He was a Dorset man who travelled halfway around the world in search of trade. An entrepreneur ahead of his time, he was sent by his father, Master Thomas Stevens in 1579 and arrived in the month of October. His journey had been long and dangerous, buffeted by storms and sustained by a combination of prayer and spells of good weather. In a letter to his father, he reported that he had been "received with great charity."

Thomas was a businessman drawn to India by the promise of trade and a fair profit. He never dreamed that his efforts would help establish an Empire on which the sun would never set.

Even though the furnace-like heat of the summer was still several months away, the air was hot enough to sear my face. After spending so long cocooned in the darkness of the plane, the strength of the morning sun was almost too much. As my eyes struggled to adjust to the glare, I became aware of a jostling mass of people laden with huge piles of luggage fighting to get into an armada of battered taxicabs and multi-coloured buses. The sunlight, noise and heat assaulted my senses, leaving me dazed for a moment. This was the first impression of the Indian sub-continent that seemed to fit in with my preconceptions.

In the midst of the chaos, my eye settled on a fat American in a business suit squeezing into an air-conditioned taxi as his stick-like porter struggled to lift his designer suitcases into the boot. As the porter battled with his cases, the American sat back, perspiring heavily. When he noticed the porter heaving his precious bags ungraciously into the back of the taxi he opened the taxi door and leaned out, his face quivering with rage, I heard his voice rise above the background din.

"Mind you don't bust my fucking cases."

He glowered menacingly, wiped of trickle of sweat off his face and picked his nose with his left forefinger. The porter collected his tip and smiled at the American.

"Thank you, sir," he said and bowed his head.

The fat American was beyond and above the world around him and was already planning a hot shower, a cold beer and a club sandwich in his air-conditioned five-star hotel. He would use bottled water to brush his teeth and keep his mouth tightly closed when he showered. His waking minutes would be filled with negative thoughts about the Vice President of Sales and Marketing who sent him to spend a month in Pakistan to install a computerised billing system.

Watching this scene reminded me that I had decided that when possible on this journey, I would use local transport. Somehow, I thought that it would be more interesting to take a local bus to Karachi and find a traditional Pakistani hotel in the heart of the city. The club sandwiches would have to wait.

Among the cluster of buses filling up with people and bags was one heading for the centre of Karachi. The bus was short, squat and ugly, but had been transformed into a work of Islamic art by the addition of burnished aluminium sheets decorated with the many names of Allah in Arabic script.

A voice from within the bus beseeched me to get on board and for some reason, I felt unable to refuse. I clambered on board to find only standing room left. For the princely sum of a rupee and a half, I found myself crammed into a bus designed for twenty with forty or fifty silent Pakistanis and their luggage. The roof of the bus was so low that I had to stoop with my face crammed against the back of the man in front of me. As the sun rose higher in the sky, the temperature and humidity in the bus began to rise slowly, inexorably.

This could almost have been the commuter crush on the Northern Line, except that while the men were crushed together in the back of the bus, women and children were sitting in comfort on reserved seats by the driver. Sweat soon began trickling down the small of my back and I felt in dire need of a shower. The silence around me was deafening.

As soon as the driver set off, the uneasy silence was broken and my fellow passengers greeted me with a flurry of shy, toothy grins and questions. Pressed tight against me on all sides, my immediate neighbours fired their questions at me in quick succession, shouting to be heard over the clatter of the engine. The resulting din was almost overwhelming.

"Hello sir!"

"What is your country?"

"Where are you coming from?"

"What is your name?"

The impassioned voice of a fat student with rivulets of sweat running down his face penetrated the cacophony.

"I am tw-tw-twenty one. W-w-what is your age?"

The fat student could hardly get his words out as he shivered with excitement. Moist fingers clutched my hand as he peered at me with a wild intensity, but he could not look me in the eyes. He pressed his body against mine and I began to feel like a sacrificial virgin trapped in a rugby club changing room.

As I was too tall to stand upright, I had to crouch with my chin trapped against my chest, which only made matters worse.

"What is your country?"

He was very persistent. I felt his fingers squeezing my hand and sweat collecting in the small of my back. If this had been the Tube, I would be very, very concerned, but this was a different culture and I did not know how to react. Nevertheless, when I replied, he smiled and passed my answer around the bus with a certain style. I caught a few words of Urdu.

"*Yi admi Britannia hai.*" His friends laughed and flashed their teeth at me.

"This bus is going Sadaar side. Where are you going?"

A schoolmaster, who appeared from behind me, rescued me. He was earnest and worried that I might miss my stop or even worse not know where I was going. He grasped my other hand and stared into my face, waiting impatiently for my reply. Crouched in an overcrowded, rickety bus, with two strange men holding my hands, was not quite the entry into India of my dreams. Well, one of them was very strange.

"You know that they were planning to replace all these old buses with new ones?"

The student paused briefly, not waiting for my reply.

"I think the new buses will not be so beautiful."

The fat student released my hand, coughed politely and gazed out of the window in silence until he got off. The stickiness left behind on my hand was hard to remove.

The new buses were already being built in a factory on the outskirts of Karachi. I was sure that these old buses would be missed and I suspected that the local bus drivers would delay their replacement for as long as possible. The caring hands of the mechanics had already kept these old buses running well beyond their normal life expectancy and I had a feeling that their work was not over.

As we picked our way through the crowded suburbs, the ticket boy wriggled between the passengers and did his best to make us all feel at home. Creating an atmosphere more like a private party, he collected fares, shared jokes and spread outrageous snippets of gossip. When all fares were paid, he stood in the open door, holding on with one hand so that he could hang out over the traffic and proclaim our triumphant entry into the city.

"Sadaar! Sadaar! Sadaar!"

Beyond the grimy windows of the bus was a world of half-finished buildings, bustling shops, brightly painted billboards, engine fumes, dust and noise. Whenever the bus slowed a little, he leant right out over the pavement and called out to the passers-by, imploring them to leave their lives and join our pilgrimage to the heart of the city. Mostly, they grinned and waved back their refusals. Those brave souls that did choose to leave their lives behind were hauled on board and packed in place with the rest of us.

"Sadaar! Sadaar! Sadaar!" The song continued.

As he clambered through the bus, he caught my eye, grinned conspiratorially and was off again.

"Sadaar! Sadaar! Sadaar!"

Carried onwards by the rhythm of his song, the bus careered towards the dark heart of the city.

The ticket boy kept in touch with the driver by thumping on the roof of the bus. After a while, I began to catch the meaning of his signals.

One thump for "STOP!"

Three urgent taps for "ON! ON! ON!"

And a special tattoo of celebration for "*Sadaar.*"

In the midst of this confusion, I tried to glimpse the streets outside, to breathe the air and get a sense of the place.

In a matter of minutes, the bus had transported me from a world of jet engines, electronic control systems and plastic airline meals into a world still partly rooted in another age. Here, in the crowded streets of Karachi, air-conditioned limousines gave way to camel carts, which in turn gave way to bullock carts. It was a frantic world trying, but not quite succeeding, to hurl itself headlong into the twentieth century.

"Now," I thought, "now, at last, I am here." This was more like it.

Chapter 3

The bus finally stopped in a narrow street deep in the heart of Karachi and it was time for me to leave the party. The schoolmaster helped me clamber down on to the pavement and shook my hand to wish me a safe journey. The ticket boy gave me a thumbs-up as the bus pulled away, leaving me standing alone by the road in a cloud of exhaust fumes. A solitary hand appeared against the rear window and waved.

Taking stock of my situation, my first priority was to find somewhere to stay. With the help of a passing arms dealer who gave me his card, I made my way through the Empress Bazaar to the Khyber Hotel, where for the princely sum of sixty rupees, I had a room with en suite bathroom and lavatory. The bathroom was primitive, but functionally adequate. The bath turned out to be nothing more than a pair of taps sticking out of the wall and a galvanised bucket. The lavatory was a hole in the ground. There was no paper, just a small plastic jug. As I surveyed my new domain, the resident gecko flitted across the ceiling and stopped to stare at me with baleful eyes.

As I explored further, I found I also had a hand basin and a bedside table. Both the fan and bare strip light worked. The decor was austere, with rough wooden floorboards and painted walls creating a comforting rustic atmosphere. From a distance, the green gloss on the wall next to the bed seemed to be speckled with red paint. Closer inspection revealed the squashed remains of countless engorged mosquitoes, bedbugs and cockroaches, bound together with a thin layer of scented hair oil to create a decorative veneer.

It was now early afternoon and I needed a wash, a shave and a change of clothes. With some trepidation, I stripped off and washed. For the first time for what seemed like an age, I felt clean and refreshed. The shabbiness of my room faded and I gave in to the embrace of a dreamless sleep.

When I next opened my eyes, it was already dark outside. Leaving the hotel, I set out into the night, but in the darkness I was soon confused and for some reason, very afraid. I dared not wander too far from the hotel in case I lost my way.

Beneath my feet, the pavement was dotted with red stains of betel juice that in the glow of the neon streetlights looked suspiciously like pools of dried blood. Beyond the streetlights in darkened alleyways, shadowy, sinister figures dressed in long shirts and baggy trousers stood in huddles, talking and smoking.

Stalls selling plastic suitcases, nylon bags, cheap radios, digital watches and pocket calculators competed noisily with each other. Cheap bare bulbs and neon tubes created pools of light that blocked out the darkness beyond. Wailing Pakistani love songs blaring from tinny speakers competed with each other and the sound of heavy traffic. As I began to take in this new assault on my senses, I began to relax and enjoy my first experience of life on the streets of Karachi.

Feeling tired and hungry, I was ready to try some real food. After the dubious delights of Egyptian cuisine, I was sure that anything would have been an improvement. An eating-house in a side street welcomed me into its grubby interior and when my food arrived, it was a delicious minced lamb curry, delicately spiced and served with perfect *basmati* rice.

A middle-aged, fleshy, balding salesman in a white *shalwar kameez* sat down at my table and peered at me with a toothy smile.

"Kamil Aziz, plumbing and bathroom equipment."

He showed me a battered business card and asked if he could practice his English. Within minutes, he steered the conversation to his favourite topic, the dismal state of tap water in Karachi.

"You must under no circumstances drink water from the ruddy tap. In Britain, the water from the tap is clean and safe. But if you, a British man, drink tap water in Karachi it will most probably kill you."

He laughed at the idea. This was cheering news. However, there was more.

"You see, they put in a water treatment system and chlorinate all the water for the city. Do you see?"

I nodded in agreement and chewed a mouthful of rice. It was delicious, especially when mixed with the spicy lamb curry.

"The problem is that the water pipes in Karachi put in by the British have never been modernised. They were made of cast iron and are now rotting. All that clean water is made dirty because it was mixing with the water leaking from the sewage system. This was why you should never drink water from a tap."

The lamb really was very good and the rice perfectly cooked, light and fluffy.

"There are so many leaks in our sewage pipes that the whole city is floating on shit. Human shit. And that is where this tap water comes from."

He poured out a glass of tap water and drank it with a flourish. For an hour or so, he entertained me with tales of the city authority's inability to deal with the biological waste produced by seven million people.

In the end, I could take no more and left him to enjoy the rest of the evening on his own. Back at the hotel, I crawled into bed with a feeling of relief. Above my head, the electric fan stirred the limpid air, gluing the mosquitoes to the walls. Beyond the shutters, the city stayed awake, as I slept like a baby.

In the middle of the night, a sudden spasm brought me back into the real world. I rushed to the pit and the agony began. By morning, I was literally drained.

The sickness lasted most of the day and my plight soon roused the curiosity of my neighbours, two Pakistani students studying at a local technical college. They were very concerned about my health and offered to call a doctor. Late in the evening, the hotel manager came to see me.

"You cannot spend twenty-four hours sleeping. It is not healthy. Are you sick?"

He spoke quietly, with a worried look on his face. I nodded feebly. I explained that I was tired after a long journey and that I had some problems with my stomach. He persisted and asked, "Do you need tablets?"

I shook my head and I told him that I had some.

"It is probably just the change of water. You will be all right. I will have some tea sent to you. It will make you feel better."

The *charwallah* soon appeared with the promised tea served on a stainless steel tray. He poured me a cup of a nectar-like infusion that was sweet, milky and delicious. When it was finished, I had just enough energy to turn over and fall asleep.

In the morning, my newfound student friends dropped in to find me feeling hungry and in good health. They looked at my Western clothes with polite disapproval.

"We will take you to Bohri Bazaar to get you fitted out with a *shalwar kameez*. You will be more comfortable."

Bohri bazaar, established around 1890, is a maze of narrow streets with hundreds of small shops selling a wide range of variety of household goods, including: pots and pans; crockery; cutlery; plastic items; silk flowers; cotton sheets; buttons; threads and all the paraphernalia of dress making.

My friends led me through a labyrinth of alleyways into a tailor's shop and explained that I was an Englishman in need of sensible clothing. With great care, the tailor measured my waist and produced a pair of baggy trousers with a fifty-six inch waist. He gathered in the waist with a pyjama cord that pulled the cloth into a cascade of graceful flowing folds. Over the kameez, I slipped on a shalwar with long sleeves and shirttails. It was a wonderfully comfortable garment and ideally suited to the heat of Karachi.

My hosts liked the effect and insisted that I wore nothing else while I was in Pakistan.

"You are very beautiful in Pakistani dress."

Another first, no man had ever called me beautiful before. Happy that I was now properly dressed, the oldest student revealed their plan to take me on an expedition. There was nothing for me to do but allow myself to be swept along by their enthusiasm. I was touched by their kindness.

"This afternoon, we will visit the Mausoleum of Quaid-I-Azam, founder of Pakistan."

Several student friends eventually joined us as we waited for a bus. They refused to get on one bus because they thought that it was too crowded for me.

Nazir explained, "You are too tall to stand. We will wait for the next one."

Eventually, a less crowded bus arrived and they helped me find a seat. I could not have thanked them enough for their kindness and consideration.

After a short ride, we left the bus near a gate opening into a large parched park. The park marked the site of the Tomb of Al Jinnah, *Quaid-I-Azam* otherwise known as Pakistan's Father of Nations. The tomb is in a tall domed building with blue ceiling tiles made in Japan and a large crystal chandelier donated by the People's Republic of China. The silver railing around the marble sarcophagus was donated by Iran. Despite these small tokens of grandeur, the tomb was actually quietly modest, at least when compared with the tombs of some great leaders.

Jinnah was Governor-General of Pakistan after Partition in 1947 and died of tuberculosis a little more than a year later. I was struck by the irony of the occasion. I had left home to search of my colonial past and instead found myself visiting a monument symbolising the end of the British Raj.

Four skinny soldiers stood to attention in the merciless heat of the afternoon guarding the marble tomb itself. They looked through me and only moved when their replacements arrived. After a short ceremony marking the changing of the guard, they marched off.

After the pleasant warmth of Cairo, the afternoon heat was almost overpowering. It was a sobering thought that the hot season was still a long way off.

I returned to the hotel feeling healthier and happier. I thanked my friends for their company and fell on to my bed in a state of exhaustion. The gecko darted across the ceiling and stared down at me as I fell into a fitful sleep. In my waking moments, the events of the day flashed before me in a kaleidoscope of memories.

As arranged, after the visit to the Tomb, I had joined the students for tea at their technical college. Despite knowing that my hosts had planned the event with great care, I faced the whole business with a sense of impending dismay.

The whole thing had started when the two boys in the room opposite mine knocked on my door to invite me to join them for tea after our visit to Jinnah's tomb. When I accepted, the eldest, Nizar, the trainee pipe-fitter, looked me in the eye and with great majesty announced:

"I am responsible for the management of your refreshments. What shall we obtain?"

After the sickness of the day before, my appetite had not fully returned and my insides began to churn at the prospect of having to face spiced food or sickly sweet desserts. I was also aware that as students, they probably did not have much money. What could I possibly have suggested? I tried to be diplomatic.

"What is available?" I asked lamely.

It was no good. A pained expression crossed Nazir's face and with a sinking feeling in my stomach, I realised that they would not let me get off that easy. He shook his head.

"As it is you who are invited, it must be your choice."

I was learning nuances of etiquette of which I had been blissfully ignorant. A culture chasm opened and I began to sweat. In growing desperation, I tried another tack.

"Could you help me with some suggestions, I had not been here very long yet and I do not know what would be appropriate?"

Nazir considered my request a moment and then to my relief suggested a choice of different fruits.

"Fruit? Apples . . . Mangoes . . . Bananas . . . Oranges . . . ?"

The list continued, but then I remembered that I had read somewhere that bananas were good for upset stomachs. I was very glad that he had not suggested that we went out for a spicy meal.

"How about bananas?" I suggested hopefully. Nazir smiled and I knew that I was making progress.

"Aachaa, bananas."

With great care, he made an entry in his notepad and then looked up at me with large brown eyes.

"What else?"

In desperation, I looked at the two faces now staring intently at me for some inspiration. Hazan, the youngest of the pair, grinned and suggested pistachio nuts. It was agreed.

I watched as the 'refreshments list' was finally committed to paper in laborious English. The letters were misshapen, but the spelling was faultless.

"Bananas . . . pistos . . . tea."

At the technical college, they treated me as an honoured guest and gave me a comprehensive tour of the facilities. We visited a gymnasium, science labs and spotless classrooms, ending up in a dormitory where I was introduced to students lounging around on their beds. With great ceremony, tea arrived and was as promised:

"Bananas . . . pistos . . . tea."

They were kind people and after only a few days in Pakistan, I could already see vast differences between Karachi and Cairo. While Cairo was a tumbledown city crumbling into the dust of neglect, Karachi was a city on the brink of escaping its past. The streets, at least in the parts that I had seen, were clean and well maintained, not potholed and bordered by cankerous piles of stinking rubbish as in Cairo. In Karachi, even the older buildings seemed to have been well maintained and showed few signs of the neglect that I had seen in Cairo.

Later that evening, I woke up feeling hungry having had a short nap and set out in search of food. In the hotel courtyard, I bumped into Alan Cox, an Englishman staying at the Khyber Hotel. A wiry Northerner from Oldham in Lancashire, with thinning red hair, an orange tipped moustache and National Health steel rimmed glasses, he was engaged in an animated discussion in Urdu with a group of students. After we exchanged greetings, he paused to help me order dhal and chapattis.

After the students finally drifted off, Alan joined me at my table.

"Do you mind if I join you? I've ordered a pot of tea."

The proprietor arrived shortly afterwards with a tray laid out with tea for two and chatted with Alan in Urdu. They laughed at a joke and shook hands as old friends.

He poured me a cup of tea. I told him my story and he listened attentively, asking polite questions from time to time. We exchanged tales as only two travellers meeting in a foreign land could, knowing that this was a ritual and the questions were those that travellers have always asked each other and always will.

"Where are you going?"

"Where have you come from?"

"Why did you leave?"

"Why are you here?"

"What were you doing before you left?"

We chattered on. When my food finally arrived, Alan told me about himself and it soon became clear that he had an interesting past.

"Me? I was a bit of a mixed bag really. I got a third in Chemistry so I took a two-year postgraduate Theology course. I passed that and became a bloody vicar."

With a flourish, he poured himself another cup of tea.

"My heart wasn't really in it. I was more inclined to the House of the Pope, than the Church of bloody England. I was always a bit too much High Church for some, but sod 'em."

He took off his glasses and gave them a good polish with his shirttail. His eyes were pale, half hidden behind long eyebrows.

"As a Northern vicar, I spent much of my time meeting my parishioners in pubs over a few beers. It was a good way to chat with 'em. A pub was sort of like neutral territory. I saw many parishioners that way. Perhaps too many. Anyway, I got done for drink driving twice."

He grinned wickedly at the memory.

"After the second offence, the Judge decided that he liked my licence so much that he told me that he was 'going to look after it' for three years. The first time, he only kept it for one year. I suppose he must have grown to like the damned thing."

"After the court case, the bishop sent for me and asked me what I was going to do with my drinking problem. I told the bishop that I did not have a drinking problem, just a driving problem. He was not amused."

Alan laughed aloud at the memory.

"The bastard had no sense of humour. Anyway, it did not really matter. I left the church not long after that. I saw a Catholic bishop about becoming a priest, but he told me that I would have had to wait six months before I could take any vows. It was no use. One day I walked out of my church and said 'fuck it'. I've never been back."

The students came to say good night and left us talking under a star-studded sky.

"I got a job with the Department of Health and Social Security (DHSS) and then trained for a year as a maths teacher, because I got twenty pounds a week more doing that than I got working for the DHSS. I took Urdu classes because most of the kids I taught could speak more Urdu than English."

The waiter cleared the table and left us.

"I started coming to Pakistan to practise my Urdu and keep coming back. I really like the people and the country."

"I came here this time to escape Christmas in England. I 'ate Christmas."

He paused for effect.

"It's nowt but bloody baby worship."

To emphasise his point, he twisted his moustache to a fine point and adjusted his glasses.

"It's disgusting. But while I was here in bloody Karachi, I wanted to go to Midnight Mass on Christmas Eve. I found out that there were two services. One in English in the Cathedral and one in Urdu in some slime pit village hall. Being as I wanted to practice my Urdu, I had to pick the slime pit. Caused some problems while I was there."

Old habits seemed to die-hard.

"I asked them if they thought it right that the posh people should have the Cathedral for a service in English, while the other people in a country speaking bloody Urdu had to make do with some crappy village hall. I had a feeling that I might have stirred up something there. Funny thing was that they said that many people at the Cathedral service couldn't even speak bloody English."

We parted company and I retired to bed. The overhead fans turned noisily in the sticky air, grounding the mosquitoes and I fell asleep thinking about Alan and his fight with his internal demons.

Alan lost his faith struggling against an ecclesiastical authority that seemed to have made little effort to understand him. He did not fit into the cosy world of the parish priest. In Pakistan, something had reached out to him and he stood once more on the very brink of faith.

At the same time, he was both profane and profound. He was a man at conflict with himself and with the world at large. However, it was a healthy conflict. There should be more priests like Alan who do their work in smoke-filled northern pubs, or in shabby Karachi hotels, so that sceptics like me can talk about faith without having to go to a church.

I awoke to find the sun shining through the window slats and a city that was both warm and friendly. The hotel manager served me breakfast in my room. It was very good. In England, there are many restaurants serving *authentic* Indian and Pakistani dishes. In a quiet hotel in Karachi, my host presented me with an "authentic" English breakfast: piping hot porridge, pallid fried eggs on flaccid toast, topped off with a pot of piping hot milky tea.

After breakfast, I escaped and set out to explore Karachi on my own. My first stop was the Empress Bazaar, a thriving market, built in Victorian Gothic style in 1889 and crowned with a clock tower one hundred and sixty-five feet high. This was Southend-on-Sea in the East.

The difference was in the smell of the place. With every breath, I absorbed a heady concoction of market smells: rotting vegetables; over ripe fruit; cardamom pods; ground coriander; cloves; fenugreek; star anise; and chilli powder, mingled with the less than delicate odours rising from the gutters. Looking around, I saw that the market was light and airy, full of colour and buzzed with the sound of people going about their normal business.

My path took me towards the station along a street lined with bookshops. In one shop, I bought myself an Urdu primer and promised to try to learn some of the language before I left.

A quick glance revealed that the primer had been written for the British Army before Independence, probably in the thirties. I could imagine my father using the primer to brush up on his Urdu when he returned to India as a young British Army officer in 1942. There were many phrases with a strong military flavour that would have been useful during the First World War.

"The airship arrived on time". *Hawai jahaz waqt par pahuncna tha.*

"We have dug many trenches". *Ham ne bahut morche khode nain?*

The only text that had been updated in this modern reprint stated, "The Pakistan Army gets more efficient every day."

In one of the more upmarket shopping areas, a crippled beggar scuttled past me on all fours. All the long bones in his arms and legs had been carefully broken in the middle and reset at right angles, so he could only crawl on all fours. He smiled at me and held out a twisted hand.

This was professional begging where healthy children are mutilated and supplicants cultivate open sores by painting them with sugar water to attract flies. Not wanting to support a practice that I found abhorrent, I chose not to give him any money. He cursed me and scurried away.

At the Cantonment Railway Station, I launched myself into the task of getting an onwards ticket for Lahore. Getting a ticket was a simple matter. Getting my hands on the appropriate forms and permissions was another matter.

At first, I was passed from office to office like a bad penny, collecting forms and permits. It was bureaucracy gone mad, a world of ancient manual typewriters, sheets of wrinkled carbon paper and endless numbered forms.

In every office there were shelves piled high with ancient piles of loose-leaf files tied with faded ribbons. The oldest files were in an advanced stage of decomposition and were entombed in a thick layer of dust. In these crumbling archives were records of journeys taken by long dead travellers carefully logged by forgotten railway clerks. Perhaps in these decaying records were details of the movements of spies, political activists and rebels. In reality, no one seemed to care about the past any more.

I watched rows of clerks filling in forms; typing out travel permits on ancient manual typewriters with two slow fingers; and recording details of journeys in great bound ledgers that they would one day be laid to rest on the shelves above their heads

Despite any of my misgivings and repeated refusals, I left the Booking Office with a ticket for the overnight Shalimar Express to Lahore. I rushed back to the hotel and said my farewells to my friends.

Returning to the station with my luggage, I found my seat in First Class Air Conditioned. To my surprise, the train left on time.

Chapter 4

By train, the distance from Karachi to Lahore is some twelve hundred kilometres. The track, originally built by the British, crosses the Sind desert roughly following the course of the Indus and some of its larger tributaries.

The Shalimar made steady progress through the urban squalor of Karachi's suburbs, out into the Sind desert, a barren landscape of sand and scrub from horizon to horizon. The monotony was broken only by sight of the occasional village and more rarely, by a solitary camel loping across the landscape, so I fell asleep to the mutterings of the wheels on the track.

"Go-ing north. Go-ing north. Go-ing . . ."

Gone.

After several hours of nothingness, the train halted briefly in Multan, a dreary-looking town isolated in the heart of the Sind desert. The station was clean, tidy and well maintained.

Beyond the neatness of the station was a depressing landscape filled with ramshackle buildings and faded billboards giving an impression of a town fallen on hard times. This was a place of desolation with drab buildings devoid of colour and dreary streets haunted by ashen-faced people in robes of grey. The buildings seemed out of place in the vastness of the desert, which seemed to be waiting for the men to move away so that it could reclaim the land for itself. Looking around I found it hard to believe that there had ever been any good times in this place, but Multan was no place to be judged by first impressions.

Behind its crumbling façade, the city was very much alive and was home to artisans and workers who produced silk, cotton, carpets, glazed pottery and enamel work. Surprisingly, given its position in the heart of the Sind desert, Multan is an important centre of trade for the farmers of the region, handling crops of cotton, wheat, wool, sugar, indigo, oilseeds, as well as a producer of manufactured goods, many of which were shipped by rail to other parts of the country.

The rows of crumbling houses of mud and straw created a patchwork of shadows that blended seamlessly into the shimmering heat of the desert. These structures stood as evidence of the age-old struggle between countless generations of builders and an unrelenting climate.

The desert wind carried an abrasive cloud of sand particles that rasped like the tongue of a cat at the very fabric of the town. When the torrential desert rains came, the raindrops ate into exposed surfaces, leaving behind gaping wounds in walls and roofs. Wooden window frames shrank in the searing heat of the sun, shedding shards of blistered paint. Little by little, the town was being devoured by the desert. Without the untiring efforts of the town's builders to repair these ravages, Multan would have been taken back into the desert centuries ago.

As the desert consumed abandoned graveyards, the remains of the dead were recycled, helping to nourish the generations that follow them. How many people had lived and died here over the millennia? Hundreds of thousands certainly. Millions? Perhaps. A sobering thought occurred to me that all that remained of these countless hordes was dust and perhaps a few bones. For a fleeting instant, a sense of the weight of all of these lives and deaths passed through my consciousness and was gone. My senses reeled under the impact of Multan's past and a shudder passed through me. This was the impact of this vast, forbidding and above all, humbling landscape. From the air-conditioned isolation of my railway carriage, I was filled with an unexpected sense of horror.

With a jolt, the carriage began to move and we crept back into the purity of the desert. Progress was slow as the train broke down with monotonous regularity and eventually as we waited in a siding for the engine to be repaired, the slow train from Karachi overtook us.

The Punjabi sitting next to me explained, "The Shalimar is supposed to have three engines. They have taken away two of the engines and the strain is too much for one engine. There was an article in the newspaper about it last week. It is disgraceful. You would have been better off taking the slow train."

The train eventually pulled into Lahore several hours late and I stepped out of the air conditioning into the kiln-like heat of the plains. The air sucked the moisture from my lips and for a moment, it was almost an effort to breathe. But it was a dry heat and after a few moments, my body adjusted and a pleasant sensation of warmth embraced every pore of my body.

The railway station was a delight, an ageing collection of bricks, cast iron and glass piled together in the Victorian Gothic style by British engineers.

The din was almost overpowering, with porters in uniform fighting with each other for business. It was a wonderful sight. There was a buzz in the air that set my pulse racing. The collective energy of the hundreds of passengers streaming off the platform was almost tangible. I watched in amazement as many of my fellow travellers sprinted away from the Shalimar as if their lives depended on somehow making up for the delay.

Within the chaos was a sense of purpose that propelled me along the platform, over the footbridge and ejected me in the open area to the front of the station. Taking heed of the many warnings I had been given about the level of violent crime and police corruption in Lahore, I took a room in a small hotel close to the station.

My refuge from the terrors of the night was a windowless cell, furnished with a single cot and sheets that were freshly laundered, but still looked grey and well used. No matter. The electric fan worked and the taps in the bathroom ran with both hot and cold water. There was no bath, just the usual bucket and plastic jug. I washed and lay back with a pot of milk-tea, thankful that one more stage of this journey had ended. What was better was the knowledge that tomorrow would bring the prospect of another new horizon.

As daylight faded, I felt rested enough to look for food and brave the streets. It did not take me long to discover that in Lahore, there was a wealth of food to tempt even the most jaded palette and that I felt as safe there as I had in Karachi. In the McLeod Road, chicken tikka Lahore-style was served in the stalls that lined the pavement. The smell of cooking and the sight of dozens of live chickens in cages drew me off the street to a pavement stall.

As my chicken was selected, slaughtered, skinned, gutted, marinated and grilled in front of me in a matter of minutes, it occurred to me that this was not a really treat for the squeamish. At least I could be sure that the meat was fresh. It was also delicious.

There was something unnerving about eating one chicken as its relatives were being slaughtered in the gutter just a few feet away from my table under the nervous gaze of its surviving brethren. On the other hand, it was better than most fast food served in the West.

Lahore is second largest city in Pakistan and the capital of the Punjab, with a population of some three million. The name Punjab was derived from the Urdu words *punj* meaning five and *aab* meaning waters. Five major tributaries of the Indus flow through the Punjab: the Sutlej; Bea; Ravi; Chenab; and the Jhelum.

Each year, the flood-waters carried by these rivers deposit silts on the farmland of the flood plains. The fertility of the Punjab is maintained by these mineral-rich silts.

Recognising Lahore's strategic and economic importance, the British built a new city centre that became the Cantonment. The old city centre was the antithesis of the new centre with its broad, open avenues and solid British-built administrative and commercial edifices built in Mughal Gothic style.

With this history in mind, I got up early and headed for the old city. The walk from my hotel took me through a thriving industrial zone crammed with small workshops and factories. One street was filled with workshops rewinding electric motors, generators and car alternators. In the next street, oily mechanics were hard at work repairing and refurbishing worn-out gearboxes. This was a "mend and make do" recycling culture. Nothing was wasted. Instead, skilled workers performed miracles on worn-out machines that would have been consigned to the scrap heap back home.

The old town was a cluster of narrow streets and twisting alleyways that had escaped the passage of time. In one darkened corner, an ancient tailor with missing teeth grinned at me from his open fronted workshop. Leatherworkers plied their trade in harmony with greengrocers, butchers and ironmongers. Friendly faces called out to me as I wandered through the maze of alleyways. Children pointed at me and giggled, hiding their faces when I turned to look at them. A few called out and asked for pens. The alleyways were the domain of the men sent out by their wives to do the shopping. The few women I saw wore shawls wrapped closely around their faces.

The old city sits in the shadow of Lahore Fort, a massive structure that had guarded this centre of commerce for the best part of a millennium. The fortified walls of Lahore Fort speak of centuries of turbulent times. The fort pre-dated the coming of Mahmud of Ghazni in the eleventh century, was ruined by the Mongols in 1241, rebuilt in 1267, destroyed again by Timurlane in 1398 and rebuilt once more in 1421.

The great Mughal emperor Akbar replaced its mud walls with solid brick masonry in 1566 and extended it northwards. Later Jehangir, Shah Jehan and Aurangzeb added the stamps of their widely differing personalities to its fortification, gateways and palaces.

The Elephant Gate was built by Shah Jehan and opens up onto the Hathi Paer, or Elephant Path, a stairway with fifty-eight steps that allowed access by royalty mounted on elephants to the forecourt of the Shish Mahal, the Palace of Mirrors, which lay within the fort. Climbing these broad, shallow steps gave me a brief glimpse into the power of the Mughal Empire. The sight of heavily decorated elephants carrying the power into the inner sanctum of the fort and away from the bustle of the narrow, crowded streets must have been stupendous.

The fort encloses an area of approximately thirty acres and the buildings within its walls stand as a testament to the gracious style of Mughal rule at its height, in which every man knew his place and where courtly behaviour had been refined into an elaborately stratified social code. Much of the architecture reflects this code.

From a raised balcony in the Diwan-e-Aam, or Hall of Public Audience, built by Shah Jehan in 1631, the emperors looked down on the common people over whom they ruled when they came to present petitions and to request the settlement of disputes. Wealthier citizens and the nobility were allowed to meet their emperors on a level floor in the Diwan-e-Khas, the Hall of Special Audience, which was also built by Shah Jehan, in 1633.

While the Hall of Audience was characterised by its strict functionality, other buildings raised under Shah Jehan's patronage were styled in a more imaginative and fanciful manner. Of these the Shish Mahal, which stands on the fort's north side, was by far the most splendid. It consists of a row of high domed rooms, the roofs of which are decorated with hundreds of thousands of tiny mirrors in traditional Punjabi "Shishgari" style.

As I peered through an ornate archway in the Shish Mahal, the voice of a tour guide echoed across the plaza.

"A candle lit inside any part of the Palace of Mirrors throws back a million reflections that seem like a galaxy of far-off stars turning in an ink-blue firmament."

The fort is no longer a haven for the wealthy and is instead a meeting place for the people of Lahore and a museum to a way of life that is no more.

Outside the fort, the heat was almost overpowering and I needed to drink something. Parisians meet in cafes to pass the time of day over a glass of wine or a cup of coffee. The British congregate in pubs to chat and enjoy a pint or two of warm beer. In Lahore, men stand in the street drinking glasses of freshly crushed juice from sugar cane stalls, so I felt obliged to join them.

In the alley next to the exit from the fort, several companies competed for business. Their stalls exuded the sweet, sour smell of crushed sugar cane. Designed as a fusion of wood and stainless steel, the stalls were utilitarian works of art. They were uniformly equipped with stacks of raw green cane, great blocks of ice and an assortment of grimy glasses. The raw cane was skinned and chopped into bite-sized chunks or fed into steel rollers that crushed the cane and extracted the juice.

On the superior stalls, the rollers were driven by a popping two-stroke engine and the juices stored in an ice-filled tank below. On the older stalls, men turned the rollers by hand.

The juice had an odd taste, but when chilled was delicious. The only problem was the quality of the water used to make the ice and to dilute the juice. It was good, but I knew that there was a good chance that I would pay for these thirst-quenching delights.

Far from Lahore, the mountains of the Hindu Kush beckoned and I knew that it was time for me to move on and escape the delights of urban Pakistan. I knew that the cuisine of Lahore was good enough to make me want to return one day.

As soon as I could, I left by Flying Coach minibus, arriving in Rawalpindi in darkness. One of my fellow travellers directed me to the centre of town, but somehow in the darkness I managed to get lost. As I wandered around unlit back streets trying to find my way, I was shaken by the rumble of a distant explosion, but dismissed it as a firework. Eventually, I found a hotel and bedded down for the night.

Breakfast was a real treat, with a generous serving of porridge, eggs, toast and tea, delivered by an elderly Pakistani. Placing the back of his hand on his forehead, he bowed deeply and backed away from me. He was always there just outside my room, eager to change the linen, bring me food and sweep the floor. He was very attentive and watched my every move with great interest. I could not decide whether all this was just in the hope of a good tip or if he was just anxious to please a guest from overseas. In the end, I decided that he was just trying to make my stay as pleasant as he could.

A brisk walk took me from my hotel towards the commercial centre of Rawalpindi. The sight of black and orange Morris Minor taxis competing for trade with horse drawn *Tongas* was a reminder that this really was a country in transition from another age enjoyed at a slower pace.

At the junction between City Sadaar Road and the Kashmir Bazaar, I came across a large unusually silent crowd held back by the police with *lathis*. Intrigued, I pushed my way to the front, to find that they were all watching an elderly cleaner sweeping a section of the road that had been cordoned off.

I asked a police officer to tell me what was going on. It was not until he turned to face me that I noticed that he had been crying. His English was poor, but good enough to tell me what had happened.

"Bomb. Big bomb. Many dead peoples."

Mystified, I looked around for any sign of an explosion. The windows in the buildings around the plaza were intact and there was no sign of any damage to the road. At a rough guess, there must have been at least a hundred police officers armed with batons and *lathis* holding back a crowd of onlookers. It was all very confusing. Finally, I found a businessman who could tell me what had happened.

"There was an explosion here last night. Fifteen people were killed and one hundred wounded. The bomb was planted at the entrance to the bazaar and went off in the crowd."

He was in a state of shock and his eyes were filled with a mixture of anger and sorrow.

This was why there was so little visible evidence of the explosion. The people in the bazaar had absorbed much of the force of the blast, helping to limit the damage to property. The old man was still washing and sweeping the sandy road surface.

"Why is he doing that?"

"He was washing away the blood of all those dead and injured people. This was the first bomb here in Rawalpindi, but it was not the first in Pakistan. It is the work of the enemy."

"Who is the enemy? India?"

"No, no. Afghanistan. The Afghans are our real enemy. They train people to leave bombs in our cities. But it was a terrible thing for any man to do."

I could imagine the chaos caused by an explosion in a busy Pakistani bazaar: the violence of the blast, the stunned silence and the sound of screams that followed. The sight brought back memories. The Zephyr and I had been staying in a Paris hotel just twelve months before, when a bomb exploded in the bookshop next door. The blast shook our room and set the bookshop on fire. Memories of the anger of that explosion and the screams of the injured in the street below our window flooded back to me and I shivered even though the air was warm. Had I not lost my way in the darkness, I could very easily have been caught in the blast.

I walked away from the crowd feeling just a little sick and took a bus to Islamabad to get away from a place filled with sadness.

Islamabad was an enigma, in some respects like an exotic version of Milton Keynes, but built on a monstrous scale with imposing public buildings housing ministries of state; one of the largest mosques in the world; wooded areas; and private villas set in high walled compounds.

Construction began in 1961 using plans drawn up by Doxiadis Associates, a Greek firm. The city was built in a triangle facing the Margala Hills to the North. Within the triangle was a grid divided into eight zones, designated governmental, diplomatic, residential, commercial, educational and industrial. Islamabad forms a sprawling conurbation with Rawalpindi and is the capital city of Pakistan.

My first impression of Islamabad had nothing to do with great architectural designs. Instead, the reek of cannabis bushes growing in lush profusion on every scrap of waste ground almost overwhelmed my senses. The smell was aromatic and sickly.

The sheer scale of Islamabad was daunting and it took me half a day to realise that it would take me too long to get around on foot. Instead, I worked how to use the local minivans that served as taxis. Eventually, with the help of a local businessman, I located the Chinese Embassy and dropped off my passport. With a sense of relief, I took the bus back to Rawalpindi to wait for my first Chinese visa.

There were still a few signs of the old colonial days: the remaining Gothic buildings and the cricket pitch next to the spire of St. Paul's Church of Scotland, which had been converted into a garden centre.

Without my passport, I was stranded in Rawalpindi. Time seemed to crawl past and the sight of buses full of people leaving Rawalpindi left me with just the slightest tinge of envy.

Eventually, my visa was ready for collection and there was nothing more to do but collect my passport and book a seat on a minibus to Peshawar. For once, the journey started at a reasonable hour and I left Rawalpindi and its neighbour Islamabad with as much desire to return as I had for a visit to Milton Keynes. The open road was somehow more welcoming. The Flying Coach minibus soon left the grand, soulless avenues of Islamabad behind and made steady progress.

This was Kim's road, the Great Trunk Road, described by Kipling as *"the artery that throbbed with the lifeblood of all of India"*. The traffic on the road was less exotic than in Kipling's day. There were no elephants, no wedding processions and no sign of any pilgrims, horse-traders or spies.

Instead, the road was mostly empty. The traffic was made up of the occasional wheezing bus; brightly coloured trucks; four-wheel drive Land Cruisers; minibuses; whining mopeds; tinny Japanese cars; and bicycles held together with string. Less romantic perhaps, but more practical.

The minibus crossed the mighty Indus, driving past warning signs forbidding the photography of bridges. The army clearly thought that spies were still travelling along the Great Trunk Road and that those spies would heed notices asking them not to photograph strategically important bridges. It was nice to know that we lived in such a trusting world and one that seemed to be ignorant of the capabilities of military satellites.

As we approached Peshawar, I strained my eyes for a first sight of the Hindu Kush to the north. To my continuing frustration, the mountains remained hidden in the distant haze.

Instead, the landscape was flat, brown and dusty, bisected by the great flow of the Indus, its many tributaries and by treacle-black streams choked with pollutants. Beside the road, windblown plastic bags hung in trees like rotting fruit. Through the dusty windows of the bus passed visions of dilapidated villages half buried in the detritus of modern life. The spread of urban squalor into the countryside seemed unstoppable and I felt a great sense of disappointment.

Nevertheless, beyond the filth was great beauty. As the hours passed, I sank into a dreamlike state, absorbed by the majesty of this great landscape and the knowledge that it would outlive all those who despoiled its magnificence.

My daydreaming was rudely interrupted when we stopped to pick up new passengers and a young man came to sit by me. Despite his manner which seemed cold at first, he immediately struck up a conversation with me.

"What is your country?"

His demeanour was all too serious and did not suit his boyish features. He seemed pleased that I was British or at least he was indifferent. As usual, he wanted to know all about me. His tone of voice became increasingly accusatory as I failed more and more of the questions in his instant test of good character.

"How many children do you have?" None.

"Are you married?" No.

"Why are you not married?" He seemed to be worried that I might have been gay. When I told him that I had been married, it was clear that he did not believe me. With each answer, I condemned myself further in his dark eyes.

"Are you Muslim?" No.

"Have you read the Qur'an?" Not really.

This was almost the last straw.

"Do you drink wine?"

The question provoked a vision of a glass of good red wine, perhaps a heavy-bodied Bordeaux or a raw, fruity Burgundy fresh from the vine. I could smell the bouquet and almost taste the grapes on my tongue. I nodded weakly. His reaction took me by surprise. He reproached me firmly and waved his fist in my face.

"You are a slave to wine. It rules your life." He glowered at me, shaking his head.

"You should not drink wine."

He was clearly convinced that I was a slobbering gay alcoholic and that I was planning to pollute him with my Infidel ways. With a shrug of his shoulders, he got up in disgust and moved to an empty seat at the front of the bus. He was right of course, I was a reprobate and probably beyond all hope.

As a religion, Islam expects its followers to have Faith and to do good works. When these high ideals are cast aside and the ritual of prayer takes over so that only outward demonstrations of Faith are important, something of the beauty of Islam is lost. The Islam preached by the fundamentalists seems to focus more on these outward signs and less on the inner warmth felt by many converts to Islam when they experience the splendour of the Qur'an.

Extremists lack the compassion shown in true Believers and do no good works. Theirs is a twisted expression of Islam that is 'all show and no action'. Like Alan, the ex-priest from the Khyber Hotel, I found Islam as practised by extreme fundamentalists overbearing and repressive. It is the fundamentalists who are overbearing and repressive, not Islam.

Eventually, the countryside ended and after a long haul through sprawling suburbs, the bus stopped in the shadow of the Great Fort, a couple of miles from the centre of Peshawar.

Stepping out into a seething mass of travellers, I was almost choked by a blue-grey cloud of exhaust fumes. The worst polluters were spluttering three-wheeler Vespa taxis and ancient, wheezing trucks. The crowd was in constant motion as more minibuses arrived and dumped their passengers into the fray.

Grey haired men with grizzled beards loading bags into brightly decorated trucks, argued with self-appointed marshals, who seemed to do nothing but make the chaos worse. Would-be travellers waited patiently by piles of boxes and suitcases, hoping that they would eventually be able to make their escape.

The noise and bustle engulfed me and filled me with a sense of arrival. With some trepidation, I pushed through the throng and took a three-wheeler to the central Sadaar district, where I found a small hotel close to the main bazaar.

Located at the top of a flight of painted concrete stairs leading off the pavement, the hotel was basic, but clean. The receptionist showed me to my room, which had an electric fan that worked. Even better, was the bathroom with a bare concrete floor, a plastic jug and a bucket that served as a shower. Around me, the sound of my fellow guests coughing, clearing their throats and spitting mingled with the hubbub rising from the street outside.

My lower bowel was still being a nuisance. After five days of misery, I had resorted to a treatment of antibiotics. Food was sliding through my system in a matter of hours, so I was not able to absorb much in the way of nutrients. If I had had the sense to see a doctor, he would have told me that I was supporting a large colony of unfriendly protozoa in my gut that were damaging my intestines and helping me to lose more weight than was safe. He would have told me that antibiotics would not help and I should expect to continue to lose weight until I got the right treatment. The trouble was that I was too impatient to get up into the mountains and did not want to waste time seeing a doctor. There would be time for that in the coming months.

In the evening, I strolled through the bazaar and ended up with a meal of chicken and sweet corn soup at the Hong Kong on the Mall, Peshawar's "best" Chinese restaurant or so the billboard claimed.

I woke up in the middle of the night with a splitting headache, a fever and the first signs of bronchitis. I also had dysentery. As the discomfort passed in waves through my lower bowel, I began to understand why the Victorians became so obsessed with the regularity of their movements; the habit must have been brought back to England by the early colonialists.

Lying awake in agony, I tried to distract myself by imagining what it must have been like for my father coming here as a young man. His journey had started in a Drill Hall just off the Euston Road in London.

In September 1939, my father enlisted into the Artists Rifle Brigade and was eventually commissioned into the Royal Berkshire Regiment. After completing his initial training, the Army posted him to Northern Ireland.

The increasingly aggressive statements coming from Tokyo had forced the British to begin building up their forces in India and the Far East. All major units were asked to provide two officers and my father and his brother were eager to put their names down. My father had become utterly sick of the endless training exercises, the rain and the icy winds of Colraines. The chance to volunteer for a transfer to India was too good to miss.

In India, he reasoned, it would at least be warm. He sailed to Bombay in 1942, stopping briefly in Durban on route. After a six-week period of acclimatisation, he was posted to Landi Kotal on the North West Frontier to spend a year attached to the Royal Garwhal Rifles. When he got there, he found that the weather on the Khyber Pass was as cold, wet and miserable as it had been in Northern Ireland.

In those days, Land Kotal was a desolate garrison town, a few miles from the Khyber Pass on the key trade route between India and Afghanistan. He arrived there in the late spring of 1942 to find the last of the winter winds slicing through the Pass and six-foot high drifts of snow. When his tour of duty at the Khyber Pass was over, he returned to Karachi and was transferred to the Intelligence Corps, probably because he spoke Urdu fluently.

For me, the route into Afghanistan from Peshawar was closed because of the Afghan-Russian conflict. I would have liked to visit Landi Kotal, the garrison town for the Khyber Pass to see where my father was stationed, but had to come to terms with the idea that Landi Kotal would have to wait until the fighting was over. In any case, I had other plans.

Ahead of me lay Chitral, once the capital of the princely state of Chitral in the North West Frontier Province; the mountains of the Hindu Kush; and a tribe of pagans who lived in three valleys close to the Afghanistan border and believed in snow frogs that lived above the snow line.

Chitral is a frontier town with a history steeped in violence, death and bloodshed. In 1895, Pathans besieged a small British force in Chitral fort for seven violent weeks. The problems had been triggered by the death of the Mehtar of Chitral after a thirty-two year reign. His succession was being fought over by his sons, threatening the fragile peace that the British had won only two years before.

Aware of the turmoil in Chitral, Umra Khan, ruler of Jandol and Dir crossed Lowari Pass between Dir and Chitral territories and declared a Jihad on the Kafir Kalash in the Bashgol valley to the south west of Chitral. According to a contemporary British account, his army of four thousand created panic in the villages and "poorer classes."

The British Political Agent in Chitral, Lieutenant B.E.M Gurdon realised that he was at grave risk. A retreat to the safety of the fort in Mastuj was out of the question as he had no supplies, no transport and only a handful of troops. He had to stay in Chitral and face a very uncertain future.

In Gilgit, Surgeon-General George Robertson, the Political Agent, viewed reports of the situation in Chitral with increasing concern. With a small force of Indian troops, he double marched towards Chitral, crossing the twelve thousand, five hundred foot Shandur Pass in deep snow. They arrived at Mastuj Fort on 26 January, 1895. Placed at the junction of three main roads, one to the Shandur Pass, one to the Bargil Pass and one to Chitral, the town of Mastuj is located at a key crossroad and is guarded by Mastuj Fort.

When news arrived that Umra Khan had crossed the Lowari Pass from Dir into the Chitral valley and attacked the village of Kila Drosh, twenty-five miles south of Chitral, Surgeon-General Robertson decided that he had to make a move. He knew that Gurdon could not leave Chitral without help and that if he stayed, Umra Khan's forces would probably kill them.

Robertson ordered more ammunition to be brought up from Gilgit and as soon as was practical, his soldiers set out on the sixty five-mile march to Chitral, arriving four days later on 31 January. The journey had been made nearly impossible by the poor state of the track and by the freezing conditions that made the roadway very slippery.

Umra Khan was still occupied with the siege of Kila Drosh Fort, giving Surgeon-General Robertson time to set up camp in Chitral itself. The siege of Chitral Fort started after a skirmish on 4 March and ended with five hundred and fifty men retreating to the Fort where a number of Pathans surrounded them.

When Robertson's request for ammunition arrived, it was clear to Captain Ross in Gilgit that the situation in Chitral was worsening. He set out from Gilgit with a company of the 13th Sikhs, arriving in Mastuj on 2 March, where he took command of the Fort. His troops brought with them the ammunition and supplies needed to support Surgeon-General Robertson's planned mission to relieve the troops in Chitral. The main problem was that they did not know how much the situation in Chitral had deteriorated and that the siege of Chitral Fort was to start in just two days.

Ignoring good advice from a more experienced Captain Bretherton, the commissariat officer, Captain Ross left the security of Mastuj Fort and set out for Chitral. He reached the village of Buni and was killed after a fierce battle with a large enemy force. Fighting continued up and down the valley and the vital lines of communication between Chitral and the outside world were effectively blocked.

Ahead of me, the roads were equally blocked by snow and the one-hour flight from Peshawar to Chitral was potentially dangerous as the route winds though mountain passes in an area known for its unpredictable weather. The only other way in to Chitral from Peshawar in March is to take bus or truck to Dir and then set out on the long hike over the snow bound Lowari Pass at twelve and a half thousand feet.

After the squalor and filth of lowland Pakistan, I was looking forward to breathing fresh mountain air and walking by streams that were not stinking sewers. Although, I was impatient to leave, I knew that I was in no fit state to face the walk over Lowari Pass. If I was to get to Chitral, I had to get a seat on the next flight and the weather had to be good enough for the flight to leave.

Late in the evening, I reflected on what had been a trying day. The antibiotics seemed to have been having an effect and while I felt much better, I was still very weak. Apart from two visits to the PIA Northern Area booking office, I had been in bed with a fever for most of the day and had seen nothing of Peshawar.

On a more positive note, I had a ticket for the first flight to Chitral in the morning. My first visit to the PIA Northern Area Booking Office had been a disappointment. The clerk had told me that the next available seat was on a flight in six weeks. When I told him that I really needed something before then, his best advice was *"come back tomorrow"*. I tried asking the question another way and was as persistent as I thought I could be. In the end, I had to give up.

His optimism was not convincing, there was something in his face that made me suspect that he would not be able to help. He strengthened my suspicions even more when he explained that a backlog of three hundred passengers had built up because of a run of particularly bad weather and that I would have to be *"patient and wait"*.

When I am in good health, I have been known to be a bit stubborn, but when I am not, I can be impossible. Outraged at what I saw as the dreadful service provided by staff in the Northern Area Booking Office, I stormed off and tried the PIA Central Booking Office next door. I demanded to see the Officer in Charge. After a few minutes he arrived, immaculate in his uniform and asked me to explain the "nature of my problem". I explained my predicament and asked if he could help. He shook his head, paused for a moment and then beamed at me.

"Come back this afternoon at two o'clock and I may have some good news for you."

The discomfort inside my belly increased and a sense of urgency entered the proceedings. All I could do was hope that this young man with his open, honest face really could perform miracles.

The journey back to the hotel was almost unbearable. My insides began to heave ominously and a feverish sweat covered my body. My head ached and I shivered despite the heat. I crawled up the stairs and collapsed into the sweaty comfort of my room.

I woke up later in the afternoon with a blinding headache and in time to meet the "Officer in Charge." As I approached his office, I saw that a crowd of two hundred Afghans and Chitralis had gathered outside the PIA Northern Area Booking Office. Most of them had been delayed in Peshawar by the bad weather, some for several weeks and quite a few of them were in an ugly mood. Trying not to think too much about the discomfort in my belly, I walked into the Central Booking Office and asked to see the Officer in Charge. He did not come immediately and I began to doubt his powers of influence. To my amazement, he turned up and marched me through the throng to the head of the queue in the PIA Northern Area Booking Office. There he told the clerk to issue me with a ticket.

The clerk was clearly annoyed, but took my fare and told me to be at the airport before seven in the morning. We escaped in a hurry and left the clerk to continue trying to placate those unlucky enough to have to wait. It was a miracle and I felt just a little guilty that I had deprived someone of a seat.

Chapter 5

Another early start. My alarm woke me at five thirty and an hour later, I was in a noisy three-wheeler taxi heading for the airport. The air was fresh and the streets mostly deserted. Best of all was the sight of a cloudless sky.

A crowd of squat, bearded Afghans and Chitralis stood in lines at the check-in desks waiting to check in. My immediate thought was that they looked like hobbits. At six foot four, I towered over them, much to their collective amusement. I half expected to see Gandalf sweep in at any moment.

Inspecting my ticket more closely, I noticed that my flight number was C130-I. Judging from the departure board, this was the second of three flights to Chitral.

There was a short delay and the almost orderly lines broke down into a scuffle. The cheerfully rowdy Afghans and Chitralis jostled each other with fierce determination to get to the front and the little order that had been established broke down. Gandalf in the form of a uniformed airport official arrived and managed to calm everybody down. Barking his orders in Urdu, the officer soon had the mountain men standing, albeit reluctantly, in orderly queues. As soon as he moved out of sight, the scrum reformed and pandemonium returned to the sound of howls of laughter.

A pair of glowering security guards fed our bags through the X-ray machine. As one security guard checked my bag, his colleagues jostled me for staring at the monitor, which they had not switched on. Somehow, it did not matter and the technician continued to pretend to stare at the blank monitor as each bag vanished into the machine. I took some comfort from that fact that they opened and searched some bags manually. I later discovered that vegetables and fruit were among the goods banned on the flight. They were also looking for guns and explosives. After all, this was the North West Frontier.

In the departure lounge, an ancient, gaunt-faced attendant served tea and cakes. I was certain that there would be no room for an in-flight meal on a Fokker and made the best of what was on offer. Time passed and we waited anxiously for confirmation that we would take off on time. If a mountain storm swept in, the flight would be cancelled and we would all have to return to Peshawar. It was a depressing thought and we waited in almost total silence with our eyes fixed on the weather. The sight of solitary cumulous cloud forming in the distance was greeted with a murmur of dismay.

The attendant collected the dirty cups and plates. I watched him carefully sweep the crumbs on to the floor and drain the dregs from half-empty cups back into the teapot. The sole comfort I could take was that this was only the second flight of the day.

Finally, a message came through a crackling tannoy telling us to board the flight. It was not until we stepped out on to the runway that I saw that flight C130-I was not a commercial Fokker as expected, but a Pakistan Air Force C130 military transport plane.

As Air Force ground crew carried mailbags and assorted bundles of luggage up the ramp into the hold, I took the time to look more closely at my fellow passengers now waiting in an orderly line on the tarmac under the fierce gaze of an Air Force officer from 6 Squadron. There were around ninety men, women and children. The men were mainly bearded, with round flat caps perched on their heads and woollen blankets wrapped tightly around their shoulders. As we waited, the mountain men wound and unwound their blankets like bats furling and unfurling their wings before a long flight. They were not the only ones feeling nervous. The women, faces hidden behind coloured scarves ignored them and talked amongst themselves in low voices.

We entered the aircraft by a small door at the rear and found ourselves in a darkened cavern already packed with mailbags and luggage. The seats ran the length of the aircraft in four rows. I sat in one of the two inner rows with my knees jammed up against the Chitrali facing me. He grinned and made room for me. The seats were not designed for comfort. They were little more than nylon webbing and plastic, made for soldiers rather than civilians. As we waited nervously in the gloom, uniformed Air Force ground crew crammed even more baggage onto racks above our heads.

A portable generator the size of a small van had been loaded on the ramp. The Flight Engineer supervising the loading of the hold noticed me looking at it and stopped to explain.

"It is needed in case we have to shut off the main engines in Chitral. The facilities at the landing strip are very primitive and they do not have a generator powerful enough for a C130. So we take our own."

The violence of the take-off was brutal. All four Allison T-56-A-15 turboprop engines, each capable of generating over four thousand horsepower, were run up to full power. As the aircraft strained against the brakes, the vibrations ran up my back and shook me so hard that my fillings rattled. Just when I was convinced that the aircraft was about to tear itself apart, the pilot released the brakes and we shot forwards with a jolt. We bumped and crashed down the runway for what seemed an age.

Looking at the scared faces around me in the packed interior, I began to wonder if the pilot had been just a little bit optimistic. Then the bumping stopped abruptly and the plane climbed sluggishly into the air. Around me, the darkness was broken only by shafts of light streaming through the tiny portholes on our side of the hold. The noise from engines made conversation all but impossible, so I leaned back in my seat and tried without much success to sleep.

Beyond the darkness of the hold, the views must have been spectacular as we flew along the Pakistan-Afghanistan border and between the peaks of the mountains of the Hindu Kush. Every now and again, glimpses of snow-capped peaks and great slabs of rock revealed themselves through the nearest porthole as the aircraft banked. We flew over Lowari Pass and then turned into the Chitral valley.

The landing was every bit as spectacular as the take-off and twice as stomach-wrenching. The aircraft twisted and turned as the pilot descended into the narrow valley and lined up for his final approach. The noise of the flaps coming down and a noticeable drop in speed told us that a landing was not far away.

The plane landed heavily and what seemed to be the sound of the fuselage scraping along the runway for a second of two of ear-splitting agony made me wonder if this was to be my last moment. The pilot braked heavily and the airframe shuddered even more violently. With a final bump, we came to a halt and there was silence. For an instant no one moved. Then we were like waking statues, each returning from our private prayers for a safe landing. As soon as my fellow travellers finally started moving, I clambered out of the hold and stepped out into the clear, fresh mountain air.

The sky was a perfect blue, sullied only by the white trails left by two F16 jet fighters. The navigator was keen to tell me why they there when I asked.

"Making sure that we didn't get shot down," he explained cheerfully.

"You see, last month we shot down a Russian military transport plane that entered Pakistan airspace and would not respond to any of our attempts to warn them away. The Russians claimed that it was carrying civilians and that we had shot down the plane in their airspace. We were worried that they might try to shoot this flight down by way of retaliation."

"Do you do this for every flight to Chitral?"

"No, but this flight was the first flight since we shot their transport down, so we thought that they might have tried something."

He turned away, leaving me standing in a stunned silence. Muhammad, the villainous looking Chitrali with whom I had shared knee space, tugged at my sleeve and pointed to a four-wheel drive jeep piled high with bags and men who looked as if they would slit my throat in a heartbeat.

"You come with us to Chitral," he called.

With only a fleeting hesitation, I threw my luggage into the back and let them haul me on-board. As the jeep rattled along the main road to the town of Chitral itself, I lay back on sacks of grain and looked around, absorbing, for the first time, my first views of the valley.

In his account published in 1895, Surgeon-General Robertson described his overall impression of Chitral as one of *"bigness combined with desolation; vast silent mountains cloaked in snow, wild glacier-born torrents; naked rock and pastureless hillsides on which ibex and markhor were once common. It takes time to recover from the depression that the stillness and melancholy of the giant landscape at first compel. All colour is purged by the glare of the sun; and no birds sing. Great eagles, circling slowly aloft represent life."*

It does not take long to see what he meant. The town of Chitral is a sprawl of flat-roofed dwellings perched precariously on the cliffs that form the banks of the Kunar River. This was a landscape dominated by water and yet, it was a landscape as parched as any desert. The barren slopes were testament to the fact that vegetation can only exist where there is water.

Confined by walls of rock, heavy with boulders, silt and a burden of melting snows, the Kunar River boiled and bellowed with rage, a sound that did little to lift the sombre atmosphere. The swollen waters were the colour of milky tea and the sound of the dull ceaseless roar of the river filled the air.

This was the age-old struggle between rock and water. The sound of thunder was nothing less than the mountain crying out in pain as the rasping tongues of the torrent ripped into its living rock. Each grain of silt would eventually find its way to the coast and spill out into Indian Ocean as a milky cloud of sediment. Even as these mountains were ground down by the elements, new rocks were being formed under the sea, biding their time until tectonic movements would cause them to rise again out of the water again into the light of the sun.

From a distance, the buildings that made up Chitral were devoid of all colour and blended so well into the barren hillside so that it was impossible to tell where the town ended and the rocks began. Scattered between the mud-walled houses and shattered rocks were fields of green that defied the order of greyness. Between the fields were poplar trees standing in elegant lines beside the water channels that brought life to an otherwise barren landscape.

Where irrigation channels fed the soil, the fields were impossibly green and fertile. Elsewhere, there was little but ice, bare rock and the stark emptiness of the shale slopes above.

The town itself was overflowing with Afghans, hill tribesmen and supposedly, foreign spies, giving the main street the feel of a frontier town. The sight of so many men carrying guns was a little disconcerting at first. The range of weapons on display was remarkable. Within a few minutes of walking around the bazaar, I had seen shotguns; mother-of-pearl handled pistols; ancient muzzle-loaded muskets; World War II vintage 303 Enfield rifles; and modern AK47 automatics.

The sight of Afghans wearing Russian fur hats and army belts with brass buckles looted from the bodies of dead soldiers was a reminder that there was a war going on just a few miles away over the border.

Beside the street were gutters carrying streams of water and sewage down to the river. The sight of a man defecating directly into the flow a few yards upstream from small children playing barefooted in the murky waters caught my eye. A woman washing cooking pans in the stream watched them play.

The boy with a bored expression behind the reception desk looked up briefly as I approached and then pulled out a beautiful chrome-plated pistol. He closed one eye, aimed at some imaginary target in the hotel garden and squeezed the trigger. There was a sharp click, followed by silence. He held out the magazine clip to show me that the weapon was not loaded and laughed. Click. Click. Click. Three more imaginary enemies fell dead before he was ready for me to sign the hotel register. I duly recorded the date and time of my arrival, as well as my name, nationality, address and occupation.

The receptionist was friendly enough and was happy to tell me that six people had been killed in a shooting incident in the bazaar twelve months before, apparently because of one of many disputes between the local Sunnis and Shi'ites.

For all the guns and the ever-present tension, Chitral was a real breath of fresh air after the suffocating fumes of Peshawar. Even the filtered tap water seemed to have a magical quality in Chitral.

In a dining room off the main street, I bumped into a freelance Australian photographer. He was in Chitral after paying a visit to Kila Drosh to the south to take photographs of the aftermath of a Russian air raid. It was not much of a raid by some standards. A single MiG had dropped four bombs on a mud-walled village in a country that was not at war with Russia. A few houses were damaged and several people killed.

It was strange to think that Kila Drosh was less than two hundred miles from Kabul and less than twenty from the Afghan border. Perhaps the bombing was retaliation for the loss of the Russian transport plane. Perhaps the raid was to discourage the Pakistanis from giving refuge to Afghans. Perhaps it was a mistake. No one really knew.

The photographer stopped and twisted his camera excitedly.

"I got there two weeks after the raid. There were still bodies in the rubble."

I could not tell whether that was a good thing or not. His attitude left me feeling uncomfortable and even a little sick. After two weeks, who would be interested in a story like that anyway? Old news was dead news.

As darkness fell and the chill of night began to work its way into my bones, I explored Chitral's nightspots, which did not take long. Tucked away off the main street was a very good Afghan eating-place. The dining room was laid out with tables and chairs at one end and a raised platform covered with rugs and carpets in traditional Afghan style at the other. The diners sat cross-legged with their food spread out before them on a long plastic mat. Most of my fellow diners were Afghans, distinguishable from the Chitralis by their black turbans and shaggy beards. A few wore traditional rolled woollen caps and woollen blankets furled loosely over their shoulders in Chitrali style, but the sheer length and volume of their beards betrayed their Afghan origins.

The building was old and the dining room decorated with faded Chinese tourist posters showing scenes of everyday life in the paddy fields. An elderly and temperamental cassette player churned out a selection of the popular Afghan songs. The waiter was the final arbiter of taste and kept cutting off songs he did not like. Each time this gave rise to an argument as the diners discussed which song he should play next. The waiter even asked for my opinion, but I thought that it would take me a while to grow to like popular Afghan music.

There was no menu but after a short wait, the waiter placed a feast of steaming white rice served with beef stew and *naan*-style bread on the mat in front of me. The bread was delicious and freshly baked an open-air oven in the street outside. Earlier, I had watched the baker flatten lumps of dough and throw them against the inner walls of the oven. As soon as the breads were cooked through, he peeled them off with a long stick and pricked them with a delicate floral pattern.

Trying to eat stew and rice with my fingers was not easy and at first, I was no more skilled than a two-year old. Watching the others eat, I noticed that the trick was to mould a stew and rice mixture into a ball with my thumb and forefingers and then use my thumb to push the pellet of food into my mouth. I also had to remember that I could only use my right hand. My left hand had to be kept well away from the food. No matter how hard I tried, I could not stop bits of rice falling from my fingers. The other problem was that I was not used to sitting cross-legged for any length of time and it was not long before my muscles began to cramp and my knee joints ached. In the end, I managed to clear the plate and get slightly more food in my mouth than I spilled on the mat.

Outside, the night air tasted cold and smelled of cooking fires and kerosene stoves. Overhead, the stars shone with the clarity only found in high places far away from the dust and pollutants of the plains. The mountains flowed like a dark river between the twinkling beacons of hurricane lamps in homes scattered over the hillside and the stars above.

Chitral at night was a huddle of windswept shadows. The icy wind that swept through the valley at night chilled the unlit streets and stirred dust devils that glittered in the starlight. Afghans and Chitralis wrapped in blankets shuffled past in the gloom, gaunt figures pausing every now and again to cough and spit into the gutter. A dog appeared out the darkness silhouetted in the dust swirling in the headlights of a passing jeep and barked into the night. The shops in the bazaar were shuttered and locked with heavy steel padlocks. A thickset *chowchidar* armed with a torch and a cudgel checked each in turn, coughing and spitting as he worked. The Chitral lunatic stormed past in silence, shaking his fists at the wind as the river growled angrily in the distance. It was time for bed.

In the morning, I felt well enough to start thinking of the next step of the journey, the trek from Chitral to the villages of the Kalash. What was it about these people that they had managed to maintain their old ways in a land where the majority had been converted to Islam? What kind of people believed in fairies and snow frogs that lived in the mountains? There was only one way to find out.

As I needed a permit to visit the Kalash, I paid a visit to the Commissioner's Office. A burly police officer showed me the way to office of the Deputy Commissioner's Clerk who recorded the details of my planned visit to the Kalash and gave me a permit valid for two weeks.

On the office wall was a wooden plaque on which the names of political agents and Commissioners, past and present, had been painted. The earliest names were very British: Captain F.E. Younghusband, the soldier-explorer and Lieutenant J.L.R Gordon, who had stayed behind following Surgeon-General George Robertson's first visit to Chitral in 1893 and Lieutenant B.E.M Gurdon of the Political Department who arrived in Chitral in December 1894. Their presence on the plaque suggested that these young men of the British Empire who came here and fell in love with these wild mountain people and their beautiful valleys were still remembered and respected by the Chitralis.

The day slipped by as I explored Chitral. The town was small, but had an impressive fort, a large mosque and a bazaar, where I bought some supplies in preparation for my hike up into the valleys of the Kalash.

Rising just before dawn, I left the guesthouse and sought refuge from the cold in a teashop. With its simple earthen floor, rickety wooden tables, battered benches and raised cooking area, the teashop was a haven of warmth. I ordered a cup of sweet milky tea and a slice of cake, which was just what I needed before setting out on the road.

The owner sat cross-legged by the fire surrounded by the paraphernalia of tea-making. From time-to-time, he raked embers out of the fire and placed them under a cauldron of simmering milk. He kept the kettle warm over a small oven. Behind him were freshly-baked cakes, neatly stacked in rows. I sat on a bench with my hands around my mug of tea and watched as the sun rose in a flawless sky. It was still cold and the last remnants of mist clung to the poplars bordering the fields that flowed down to the river. When at last I heard a bird sing, I felt ready to face the day.

The road out of Chitral headed south towards the village of Ayun, closely following the river as it twisted through deep, narrow gorges and wide-open valleys. A short distance from Chitral, the metalled road gave way to a rough track. Almost imperceptibly, the modern world slipped behind me. Every step took me further away from Chitral with its landing strip, radio mast, wool mills and modern amenities. This was a journey back into time, to a world without telephones, fax machines or power showers. Ahead of me lay a community that had escaped the ravages of the Industrial world and knew little of the Technological Revolution that was sweeping the "civilised" world.

My route took me against the flow of commuters into Chitral: schoolchildren on foot, students on motorcycles, traders in four-wheel-drive jeeps and hauliers driving brightly-decorated trucks. The track carried me through fords; past fields of ripening barley and wheat; and into tiny villages of stone, timber and mud houses and the occasional government-built primary school, with its roof of corrugated iron, painted in Pakistan's national colours, green and white. In each village, there was a strong sense of order and pride. There was no litter and the streams were clean. The villagers themselves were very friendly and greeted me with open smiles and warm handshakes.

Beyond the villages with their neat, irrigated fields of barley, the landscape became forbiddingly dry and barren. Overhead, rocky crags spewed great fans of scree thousands of feet down to the river's edge. In the far distance, the snow-capped peaks of Tirish Mir glistened in frozen splendour. The river thundered past churning with a heavy load of glacial silt washed out of the mountains by the melting winter snows. The scenery was vast and beautiful.

After two hours of walking, an Afghan refugee camp appeared in the distance. As far as the eye could see, their tents sprawled along the river's edge, perched on ledges high above the torrent. As I approached the first of these camps, an Afghan on horseback galloped out to greet me. His horse skittered to a halt in a cloud of dust and flashing hooves just in front of me, blocking my way forward.

"A salaam alikum." He placed his hand on his heart and welcomed me.

"Alikum salaam," I replied, placing my right hand carefully on my heart.

"What is your country?"

His tanned face was half hidden in a wild beard. I noticed that he was riding without reins or a saddle.

When I told him he smiled, "Britannia? That is good. America not good. Russian not good."

He pointed to his horse and jokingly asked, "You want to ride?"

The sight of the pony's laid back ears, rolling eyes and foaming mouth put me off, so I grinned and declined his offer. As he walked with me into the village, we talked about his life as a refugee.

"It is not so bad. We have plenty of food. The UN pays for half the food we eat. We have fresh water from our new well and the government has built schools for our children."

"Will you go back to Afghanistan when the war is over?"

"Of course," he laughed politely at my question.

"The Pakistani people have been very good to us, but our homes are back in Afghanistan. When the fighting is finished, we will go back."

As I walked on through the camp, I noticed that the camp shop had been constructed using empty wooden ammunition cases, mainly land mines and rocket grenades, which had been made in China. It was yet another a reminder that the war was being fought a short distance away and that this village was full of fighters, many of whom would be crossing back into Afghanistan at the end of May, just after the end of Ramadan. Then the high passes would be clear of snow and the fighters would set off on the long walk towards the killing fields carrying heavy loads of guns, rocket grenades, mines and ammunition over fifteen thousand foot passes.

From a distance, the tents looked as though a strong gust of wind would blow them away. As I got closer, I could see that hard work had turned basic refugee tents into solid structures. An evolutionary progress began when the refugees first arrived and UNHCR gave them a canvas tent and ended when the tent had been converted into a stone-built house.

Below the village, I could see a group of men working together to build one of these houses. They had formed a chain that stretched from the river to the construction site. Rounded stones flew between their hands and were dumped in a pile by the road.

The builders had dug out trenches for the foundations into which the stones were carefully placed. The first layers of the dry-stone walls had already been built under the canvas walls of the UNHCR tent. Eventually the tent would only be needed as a temporary roof covering. The final stage in the development of a refugee house was the construction of a permanent roof, made with stout logs criss-crossed and covered with a layer of rocks and mud. As time passed, more families with UNHCR tents would arrive and the men would gradually turn them into houses of stone and mud. They joined the houses together and shared walls wherever possible. I could see that the village was becoming a miniature fortress

As long as snow blocked the high passes into Afghanistan, the fighting men in the camp had little else to do and seemed happy expending their energy making homes for their families and friends.

Moving on, I came across a cemetery on the edge of the village, with its many tiny graves symbolising the bonds that had already formed between these people and the land. When they eventually go home, they will leave behind more than just memories. They will leave behind their dead as memorials to their long years of exile. Perhaps they will never go home.

For the next six kilometres, I walked through several camps. In the graveyards in each camp, I saw that there were relatively few adult graves, suggesting that infant and child mortality rates were high. It was clear that healthcare for the refugees was a problem and while the pharmacy in Chitral had a good supply of antibiotics, anti-malaria and anti-amoebic dysentery drugs, there was a shortage of qualified doctors. As there were some two thousand refugees in the Chitral valley alone, it looked as though the medical facilities available in Chitral could not meet the needs of the refugees.

While the camps in Peshawar were bigger and more permanent, I suspected that these rough camps were more like home to these mountain-dwelling Afghans.

The camps stretched out along an eight-kilometre stretch of the track. In each camp, I saw evidence that at least some of the aid money was being spent shrewdly. New wells had been sunk; schools had been built; and in the camps were Afghan shops that had been stocked by the UN and other organisations. There may have been distribution problems, but I saw no signs of any food shortages. I even saw Pakistanis in jeeps stopping at the camp shops to buy supplies from the refugees. But there were no fields. There were no crops and they had no means to survive without outside help.

These observations were made just a few days after my journalist friend came here. He returned with tales of food shortages, starvation and sickness. He planned to write about the misery of the lives of the Afghans, the incompetence of the aid agencies and the inadequacies of the representatives of the Pakistani government.

I left the camps torn between two truths. His vision of the truth and my own. He met different people, perhaps political leaders, who perhaps gave him accounts that suited their own purposes. Had he invented his story of the misery of life in the camps because it was the only politically acceptable version? Or was his version the one that would sell most column inches?

Or had I been deceived by my own eyes and seen good, where I hoped to find good? More likely was the truth that we both saw the same truth and chose to focus on different aspects of that truth. One truth that was indisputable was the fact that between these truths was a people who were far from home and victims of a wider political struggle that would continue for a very long time.

Chapter 6

Beyond the bustle of the camps, the peace of the mountain returned and I was soon alone again in this desolate land of rock, water and ice. Here, man was dwarfed by the majesty of the landscape.

Little by little, the main body of the river began to break down into a series of steams that flowed under and between vast gravel deposits, some of which were half a mile across. Eventually, the river vanished, half-choked by the very debris it had carried out of the mountains. The sound of the wind and songbirds replaced the roar of the torrent. Between rounded banks of gravel, still pools of clear water reflected white clouds outlined against a blue sky.

When the river finally broke out of its burial chamber, its roar once again filled the air with the feeling of great power and I walked on towards Ayun with a spring in my step. At midday, I halted on the riverbank and made a fire to cook up some dhal. There was not much wood, but enough dried roots and twigs to make a small fire. The dhal began to simmer and I lay on my back surrounded by mountains and blue skies with a fresh breeze across my face. It was a sublime moment.

When Bez appeared from nowhere, he gave me quite a start. A tall, rangy man in his fifties or sixties with a thick grey beard, dressed in a battered shalwar kameez and calf-length leather boots. He somehow reminded me of one of my uncles. Perhaps it was his beard or was it the twinkle in his eye?

On his head, he wore a Chitrali *pagora*. We *salaamed* each other and he accepted my invitation for him to join me. He took my hand and introduced himself first in Pushto and then in Urdu.

"Meera nam Abdul Bezakhamah hai. Ham Afghan." (My name is Abdul Bezakhamah and I am an Afghan.)

The way he pronounced the word "*Afghan*" was guttural, almost Arabic. He listened gravely as I introduced myself and seemed pleased to find that I was English. He pulled up a flat rock and sat down on his haunches beside me.

As we watched the dhal cooking, he told me about his flight from Afghanistan and his life in Pakistan.

"I walked to Chitral from Kabul in three days. Young men told me that I would take at least five days, but old Bez showed them."

Three strong fingers served to emphasise his point. The journey from Kabul to Chitral is well over a hundred miles and the route crosses high passes where the going is very hard. He must have averaged over thirty miles a day over very difficult terrain.

In one sense, our conversation was limited because he spoke no English and I spoke no Pushto, but somehow we got by. He showed me a packet of pills and explained that they were for a friend. It suddenly dawned on me that this remarkable man was prepared to walk the twenty-five miles from Ayun to Chitral and twenty-five miles back again as a favour to a friend. The return jeep fare would have cost him seventy rupees and the medicine just five rupees.

As we talked, the fire died down and soon there was nothing left to burn. With a smile, Bez wandered around our camp and soon found enough roots and twigs to make a tidy bundle. He piled them on the glowing embers and turned my neat little fire into a bonfire. The dhal bubbled and boiled. When it was cooked, we ate. It tasted dreadful, but Bez tucked in with gusto and smiled encouragingly anyway.

Bez tried to teach me some Pushto as we cleaned up and made me count laboriously from one to a hundred. Under his watchful eyes, I wrote the numbers down in my notebook. When the lesson ended, my newfound friend indicated that we should continue our journey together.

The sun was now high and I soon began to perspire profusely. Rivulets of sweat laden with dust ran into my eyes. Bez marched on and I found myself struggling to keep up with him. When I tried to stop to rest a little, he shook his head and told me to keep walking. He was without mercy. When the jeep track looped around a tight curve of the river, Bez showed me a short cut that took us up a goat path cut into the side of a near vertical cliff. Like a mountain goat, he bounded upwards, stopping only to urge me to follow. In places, the path was only a few inches wide and I trod carefully knowing that a slip would mean a nasty fall.

Looking down to the river, I noticed a man crossing a makeshift bridge across part of the river. He was dwarfed by the landscape. The bridge looked fragile and seemed to hang in mid-air without any form of support. In fact, the bridge was a triumph of engineering.

Wide enough for one man, the bridge looked as though it was there to dare the river to sweep it away, just as the rising tide will wash away footprints on a deserted beach. For the time being, the bridge remained to taunt the river, but in the end, there would be only one winner in this contest.

With the thin air rasping in my lungs and my pack cutting into my shoulders, I staggered along behind Bez. When I got to the top, I found him sitting on a rock admiring the view. I felt terrible, perhaps even close to death. My lungs were bursting and my mouth was dry. When I reached for my water bottle, Bez reached out to stop me and spoke to me in Pushto. Although I did not understand his words, I easily understood what he meant.

"Wait," he said. "If you drink now, you will get stomach cramps. Rest first and then drink." To emphasis his point, he held his gut and grimaced.

I had no choice and obeyed. He distracted me by showing me wild flowers and named each one in Pushto. Not until my breathing had eased to a normal pace did he let me drink. The cold water was like nectar.

We descended a narrow track towards Ayun several thousand feet below. At a distance, the fields of ripening barley surrounding the villages were impossibly green. The sharp contrast between the living cloak of green and the bleakness of the barren slopes of scree was breathtaking. Long lines of poplars introduced by the Moghuls enclosed the fields, trapping moisture and stopping the wind from blowing away the thin soil.

As we scrambled down the gravel path towards the valley floor, the sound of running water filled the air with music. The fields were only green because of the irrigation channels that keep them watered. The network of interlinked irrigation channels was ancient and a remarkable feat of engineering. Without water, there would have been nothing but rock and scree.

As we neared the village, Bez sang an Afghani song and kept me close by his side. Young children ran behind us, full of giggles and shy laughter. A small boy held Bez by his hand and skipped along with us. Bez was clearly well-known and loved. The sight of Bez with an Englishman stopped people in their tracks and they stared as we passed. He greeted them all with a polite wave and a salaam. He introduced me to a few of his friends.

"He is an Englishman and like me, he is a walker." He pointed to my feet and laughed, "No jeep for this man."

We walked on through the centre of the village and stopped at a cobbler's hut because one of Bez's boots was coming apart at the seams. A Chitrali, an educated man who knew Bez and spoke good English, joined us. It turned out that he was one of Chitral's two artists.

"I make signs for everybody. I am here to paint a sign board for a businessman."

As we spoke in English, Bez began to show signs of mild impatience and asked the artist to repeat the story about his escape from Kabul, to make sure that I had understood him earlier. When he was convinced that I really had understood him earlier, he clasped my hand and laughed.

"Who needs language, when you are a walker," he proclaimed.

The cobbler quickly repaired Bez's boot as we sat drinking tea and eating cakes. It turned out that I was the same age as the artist, but he was married and had three children.

"Tell me", he asked, "why do you not have a wife?"

When I told him that I had a wife once, he laughed and clapped me on the shoulder.

"And now you are ready to look for a new wife?"

"I am always looking for a new wife. The trouble is that I had not found a good one yet who wants to marry me."

Bez gave a look that told me I had better stop looking and find a wife soon. As he was about to give me more advice, a man came in with a child's shoe that needed a new sole and I escaped another Bez lecture. The newcomer sat down next to me and we chatted as the cobbler patched the child's shoe. After a few minutes of idle chatter, the artist moved the conversation around to politics.

"What is the opinion of the English people about the Russians in Afghanistan?"

I answered as well as I could.

"Most of my friends want the Russians to go home as soon as possible. They also think that even the Russians now have doubts about the cost of the war. They want to pull out, but they do not want the loss of face endured by the Americans in Vietnam."

"Here in Pakistan, we believe this also. They are now just looking for a good enough reason to leave and then the Afghans can go home."

Bez had been following the conversation and interrupted in Pushto. The artist translated his comments into English.

"The war is not a war for the Afghan peoples. It is a war for the American and the Russian peoples. No matter who wins, it will be the Afghans who will lose."

Bez finished his tea and shook my hand before leaving to deliver the pills to his sick friend. The artist and I stayed, chatting as the cobbler worked. Time passed quickly and almost too late, we realised that I had another four and a half-hour walk ahead of me. If I was to get to the valleys of the Kalash before dark, I had to get going. As I prepared to set off, the artist introduced me to a man planning to walk to the Kalash valleys that afternoon.

My new friend showed me a short cut through Ayun that took us through maze of narrow alleys and climbed steeply with every step.

Occasionally, a flash of colour at the end of an alley betrayed a woman fleeing from my gaze. My guide was a great help and we eventually re-joined the jeep track several hundred feet above the valley floor. We both stopped for a drink at a tap, giving me time to size up the route into the valleys of the Kalash. At first glance, the track seemed to vanish into the side of the mountain. On closer inspection, I saw that it disappeared into a gash cut into the side of the mountain cut by a wild mountain stream.

As I walked along the track carved into the side of the gorge, vertical walls of rock blocked out the light and amplified the terrible sound of the torrent in the blackness below. The river was in full spate and the colour of milky tea. The thunder was at the same time savage and awesomely beautiful. It was the sound of a powerful torrent tearing the heart out of the mountain. Boulders carried deep within the torrent thundered against the riverbed as they were swept downstream. The noise reverberated in the shadows and filled the air with howls of crunching pain.

For two hours, we hiked up the gorge in silence. It was a desolate place of darkness, shadows and cold rock, devoid of all life. For most of the way, there were no villages, no fields, no living creatures, only cold rock and the ceaseless roar of the river. I trod carefully, with the torrent visible some twenty feet below my feet. In places, the track was nothing more than a ledge cut into the side of a sheer cliff.

As the sun sank behind the mountain, the gorge became even darker and my companion started checking his watch. He was worried that we would still be in the gorge at nightfall. Was it demons or mountain spirits that he feared?

Just as he started to get nervous, a passing jeep stopped to pick us up. A short while later, we stopped again and picked up two men, who were walking ahead of us. I gave up my seat in the front of the jeep and stood in the back. In places, the track was cut so deeply into the cliff face that I nearly smashed my skull on an overhanging rock. The only safe option was to crouch down and hang on as best I could.

After a couple of miles, we stopped because there was no more road. The river had washed away the track, leaving only a narrow ledge, just wide enough for a man. A log had been used to bridge a short section where there was no ledge. With my heavy pack on my shoulders, I walked along the log with great care keeping my eyes on the raging waters below my feet. Beyond this ledge was short, intact section of track that led to a bridge. On the other side of the bridge was a police checkpoint. Nothing grand, just a hut.

A solitary policeman sitting on the bridge with a battered Lee Enfield .303 rifle slung over his shoulder stood to watch us approach.

He waved the others past and stepped in front of me to block my path. He checked my pass and copied my details into his logbook. I noticed that I was only the twenty-second visitor of the year.

"You have hashish?" He asked and I wondered if he suspected me of being a drug trafficker. But as is so often the case, I was wrong.

"I do not have hashish," I answered truthfully.

"Damn it," he exclaimed and showed me a lump of hashish no bigger than a pea.

"This is all I have left."

He rolled a joint anyway using the last of his hashish and smoked it with a look of misery on his face. He inhaled the spicy smoke and let the waves of relaxation sweep him into a better mood. I left him sitting on the bridge in a cloud of smoke.

The cleft opened up and revealed entrances into the Bumburet and Rumbar valleys. My travelling companions had waited for me and together we walked up the Bumburet valley.

The Bumburet valley was broad and luxuriantly green, a hidden Garden of Eden deep in the mountains of the Hindu Kush. This was a place that exuded fertility. Fruit trees, including walnut, apricot, mulberry, apple and pear, grew in abundance in and around the villages. Fields of ripening winter barley stood tall against a backdrop of snow-capped peaks. Above the snow line, pine and deodar forests filled the air with the sweet smell of resin. This was a land of magic and according to local legend, fairies, elves and spirits lived in the high mountains.

The Kafir Kalash are almost all that remains of a group of tribes that until the latter part of the nineteenth century occupied Kafiristan, a mountainous region that straddled the border between Pakistan and Afghanistan and is today called Nuristan. They always had been fierce fighters and repelled the armies of Timur in the fourteenth century; Akbar in the sixteenth century; and Nadir-Shah in the eighteenth century. The arrival of Islam finally brought them close to the edge of oblivion.

In 1895, Amir Abdul Rahman, the "king" of Afghanistan, finally conquered Kafiristan and forced the Kafir to convert to Islam. Many of those that would not convert were decapitated. Only the Kafir who lived on the British-India side of the Duran line escaped conversion. There may once have been two hundred thousand Kafirs. In 1987, there were less than two thousand left. Those that lived in Nuristan may have converted to Islam but they retained their warrior traditions. Many of the descendants of those warriors were fighting the Russian forces in Afghanistan.

The origins of the Kalash remain a mystery and stories that they were the descendants of the armies of Alexander the Great abound. Their language has roots that seem to predate both Indian and

Iranian languages, suggesting that the ancestors of the Kafir may have moved south from lands around the Caspian Sea in BC 1500-1000. The language spoken by the last of the Kafir is called Kalasha, which is closely related to the Khowar language spoken by the Chitralis. The Kafiri language spoken by the ancient Kafir tribes is different and is not part of the Indian group of languages, suggesting that they may not have had Indian roots.

The chroniclers of the invasion of Alexander the Great, Arrianus and Plutarchos, suggest that they may have come across the Kafir and described them as the descendants of Dionysus who came from Greece long before. If Alexander's armies had encountered the Kafir and their enchanting young women, it may be reasonable to assume that his soldiers left behind more than traces of their culture.

After two more hours tramping along a rough track, a passing jeep picked us up. After a brief discussion, most of which I did not understand, the driver threw my bag on board. Half an hour later, he dropped me off outside a mud-walled single storey building. A painted sign hanging at an angle from a bent nail told me that my driver had delivered me to the Hotel Du Paix.

Its owner, a slightly built man with a nervous smile and dark, closely set eyes came out to meet me.

"My name is Sher Wazir. You stay here and I will give you a good room. You can take breakfast in the morning. Very good prices."

He ushered me into the hotel garden and set me up with a pot of cardamom-flavoured green tea, which he explained was *gowah chai,* at a table set under the spreading bows of an ancient walnut tree. Having walked nearly forty kilometres, I drank far too much of the golden nectar and too late, I sensed the caffeine seeping out into my tired body. At six and a half thousand feet, the air was just thin enough to give me a slight headache, which the caffeine only made worse. I knew that I would sleep badly.

There were only three other guests and at first they kept their distance. As the sun settled behind the mountains, the air chilled and Sher Wazir moved us all into his kitchen where we welcomed the warmth of the open fire. The kitchen had a stone fireplace, a homemade cupboard, three walls, a roof and little else. Still, it was just big enough for the four of us to sit around the fireplace with Sher Wazir in close attendance.

As we sat in silence watching the flames dancing in the wind, Sher Wazir reappeared with the evening meal. Like any perfect host, he introduced me to my companions, all of whom were in their twenties. One was French, one German and the other Swiss.

Sher Wazir was very uncomplicated in some ways and tended to forget his guests' names. Instead, he called every one by their nationality. He introduced me as "English".

The food was plain but wholesome. Sher Wazir gave us each a bowl of spiced, boiled potatoes with boiled rice and chapattis. We ate in silence, our faces glowing in the light of the fire. Outside the valley sank into darkness. The Frenchman and the Swiss man picked at their food. The silent German tucked in with relish, carefully wiping his beard after each mouthful. It was only after Sher Wazir had cleared away the plates that conversation began.

Peck, the Frenchman was staying with a Kalash family and only came to the Hotel to eat and socialise with the others. Peck told me that the German was a carpenter. The German was the strong silent type and hid behind his beard most of the time.

As soon as the meal was over, I dragged my aching bones into bed. My room was simply furnished with a paraffin hurricane lamp, a charpoi, a grimy quilt and an earthen floor. I read for a while in the light of the flickering hurricane lamp and then tried to sleep. Outside, I could hear the sound of thundering water, the wind tugging at the door and wild birds calling in the night.

As expected, I slept badly, tormented by a combination of an excess of caffeine and aching bones. The night passed slowly and as soon as the sun started to rise behind the snow-capped peaks of Tirish Mir, I crawled out of bed to face the day. The cold seeped into my bones and my breath froze in the still air.

The others were still sleeping and for a few moments, I had the place to myself. Sher Wazir appeared and showed me how to light the fire. We soon had a kettle boiling on the hearth. As the pink sky turned blue against the mountains, Sher Wazir remembered breakfast.

"English, you want breakfast? Sher Wazir will give you the best breakfast."

He paused for effect and stoked the fire sending sparks into the crisp morning air.

"Sher Wazir can give you the best breakfast in the valley. You can have marmalade and pancakes, with eggs and tea."

With a sniff and a sly grin, he leaned forward and added, "Only two rupees."

He cleared his throat noisily and spat over the veranda. In fact, there was nowhere else to eat and the idea of pancakes sounded good. Besides, I was hungry enough to agree to anything.

When it arrived, breakfast was not quite what I expected. The marmalade turned out to be stewed dried apricots, but was delicious anyway. Wrapped in a filthy rag, the pancake was warm and as big as a dinner plate and was somewhere between cake and bread in consistency. Later, I discover the pancake was called *tikki* in Chitrali and was made from a flour and water mixture, fried in oil or ghee. When I broke the pancake open, I found that it was filled with a mixture of crushed walnuts, ghee and honey. The tea was milky, sweet and delicious. Served with a plate of fresh fried eggs, it was the perfect Hindu Kush breakfast.

Sher Wazir sat down in front of the fire and was eager to chat. He was, I was soon to discover, quite a gossip.

"An old woman died yesterday and the Kalash are mourning her death. The feasting started as soon as she died and continued overnight. There was so much food: six-month-old cheese, milk and meat."

He continued and told me that there was a rumour that there was a man who was even older and richer who was expected to die soon.

"He was already one hundred and twenty years old and nearly died before, but he recovered," Sher Wazir grinned.

"When he does die, they will kill forty sheep and the celebrations will last four or even five days."

He explained that the death of a Kalash man was considered more important than the death of a Kalash woman.

"When they die rich, there is always a big festival."

The Hotel Du Paix was grandly named, but lacked many of the amenities found in even the most modest hotels: running water, electricity and telephones. The only lavatory also doubled as the only bathroom and was a simple lean-to with a hole in the ground. A bucket filled with water collected from the nearby stream was the only plumbing. Nevertheless, the hotel was in a magnificent location, with fine views of the valley and in the distance, the snow-capped peaks of Tirish Mir.

After breakfast, I explored the valley, enjoying its peace and solitude. This was a rural community living in harmony with nature and itself. In a small field by the river, a man with a twisted back steered an ox-drawn plough over the rocky soil in preparation for the spring planting of corn. Elsewhere, tiny fields enclosed by neat dry-stone walls nurtured young shoots of winter wheat and barley. Ancient walnut trees stood like guardians in gardens filled with fruit trees in blossom, leaves fluttering in the breeze. The landscape was a wild profusion of greens, crimsons, chestnut and pewter laid out on a backdrop of shattered rock and snow-capped mountains. Overhead, fluffy clouds sailed across a clear blue sky.

As the sun rose, the watercourse cut into the side of a vertical rock face on the other side of the valley was brought up in sharp relief. It was built on a monumental scale and visible at this distance as a thin line traced across a sheer rock face. Someone long ago must have crawled on hands and knees to carve the watercourse out of the cliff face, with a drop of a thousand feet below him. The watercourses, without which the fertile fields would be barren, were magnificent feats of engineering.

An intricate web of irrigation channels carried water to homes and fields alike, filling the air with the ever-present sound of running water. Spring water gurgled in a channel running alongside the jeep track. Beyond the fields, the river rumbled in full flood filling the valley with its presence. In the distance, it narrowed and crashed into a gorge with a thunder that shook the ground.

When I closed my eyes and listened carefully, I could hear birds singing, children playing, a cock crowing, women laughing and the crackle of fresh wood burning in the grate. The breeze was warm on my skin and perfumed with the scent of deodar resin, wood smoke and apricot blossom. Close by, scrawny chickens pecked at the ground. Ducks paddled against the current in the water channel that drove the flour mill. Goats, sheep and cattle wandered freely. Overhead, delicate butterflies floated in beams of sunlight.

There was a balance in the valley between the forces of nature and the ways of man. When the Kalash felled a tree, they planted a seedling to replace it, preserving both the forests and the fragile soil. They used manure instead of synthetic chemicals in their fields and harnessed the power of the river to drive the water mill perched on the edge of the torrent. There was none of the pollution and rubbish found in the villages on the plains. Nothing was wasted.

In the evening, I joined the others, Peck, the Swiss man and the German, in the kitchen to watch the sun sink behind the mountains. Sher Wazir brought us a tray laden with food and we ate together, sitting cross-legged in front of the blazing fire. The Swiss man grumbled constantly.

"Sher Wazir, this is shit food you are serving. Why you no give us any meat? No one can live on this kind of shit."

Sher Wazir grinned nervously and treated the Swiss man's comments with diplomatic disdain.

The Frenchman winced as he ate, "It is my fucking tooth. It is bad, man."

The German chewed his food in silence as the night wind blew down from the mountains above, filling the kitchen with its icy blast. The Frenchman shivered and moaned pitifully, a pathetic sight with his hands wrapped around his swollen face.

As soon as we finished eating, we all moved into the room shared by the German and the Swiss man to escape the cold. Between the four of us there were only two hurricane lamps, so they needed my lamp and to a lesser extent, my company.

Sher Wazir had given them his best room, which had a concrete floor and a single glazed window. When the door was closed, the chill of the night was kept at bay. Lying full length on his bed, the bearded carpenter flew high on Pink Dreams, which he told me was an LSD derivative, while the others smoked hashish. At first, conversation was limited, so I read. I sensed that they were wary of me because I had declined their offers to get stoned with them. Ignoring me, they retreated into their own private worlds.

They seemed intent on destroying themselves in this desolate place and were falling into the darkness as I watched. Peck, the Frenchman chewed endlessly on opium to dull the pain of his rotten tooth and complained about everything around him. The Swiss man sneered at the world, while the German lay back and said very little. For some reason, I decided that they reminded me of the pilgrims in Conrad's Heart of Darkness who hated each other and mistreated the 'natives.' Despite their faults, the Pilgrims were good company, if only because they were entertaining.

The Swiss man told me that according to local gossip, Sher Wazir's father, Sher Wazir Babu had come to the valley after partition from India. Life as a hard-core Muslim did not really suit him. He bought land in Bumburet in 1977 using what was left of the money given to him as compensation at partition. Apparently, before becoming a landowner, he had frittered away the lion's share of his money on women, drink and drugs, but somehow saved enough to build the Hotel du Paix. Whether any of these stories were true, was hard to tell.

When he retired, Sher Wazir took over and worked hard to upgrade the hotel to attract a better class of guest. His first move was to glaze the guest rooms. He was in the process of expanding the hotel by building an extra room with a wide bay window. His entrepreneurial spirit was indomitable. As well as being a hotel landlord, he was also the village postmaster. His shop sold stamps, cigarettes and batteries, all with a healthy mark-up.

All cooking was done at the Wazirs' home by his wife and carried to the hotel by Sher Wazir on a tray. In the height of summer, the hotel may have had as many as thirty guests. It was hard to see how Sher Wazir, or his wife, coped.

The food was basic, but wholesome. Breakfast was "cake" or *tikki,* a kind of bread stuffed with walnuts and honey and fried in a skillet with ghee, served with "marmalade", stewed dried apricots and *dud chai*, sweet milk-tea.

As the days passed, Sher Wazir's wife varied the meals as much as she could and given the limited range of ingredients at this time of year, she did a great job. Each day brought a different dish: boiled spinach with potatoes; spicy potato stew; potatoes with eggs and tomatoes; eggs and tomatoes with fried dried onions; and boiled rice with beans. Each meal was served with *tikki*, maize meal cakes or *chapattis* and tea, either milky black tea or sweet, green *gowah* tea with cardamom.

Sher Wazir also offered a number of chicken dishes, at a price. In Chitral, they were half as expensive and cheaper still in Peshawar. He told me that he used the number of chicken meals ordered as a measure of the wealth of his clients. According to the Swiss man, he also had mutton and beef to offer, but they were even more expensive. There were a couple of other similar hotels nearby, but they both appeared to be closed.

I discovered that the Pilgrim's had not helped by insisting that the food should not be too spicy and that little or no ghee was used. The opium had made the Swiss man's stomach very sensitive to spicy food and he could not keep anything down if it was too spicy. Consequently, the food was fairly bland.

Other vegetables were available in Chitral, but until Lowari Pass was open to vehicles, the quality would remain poor and prices three times higher than normal. Most of the fresh fruit and vegetables in

Chitral bazaar had been carried on someone's back over Lowari Pass, which was likely to be snow-bound for another two months.

The climb over the Pass involved an arduous three-hour ascent, followed by a similar descent on the other side. The porters charged the traders heavily for their services and the traders passed on those costs to their customers. Sher Wazir was not the kind of man to pay more for anything than he considered it was worth and anything that could have damaged his profit margins was shunned vigorously.

There were bazaar rumours that the Chinese government was to fund work on a tunnel through Lowari Pass, perhaps when the Karakoram Highway was complete. Until the Pass was constructed, the valley would remain cut off from the rest of the world during the winter months.

The secretive Pilgrims eventually revealed that they were planning a trip to Chitral as their supplies of hashish, opium, heroin and Pink Dreams were running low. The first signs of their plans had appeared when they started pestering me to change money for them. In the end, I decided that I would rather not get involved in their business dealings, much to their annoyance. The best thing that I could do was to leave the Pilgrims to their drugs and stay with my own, one small tin of instant coffee carried all the way from Jerusalem.

Sher Wazir had caught wind of their plans and cornered me in the kitchen.

"When do you think they will be going? Are they really coming back? Tell me what you think."

He could see a revenue stream about to walk away and was understandably concerned. The trouble was that I had no idea when the Pilgrims planned to leave or when they would be back.

On a good day when the roads have not been washed away and jeeps with fuel are available, the journey to Chitral only takes a couple of hours. The Pilgrims looked forward to the journey because in Chitral, hashish cost only one rupee a gram. This was the equivalent of just forty dollars for a kilogram. They could also get heroin. They told me that drugs were even cheaper in Peshawar.

The Pilgrims knew that the poppies were already flowering in the opium fields around Dir, south of Chitral. Most of their conversations revolved around the availability and cost of drugs in different places. Sher Wazir as ever was able to cast light on government policy towards the drug producers.

"The US government has promised F16 fighters if the Pakistan government does more to control the drug trade. By all accounts, the US government is pressuring the Pakistan government to pay farmers more for growing tomatoes, than they could get for growing hashish or opium. The plan is probably doomed to failure, as any attempt to restrict the growth of hashish or opium pushes up the price and eventually it is better to grow drugs than tomatoes."

In this bucolic paradise, there were problems nearer to home. The lack of clean drinking water and medical facilities had contributed to a high infant mortality rate in the valley judging from the high proportion of tiny graves in the Muslim graveyards. While the Pakistan government had built a free health centre in the village, there was a shortage of medical staff able to offer advice and care. While the free medical care that was provided was a good start and modern drugs would help relieve some of the suffering of the elderly and infirm, I wondered whether the health centre would provide as much as the good people who built it would have hoped.

The Kalash had resisted change for so long because they had never really wanted for anything and had achieved a way of life that was close to being in a state of equilibrium. Their fertile fields, pounding rivers and mighty mountains had given them enough food to eat, water to drink and isolation from the world at large.

At the end of the valley was a Nuristani village balanced on a promontory at a fork in the river. The buildings were grey and angular, with flat roofs. From a distance, the houses seem to dissolve into the hillside.

I walked there and was hounded out of the village by a crowd of children who stoned me when I told one of them that I was not a Muslim. An old woman joined them, puked a torrent of venom in my direction and managed to hit me on the leg with a well-aimed sliver of slate. They had clearly been taught to mistrust strangers and in particular those who were not of the Faith.

Limping a little, I returned down the valley and passed Kalash women who greeted me with broad smiles and ribald catcalls. As I passed, they waved and hailed me.

"Schparta baya!" (Hello brother!)

"Schparta baba!" (Hello sister!)

My response was greeted with a cackle of raucous laughter and knowing grins. The stark contrast between the Muslim and Kalash cultures was an ever-present reality in the valley. This was a community in a state of uneasy equilibrium.

At times, it seemed as though the Prophet's message had been subverted by some darker forces intent on dividing people with barriers of fear and hatred. In its purest form, the Qur'an is a spiritual guide as well as being a good code for living with oneself and with other people. The Qur'an teaches tolerance to other peoples' beliefs and offers a way of life based on obedience, discipline and cleanliness.

Muslims believe that the Qur'an is the word of God and as such cannot be changed or challenged. The Qur'an also sets out a code for living, which was based on life in the Middle Ages.

Islamic fundamentalists want to live in a world governed by a code of conduct from an older Golden age, when the Truth was the Truth and the people who believed in the Truth lived the Truth. They also believe that if the Truth is good enough for the individual, it must also be good enough for the state. The fundamentalists believe that Islam is the one true religion of God and that all other belief systems are no more than idolatry, creating the basis for their Jihad against all other religions.

The Middle Ages marked the Golden Age of Islam, when Muslims were powerful and the Islamic Caliphate expanded across northern Africa, Southern Europe and into Asia Minor. Given the poverty and hardships endemic in many modern Muslim countries, it is perhaps no wonder that there are people who want to turn back the clock to a time when Muslims were in the ascendant.

I first came across this face of Islam in Turkey where teachers sent by the government to villages in Eastern Turkey were stoned. The stonings were led by elders of the mosque intent on protecting their power over the people. They knew that fire and brimstone preaching did not work well on the educated.

This was nothing new. Christianity fought against science and learning for centuries. Scientists and thinkers like Galileo were imprisoned for suggesting that the teachings of the Church did not tell the whole story. Darwin is still ridiculed by the Creationists for questioning the idea of the Creation, for suggesting that life evolved from humble beginnings and for showing that Mankind had evolved from apes.

The Church taught that the only way to avoid hell and damnation was to follow its teachings. The Inquisition, representing the Roman

Catholic Church, hunted down, tortured and killed those who it deemed to be heretics.

Education is the only cure for the state of mind that is religion, which is why fundamentalists of all faiths strive to limit the flow of knowledge into the hearts and minds of the Faithful.

The power of religion is that believers are encouraged to stop thinking and believe what they are told. History has shown us that in the wrong hands, this religious power has been used as a means for political, rather than spiritual control.

With my leg still smarting from the impact of the old woman's stone, I limped back to the Hotel du Paix.

Sher Wazir and I made tea. He told me that apart from the three Pilgrims, I was the only outsider in the valley. The French researchers who had been making a documentary film about the Kalash had left in the morning. They had been staying at a rival hotel owned by a Kalash family. According to Sher Wazir, the hotel was not as clean as the Hotel du Paix. Perhaps they had a lower class of bed bug. The researchers were due to return in two weeks to film Joshi, the Kalash festival of spring.

Back at the hotel, the health of the Pilgrims continued to deteriorate: Peck was wracked with the pain of his disintegrating molar; the Swiss man kept vomiting because of the opium he ate; the German alone remained healthy, but he was withdrawn and kept himself to himself. He was living in a different world most of the time.

Drugs continued to form the focus of most of their conversations. They talked for hours about the availability of drugs, the effect of drugs, the drugs they had tried and more rarely the drugs they would not try. The Swiss man told me that the opium he had been buying only cost him three rupees a gram and that he usually bought ten grams at a time. The heroin he had been buying was only marginally more expensive.

They smoked hashish, ate opium and did little more than stay near the hotel all day long. The air in their room was pungent, reeking with the odour of hashish smoke and unwashed bodies.

My head remained clear and I lived a little apart from my European neighbours. Life without any vice was not so bad. No drugs, no alcohol and no women. Perhaps my breakfast cup of instant coffee, counted as a vice, but for the time being, it was the worst of my sins.

Bumburet was doubly cut off from the outside world because part of the jeep track to Chitral had fallen into the river and was not likely to be repaired for several weeks.

As Ramadan was to start in four days, it seemed like a good time to return to Chitral to extend my permit and gorge on spicy meat and vegetables. This time, I decided to be lazy and travel by jeep. Bez would not have approved.

A jeep took me down to the foot of the valley. From there, I walked down to Ayun to wait in the teashop for a jeep to Chitral. Beyond the teashop, a small group of Islamic fundamentalists were staging a demonstration.

Watched by wary police officers, the small, but noisy crowd, bearded Islamic hardliners hammered out their demand for the removal of General Zia Ul Haq. They were angry because in ten years of government, he had failed to implement the full power of Sharia, absolute Islamic law, in Pakistan.

Sharia binds the governance of the state to the code of conduct prescribed in the Qur'an, creating a system of government in which religious and secular sources of power are brought together.

History has few examples of societies that work well with this style of government. In fact, the past is littered with societies that placed too much power in the hands of a few and suffered years of human misery as a consequence.

The teashop crowd watched with detached interest as the speakers mounted an increasingly agitated verbal attack on their Head of State. Sitting next to me, a Pakistani seaman home on leave shook his head.

"The trouble with this country is that we have too many political parties. This party wants Muslim law, another Russian law and another wants Reagan's system."

His friends grinned because they had heard this speech before.

In the square, the speakers changed from time to time, but the tirade continued and the message remained the same. One of the police officers took notes and shook his head at the prospect of having to write up a report on the rally, with a full list of the names of the speakers and an outline of their key points. I could imagine a summary of the report being added to a fat file marked "Political Activists - Secret" in the District Commissioner's office in Chitral.

From their vantage point in the teashop, the seaman and his friends were amused by the spectacle and provided a running commentary.

"They are only a few. You see they have to bring children to make any noise."

He was right; almost half of the people crowding around the speakers were young children who chanted political slogans in shrill discord.

"It is all such a waste of time. No one wants to listen to these people."

He finished off his tea and tipped the dregs onto the ground.

"My friend and I want to go to America. We will collect semi-precious stones from here and sell them in America. Then maybe they will give us a visa."

His friend grinned and interrupted.

"But every time we go to US embassy in Islamabad, they give us no visa?"

When more tea arrived, sweet milky nectar in grimy cups, the seaman leaned forward.

"When you get there, it is not a problem. There is always work. In New York, I once worked in a hotel. I showed them my seaman's book and they see I worked as a steward and gave me a job. No problem."

Looking around at the teashop with its mud walls, mud floor and sun-blackened wooden benches, he remembered his time in his New York hotel and looked at me with a wry smile.

"Look at this place. It is disgusting. It is a very dirty place."

In fact, it was a particularly grand highland teashop, with seating on two levels. On the ground floor was a dark room that was ignored by all. A wooden ladder darkened by years of exposure to the elements led to an open first floor balcony facing a courtyard. This was clearly the place to be and with some trepidation, I had clambered up the ladder to join the other tea drinkers.

An ageing *chai wallah* brewed tea on a raised mud-oven screened from the drinkers by a few lengths of sacking marked with the faded letters "UNHCR". A small boy washed the dirty cups in a plastic bowl and set them to dry on a mud-shelf in the kitchen. Our seat was a split-plank balanced on a couple of rocks.

"Even Macdonald's is better than this," he sniggered, conjuring lurid images of plastic and chrome temples to fast food in stark contrast with our surroundings.

We shook hands, sharing a moment of amusement and in the background, the children launched into yet another frenzy of chanting.

The jeep to Chitral arrived and fifteen of us climbed aboard, crammed shoulder-to-shoulder, knee to knee, rifle-butt to rifle-butt. The passengers harangued the driver with constant calls to get going.

"Chalo, chalo, chalo...."

Encouraged by the enthusiasm of his passengers and countless good-humoured jibes about his driving skills, the driver kept his foot down and the jeep flew over the track, floating like the wind over the rocky surface. Surrounded by the ravishingly beautiful mountains of the Hindu Kush, we fell silent and soaked in the magnificence of the landscape. Before too long we arrived and came to a jolting halt in the Chitral jeep depot.

After the dearth of choice in Sher Wazir's kitchen, the bazaar offered delights that tempted my eyes and my stomach. A bag of over-ripe tangerines was swiftly demolished and followed by spicy Afghani kebabs served with hot *naan* bread.

The choice of vegetables in the bazaar was outstanding: a cornucopia of aubergines, red peppers, dried chillies, tomatoes, purple-skinned onions, mustard leaves, spinach and cloves of garlic. Elsewhere were stalls selling sacks of rice, beans, salt and mustard seeds, aluminium-cooking pots, bars of hard pink soap, crockery, lengths of rope, knives and cheap plastic bowls of all sizes.

As I walked down through the bazaar, a tailor saw me and called me into his shop. Sitting cross-legged on a rug, he was surrounded by bolts of brightly-coloured cloth, blankets woven in Chitral and stacks of the round woollen Chitrali hats known as *pagoras*. He invited me to join him.

"You look very beautiful in Pakistani clothes."

Coming from a tailor, I accepted the compliment with grace and sat down with him. Back home, the same comment might have been seen in a very different light.

His English was very good and his manner polite, but direct. After our initial introductions, he sold me a *pagora* and moved straight on to religion.

"You are not a Muslim?" I shook my head.

"Then why do you not become a Muslim?"

He held my hand. "You must read the Qur'an so you understand. Then you will believe. Islam is a good religion. Do you believe in God?"

His accent made the word "God" sound exactly like the word "cod" and I had to try hard to conceal a smile.

"I suppose I do."

"Do you pray five times a day to God?"

"Not in the way that you pray."

"Do you fast during Ramadan?"

"I do when I am in a Muslim country during Ramadan."

That was partly true, but for this conversation, my answer was truthful enough.

"If you do not pray five times a day, you will not go to heaven." He seemed genuinely concerned and was eager to convert me to Islam. Not wanting to stir up a religious argument just before Ramadan, I remembered my conversation with Mr Orman in Cairo.

"Have you got a Qur'an?" He nodded.

"Can you find Sura 109 and read it to me?"

With great reluctance, the tailor brought out his Qur'an wrapped in several layers of cloth from a recess behind him and proffered it to me. As I reached out to take it from him, he pulled it away from me.

"Have you performed the proper ablutions?"

It slowly dawned on me that he expected me to find and read the prayer, so I tried to explain why he should hold on to his precious Qur'an.

"I am sorry, but I can't read Arabic. Could you read Sura 109 for me?"

The tailor seemed oddly hesitant, but together we searched for the Sura anyway.

After a short while, we found it, but after reading the text for a few minutes, the tailor announced that he could not translate the text into English. When I looked at him in disbelief, he avoided my gaze. I could only guess that while he could read the Arabic script phonetically, he did not understand Arabic. To him, most of the Koran was just a series of words that had meaning only in a language he did not speak.

Was this the real source of the power of the Mullahs?

I was reminded of the Roman Catholic Church in the Middle Ages, which demanded that the bible and prayer book were written in Latin, a language that an illiterate population could neither read nor understand. The church maintained control by ensuring that access to learning remained a privilege of the few. The church and state shared power and shared the taxes collected from the people. In many ways, the Roman Catholic Church was more powerful than any of the rulers of the lands in which it had influence. Like Islam, the Roman Catholic faith transcended national borders. In many ways, the Roman Catholic Church was the first multinational corporation.

At a local level, the priest acted as local sales manager. He reported to the regional sales director, the bishop, who in turn reported to the country-level Head of Sales, the Cardinal. The Cardinal reported directly to Head Office and if his sales operation was large enough, to the global Head of Sales and Marketing, His Holiness, otherwise known as the Pope.

The Roman Catholic Church also offered a narrowly-focused product range: christenings, weddings, indulgences, funerals and the absolution of Sin, all at a price. The most impressive of all the services offered was the promise of a place in Heaven in the afterlife to those customers that remained most loyal to the brand. This was the ultimate promise and never once did anyone come back to complain.

To enforce an already powerful marketing message, the Church also sold the idea that anyone who was not loyal to the brand would face eternal damnation in the fires of Hell. As an additional bonus, the Church led people to believe that regular attendance at church and the payment of tithes contributed to a kind of Air Miles scheme that helped pay for a place in Heaven.

In the Middle Ages, the Church discovered merchandising and made a fortune selling images of Jesus, the Virgin Mary and the saints. The business of packaging relics filled the coffers of the Church to overflowing. The power of the Church was further magnified by the development of strategic alliances with heads of state in most of the countries in which they operated.

Following the example set by the Catholic Church in the Middle Ages, extremist Islamic sects were able to quote those parts of the Qur'an that helped them to maintain control and ignore those that presented a softer, more humanistic view of Islam.

I dined in the Afghan eating-place as usual and returned to my room to write a letter. Halfway through the letter I began to shiver violently and could write no more. The onset of the illness hit me like a train. The symptoms were the same as last time: a chest infection, a dry mouth, loss of appetite, a headache and a general feeling of exhaustion. I crawled into bed coughing and trembling with cold. I was freezing. From time to time, I had to crawl to the bathroom to empty my soul into the darkness.

Back in bed, I felt warm for a while, but the cold got to me again. Using the last remains of my strength, I got up and put a second quilt on the bed. I shivered uncontrollably and I could not stop my teeth chattering. My head throbbed and all strength drained from my body. There was a knock on the door and to my horror, I found that the shivering was so violent that I was too weak to get out of bed or call out for help. I was imprisoned by the weight of the two quilts. My unseen visitor left me to my torment. It was a hard night, mostly spent in a state of delirium. Shortly before dawn, sleep came and the real suffering ended.

Although I did not know it, I was not the only one with health problems. Far away in Wisconsin, my Zephyr had become so ill that she had been admitted into hospital. Separated by more than seven thousand miles, I struggled against my demons not knowing that at the same time she was fighting a hard battle against hers. As she recovered a little, she picked up a pen and started writing. When she finished, she folded the letter and sealed it in an airmail envelope addressed to me in Chitral. She then posted the letter, not knowing if her words would ever find me.

The mailman eventually came, took her letter and fed it into the US postal system. Before long, the Zephyr's words were waiting in silence in the hold of a 747 heading for Islamabad.

By morning, my fever had broken and apart from a blinding headache, the worst seemed to have passed. The local pharmacist prescribed me a cocktail of drugs: Paracetemol for my headache, a broad-spectrum antibiotic for my chest infection and entramiazole for the amoeba in my guts.

Later that day, I managed to phone my Mother on her birthday. I wondered if she had any idea how much effort had been put into making that call. It was nothing short of a miracle that a combination of radio and satellite links managed to link Chitral, in the North West Frontier Province of Pakistan, with my mother's phone in rural Gloucestershire. It may also have been a miracle that I had been able to make the call at all.

All that was left for me to do in Chitral was to renew my permit so I could return to the peace and solitude of the valley. The journey back by jeep passed in a blur and when I got back to the Hotel du Paix, I spent the rest of the day recuperating on a charpoi in the shade of the veranda. With little else to do, I read and watched the villagers going about their business.

On the other side of the jeep track was a Kalash house surrounded by fields and fruit trees. In front of the house was as perfect a lawn as any I had seen in England. Bibi, an attractive Kalash woman and her eighteen-month-old child sat playing on the lawn all day long. They stayed close to each other, constantly touching and holding each other in that secret way that is known only to mothers and their children. She was a widow. Her husband had died of tuberculosis not so long before. Her smile lit up the valley and hid the pain of loss that lay within.

By the end of the day, the valley had worked its magic on my body and I felt fully recovered. This enchanted place seemed to protect me from the ravages of the sickness that had laid me low in Chitral. As long as I stayed, I knew that I would be healthy.

A sudden noise in the middle of the night woke me. It was the sound of someone being violently sick. I got up and found the Swiss man slumped over the veranda, with trails of vomit hanging from his mouth.

"Are you all right? Can I get you anything?"

He turned at the sound of my voice and looked at me. In the moonlight, his eyes glittered.

"No, no, it's just the fucking opium. Go back to sleep." He vomited again.

I crawled back into the comfort of my sleeping bag and listened to him retching into the night. In the morning, he appeared in time for breakfast and looked terrible. I noticed that dark patches had sunk into the skin under his eyes and his face looked noticeably thinner. He sat down by the hearth, warming his fingers in the flames.

"This shit opium is bad for my stomach, but it will be all right when I'm used to it. Sorry if I disturbed you."

He showed me a ball of black goo and squeezed it into a sausage shape.

"You want to try some?"

He pushed it towards me and I took it from his fingers. It was like plasticine and smelled of poppy juice. It was foul. I could not imagine how he could bear to eat it and understood better why he had been sick. He seemed relieved when I gave it back untouched.

"Today, I am going to Peshawar with the Frenchman. We will back in about ten days."

He grinned and clasped his arms around his chest.

"There, we will really have some fun."

It sounded good to me. Ten whole days of peace and quiet, but I was sure that I would miss them anyway.

After they left, the valley was even more peaceful. The official who issued me with my permit had told me that there was no crime in the valleys of the Kalash, other than the murder of a tourist a year before. The only other crime was the local sport that involved relieving rich Punjabi tourists of a rupee or two. There was no vandalism, no graffiti, no mugging and no violence.

Sher Wazir came to me after they left and reminded me that Ramadan had started. He was keen to tell me that he was still happy to sell me food and in many ways, life continued regardless.

The Pilgrims were replaced by Kevin, a young Englishman, who had studied philosophy at university and had then worked as a forester on a large estate in the heart of rural England. For the past year, he had been teaching English in Peshawar. When he returned to England, he hoped to be ordained in the Church of England.

As darkness fell, we sat in Sher Wazir's kitchen and toasted our faces in the glow of the fire. Sher Wazir seemed relieved that the Pilgrims had gone and was in a good mood. As we settled down for a post-prandial pot of tea in front of the fire, he kicked off the night's conversation with an unusual question.

"English, you want an AK47?"

He grinned and his eyes danced with glee. The idea of talking about selling me an AK47 was almost as exciting as actually selling me one. He could not really have believed that I would buy one, could he? There was nothing to lose, so I played along.

"How much?"

"Of course it depends. A Darra-made AK47, which might explode in your face, would cost maybe 9000 rupees. An Egyptian AK47 is next at around 10000 rupees. Then the next best is Chinese-made at 11000 rupees. A Russian-made AK47 with a metal stock would be 12000 rupees and 13000 rupees for one with a wooden stock."

For the technically minded, the AK47 is a gas-operated, selective-fire, reciprocating, rotating-bolt design, with dual lugs locking into the front of the receiver. The gas system is "over barrel" with the piston and operating rod fixed to the bolt carrier. Its practical rate of fire in semi-automatic mode is 40 shots per minute, in automatic mode, 100 shots per minute with a cyclic rate of 600 shots per minute. Its effective range is around 300 metres. It works well in the dustiest of environments and rarely jams. It is a perfect guerrilla weapon.

Local estimates were that the numbers of Russian and Mujahideen killed in the war so far were one hundred thousand and fifty thousand respectively. Everyone in the valley was sick of the war, of the exile and the never-ending toll of the dead and wounded, but some of the effects of the fighting I could not have imagined.

"The price of a Russian Kalashnikov is always falling. When the Mujahideen are winning, they bring back many Russian rifles. Then the price goes down. I can remember when a good Russian Kalashnikov was worth 25,000 rupees."

This was nearly one thousand dollars. It was strangely comforting to find that market forces affected even the price of rifles.

"Until the Pakistan Air Force shot down one of their planes, we saw MiG's flying in the Chitral area all the time. We had a couple of MiG's flying up this valley just a few months ago. You know they bombed Kila Drosh? That is only a few miles from here."

Living in the peace of the valley, the nearness of the war was hard to imagine, but a few miles away in Afghanistan children were being left without parents and in Russia, grieving parents were struggling to come to terms with the loss of their sons.

The valley had become a holding area for fighters waiting for the Spring offensive. When the passes into Afghanistan were clear of snow, there would be a steady stream of Mujahideen fighters moving up the valley and into Afghanistan. There was a token police checkpoint close to the border, but it was only manned between the hours of nine to five. The main reason for the checkpoint seemed to be to ensure that only Mujahideen passed into Afghanistan. Too many intrepid travellers had been lured into Afghanistan only to be robbed and killed by their erstwhile 'friends' or picked off by Russian snipers. The war was a real war and the value of life had fallen, along with the value of the rifles that took life.

Dinner that night was especially good, because Sher Wazir had somehow managed to get hold of a kilo of aubergines at a good price. We ate in style with a feast of rice with beans, served with potatoes, fresh tomatoes and aubergine. Maize bread and black tea completed our banquet. There was a reason for his generosity, he was celebrating. I also realised that this was the first time that a few aubergines had made me so happy.

"English, tomorrow you will see water in a tap at Sher Wazir's hotel. The water will come in a metal pipe all the way from the tank at the top of the valley. The water in the tank will be purified and will be clean. You will be able to drink as much as you like and never get sick."

The night passed without incident and the light of day brought the prospect of having purified water from the head of the valley on tap at the hotel. Sher Wazir was in a state of barely-contained excitement and oversaw the workmen manoeuvring the steel pipes into place alongside the jeep track. When the pipe reached the hotel and the tap was finally connected, Sher Wazir celebrated by washing the teacups and making a fresh brew of milk-tea. Villagers passing by stopped to admire this wonder of steel and chrome. I drank large quantities of water and enjoyed its sweet freshness on my throat.

Several weeks passed before Sher Wazir discovered that the man responsible for purifying the water tank had gone to Chitral on business and had locked the purification tablets away for safekeeping. The water was still untreated and infected with *giardia* protozoa and other unpleasant creatures.

The afternoon was spent working with a group of Mujahideen who were "improving" a batch of Chinese land mines. Their commander was happy to explain why the improvements were needed.

"The problem is that these mines will not penetrate the bottom of the Russian Armoured Personnel Carriers. We have to make them better."

He packed a short coil of plastic explosive around the top of the land mine to create a shaped-charge that would concentrate the blast so that it would cut through Russian armour like a knife through butter. Carried on the backs of the fighters, these devices would soon be in Afghanistan. In these hinterlands, the war was never really very far away.

Sher Wazir was keen for me to move to his new room, which had a bay window that framed the distant mountains. The problem was that there was no glass in the windows and the new mud floor was still quite damp. At night, the temperature in the valley often dropped below freezing point, but it seemed a perfect place to escape the Pilgrims when they returned. The bitter cold at night was kept at bay with a down sleeping bag and one of Sher Wazir's grubby quilts. The freezing air also helped keep his bed bugs, which lived in the quilts, at bay.

Every now and again, Sher Wazir started to talk about going on a hunting trip. He seemed keen for Kevin and me to go with him up into the mountains and shoot some game. We soon realised that his enthusiasm for hunting had more to do with talking about hunting than actually going hunting, as he always found a reason to postpone.

As we waited for Sher Wazir's enthusiasm for hunting to return, Kevin and I decided to go off in search of a waterfall in the mountains above the valley that he had described to us. Heading north through fields of winter wheat and barley, we found the path beside a stream. The path steepened and took us into the pine forests high above the village. Eventually, we climbed above the tree line where the path broke down, leaving the sound of the waterfall as our only guide. After ten more minutes of scrambling up the slope, the waterfall finally appeared in sight.

The icy glacier melt water cascaded in a spray from a notch in the cliff face a hundred feet above us and plummeted into a pool enclosed by rocks. Despite the cold, we both stripped off and took turns to shower in the freezing water, screaming and yelling as the icy jets of water sprayed over our bodies.

The atmosphere was magical. Rainbow shards glittered in the sunlight and danced between droplets of spray. Had we looked closely enough, we would have seen snow fairies dancing around our heads and snow frogs swimming in the stream.

Refreshed, we sat and looked down across the valley and beyond to the snow-capped peaks of Tirish Mir in the distance. The Zephyr would have loved this place.

For a while, birdsong and the roar of the waterfall were the only sounds that disturbed the silence. Then, below in the valley, the sound of Mullah calling the faithful to prayer filtered up through the pines. His voice sang out into the still air powered by a battery driven loudspeaker. Sher Wazir had told me that some of the Kalash had been so fed up of the noise that they had once stolen the batteries.

After a while, we chatted and my curiosity soon got Kevin talking about his faith and religion, including Christianity, at great length.

We disagreed quite a lot, but did agree that most of the major religions had three main parts: a code for living, a system of beliefs and a way of dealing with death.

Kevin was a very patient man and tried his very best to fill in some of the many gaps in my knowledge about the world of religion.

"In most religions, these parts are linked together in a complex series of rites and rituals. Many religions have a Holy Book in which these rites and rituals are prescribed. Most of these Holy Books are hundreds, if not thousands of years old and were written for a way of life that existed at that time. They were also written at time when ignorance was rife and education was a privilege available to the wealthy and the influential. When we read these books today, we must try to also understand the world in which they were written."

When I challenged Kevin about the crimes that had been committed in the name of Christianity in the past, he kicked a pebble into the clear water.

"Terrible things had been done in the name of Christianity, but if a man uses a beautiful porcelain statuette to smash someone's skull, he is wrong, not the statuette and the statuette would not become less beautiful. It is the same with Christianity. Can Christianity be blamed for acts committed in its name that not only deny its teachings, but make a mockery of them?"

Overhead, a bird of prey circled, searching for food.

"You have to look beyond the medieval interpretation and portrayal of the beliefs behind Christianity to see the teachings hidden within the symbolism of the parables."

As we clambered down the steep valley sides to the villages of the Kalash, the sound of the Mullah calling the faithful to prayer continued to resonate through the pine forests, guiding us back to the village.

This was a strange place. Christians, Muslims and the Kafir Kalash living together, each convinced that theirs was the only true religion. At the same time, they were all linked by the fact that they had faith in a version of God that fitted in with their beliefs. Some worshipped one God. Others worshiped many Gods. The Christian worshiped a single God seen as a Trinity: the Father, Son and Holy Ghost. According to Sher Wazir, Christians worshiped three Gods. He did not believe their claims that they only worshiped one God. He had been adamant on that point.

"If Christians believed in One God, they would not have the Father, Son and Holy Ghost. They would just worship God. Some Christians worship the Mary god and other the baby god. They should just worship God."

The Muslims worshiped Allah, their only true God. As far as I could tell, the Kalash worshipped one God, but also believed in goddesses, prophets, demons and fairies. Their God was Imra, the Creator of all things in heaven and earth. Imra had also created "prophets" by the breath of his mouth. Their goddess Dizane sprang into existence from his right breast. According to the Kalash, Imra also created the demons and fairies that brought so much trouble to the world.

As Ramadan progressed, Sher Wazir continued to serve meals as normal. He even introduced more variety to our daily fare. New breads appeared, as well as mouth-watering dishes made with aubergine and okra. The arrival of curry soup with morsels of beef and chicken was an indication of how much life had improved.

As darkness swept into the valley again, I retreated to the crude comforts of my room and tried to sleep. Instead, I found my mind throbbing with thoughts. Kevin's departure back to the routine of teaching in Peshawar left me with a future in which the only certainty was that I was alone with Sher Wazir again. Ahead of him was a future that would take him back to England, back to University, through curacy and eventually to his first parish.

He would be a better priest for his time in Pakistan, where he had seen a Christian church wrought with corruption and ambition. He had seen that, despite many problems, the Church survived and continued to support and cherish the faithful few. He had also seen a Christian community living under siege, persecuted by many of their neighbours, but tolerated by some. I was comforted by the idea that there would be a day when he would think back to his days in Pakistan and remember the lessons that he learned.

Even disbelievers like me need people of faith like Kevin. They serve to challenge our ideas, which is good, because it is always possible that they are right.

His absence brought back memories of our long discussions about religion and faith around Sher Wazir's fire after the sun had retreated behind the mountains. We had talked for hours as the flames crackled in the freezing night air. I was sure that he would be a great teacher one day.

Faith is a strange thing that both binds and separates people. The majority of the religious sects around the world are all convinced that they hold the only version of the truth. What was most puzzling to me then and even now, was that most religions are not that different. Some believe in one god, others believe in many gods. Most believe in at least one god. As a biologist by training, I wondered if there was there some evolutionary advantage to those individuals who had Faith. What if there was a Religion gene? A special gene that curmudgeons like me did not have?

For there to be a God gene, there would have to be an advantage to the species that the gene provided. If there was such a gene, it may have given us the ability to form communities in which we shared common beliefs and could live in peace with each other.

Faith has certainly bound communities together and helped temper the stronger of our animal instincts. Somewhere in the past, I had read about the mutineers of the Bounty who settled on Pitcairn Island. They were a rough and ready crowd. English seamen, South Sea Island men and a smaller number of South Sea Island women.

At first, the white men took a wife each and left the South Sea Islanders to share the remaining women. This worked until one of the wives of the white men died. The white men then insisted that the South Sea Islanders gave up one of their women. This demand led to a period of violence marked by murder and rape that ended only when one of the white men discovered God and led the survivors down the path of righteousness. The murders stopped and peace returned.

Science has yet to demonstrate either that there is a god or that there is no god. The mathematical patterns that exist in physics, chemistry and biology serve to prove to some that there is a god and that we are all part of a greater plan. To some, the same patterns serve as proof that there is no God.

As far as we know, the entire universe follows a common set of mathematical laws. Did these laws predate the universe? What if there were other universes? Would they follow the same laws? Would the disintegration of one universe lead to the creation of another? If there is a God, is it the God of all universes? Is there a God of Gods? If there were a God, would the God really care how we dressed or how we ate?

We live in a universe that has several separate parts. One part is the sum of everything we know. The other part is the sum of things that we do not know. There seems to be another part that is the sum of the things that we believe. As our shared knowledge expands into new areas, we discover that the part we do not know is bigger than before. The more we know, the more we know that we do not know. Also the more we know, the part in which we believe seems to get smaller. Moreover, where did snow fairies fit into all of this?

The more I thought, the sleepier I got. Outside, the river growled and the rustling leaves of the walnut tree whispered sweet nothings to the passing wind.

The days passed and I used the time to explore the valley, climbing through the pine forests to the snow line where the thin air made my head spin. This was a time of great freedom. I went where I pleased, when I pleased and did what I pleased. This was a time to remember and to cherish

Sher Wazir taught me that life in the valley moved at a gentle pace. Just taking a shower was a major exercise that needed careful planning, rather than just "going with the flow". The joy of a warm shower was worth giving up just a little of the freedom from planning that I had been trying to work into my life.

Firewood had to be gathered and chopped; the fire had to be made up; a bucket of water pulled from the spring; and the kettle boiled. Timing was essential as the sun only shone directly into the open shower room for a few brief minutes. The trick was to grab a bucket of cold water in one hand, a kettle of boiling water in the other, toss a towel over my shoulder and strip off in the shower room just as the first rays of the sun shone through the open roof.

Balancing on the plank floor of the shower, I had to mix the water to a comfortable temperature in a bowl and for a few moments, I could enjoy the wonderful combination of the sun on my back and warm, soapy water around my feet. For a few minutes, time would slow and I would picture the world around me: a man ploughing his field with a pair of cattle; Bibi sitting on her lawn and playing with her child; and chickens pecking at the weeds among the growing shoots of winter barley. Every shower was a moment to savour.

Sher Wazir's wife was a mysterious creature. She was almost never mentioned and never seen. I tried many times to get Sher Wazir to show me where he lived, but each time I asked he just smiled and gave me a look that made it clear to me that this was one aspect of his life that was private. She remained one of Sher Wazir's great secrets, but I persisted.

After a while, I managed to get Sher Wazir to pass on messages from me to her. I asked him how she made our cakes. He did not know, but soon returned with the recipe.

"You take flour, eggs, milk, ghee, salt and a little yeast. Then you mix it and knead it until it comes like elastic. You take a round lump of dough and flatten it into a pancake as round as a dinner plate and an inch thick. Then you pop it into a slow oven or cook it on a thick iron pan."

The result was a pancake that was halfway between bread and cake. The different breads were made using different grades of locally milled flour. The stuffed breads were made in the same way, but in two halves. The cooked stuffing was placed between the two halves, which were then sealed. For the plainest bread, his wife did not use eggs or milk. The mysterious Mrs Wazir remained out of sight, but at least I now had started a conversation.

Rising with the sun, I got up at half six to find that for once Sher Wazir had already started the fire and filled the kettle. The reason for this unusual behaviour was that he had visitors. Two Nuristani men walking towards Ayun had stopped to chat with Sher Wazir. They had been visiting friends in the Nuristani village at the head of the valley. The older of the two was about my age and wore a US army jacket over his shalwar kameez. The other man had a Kalashnikov with a wooden stock slung over his shoulders and was clearly his subordinate. The older man spoke some English and a little Russian, which he had learned before the war and talked about the fighting in Afghanistan.

He watched me admiring the rifle and held it out for me to hold. It was Russian-made and had been manufactured in 1972. The polished wooden stock and pressed steel body felt curiously reassuring in my hand. After a minute to two, the Nuristani took the rifle from me and cradled the weapon with his beautifully manicured hands. There was no sign that he had been doing any work in the fields over the winter months. He was a fighter, not a farmer.

A crow in a distant field caught the Nuristani's eye. With a wicked grin, he readied his weapon, aimed and fired. The sound of the shot rattled Sher Wazir's kitchen and a cloud of dust exploded behind the crow. The startled bird jumped, defecated and flew off unharmed. There was a cackle of laughter from Sher Wazir. The Nuristani grinned and yelled at the bird as it made its escape.

A white patch of rock on the mountainside on the other side of the valley was the next target. Sher Wazir and I crouched down beside him and looked to see where the round hit. He fired, deafening us and covered us both in a shower of tiny fragments of paper. Perhaps, I was looking at the wrong patch of white rock, but I did not see the round hit. We each took a turn to blast the distant mountain. The bullets were Russian made, presumably war booty.

A passing tailor joined us and placed a bundle of brightly coloured fabrics on the table. Sher Wazir scurried off in search of our breakfast and the Nuristani examined each of the bolts of cloth in turn.

"I would like something for my wife."

Sher Wazir returned with breakfast and the Kalashnikov was placed on the table next to the bolts of cloth. The man with the jacket finally settled on a yard and a half of blue silk for his wife. With the business done, we turned to breakfast, which was better than normal, with three kinds of bread, apricot jam and milk-tea. The Nuristani and his silent acolyte set out on the long walk to Ayun and after eating my fill, I returned to the waterfall.

As I clambered up into the pine forests, a fox stopped to stare at me for a moment and strolled away. As he left, I banged a rock on the path and he stopped to turn and look at me again. Our eyes met for an instant before he vanished into the trees.

After a short rest by the waterfall, I went back into the pine forests and found a trail that I had not noticed before that took me to Sher

Wazir's father who was collecting firewood. An old donkey with a split ear stood patiently as we lifted a fearsome load of firewood onto its back and made it secure with a length of rope.

Leaving him to return to the valley floor, I climbed onwards and upwards. The trail was often buried under piles of snow, rocks and fallen trees and led to a shale cliff. Clambering up the cliff, I began to notice the thinning air and sat to rest, feasting my eyes on the Hindu Kush laid out before me. Around me, birds sang with joy and the melting snows trickled downward in a myriad of gurgling streams. The scent of the *deodar* was heady and cloying. I must have climbed to about ten thousand feet, just high enough to make my vision shimmer and sparkle in the bright sunlight. All too soon, it was time to get back to Sher Wazir's kitchen.

Sher Wazir's father had shown me a better route back that took me along a narrow winding path down to the valley floor. From time to time, I could make out hoof marks in the soft earth where he and the donkey passed earlier. The path was cut into the side of the valley and at times was near vertical. Below was a sheer drop of a thousand feet to the valley floor below. This was another truly outstanding feat of engineering.

Back at the Hotel, I found Sher Wazir asleep in one of the empty rooms. He struggled to his feet and wiped the sleep from his eyes.

"I'll get your lunch. You make your tea. OK?"

Despite the fact that it was Ramadan and already late in the afternoon, he was keen to sell me a meal. Having made up the fire, I fetched a kettle of water and brewed up a pot of milk-tea. The teapot sat in the embers to keep it warm. The food when it arrived was a tasty hash of potatoes, onions, okra, aubergine and egg, slightly spiced and served with fresh chapattis. I was getting used to Ramadan.

Chapter 7

After dinner, I retreated to bed to read by the light of the Hurricane lamp and listened to Bach on my Walkman. My reverie was interrupted by a massive shock that slammed the *charpoi* into my back. Around me, the air was filled with a rushing, roaring sound that seemed to be coming from underneath and all around me at the same time. The room shuddered violently and it took a second or two for me to realise that an earthquake had just hit.

A second, more violent blow then picked up the hotel and slammed it into the ground like a child's toy. I panicked and rushed to get outside, but found the door was jammed in its frame. The shaking continued and the door finally opened. I dived outside and skinned my shins trying to vault over the veranda rail. With a thud that knocked the breath out of me, I landed on my stomach on the lawn in front of the hotel. The ground rippled under my body for a moment and then was still.

As I lay panting and wishing that I had not tried to jump over a fence in the dark, the roar of the quake echoed across the valley. The frequency of the sound was so low that I felt it more than heard it. Like me, the hotel was shaken, but more-or-less intact. I spent the rest of the night in my room, but with the door wedged firmly open.

In the morning, I wandered around the village to see how well others had fared. The health centre and schoolhouse, which had been built using breeze blocks, were badly damaged. As far as I could see, structures built using local materials were unscathed.

In the evening, Sher Wazir told me that the epicentre of the quake was somewhere in the Chitral valley and had measured 5.5 to 6.0

on the Richter scale. News of the technical analysis of the earthquake must have moved like wildfire.

The earthquake moved Sher Wazir's wife to celebrate our survival and she treated me to a special cake filled with walnuts, potatoes and onions, served with a fried egg and piping hot apricot marmalade.

In general, Sher Wazir spoke and wrote very good English, until religion was mentioned. He then claimed either that he did not understand the question, or pretended that he had not heard. The earthquake brought out a side of him that I saw rarely, the religious Sher Wazir.

"The earthquake was God's punishment to bad Muslims. You look at the houses that were damaged and you see that only bad Muslims have been affected."

The hotel was of course undamaged. He named some the worst offenders and described their "crimes" in detail. My attempt to suggest that there might have been a more natural, rather than supernatural, explanation for the quake was met with silence. The conversation continued, but seemed to be going nowhere. Eventually, Sher Wazir announced that he was tired and sloped off to bed.

The day dawned with low clouds hanging over the valley, sealing out the rest of the world. The rain fell in a fine mist that hung in the air, giving everything a soft sheen of dampness. The mist had leached all colour from the landscape, leaving a grey world devoid of warmth.

The previous day's dust had turned into a paste that squelched between the toes and got everywhere. Locals trudged past the hotel wrapped in sodden blankets, their feet thick with mud and their shoulders hunched against the chill.

Sher Wazir's veranda was a hive of activity as four Kalash men used stones and crude punches to make holes in black PVC seedling bags. The bags had been made in Japan, but someone had forgotten to add drainage holes. This meant that they were cheaper to buy, suggesting that this may have been another of Sher Wazir's "get rich quick" schemes.

When the weather was bad in the valley, there was not much to do other than read. I had only two books: Conrad's "Secret Sharer" and "Heart of Darkness", both of which I had read many times. In the absence of physical activity, food took on a greater importance and the arrival of Sher Wazir's tray of delights helped pass the time.

The days of solitude and peace ended when the Pilgrims returned from their shopping trip. Although they had only been away for a few days, the Swiss man and Frenchman looked physically different. Their faces had sagged against their bones and they looked even more unhealthy than usual.

That evening, I joined them in their room. They had the only heater and we needed to share the Hurricane lamps to have enough light to read. The Pilgrims were excited and for the first time 'chased the dragon' across a sheet of silver foil as I read. With an expert hand, the German sprinkled heroin powder on the foil and heated it with a lighter. As a column of smoke rose from the bubbling white powder, he inhaled it through an empty plastic ballpoint pen. Next, it was the Swiss man's turn. When he finished, he relaxed by rolling a joint. He had been chewing opium earlier. He caught my eye and leered at me.

"Keeps the mosquitoes away! They don't like the shit drugs in my blood."

Peck the Frenchman squatted in a corner moaning pitifully. His rotten tooth was making him cry with pain. There was a big debate about whether he should cross the narrow footbridge over the river to his lodgings given his condition. He staggered off into the darkness anyway, whimpering and cursing with every step.

"I tell you," the Swiss man says. "He will fall into the river and that will be the end of the fucking Frenchman."

He laughed harshly, because he knew the bridge was very narrow and was worried about his friend.

The low cost of drugs here was one reason why Peck and the Swiss man had come to Pakistan. They told me that one gram of hashish cost one rupee. One gram of opium cost twenty-five rupees. One gram of unrefined opium, brown sugar, cost fifty rupees. A gram of heroin cost one hundred and twenty rupees. A dollar was worth twenty-five rupees.

"When I was in Darra, I met a man who said he could guarantee delivery of a ton of heroin. Shit, he gave me a kilo of hashish from last year. It was stale, but I cut it in half and saved half a kilo. Man, they just make so much of the stuff that they don't care."

He carefully emptied the tobacco out of a cigarette, picked out the fragments of wood and twig and mixed it with a small lump of powered hashish. With infinite patience, he packed the mixture back into the emptied cigarette and tamped it down with a match head. With a smile, he lit the joint.

"Man, Darra was fucking amazing. You can buy pen-guns there. It looks like a pen but is a pistol."

He inhaled deeply and breathed out a cloud of sickly smelling smoke.

"I knew someone who bought one and lost a finger when he tried to fire it. Man, the fucking thing exploded."

The stories continued under the flickering light of the Hurricane lamp. Eventually, I could take no more and crawled off to bed.

Conversation became a valued commodity that the German carpenter and I rationed with great care. During daylight hours, we barely spoke, saving conversation for the evening, as we sat cross-legged in front of a crackling fire. The arrival of Sher Wazir with yet another great scheme in which he became rich captured our attention. Over a pot of cardamom tea, he set out his plan.

"You see, in Europe dried morel mushrooms are five thousand rupees for one kilo. There are many in the hills around here."

In the light of the fire, his face gleamed with excitement.

"These mushrooms are very expensive because they have special powers as they are formed by thunder and lightning. You can only find them in places that are very hard. They even grow out of rock. Tomorrow, we will find morels."

Wrapped in clouds, the dark shapes that surrounded the valley hung ominously above us and it was easy to see why the laws of science did not work in this valley.

As the plan to gather morels developed, Sher Wazir decided to turn the expedition into a shooting party. The hunting trip that he had talked about earlier seemed to be back on the table.

"English, you will carry my rifle. It is British and made in 1918. If we see a turkey we can shoot it."

As the fire died down and the ashes glowed red, our ambitions took over and we all agreed to leave at six in the morning. With the prospect of a hunt ahead of us, we all trudged off to our beds to sleep.

Morning arrived with more rain and clouds that hid the mountains from view. Sher Wazir appeared with breakfast and sat by the fire warming his hands around a cup of milk-tea.

"With this rain we cannot go hunting. Maybe we go tomorrow. The rain and the lightening will make many mushrooms."

Instead, I spent the day watching the Kalash punch holes in more seedling bags. Sher Wazir explained why they were working so hard.

"These bags were bought by a government representative who is paying forty rupees to each man for half a day's work. The deal is that if the rain stops, they will return to work in their fields."

It made sound economic sense and the bags would be cheaper than if they had been bought with drainage holes.

After the interest shown in the Kalashnikov, Sher Wazir was keen to show us that he had a rifle as well. Despite his claim, it was not a 1918 English army rifle, but a Berlin-made 8.8 mm bolt-action Spandau manufactured in 1891. The barrel was pitted and filthy, but otherwise the rifle was in splendid condition. He bought it from an Afghan for the princely sum of fifteen hundred rupees, around a hundred US dollars. The rifle may have been supplied to the Afghans by the Russians during the Great Game that the British and Imperial Russian Empires played along the North West Frontier at the turn of the century. After ninety-six years of use, it would have had some tales to tell if only it could talk.

The weight of the rifle on my shoulders told me why Sher Wazir was keen for me to carry the gun.

"Where do you get ammunition for a ninety six year old rifle?

Sher Wazir grinned proudly, "No problem. In Darra, they make anything you want."

By the time the rain stopped, Sher Wazir had lost interest in the hunting trip and scurried away whenever the topic was mentioned. Instead, I returned to the waterfall and climbed higher than before. What seemed to be pounding of blood in my head became a drumbeat rising from the Kalash village in the valley below. The rhythm echoed through the trees, filling the silence with the heartbeat of an ancient culture.

The nearness of Joshi, the greatest of the Kalash festivals, had turned the valley into a religious melting pot with Pagans, Muslims and Christians coming together in this magical valley, sealed off from the real world. The atmosphere was charged with a sense of expectation and the river snarled with renewed vigour. The Hotel du Paix had become a focal point for the outsiders who were now arriving in the valley for coming Spring festival.

A potentially dangerous cocktail of different nationalities and religion was working its way into the very soul of the valley. In one camp, a family of evangelists plotted to save the Kalash for Jesus. They were ignored by the Japanese anthropologists who moved around the valley recording and logging all that they saw. Sitting in state, David and Linda, the hippies from Goa watched over the valley, passing their time chain-smoking joints and spinning yarns. There was Thierry, a gay French aristocrat with a penchant for jewellery and smack. His presence was ignored by the middle-aged German couple camping in a tent on the lawn in front of the Kalash Hotel. Further down the valley, young Sindi men were gathering at the guesthouse that had opened in the next hamlet. As the first day of Joshi neared, journalists and photographers arrived and Sher Wazir was almost beside himself with excitement.

"English, you wait. Tomorrow, you will see dancing like you have never seen."

On the morning of the first day of Joshi, Sher Wazir called me and told me to watch the girls returning from the upper pastures. As they ran towards the Kalash village, they skipped and sang. They carried green branches and bunches of wild flowers. Sher Wazir watched them with approach and grabbed my shoulder, exclaiming:

"English, this is Pushen, the start of the dancing."

As the girls dressed in their traditional costumes, long black robes, cowry head-dresses and coral necklaces, ran down the hillside waving their garlands of flowers and greenery, I was reminded of the May Day festivities of old England with their strong emphasis on the May Queen, May blossom and the Mother Earth.

Elsewhere in the Kalash village, the sound of beating drums called the dancers to the dancing area, an open space in the heart of the Kalash village.

The young Sindi men gathered on the grass next to a *charpoi* covered with cushions that had been set out for the visiting VIP's. Lesser VIPs had to make do with pine timbers that had been laid out on the ground for them. The prospect of seeing women dancing was almost too much for the Sindis and they giggled like schoolboys outside a strip joint. Their excitement was short lived because the local Mullah did not want Muslims lusting after these pagan women.

Their eyes and expensive cameras spent as much time focused on two French women dressed in Kalash costume as they did on the gathering Kalash dancers. When the French women turned their backs to the cameras, as a Muslim woman would had done, the reaction of the Sindis was one of disappointment. The Kalash women laughed at their confusion.

Shortly after midday, a mob of Muslims from the mosque by the Kalash Hotel led by the Mullah marched down the valley to the dance area. Above the beat of the drums and the singing, their angry shouts chilled the air.

As the mob arrived, the Mullah screamed at the young Sindis. The dance stopped and in the silence that followed, the Mullah's intentions become clear. He was angry that Muslims were watching women dancing during the holy fast of Ramadan. Although his spleen was concentrated on the Sindis, it was clear that the visiting dignitaries were just as guilty in his eyes. Their unease was clear and they were not sure whether to stay or leave.

With a final toss of his old grey beard, the Mullah stormed off, closely followed by an increasingly angry mob. Their mood was threatening and somehow ominous. It was very clear to me that this was not the end of the matter.

As the mob moved away, the dancing resumed, with most of the Kalash dancers grinning wickedly. The performance of the Mullah and the reactions of the young Sindis they had seen before and they really could not see why anyone should get so upset over such a minor matter. The reaction of the seated dignitaries was that of great agitation. After a short discussion, they all stood up and walked away from the dance area, looking uncomfortable and embarrassed.

Waiting around their Land Cruisers was the mob, now armed with heavy sticks, hunting rifles and shotguns. The dignitaries were bundled into the Police Jeep, which was attacked by the mob as it drove off at high speed in the direction of Ayun. Most of the Sindis slinked back to their hotel, but one of them stayed behind to argue his case with the Mullah.

"It is my choice. The Qur'an does not say that I should not watch these dances," he pleaded. The Mullah's response was drowned by the mob's angry reaction. Their mood had become dangerous and threatening.

The mob congregated around him, jostling him and shouting. Somehow, in the melee, he pulled a shotgun out of someone's hands. He pointed it at the mod and his voice could be heard telling them to keep back. They paid no attention to his warnings and continued moving towards him.

There was a sudden urgent shout, followed a silence broken only by the sound of the trigger being pulled three times. Luckily, for him, the gun did not fire. If the gun had been loaded, there would have been at least one death and several people badly injured. He would have been torn to pieces.

The mob became even angrier and surged forward, sticks flying. The sound of the man being beaten by the mob was sickening. Eventually, some of the locals managed to drag him away from his tormentors and lock him in one of the Muslim hotels for his own safety.

With no one left to attack, the mob dispersed and the dancing started again. The music was a pagan mix of drumbeats and discordant wailing pipes. As they danced, the women chanted, their shrill voices rising into the air, mingling with shafts of sunlight that made ghosts in the swirling dust. The women linked arms and danced in ever decreasing circles until they became a blur of black embroidered gowns, red coral and white cowry shells. Toothless elders and young girls moved in and out of the clouds of dust raised by their stamping feet. This was the women's dance, a spiral dance that encircled and captured the smaller band of brave male dancers.

For two days, they danced from ten in the morning until seven at night. As they danced, they sang, moving in time to the beat set by the two drummers standing in the middle of the dance.

I heard a rumour that an American family staying at the Kalash Hotel had been studying the Kalash for four years and despite their claims to be anthropologists, was actually from the Wycliffe Bible Foundation. According to local gossip, they were linguists and had been writing a dictionary of the Kalash language, but their real purpose was to use this knowledge to translate the Gospels into Kalash using the Urdu script. It had taken four years to complete a first draft of a translation of the Gospel according to Saint John. According to the rumours, they planned to distribute the translated Gospel among the villagers. Their son was in his twenties and mingled with the Kalash dancers. He had spent a long time with the Kalash and was fluent in their language.

I confronted him as he danced and he confirmed that the rumours I had heard were partly accurate, but denied that they were working as missionaries. When asked how the villagers would react to manipulation from an experienced team of evangelists, he paused for a second and then explained.

"The Bible is God's message to people everywhere. Through the words of the Gospels, Jesus Christ filled my world with light. When you have something that you believe is good, you should try to share it with as many people as possible. Don't you agree?"

I did not agree and pointed out that if he and his parents were successful, they would probably end up destroying the Kalash and their culture. His response started with a quotation from the New Testament.

"If they have eyes they will see. If they have ears, they will hear. If they come to Christ, it will not matter if their culture changes. They will have seen the Light and that is what is important."

It seemed clear to me that their goal was to convert these pagans and save their souls. They had deceived the Muslim Pakistani authorities and were evangelising under the very nose of the Mullah. Having seen his reaction to badly behaved Sindi Muslims, I could not imagine how he would react to Christian Evangelists working on his very doorstep.

Walking between the groups of dancers, I asked him how he would feel if the Kalash became Christian and these festivals were forgotten.

"It would not matter to me." He explained with great patience. "If they found the Lord, they would be saved. If they lost these dances, it would be in the name of the Lord."

I asked him what right he had to interfere with their way of life.

"I have a duty to introduce the Lord into their lives. It would be a sin for me if I did not show them the Way."

Caught in the turmoil of change intruding from the outside world and assorted groups of religious zealots trying to convert them, the Kalash danced in ignorance of the discussions that were being held about their future. Nevertheless, it seemed to me that it was the Christians and the Muslims who should shamed by the tolerance of the Kalash.

Sher Wazir was doing well and the visiting spectators flooded into his garden to eat. It was not a good time to be one of Sher Wazir's chickens.

After so many days of simple eating, I decided that the time had arrived to give in to Sher Wazir's pleas for me to try his wife's roasted Bumburet chicken. According to Sher Wazir, the roasting was done in a sauce made with garlic, chilli powder, onions and one tomato fried in ghee. His wife skinned and chopped the chicken into bite-sized pieces. The chicken was then added to the sauce and baked in a hot oven. From time to time, she took the chicken out of the oven, stirred the dish and added water to the sauce when required. The chicken was served with potatoes cooked with okra in a base of spices, garlic and onions and a round of Sher Wazir's best walnut cake.

Five of us shared the chicken in the garden under the cool boughs of a walnut tree. As we ate, we heard distant voices chanting to the beat of the constant drumming.

One of Sher Wazir's helpers spoke some English and explained how the Joshi festival was a series of ceremonies. The first was Chirikpipi, when the women collected flowers before dawn and took them to their houses, temples (Jeshtaken) and cattle byres, before moving on to the cattle byres dancing and singing where they collected milk that had been kept for ten days. At night, the men held a ceremony in the cattle byre.

There was Kuiparik Tsatak Joshi, a ceremony to purify year-old babies and their mothers in which all the Kalash gathered to dance and sing. There was also Gona Joshi with dancing and singing throughout the day.

The village throbbed with sound of drums and felt more alive than it was just a few days ago. After the long cold winter, life was returning to the valley.

On the third day of dancing, my French friends invited me to join them in a trip by jeep to the Rumbar valley to see the dancing there. The valley was narrower than the Bumburet valley and somehow darker. The dancing area was a wide terrace on the side of a near vertical slope overlooking the river several hundred feet below. As the dancing started, people crowded on to the dance platform and inevitably, someone tumbled over the edge. A minute later, she was hauled back on to the platform, bruised but miraculously alive.

The dancing continued as the sun began to slide behind the mountain. With a strange sense of sadness, we left. For some of us, this might have been our last Festival of Spring here in the secret valleys of the Kalash.

For Sher Wazir, the Spring Festival marked the beginning of the tourist season. The cash would flow into his coffers and his wife would continue to provide the best cakes and marmalade this side of the Hindu Kush. For me, it was time to move on.

Sher Wazir came to see me off and collect monies to pay for my accommodation and food.

"Good bye, English."

He smiled and shook my hand as left. He stood by the side of the track and waved as the jeep rattled away from the Hotel du Paix.

The call of the road was powerful and I was keen to set off on the next stage, which would take me over Shandur Pass, but there was just one more thing that I had to do in Chitral. To get over Shandur Pass, I needed to get another permit from the District Commissioner's office. As the Officer of the Day typed out my permit, I leant forward and asked a question that I knew would create a bit of a ruckus.

"What would the District Commissioner say if he knew there were Christian missionaries working in valleys of the Kalash?"

He stopped typing and stared at me. His response was terse and his annoyance evident.

"If that was the case, we could not allow that to continue. Even the Muslim fundamentalists are not permitted to try to convert the Kalash. It is the law."

I gave him as much information as I could and had some regrets as I had grown to like Daniel, but felt strongly that he had no right to try to destroy the Kalash culture and religion. There remained a nagging doubt in my mind that I was not doing the right things, but in the end, I felt that the Kalash did not need the help these people had to offer.

Fate is a strange thing and as I left, I passed Daniel on his way to the District Commissioner's Office to collect his permit for Shandur Pass.

"I have told them about your work. They know who you are and I must warn you that they are not happy."

He looked at me in astonishment. "Chris, I am very disappointed in you."

With that, he walked off to face the District Commissioner's office. My next step was to sort out my continuing health problems, so I visited a doctor who diagnosed amoebic dysentery.

"The problem is that the amoeba have caused small ulcers in the walls of your intestines. You will have to go on a diet of plain or milk rice, tea and porridge to give the ulcers a chance to heal. Your diet must have no vegetables and no meat."

He also prescribed a course of drugs to kill the amoeba. The diet was bad news, because I had just accepted an invitation to join an Oxfam researcher and her Australian photographer, who had I encountered at the Kalash dances, for dinner at the best hotel in Chitral. This was not a hard decision to make. The diet would have to wait until after dinner.

Not long afterwards, I shared a few minutes with a young South African of Pakistani descent. His parents lived in Singapore and he lived in Cape Town. He had a South African passport, but because of South Africa's apartheid policy, he was not able to travel to visit his parents in Singapore. In South Africa, he was discriminated against because he was not white and elsewhere, he was discriminated against because he was South African. He had problems in Pakistan because he was of Pakistani origin and did not have a Pakistani passport. In fact, there were few places in the world where he was not subject to some form of discrimination.

Over dinner, the Oxfam researcher offered to arrange for one of the doctors working in the refugee camps to "whip out" my appendix as soon as she heard that I was planning to head out of Chitral into the hinterlands of the Shandur Pass. Somehow, I felt that this was not the time or the place to lose any part of my body and politely turned down her kind offer.

"Medical care in the Chitral area is pretty poor, especially when you move away from Chitral town. If you have a medical emergency that needs a doctor, you would be in real trouble."

Her views on the medical care available in the Chitral valley were based on hard-earned experience gained working in the refugee camps.

"It is the women who suffer most. More than sixty percent of the Afghan women in the camps have malaria. There is only one female doctor for the 3,300 women in the Chitral area. One of our biggest problems is that most Afghani women will not allow a male doctor to examine them. There are plenty of drugs. What we really need are female medical staff able to administer them to the women. Women are dying of malaria and dysentery here that really should not be dying. The death rate among women in the camps is much higher than that of the men. There are no pharmacies in the camps, so trivial complaints receive no treatment and often become more serious consequently. The same is true for dental care."

As refugee camps go, they seemed to be well-run, partly because the spotlight of the world's media had focused so much attention on the aid agencies that "run" them.

"Their lives are better in some ways than they were at home. The trouble is that the war has destroyed everything that they had. What is there for them if they did go back? Many of their villages have been destroyed and the fields are covered in anti-personnel mines and anti-tank mines. I think that they will be here for a long time yet."

The Australian photographer had been inside Afghanistan on two separate occasions and his description of the devastation caused by ten years of war painted a grim picture of ruined towns and villages surrounded by fields that had been untended for too long.

Life as a journalist inside Afghanistan had become more dangerous in the past month because of threat posed by the Spetsnaz, Russia's Special Forces.

"They are using helicopters to put snipers with night-sights into positions overlooking strategic passes. They pick people off as they cross at night and seem to be targeting Westerners. The rumour is that they were out to kill as many journalists and Western medical workers as they can."

He paused to look out towards the distant mountains of Afghanistan and leaned forward.

"It is bad enough living with the risk of being killed by chance, but knowing that I am a target focuses the mind beautifully. You won't catch me going back there right now."

Life inside Afghanistan for a journalist living with the fighters was life spent living on the edge.

"They were just as likely to kill you as to save your life. They will cover your body as you lie in a shell hole listening to incoming fire getting closer and closer. Then one day you piss them off and they'll shoot you dead."

The letter that the Zephyr had posted in Wisconsin arrived in Pakistan and was making its way from Peshawar to Chitral, just as I was making plans to leave.

Chapter 8

Half-hidden in a side street off the main bazaar was a gloomy barber's shop that doubled as a bathhouse. The entrance led from the street into a steamy world bathed in flickering firelight. Standing in one corner was a massive boiler heated by an open furnace. A young boy with bloodshot eyes and grimy skin stoked a blazing pile of logs. As sparks rose into the air, he turned and flashed his perfect white teeth at me.

Against the back wall were six bathrooms, each little more than a cubicle with running hot and cold water, a bucket and a red plastic jug. Stripping off in the narrow confines of one of the cubicles, I was soon surrounded by steam and sweating heavily. The temperature rose to create a sauna-like atmosphere that seared my face and sucked the grime off my skin. After living in the Kalash valleys, where the only running water came from freshly melted snow and ice, the joy of being able to wash with soap and an endless supply of hot water was almost indescribable.

Afterwards, the bathhouse attendant took my money and watched me leave with beady eyes. For a couple of minutes, the air outside felt cool and pleasantly refreshing, but heat of the sun soon worked its way through my clothes and the sweat returned all too soon.

There was work to be done and I returned to my room to prepare for the climb over Shandur Pass. The distance from Chitral to Gilgit is around two hundred miles and as there was so little fuel in the Chitral valley, there was a good chance that I would have to walk a large part of the way.

Food and lodgings were also likely to be in short supply. There were a few rest houses en route, but given the time of year, there was no guarantee that any of them would be open. Having some food with me would be prudent, so I left my room for five minutes to buy some supplies in the bazaar, nothing perishable, just rice, lentils, sugar and instant porridge. Basic rations that I could cook up with minimal effort if needed. My diet had to start some time.

Returning to the hotel with my provisions, I discovered that someone had forced my door open and ransacked my room. The bolt and padlock had looked solid enough, but had been ripped off the door with apparent ease and hung uselessly from the one remaining screw. A frantic search confirmed that only my camera and film of the Kalash dances were missing. It was a heart-breaking loss.

The boys paid to act as doormen claimed they were "asleep" in their room at the time of the break-in. Neither of them spoke English but they soon understood that I was not happy. My request that they call the police was met with stalling tactics. Eventually the hotel manager appeared, but he too was unwilling to involve the police and insisted that we waited for the hotel owner. He had been summoned and I was assured that he would arrive "very soon".

When there was no sign of the owner after an hour, the manager moved me to the biggest hotel in Chitral, the sister hotel to my rather more basic hotel and we waited for him there. James, the Australian photographer, was there enjoying a late breakfast. When he heard my news, he rushed back to his room to collect his camera and film.

"I thought that if I locked everything in my room I could relax," he said and I felt a little less naïve. He offered me some advice that he thought might help me to get my camera back.

"I know the Area Commander of the local Mujahideen. Tell the owner of the hotel that I will ask for the Area Commander's help if he cannot get the camera back. The Area Commander is a very religious man and does not take kindly to Muslims stealing from anyone, particularly Westerners, when he is fighting a Jihad. You could have been a journalist or an aid worker. Do not bother going to the local police, they will do nothing to help and will do their best to get some kind of a bribe out of you. Take it from me, getting the police involved would be a waste of time. Anyway, the Area Commander will probably have the boys killed for not doing their job properly."

As a photographer, the loss of my camera and film had a special meaning for him and he was very keen to help. Camera thieves were not good for his business. With a slow cutting action, he pulled a finger across his throat and glowered at the hotel manager.

"Whoever took your camera knew exactly what they were looking for and went to the trouble of breaking down the door. The boys employed in the hotel will know who has your camera. They must have heard the noise of the door being forced open and did nothing. They were supposed to be security guards, which is why they are armed. If I were you, I'd go back to your hotel and get the names of the two boys."

This I did, in English and in Urdu script. The boys had started to understand why I wanted their names and were clearly terrified. They had tried delaying tactics, but I was determined to follow this through to the end.

When he arrived, the hotel manager briefed the hotel owner and a short, angry argument ensued in Chitrali. The manager looked as though he knew that he was not going to have a good day. I suggested once more that the police were called and told him that if they were not called I would be in contact with the Area Commander of the local Mujahideen.

The owner did not want to involve the police, but was more horrified about the idea that I would contact the Area Commander.

"You know that he will most probably have the boys killed? He will use them to set an example to the others. I will do everything I can to help you, but I need some time. I will make enquiries and I will be back here this afternoon at three."

The rest of the day passed slowly and I really did not hold out much hope of seeing my camera again. To my surprise, the hotel owner returned at three with a camera that was identical to the one that had been stolen. It was not my camera, but he insisted that I took it and promised not to take the matter any further. I realised that this was not the time to ask questions and accepted his offer. Much as I was annoyed by the failure of the two boys to prevent the robbery, I did not want them killed for the sake of a camera and a few rolls of film.

Late that night, the shock of being robbed really hit me. I began to wonder if the loss of my camera and film of the Kalash could have been linked to my betrayal of evangelists to the District Commissioner.

Daniel had told me all about their plans in good faith and I had betrayed his trust. He assumed that as a supposed fellow Christian, I would side with his actions, not those of the Muslim and Kalash communities around us. He had been wrong. I had taken part in the battle for people's beliefs that had been raging from centuries along the Divine Highways of the Silk Road.

The souls of the Kalash would not be saved and it was all going to be my fault. Was it possible that all those long years of planning and entomological research had been cast aside in an afternoon? It was clear to me that my treachery had been avenged by a hand reaching down from some Evangelist heaven to chastise me for my sins.

A shiver ran down my spine as the thought passed. Why would anyone in Heaven bother stealing my camera and pictures of the Kalash dances? The shock of being robbed and losing the film of the Kalash dances had hit me harder than I thought. It really was time to move on.

The word in the bazaar was that the snow blocking Shandur Pass was probably clear enough for me to try the most direct route to Gilgit. The alternative was to hike over Lowari Pass, take a bus to Peshawar, another bus to Rawalpindi and another bus to Gilgit. The journey would take a week at least and would involve going back to the heavily polluted lowlands. Worse still, it would mean leaving the mountains behind. The route over Shandur Pass would take me into the wilderness that lies between the two great towns of the Hindu Kush, Chitral and Gilgit. This seemed a far better prospect.

The main problem seemed to be that the supplies of fuel in the valley had run down to a dangerously low level and that there were unlikely to be any jeeps crossing Shandur Pass until more fuel was brought over Lowari Pass, which was still closed to vehicles.

Shandur Pass at twelve thousand five hundred feet is on the main trade route between Chitral and Gilgit. It is also the site of the world's highest polo ground. Once a year, it is the site of a polo festival between teams from Chitral and Gilgit. The contest started in the 1920's when the ruler of Mastuj was looking for a way to promote good relations within the region and thought that a polo tournament would help. The British Resident at the time, Colonel Evelyn Hey Cobb came up with the idea of a polo festival on Shandur Pass. The games would last an hour with a short break between two thirty-minute chukkas. Over ten thousand spectators make the annual pilgrimage to the polo ground and almost overnight create a tented town complete with restaurants, peddlers and makeshift hotels. Drummers, dances and bandsmen add atmosphere, creating a unique spectacle.

The distance between Shandur Pass and Chitral is about ninety miles over hard mountainous terrain and takes around nine hours by jeep. To get there, I would either have to find a jeep heading that way or walk.

There were no drivers in the jeep depot willing to offer me a lift. One driver shrugged his shoulders and shook his head. "I am not going over Shandur Pass as there is no fuel. My best advice to you is to wait. Something may turn up."

He did not sound hopeful, but there was nothing else to do. After an hour waiting in the blazing sun, a driver in a red Toyota pick-up truck turned up and told me that he was going to Mastuj. I felt a surge of excitement that increased when he let me load my bag on to his jeep. The trouble was that he then vanished. There was nothing for me to do but wait in the heat and dust of the jeep depot for him to come back.

I found a shady corner against an ancient wall and squatted on my haunches in the dust, reconciled to the idea that I might have a long wait. A moment later, I was joined by Aziz, a Chitrali in his fifties also waiting for a jeep to Mastuj. He had a long, lined face, a trimmed beard of coarse silver hair and deep-set eyes that gazed at me with a mixture of bemusement and interest. On his head was a round Chitrali *pagora* hat, tilted back at a jaunty angle. His hair was close-cropped and a distinguished whitish-grey. His long, angular and manicured fingers told me he was not a man who worked in the fields. The chestnut shades of his matching waistcoat and *shalwar kameez* went well with his tanned forearms.

We talked in broken English and Urdu, passing the time throwing small stones at a pile of pebbles lying in the glare of the sun a few feet away from us. Aziz was clearly an Anglophile and quite happy to while away the hours talking about the past glories of the British Empire. The trouble was that he did not speak much English and my Urdu was very basic, so after a faltering start, we lapsed into a silence punctuated with short statements that I could understand despite my limited knowledge of Urdu.

"Britannia acha hai." Britain is good. I nodded in agreement.

"Pakistan nahin acha hai." Pakistan is not good. I tried to suggest that he was exaggerating with little success.

Eventually, the driver returned and noticed that one of the tyres of his jeep was nearly flat. He jacked up the back of the pickup truck and took away the tyre to be repaired. The sun rose even higher and we waited in languid silence as the long morning shadows crawled back under the dry stone walls of the depot.

The jeep was laden with sacks of grain and as far as I could tell, we were the only passengers. After what seemed an age, the driver returned in triumph with an inflated tyre. When it was safely back in place, he told us that we could climb on board. The driver placed cushions covered in green vinyl on top of the sacks of grain for us and we sat in palatial comfort with our backs against the driver's cab. With a rumble, the driver started the engine and moved forwards a short distance, only to be stopped by an official and sent back to our parking place.

The problem was that the jeep was over loaded. The driver had to unload four sacks of grain before the official was willing to let us go. As we were about to leave for the second time, the driver stopped to pick up two more passengers, both Afghanis and both unfriendly. They clambered aboard and glowered at us. Once again, we set off.

Five minutes later, we stopped in the jeep depot on the other side of the river to pick up the Afghans' luggage, six heavy tea chests. With a great deal of grunting and straining, the driver and the Afghans began piling their tea chests on top of the sacks of grain. When only three chests had been loaded, it was clear that there would be no room left for any passengers. It was soon clear to everyone else that the task was impossible, but the Afghans had to try every combination of positions before they saw what common sense should have told them. After twenty minutes, only three chests had been loaded. The remaining tea chests would not fit, no matter how hard they tried. The driver finally lost his temper and unloaded all the chests. Reluctantly, the Afghans helped him. Aziz joined me to watch the tea chests being unloaded. Under his breath, he continued his tirade against the disorganisation that bedevilled his country. In his crazy mix of English and Urdu, he bemoaned the passing of the British Raj.

"This would never have happened when the British were in charge. The trains always ran on time. You could trust the courts and the police were honest. Now this is Pakistan. Nothing works anymore. Everything is always chaotic like this."

He shook his head and muttered, "Pakistan!" in a disparaging tone of voice and then moved across to the jeep to offer his advice. He stared balefully at the Afghans as they moved their tea chests away from the jeep.

With a feeling of relief, we clambered back up to our seats and left, to the dismay of the Afghans, who watched in silence as we passed. We got only as far as the fuel station on the edge of town. When the attendant refused to serve us, the driver stormed off into the office and stayed there for half an hour to argue his case, without success. Before we left, the driver checked the radiator and then without checking, topped up the brake fluid, leaving me wondering if this was a good sign or not.

After a last futile plea for fuel, the driver announced that he was ready to leave for Buni, part way to Mastuj and a long way from Shandur Pass, but better than staying in Chitral. Despite the tribulations of the morning, he was optimistic and eager to please. Whether he believed any of this or not, I could not gauge.

"If I can get more fuel in Buni, then I will drive on to Mastuj tomorrow and maybe then we can go on to Shandur Pass."

The metalled road quickly gave way to a rocky track that punished both suspension and seating systems. Riding on sacks of grain in the back of the jeep, I was protected to an extent against the worst of the jolting.

From time to time, the driver stopped to pick up people walking along the track. Mostly, we picked up people travelling from one village to the next. One stop gave us a man travelling with a small boy who stretched out full length on the sacks of grain and promptly fell asleep, despite the jeep's erratic movement and the constant pounding of tyre on rock. His ability to ignore the noise and violent motion of the jeep on the rocky track was almost unbelievable.

As we moved away from Chitral, the road became rougher and harder on everyone, except the boy who continued to sleep. In places, the valley narrowed into a gorge and the road was little more than a notch cut into the side of a sheer cliff. Where the rock was too hard to quarry, the track ran over a bed of branches and gravel laid over tree-trunks driven into deep holes cut into the cliff face. Just a few feet below our wheels, the churning river thundered and boiled.

The track wound its way up a narrow valley hemmed in by desolate walls of bare rock and fields of scree. Above us, a perfect sky set with snow-capped peaks dominated the landscape.

Only those valley floors that had been irrigated and tended showed any visible signs of life. The rocks themselves were streaked with blazes of colour: greens from copper oxides and reds, yellows and blues from different oxides of iron.

Out of this world of minerals came two tiny men with sharp pointed features, large ears and eyes like black pearls. For all I knew, they were elves or pixies from the land of snow frogs in the high mountains. They grinned when they saw me and settled down on the sacks of grain.

When they spoke English and were keen to talk, I was genuinely surprised.

After the usual questions about my "country of origin", they wanted to know why I was travelling alone. When I told them that I was travelling with many friends, their faces could not hide their innermost thoughts. They thought that I was mad.

The elf with the pointiest face leaned forward, grasped my hand with his tiny, bony fingers and asked, "Where are your friends then?"

I pointed at each of them in turn and smiled.

"You are my friends."

He shrieked with laughter and translated my response for the other travellers sharing space among sacks of barley and we shared a sense of fellowship. For the duration of each of our shared journeys, we were indeed friends.

Several hours later, the jeep turned off the Mastuj road, crossed a new suspension bridge and struggled up the final hill leading to Buni. Aziz, my travelling companion from Chitral led me to the rest house and made sure that I was made welcome. Despite Ramadan, he asked the cook to make me some tea. With a kindly smile across his face, he brought me a pot of milk-tea and watched me drink.

"Please drink and enjoy. I will drink later."

The tea was hot, sweet and very, very good. With my head still ringing from the pounding of the journey, I rested on a charpoi at the front of the rest house and took stock of my surroundings.

The rest house was a simple single-storey building facing a gravel track and surrounded on three sides by fields of ripening barley. A few hundred feet away, a line of poplars marked the boundary between the fields and the distant foothills. The bare rock of the lower slopes had been rounded by centuries of ice, wind and rain. In the distance, the angular snow-capped mountains of the Hindu Kush were shrouded by a fine grey mist. Beyond their snow-capped peaks, just forty-six miles away as the crow flies, were the burly shoulders of Karl Marx Peak in Soviet Tajikistan.

A chill wind swept down from the icy slopes above, bending the poplars and raising dust angels in the yard. Five boys from the village appeared on the gravel track, standing perfectly still in silence, watching my every move. The oldest boy approached me with caution, stopping just a few feet away from me before running back to join his friends. The boys turned and left, trailing behind a flurry of giggles and catcalls.

This was a place with a small footnote in the history of the British Empire. Captain Claye Ross was killed in a small village nearby on 11 March 1897. Sent to help lift the Chitral siege, he was shot when his force of one hundred and ten officers, men and porters were cornered by a group of Chitrali tribesmen. Sniper fire had forced them to seek cover in two caves close by the river for two days. The main body of troops led by Lieutenant Herbert Jones, his second in command, escaped and arrived in Buni later that night.

Back in Chitral, the Zephyr's letter finally arrived, having been carried in a mailbag in the hold of a C130 transport plane. The postmaster had remembered my request that any mail for me should be forwarded to Gilgit. He readdressed the envelope and dropped it into the Peshawar mailbag. When the weather was good enough, the letter would be on the next plane back to Peshawar. The Zephyr's words lay in the darkness of the mailbag and waited for the next stage on their Odyssey, which would take them from Chitral to Peshawar and then onwards to Gilgit by road.

My reception was very different and as ever, I was treated with kindness and respect. The Buni rest house was new but basic, with no running water, no electricity and no bathroom. There were two sleeping rooms, each equipped with a half dozen *charpois* and a pile of red blankets stuffed with raw cotton. The only other room was the kitchen, a tiny annex barely six feet long and twelve feet wide.

Despite its size, the kitchen was divided into two parts, one for storage and the other for preparation and cooking. There was little in the way of furniture or equipment: just a couple of low benches; a board for rolling chapattis; and a simple platform on which there was a sack of flour and cooking pans. The mud walls and floor filled the rooms with an earthy aroma that mingled with the wood smoke and the smells of cooking food, bringing back memories of a farmhouse in a remote French village in the Massif-Central.

A simple, but effective wood fire burning in a mud brick fireplace provided cooking facilities. A blackened kettle stood balanced on the grate with one side over the heat. The cook squatted on his haunches rolling small balls of dough between the palms of his hand. With a few rapid movements of his hands, he flattened each dough ball into a rough circle. With the help of a rolling pin and a pinch of flour, a perfect chapatti soon appeared. In the gloom of the kitchen, the flickering glow of the firelight danced on his face as he worked in silence.

He cooked the chapattis on his *tava* or frying pan and then laid them out under a grimy cloth in readiness for the feasting that would follow sunset.

Outside, fasting Muslims sat watching the shadows stretching out across the road as the sun sank behind the mountains of Afghanistan to the west. They murmured to each other and checked their watches at regular intervals. Finally, the Mullah in a distant Mosque called the Faithful to their prayers, leaving me alone with the crackling fire. As the shadows of the day blended into the darkness of the night, cigarettes were flourished and glasses of milk-tea passed around. The day's fasting was at an end.

The old man and I ate together in the kitchen facing the open fireplace. The fare was plain but satisfying, dhal and chapattis eaten in the light of the fire and a flickering Hurricane lamp. Aziz rounded off the meal with a pot of milk-tea and a freshly-rolled joint, before leaving me to go to prayers.

With my head reeling from the effects of the fumes from his joint, I crawled off to bed, my head filled with images of twisting jeep tracks and the sound of the voice of the old man bemoaning the problems that followed the exodus of the British from India. His gravelly voice echoed around in my head and for a minute or two, flowing in and out of my dreams. In a strange way, he reminded me of my father.

"No whiskey anymore, except for the people in power."

He floated before me, shook his head and spat into the fire.

"Corrupt officials."

The spittle sizzled and steamed in the ashes.

"Incompetence at all levels. Tell me, when are the British coming back? When? Tell me, when?"

Eventually, the night swallowed my thoughts and I slept dreamlessly.

Morning brought the news that the jeep was not going straight to Mastuj. What was worse was the sight of the driver leaving in another jeep. Aziz as usual knew what was happening.

"He is going to try to get some more fuel. He promised that he would be back very soon. We must wait for him."

After three hours spent waiting with the other travellers at the agreed assembly point, I decided to walk to Mastuj.

At the bottom of the hill, three workmen greeted me by the suspension bridge linking Buni with the main trade route between Chitral and Mastuj.

"Why are you walking when a jeep to Mastuj will be coming in ten minutes?"

When I just smiled and kept on walking, they tempted me back.

"Why bother starting out on a fruitless journey by foot when you could ride in a jeep? It is a long way to walk. Wait here with us."

They sounded so convinced that a jeep was coming that I waited with them for half an hour before setting out again. The sun climbed into the sky and its heat soon beat down on me and on the rocks beneath my feet. The going was easy, but the rocks were very hard on my feet. Trickles of sweat were soon running down my back.

The emptiness and silence of the mountains around me filled me with a sense of bliss that soothed away the ache of the straps of my pack on my shoulders.

Three hours later, a passing jeep stopped and picked me up. Eager hands stowed my baggage and a place was made for me in the back of the jeep between three men travelling home from Buni. With a lurch, the jeep set off and we were soon bouncing along the track towards Mastuj. The questions began in a mix of English and Urdu. They were keen to know where I came from and where I was going.

As the conversation continued, I discovered that one of them was the Family Welfare Officer in Buni.

"What do you do as Family Welfare Officer?"

As he explained, we skidded off a large rock and crashed into a shallow drain cut across the road. His response was hard to make out and was a puzzle to me.

"Wife control."

This conjured up such fantastic images that I had to know more. When I asked him to explain, he doubled up in a fit of hysterics.

"No, not *wife control*, I said *birth control*."

He translated for his friends and they all laughed. A bond of brotherhood had been created by the moment. Twenty minutes, the jeep stopped and we all got out. The Family Welfare Officer immediately took me by the hand and asked me to join him for lunch.

We walked together along a narrow path that meandered between the fields of spring barley and winter wheat. Already standing tall in the rich glacial soil, the crops soaked up the sunshine and swayed in the breeze. The sound of water channels bubbling and babbling in the irrigation channels filled the air with sweet music. The sky was blue and the peaks of the distant mountains glistened with ice and snow. Here, the air was warm and perfumed with oils from aromatic herbs growing in glorious profusion on the untilled land. Goats and sheep grazed in the pastures and chickens strutted over the stony path, scurrying out of our way at the last moment.

Five minutes later, he led me into a shady courtyard and invited me to sit on his eating platform. Sitting there cross-legged with my bare feet curled up in the dappled sunlight, my back resting on cushions, I felt like a king.

"Wait here and I will get you some refreshments."

He left me facing a garden filled with fruit trees, green grass and the sound of running water. A short while later, he returned with a plate piled high with slices of cheese; fried eggs; nuggets of herb butter; and thick chapattis. He then brought me a pot of milk-tea and a tall glass of *lassi*, a thirst-quenching yoghurt drink. It was all very good.

With great pride, he told me, "everything you are eating has been made in my house. My wife made the cheese. The eggs came from our chickens. My wife made the butter using a mix of sheep, goat and buffalo milk."

Flavoured with aromatic herbs, the butter smelled and tasted divine, it was good enough to eat on its own. When I realised that I was eating alone, I asked him if he was fasting for Ramadan.

"No, I do not fast. I am an Aga Khan Isma'lli Muslim and we do not have to fast during Ramadan. We have a very gentle version of Islam. If our hearts tell us to pray five times a day, then we pray five times a day. If our hearts tell us that it is alright to pray only once a day that is also alright."

His wife appeared briefly and she was exceptionally beautiful. I told him that he was a very lucky man and he smiled proudly.

"God has been good to me. I have land that is worth eight lakh (800,000) rupees; fourteen buffalo; forty sheep; forty goats; and I have many chickens. In my garden, I have fruit trees and fresh water."

What more could he want? This was paradise, a land of milk and honey, a Shangri La hidden in the mountains of the Hindu Kush. There was a catch. He wanted to leave this palace in paradise to explore the world that lay beyond the mountains.

"I want to travel like you. How much money do you need to travel for one year?" His question caught me by surprise.

Laughing, I told him, "From what I have seen, I would like to live your life. Why would you want to leave this beautiful place and what about your wife?"

He saw the irony of our situation and grinned, "If you ever return, I will give you some land and help you build a house. You can live here if you want."

There was a part of me sorely tempted by his offer, but the open road beckoned me onwards and I knew that I was unlikely to return.

Briefly, we talked about the differences between the Shi'ite and Sunni Muslims living in the Chitral valley.

"There are many different views of Islam in this place. Here many people are Isma'Ili Muslims with the Aga Khan. In Chitral, there are many Sunnis and others are Shi'ites. There is sometimes fighting and people are killed. There should not be fighting between Muslims. God does not want Muslims to kill each other."

The roots of many of these local quarrels go back to the very origins of Islam, a religion that developed in relatively recent times, in the seventh century of the Christian era. In its first hundred years, Arab conquests carried Islam over Western Asia and North Africa and into Central Asia, Sind and Spain.

According to most scholars, Muhammad was born in AD 570. The first forty years of his life were unremarkable; he worked in the caravan trade, married a wealthy widow and had three daughters.

His world was one in which the majority of the Arabs living in North and Central Arabia followed polytheism and idolatry. They were turbulent, violent times in which battles were fought across the Arab world, leaders routinely assassinated and war served as a distraction from the hardships of desert life.

As his daughters grew older, Muhammad seems to have become more meditative and it was not until he was forty that he received his call from God. He soon began telling his friends to give up their pagan ways and worship Allah, the one True God.

For ten long years, he preached against the pagan religions but made little headway, particularly in Mecca where he faced growing opposition. He was invited to move to Yathrib and took with him the few converts that he had made in Mecca. There the number of converts grew steadily and by the time, Muhammad was fifty-three, his followers were strong enough mount attacks on Meccan caravans.

Over the next seven years, hostilities escalated and by the time Muhammad was sixty-one, the merchants of Mecca had had enough and capitulated. The city was purified of the old religions and its ancient pagan sanctuary, which had been centred on a large black meteorite, was reconstituted as the central pilgrimage shrine of Islam. Muhammad died two years later and was buried in Yathrib, later to be called al-Madina.

Muhammad was not described in the Qur'an as a man who claimed supernatural powers or performed miracles. Instead, it is the Qur'an that is presented as the miracle. The current form of the Qur'an was written some thirty years after the death of Muhammad from various written and verbal sources.

Popular culture on the other hand demanded a more magical version of Muhammad capable of performing miraculous deeds. Orthodox Muslims still reject as heresy any kind of worship addressed at Muhammad.

When Muhammad died without appointing a successor, he inadvertently created a struggle for political and religious control of the Islamic movement. On one hand was the view that the leader of Islam should be elected by the Islamic Community. This led to Abū Bakr, one of Muhammad's early converts from Mecca being elected as his successor. The election of Abū Bakr had the effect of consolidating the transition of the religious and political power base of the Islamic world from Yathrib to Mecca, where the Meccan aristocracy still reigned. In effect, the old enemy of Islam had become its master.

Abū Bakr survived only two years, during which time he enforced the obedience of those tribes that did not want to pay their dues with the sword. Before he died, he named Umar ibn al-Khattab, another of Muhammad's early Meccan converts, as his successor.

Both men were given the title of Caliph, in which both political and religious leadership responsibilities were combined. Umar spread Islam into Syria, Mesopotamia, Persia and Egypt. In turn, Umar was replaced by Uthman, a son of the house of Umayya, which had fought against the Prophet almost until the last. According to some sources, Uthman destroyed all variant forms of the Qur'an and prepared the unified version that is in use today.

The Sunnis formed the largest group in the Islamic world. They believed in the Community and in the Community's right to elect the religious and political leader of the Islamic world. The Sunnis, or the followers of the Sunna practice of the Community, trace their origins to a civil war that started within thirty years of Muhammad's death.

Tribal factions in Iraq and Egypt resented the power of the Meccan Caliph and his governors. The civil war started when the Caliph was murdered by tribesmen and ended when the power base of the Islamic world moved once again, this time to Damascus under a new dynasty of Meccan Caliphs.

Opposed to the Sunnis were two dissident groups, the Shi'a and the Khawārij. The Shi'a believed that the Community had been wrong to elect Abū Bakr and his successors. Instead, the Shi'a believed that God would provide a divine leader, or Imam, rather than leave the Islamic world under the control of imperious leaders.

There were many who believed that Ali, the second cousin and son-in-law of Muhammad had been divinely designated as his successor. By capturing the Caliphate for Uthman, a son of the Umayya family, the Meccan aristocrats set the scene for an inevitable confrontation between the Sunnis and the other followers of the Faith.

What followed was a battle to control Islam that led to the deaths of tens of thousands of Muslims and instead of reaching a consensus, the Islamic world was torn into a series of groups, each believing that their version of the Faith was the only true version. At the same time, the conflict rooted the tenets of Islam in the Middle Ages, creating a way of life that was at odds with a changing world.

In the end, the struggle for power was between those who favoured political processes, the Sunnis and those who believed in divine intervention, the Shi'a, as the best way to designate the leader of the Islamic world.

Muhammad's original message from God had become the focus of a battle for ownership of the right to control the followers of the Faith.

As the heat of the day passed, my host bade me farewell and walked with me back to the main jeep track. He explained that I had little more than a ten-kilometre walk to Mastuj ahead of me and waved me on my way.

The route took me though a deep, narrow gorge for half of that distance. The atmosphere was oppressive and the walls of solid rock were dark and overwhelmingly cheerless. For most of the way, the track was a few feet above the torrent of blue-green anger as it gnawed its way to Chitral. The second half of the journey took me over a flat expanse of glacial deposits, lonely boulders and scattered villages. A chill wind sifted sand into my face and hair, filling my mouth with the feel and taste of the majesty that surrounded and dwarfed me.

As Mastuj appeared, the jeep track veered off to the right, but the footpath twisted its way down to the valley floor to a ramshackle footbridge that carried me safely over the raging river and guided me to a goat track leading to the town.

At first sight, Mastuj was a just a splash of emerald green in a landscape of barren glacial deposits and sombre mountains of grey granite. The town itself was little more than a cluster of shabby buildings, built in the shadow of a great fort. As I neared the town, a young man approached me and offered to escort me to the only rest house. As we walked together through the dusty side streets towards the centre of town, a small crowd gathered and watched us pass.

The rest house was a single room with a mud floor and a *charpoi* just visible in the gloom. The manager explained that I had to register with the police and was kind enough to walk with me to the police station. Leaving my bag in the rest house, I was taken out of the village to Mastuj Fort, an imposing rectangular building with walls made of great timber frames filled in with stones and mud carried up from the riverbed. After months of near isolation, I was one of the first Westerners to visit Mastuj since the start of winter and my arrival generated a frisson of excitement that coursed through the town.

My guide took me through the entrance to the fort and into an office with a long, narrow counter. A small crowd of interested bystanders crowded in behind me. The Duty Officer appeared and inspected me closely with dark eyes.

With great ceremony, the Duty Officer set the registration book on the front desk for me to sign. As I signed the register, I saw that an Australian called Gus was ahead of me by only two days.

As the noise level rose, a burly police sergeant appeared to see what was going on. He soon took charge of the situation and cleared away the bystanders. He was not happy that my arrival had caused so much disruption. As soon as he discovered that I was British, his manner changed and he became exceptionally friendly. After a brief discussion, the sergeant informed me that the rest house was not really an appropriate place for an English "gentleman" to stay and sent a constable off to make me milk-tea.

"I will send a man for your bag, if you would stay with us as our guest."

Without hesitation, I accepted his offer. How often would I have an opportunity to sleep in a police station? I also hoped that the *charpoi* in the cells were at least as comfortable as those at the rest house.

However, the sergeant had other plans for me.

"You will share my room."

He was a large man and at first, I was unwilling to put him to any trouble. When the sergeant showed me to his room, I was very pleased to discover that he had a spare bed. He told me that he was studying English and that he hoped to practise his English with me. Although it was still Ramadan and the sun was still high in the sky, he insisted that I had more tea and watched me with his textbook at the ready. I did my best to earn my keep by helping him with some grammar and by translating some of the more esoteric English phrases in his MA study book. He still had quite a lot of work to do before he would be able pass the exam, but he showed real promise and spoke far better English than I did Urdu. Later, the sergeant invited me to join him and his colleagues for dinner.

I found my hosts sitting cross-legged on the floor in a circle waiting for the food to be brought out from the kitchen. They made room for me and it was not long before the cook arrived with pots filled with steaming rice and *dhal*, piles of *tikki* bread and a large pot of milk-tea. They had no meat or vegetables, which was good for my diet. After a brief exchange between the cook and one of the younger constables, a roasted sparrow was brought out and placed with great ceremony in front of us. Little larger than a walnut it was hard to see how we would share this part of the meal.

A debate developed and was translated for me by one of the younger police officers. He spoke very good English and looked very fit. With a grin he told me why the Sunnis would not eat the sparrow and why they thought we should not eat it either.

"My colleagues told me that we should not eat the sparrow because it was not killed properly. It may not be halal. It is a question of whether it was already dead when I slit its throat."

The tiny body of the bird remained untouched on its platter until there was a mass exodus as prayer time approached. Only my translator remained behind. As soon as the door closed, he grinned and somersaulted across the dining cloth, ending up beside me. With a knowing nod in the direction of his departing colleagues, he smiled and placed his right palm against his heart.

"I am Isma'Ili Muslim and I only pray three times a day."

With a deft twist of his fingers, he divided the bird in two and offered me the larger half, which I accepted and ate. There was almost no meat, but the taste was good. It was something that they were reduced to cooking sparrows. As he sucked the bones clean, he told me more about himself.

"I am not a regular police man. I am the Mastuj representative of the Chitral Scouts, a special police force."

"You must be very fit."

"Very soon I will be taking part in a Police athletics championship. Now, I am in training and run several miles every morning."

We drank more tea and he explained why he had not joined the others at the mosque.

"I am Isma'Ili Muslim and we are taught that if our hearts tells us that it is alright to pray only three times a day than we should pray only three times a day. If we wish to break our fast and it is all right in our hearts, that is also permitted. It is better to have the right feelings in your heart, than to follow the rules just for the sake of following rules. It is who you are that matters, not what you do."

He stood up and left me alone for a few minutes, which gave me time to reflect on the fact that Younghusband had been stationed in Mastuj in 1893. To his chagrin, Younghusband had been ordered to leave Chitral and move to Mastuj in September, because officials in the Government of India had decided this tiny mountain town should be the headquarters of the Political Agent. His home was a hut, where he stayed until May 1894, when he left to take his Political Service exams in Gilgit. To get to Gilgit, he had to cross Shandur Pass and would have travelled along the route that lay ahead of me. As the only English man in Mastuj, I felt very close to Younghusband at that moment.

When the others returned from prayers, I said goodnight and retired to bed. The sergeant came to see that I was comfortable and left me to a deep sleep.

In the morning, their kindness and consideration continued and I was left to sleep until half past five, rather than Ramadan breakfast time at half past three. Breakfast was waiting for me: dhal, bread and milk-tea. By six, I was ready to leave and just caught my Isma'Ili friend as he returned from his morning run. He embraced me and kissed me on the neck. In another world, he and I would have been good friends.

"You have a long walk ahead of you. It is seven hours to Laspur, the last village before the climb over Shandur Pass and then, seven hours over the Pass to the first village. Take care and keep walking and remember your friends here."

In the solitude of the mountains, people tend to seek out the company of others and this day was no exception. Five minutes out of Mastuj, I was joined by Hazir Jan, a grandfather. He walked with the measured lope of someone who had lived all of his life in the mountains and despite the fact that he had a bad back and was in his sixties or even his seventies, I struggled to keep up with him. The combined effects of my diet and amoebic dysentery were debilitating and my stamina was badly affected. Whenever I looked too tired, we stopped for a minute or two. Hazir showed me how to drink water out of a muddy stream. He made a tiny sandbank to filter the water into a small depression and scooped out a mouthful for me with his hand. The filtered water looked clear and tasted just a little muddy, but quenched my thirst. He waited patiently as I caught my breath. The track wound upwards into the mountains through a valley hewn by a glacier in times past. Vast fields of scree swept down from walls of solid rock and tumbled into the seething waters below.

After five hours of hard walking, Hazir Jan invited me to his house in Brook, a small village just a short walk from Sol Laspur. An hour later, we stopped briefly in Harchin so that I could register with the police and drink a glass of cold mountain water. One of the benefits of having amoebic dysentery is that you do not have to worry too much about the cleanliness of drinking water.

An hour later, we arrived at Hazir Jan's home in Brook. Built in 1985, the house was a solid construction with walls of stone and mortar. Stone steps rose to an open veranda facing the track. The mud roof was flat and built using roughly-trimmed logs, over which were planks held down by a layer of rocks. A tree trunk supported the main weight of the roof. This was a house of substance.

Hazir Jan was an Isma'Ili Muslim and his family treated me as one of their own and welcomed me as if I had known them for years.

The interior of the house was dark and warm, lit only by a wood fire burning in an open grate in the centre of the living area and by a couple of spluttering hurricane lamps. The smoke from the fire rose through the house to a chimney vent formed by roof timbers laid diagonally on top of each other.

We ate together and shared a simple dish of boiled mustard leaves with *chapattis*. This was not what the doctor ordered, but it was all they had. The atmosphere was sombre because two of Hazir Jan's grandchildren were sick and there was no milk. The youngest, a baby, had a fever and lay very still, panting pitifully. Hazir asked if there was anything that I could do to help. With some reluctance, I offered him some Paracetamol and suggested that the children should have no more than half a tablet each every four hours.

"How do I get the baby to take a tablet?"

Hazir looked at me and expected an answer. All I could think of was my mother giving tablets to my youngest brother. With two teaspoons, I crushed half a tablet and asked for some milk. Hazir reminded me that there was no milk, so we tried mixing the crushed tablet with water. With great care, patience and gentleness, the baby's mother got the mixture down.

I retired to my room in an annex with the sight of the baby struggling to fight a fever weighing heavily upon me. The charpoi awaited me and carried me into the night.

The family woke up before sunrise and I joined them for breakfast and good news. The baby had recovered and was on her feet. The mother showed me the baby's sparkling eyes and smiled in gratitude. The little girl was around nine months old and walked quite well. Her laughter filled the house with music and happiness. As I sat by the fire, the young mother breast-fed her child and smiled as the logs crackled, throwing sparks over my feet. She kept an anxious eye on her other child who was still not well. She still had a fever but I had run out of Paracetemol and could offer nothing more to help.

As the little girl played around the fireplace, her mother prepared breakfast. When there was an "accident", she swept the rabbit-dropping sized turds into the flames and giggled and then carefully placed a *tikki* in the warm ashes. We ate breakfast in the gloom of the firelight and I mentally prepared myself for the climb ahead.

When an ancient flintlock musket hanging on one of the timbers caught my eye, Hazir's eldest son took it down to show me.

The gun told its own story, having been built for the British Army in 1857. Made by Tower, it was still in working order and used by the men of the family for hunting.

Word of my supposed healing skills had leaked out into the village and as I tried to leave, several people asked me to give them medical treatment. My personal supply of medicine was almost gone and I had to explain to them again that I was not a doctor. With polite efficiency, Hazir Jan ushered them away. As the sun rose from behind the mountains, I got ready for the long walk over Shandur Pass.

The entire family came out to send me on my way and I felt ready for the climb. They had been very good to me and I had been able to repay their kindness by playing some small part in the recovery of their baby. The mother stood in the door of the house with the baby in her arms and smiled at me. It was a fine farewell. Time was pressing and I left with the sight of Hazir Jan's family watching me firmly engraved in my memory.

The track climbed steeply at first and then curled round to the right. Seeing a well-worn path, I left the road and walked to the top of the rise ahead of me. Before me stretched the twisting gorge cut by the river and the sight of the village of Laspur dwarfed by the towering bulk of the snow-clad mountains on all sides. I clambered down and re-joined the track. Following in the footsteps of all those who came before me, I walked along the rock track as it twisted and wound its way down to the valley floor. The ground rumbled with the growl of the torrent below and the wind snatched tears from my eyes. The landscape was overpoweringly beautiful.

I pushed on through the village of Laspur, climbing steadily up the other side of the valley, following the contours and trying to shorten the route as far as I could. A herd of grazing yak ignored me as I clambered upwards. In the distance, a woman dressed in a red shalwar kameez struggled down towards Laspur, burdened with a huge pile of brushwood. At first, I made every effort to avoid her, but it soon became apparent that she was trying to cross my path. Stories of Europeans being shot in these mountainous regions for talking to women made me nervous about getting too close to her.

When she waved at me, there was no doubt that she wanted to meet me, so I took my life in my hands and walked towards her.

When we met on the side of a mountain high above the villages, she showed me an open wound on her finger that had been rubbed raw by the kindling she had been collecting. My fame as a supposed healer had spread far and wide. With a tube of antiseptic cream and a simple Band-Aid, I made her a happy woman. With her surprisingly strong hands, she grasped my hand and thanked me profusely. Her face was covered in a protective layer of ash that helped protect her skin from the sun and wind. The grey woollen shawl that covered her head and shoulders was made from the finest wool. The edges of the shawl were delicately embroidered with flowing symmetrical patterns sewn in orange and green silk. It seemed far too precious to be worn on the side of a mountain.

For a few minutes, she and I talked as best as we could, before parting on our respective ways. With a low grunt, she heaved her load on to her shoulder and set off down the mountainside towards Laspur, turning briefly to flash me a radiant smile of thanks.

Within minutes, she was little more than a splash of colour on a leaden backdrop. Other than a herd of yak, there was nothing between the Shandur Pass and me.

Overhead, the clouds were grey and ominous and blocked out the sky. They clung stubbornly to the highest peaks and pressed down towards the ground. Half-buried in snow, the mountains were blue with cold and crowded together so it was hard to see how there could be a way through them. A snowstorm would not have been helpful. I had to keep moving.

As I climbed higher, the air got colder and I had to stop to put on my pullover and down jacket. At least conditions for me were not as bad as those faced by Surgeon-Major Robertson when he crossed the Pass on his way from Gilgit to Chitral in late January 1885:

"Every care was taken of the Sepoys, who were provided with Balaclava caps and snow goggles and had their feet cased in strips of blanket, sent up by the careful Baird. Gloved, with thick wrappings on their feet and woollen mufflers on their faces, the men looked comfortable in yellow sheepskins worn over their greatcoats and trudged sturdily."

Wrapped in a down jacket, I trudged as sturdily as I could, imaging meeting Robertson's men as they crossed the flat plain at the top of the pass towards me. Today, the wind was cold, but bearable. Robertson recorded the cold conditions at his camp in Langar on the far side of the pass on the eve of his crossing:

"It was almost impossible to keep warm, even beneath a mountain of blankets and furs. Revolvers felt sticky, while iron tent pegs could not be touched with the bare hand."

The snow line was above me and if the weather held, I would be over the pass in a couple of hours. As I climbed, the effects of the high altitude began to slow me down. I had to stop to rest every five minutes and felt weakened by the combined effects of amoebic dysentery and the thin air. The effort of walking left me noticeably breathless. My muscles cramped easily and I had a slight headache. I knew that these could have been some of the first symptoms of altitude sickness. However, if all went well, I would be over the pass by two and in Langar on the other side by six or seven in the evening at the latest.

I reached the mountain plain that marks the highest point on the pass at two and found that most of the track was clear of snow. The snow that remained was frozen solid and I walked on top of it without difficulty. The air smelled fresh and as the slope levelled off, I made good progress.

The track continued past the lakes that straddle the pass and was deeply rutted by centuries of use. The silence of the mountain was broken only by the sound of snow sliding off reeds growing at the edge of the lake into the cold, clear water.

A tall, bearded rider on a brown pony heading towards Gilgit overtook me, greeting me with a polite *as-salaam alikum* and a salute. He trotted on towards the distant horizon and was soon out of sight.

"Bastard!" I thought, quite unreasonably.

"Next time," I screamed into the passing wind. "Next time, I'll bring a bloody horse."

Walking on the level was relatively easy and I made good time, passing along the length of the lake. In the distance, I could see two army huts used by the Chitral Guides standing by the famous Shandur Pass polo ground.

I decided to visit the soldiers camped in the hut, on the very good chance that they might have offered me a cup of tea. When I got there, the open hut was deserted, with only a smouldering fire providing evidence that they had been here at all. A pot of reed roots gathered from the lake simmered on the embers and looked most unappetising. The other hut was locked and seemed to be empty.

I brewed up a cup of coffee and a plate of steaming porridge and sat back to wait for their return. As I rested, lethargy set in and I dozed for a while. It was tempting to relax and think of the long walk ahead some other time. Maybe the soldiers would let me sleep in one of the huts. It would have been nice to watch the sun rising over the pass. At four in the afternoon, the door of the other hut opened and two bleary-eyed soldiers appeared.

The sergeant was not pleased to see me and made it clear that unless I paid him a substantial bribe, I would have to leave.

"This not tourist camp. This is Army camp," he blustered and shambled off for a shit. Perhaps he was right, but did he have to be so unpleasant?

"You are a little shit," I muttered as he squatted down by the lake.

As I repacked my bag, the private offered me a cup of tea from a thermos flask. I gave him a packet of porridge oats in return, which he hid from the sergeant. There was something about his manner that made me wonder what the two men were doing in bed together in the middle of the afternoon. The sergeant really was an unpleasant little man and was clearly not happy for me to be here.

When he came back from his ablutions, he repeated his demand for money. His tone made me nervous and just a little angry.

Without too much thought, I shouldered my pack and stormed off down the mountain. An hour later, I began to calm down and the reality of my situation started to dawn on me. I was at least four hours from the nearest village and there was less than one hour of daylight remaining. I kept walking, somehow convinced that I would be all right and that something would turn up. If all else failed, there were enough big boulders under which I could shelter. The clouds sank lower and a fine drizzle enveloped the world. I kept walking. This was either a moment of mountain madness or a moment of great faith.

Ten minutes later, I rounded a corner and found myself face to face with a man standing on the track. He stared at me in astonishment. As I approached him, three more men appeared and watched me approach. They were almost as surprised to see me, as I was to see them.

After a brief discussion in broken Urdu, they convinced me to stay with them. It turned out that they were driving a herd of donkeys and cattle from Laspur over Shandur Pass to the village of Teru on the other side. Their animals were well-hidden and penned inside a dry-stone wall enclosure.

The oldest herder led me by the hand into a narrow slit in the mountainside that I would had never have noticed without his help and into a cave that had been hollowed out under a boulder the size of a house. After my experience with the sergeant on Shandur Pass, many thoughts crossed my mind as I was bundled through the entrance, most of which were not very palatable.

The roof was low and we had to walk in a crouched position. As my eyes adjusted to the gloom, I made out a pot of rice simmering over a fire towards the back of the cave. Elsewhere, their bags and blankets lay scattered across on the cave floor. With a certain amount of trepidation, I squatted in an empty corner and began to wonder if they were likely to slit my throat and rob me. They were a rough-looking crowd, but their first step was to offer me hot tea and some unleavened bread. Then they began trying to find out what I was doing alone on the side of a mountain, so late in the day. Seated on their best blanket and warmed by a blazing fire, I tried my best to answer their questions. Our lack of a common language made conversation less than easy. After a while, they gave up and continued with their preparations for the night.

They were all fasting and kept a close eye on the time as sunset approached. Outside, the animals were restless and needed constant attention. When they had finally settled the animals, the men all crowded back into the cave and sat watching the minutes pass until the sun had officially set.

The oldest of the men sat under an umbrella at the mouth of the cave, watching his digital watch with great care. Sheets of rain started to swirl in through the cave opening and the umbrella tossed and turned with a life of its own. The old man kept his eyes glued on the glowing digits on his wrist.

The other three harangued him about the so-called accuracy of his digital watch, but he was resolute and until he was sure that the sun had set, he let no one near the food.

When at last, he declared that the sun had set, feasting began. The cook heated up the rice and brewed a large pot of tea. In return for my warm reception, I offered them the last of my sugar, a bag of green tea and a packet of mixed spices that I had bought in the bazaar in Chitral.

This was a mistake. For the remainder of my stay, I strived and failed to convince the cook that I did not drink only green tea and no matter what the circumstance, I did not want mixed spices added to my tea. Every time I tried to explain that the green tea and spices were a gift, I thought that they had understood me. But shortly afterwards the cook did something with either the green tea or the spices that showed me that he had no idea what I was saying.

Only one of them spoke any Urdu and his accent was so thick that I could barely understand anything he said. He was the cook, the youngest of the group and had decided to teach me to speak his local dialect. My nightmare lesson in Chitrali, or whatever language it was, began with him asking me to repeat the names of objects in the cave. If I pronounced a word wrongly or forgot, he repeated the word louder or more quickly. With his face close to mine, he screamed each word into my ear and covered me with his spittle. His grin told me that he was enjoying this bizarre form of torture.

If it had not been for the digital watches and the umbrella erected to stop the worst of the rain blowing into the cave, I could have been forgiven for thinking that I had tumbled into a Neolithic homestead. As the temperature dropped steadily, the cook piled more fuel on to the fire, filling the cave with acrid, choking smoke. Any heat produced by the fire escaped through the cave entrance and was replaced by icy draughts of mountain air. The lesson continued and my failure to learn quickly enough was irritating my instructor to the point of distraction. With eyes and nose streaming because of the fumes, I tried hard to please my tormentor and wondered how much longer he would keep up this misery.

An age later, he gave up and at last, we prepared for sleep. I was given a blanket but not allowed to use it to insulate myself from the cold, damp cave floor. Instead, one of the herdsmen placed it on top of me. Freezing rainwater soon dripped down from the roof of the cave, through the blanket and down my back. The shivering soon started and I felt like shit.

Moments after I finally managed to get to sleep, a sudden scream fractured the still of the night and I sat up with a start to see the herders scrambling into the night through the narrow cave entrance. A predator had spooked the animals, perhaps a wandering snow leopard. I could hear the men shouting to try to scare it away. Peace finally returned and I spent what was left of the night shivering under the blanket, with the chill of the freezing ground eating into my side.

Relief came at three in the morning as the herders began to stir and get breakfast underway. Once again, the cook stoked up the fire and once again, the cave filled with choking smoke. The back of my throat and my eyes felt raw and my nose ran uncontrollably. I would have preferred tear gas.

My tormentor, the young cook, brewed a pot of tea and re-heated the rice until it burned on the bottom of the pan. One of the herdsman spread out the eating cloth and we ate in silence. As the food was cleared away, my torment entered its second stage. He spoke to me in unintelligible Urdu, but his intentions were very clear.

"You have had a good sleep? Now we will go over last night's lesson."

With my head muzzy from lack of sleep, the altitude, the cold and the exertions of travel, my brain was in no fit state to learn, but he was relentless and hammered me on every word. He would not move to the next word until I had managed to produce a reasonable pronunciation. For the best part of half an hour, he screamed at me, laughing like a maniac at my many mistakes.

In revenge, I did the same to him and got him to repeat the names of objects in the cave in French. It was a futile exercise, but made me feel a little better. Eventually, the old man told him to leave me alone and pack away the kitchen.

Aching with the cold and exhaustion, I managed to crawl close enough to the remains of the fire to feel its magic working into my bones and fell asleep against a pile of brushwood.

In their world, I was out of place and they treated me like a moron to be looked after but also to be played with. In some ways, they were right. I could not speak their language at all and could only speak as much Urdu as a rather slow two-year old. To make matters worse, I had managed to get myself stuck on the wrong side of a mountain on a very cold and wet night.

When the young cook found my plastic sugar container, he asked if he could keep it, so I gave it to him. He struggled for a few minutes to close it and was red faced when I offered to take it off him and clicked the lid back in place with a single motion of my thumb. He quickly slipped the container in his bag, trying to hide his embarrassment.

Chapter 9

The rain of the night had moved on leaving a clear blue sky. Before leaving, I took a photograph of my hosts standing in front of their cave. When the posing was over, the men all wanted to look at my camera but needed help from me to operate the zoom lens. They scanned the mountains and smiled as the viewfinder brought distant objects a little closer. The young cook was still sulking. After I replaced the lens cap, he came forward and snatched the camera out of my hand. For a few fruitless minutes, he tried to see what his friends had been seeing and in the end returned the camera without a word. When I showed him how to take off the lens cap and work the zoom lens, his sullen glower was finally replaced by a smile. With a sweeping gesture, he looked out down the valley and was transfixed. When at last he gave the camera back to me, we were friends and he shook my hand. In the end, we all came to understand and accept our differences.

When I left at six, my rescuers stopped work for a moment to bid me farewell. With a mixture of relief and sadness, I left them with their animals and set off down the mountain.

Following a stream, the track meandered down a broad grassy valley surrounded by snow-capped peaks. There was a sense of space and light that was missing on the Chitral side of the Pass. After the trials of the night, I walked with joy, knowing that every step was taking me further away from the cave.

After two hours walking towards the village of Teru, I met a small group of civil servants travelling on foot from Gilgit to Chitral. They were on an important mission.

"We are going to Chitral to start organising this year's polo match on Shandur Pass."

When they heard that I was going to Gilgit, they had some news for me.

"You will catch the visit of Pakistan's Prime Minister and that will mean good polo. There will be celebrations, music and games. You should try to see it if you can."

We went our different ways after a few minutes rest, conscious that we all had a long walk ahead of us.

The first sign of any human habitation came into view four hours later. At first, there were only orderly fields of winter barley enclosed by dry-stone walls. Eventually, I started to meet people, who all stopped to greet me and shake my hand. There was also a real sense of prosperity and happiness here. Even the women working in the fields stopped briefly to watch me pass and some waved. Their coloured dresses and distinctive red fez-like hats were very different from anything I saw in the Chitral valley. As men walking up the track passed me, we exchanged *salaams* and saluted each other with our right hand on our hearts.

Six hours after leaving the cave, I finally arrived in Teru feeling hungry, tired and thirsty. The sight of the rest house filled me with joy. Visions of cups of hot, sweet tea, hot food and a comfortable *charpoi* danced before my eyes. Almost more tantalising was the prospect of a good sleep.

With a tremendous effort, I threw my bag to the ground and shook its weight out of my bones. A young, smartly-dressed man came out of the guest-house to welcome me and invited me to sit on one of the garden chairs to rest while he finished vaccinating children from the village.

When his work was finished, he was happy to stay and chat with me for a few minutes. His English was excellent and he was very well spoken. However, when I asked how much the rest house was for one night, he looked through me and pretended not to have heard me. When I repeated the question in Urdu, he ignored me again and tried to change the subject. I pressed him once more, he told me that the price was twenty-five rupees. When I asked him if he had a room, he again ignored me.

Deep within me, a surge of anger and suspicion welled up and I felt sure that he was trying to cheat me somehow. The voice of sanity in my head was being swallowed by a wave of fury boiling up from deep within me, fuelled by tiredness and acute hunger. I was not thinking rationally and could not see that he was trying to help.

Instead of answering me directly, he tried to steer the conversation in a different direction.

"If you are going to Gilgit, you should go to Phandur. A jeep will be going to Gilgit tomorrow morning."

"The driver lives in Phandur and is coming now. He will take you to Phandur and you could stay in the guest house there tonight if you like or we could walk there tomorrow together."

My rage subsided and I knew that this was too good an opportunity to miss. Sure enough, a jeep soon appeared and my host flagged down the driver. They spoke for a minute or two and then the jeep drove off without giving me a chance to say anything. My host returned with an explanation.

"The driver told me that he is not going to Gilgit, so you will stay here tonight. Later, we will walk to Phandur and there you will find a jeep to Gilgit."

This news made no sense to me as he had told me that the jeep driver lived in Phandur. He could have given me a lift there at least. Was this little more than an attempt to get a twenty-five-rupee fee out of me here in Teru, at the expense of a ride to Phandur?

"Why couldn't he take me to Phandur? It would have saved me a fifteen kilometre walk, even if he isn't going to Gilgit?"

"But the driver does not live in Phandur."

"Ten minutes ago, you told me that he lived in Phandur." The rage that had been brewing in me began to seep out in explosive bursts.

"I was mistaken."

"Alright then, would it be possible for me to get a cup of tea? I walked for six hours to get here and had almost no sleep last night."

"I am sorry; there is no tea here because it is now Ramadan."

"But I am not a Muslim. I had been travelling and have been sick."

These were all good reasons for me to break the Ramadan fast in some eyes, but he would not be swayed and out of desperation, I harangued him and accused him of not being a good Muslim. With a rush of energy and very unreasonable anger, I picked up my bag, stormed out of the rest house garden and headed down the jeep track towards Phandur.

After a while, my host and a friend appeared behind me and soon caught me up, despite my rather pitiful attempt to walk faster than them. As they passed me, he tried once more to talk to me. All I could do was growl. He laughed and walked on past me, joking with his friend.

Ten minutes later, I passed the jeep, which was being loaded with timber to be taken over Shandur Pass. Gradually, my anger subsided and I began to pull the pieces together. My "host" almost certainly had nothing to do with the Guest House and had been telling me the truth about the jeep.

Ahead of me, several more friends had joined the young man and they soon pulled away from me. After a while, the young man slipped away from the main group and vanished into a rocky outcrop. There was no sign of him when I passed the spot where I last saw him, but he soon reappeared and caught me up with me again. As he drew level with me, I made my peace and apologised for my appalling behaviour.

"No problem. You had travelled a long way and I could see that you were tired. Forget it, please. In the next village, you will find shops. You will be able to buy biscuits and take a rest. You will reach Phandur at four or maybe five o'clock tonight."

That meant another three or four hours on the road, but his good intentions had become very clear to me.

"What were you doing in Teru?"

"I am the Vaccination Officer. I work for the government and was doing my duty in Teru."

We parted on good terms as he set off down a narrow path to a village where young mothers waited anxiously for his arrival.

As promised, the next village soon appeared and I was besieged by a group of children, four girls and six boys. Their coloured clothes made a welcome change from the drab shades worn in the villages of the Chitral valley. One of the boys wore a green Chinese cap on his head. They gathered around me and practised their English. All at once, I was swamped by questions, leaving me no time to answer.

"How are you?"

"What is your name?"

"What is your country?"

"Bye, bye."

"Pen? Rupee?"

"Phototi-colour?"

Finally, a small boy with a shaven head and a cheeky grin took me by the hand and announced, "This is a table."

The children giggled and laughed, their words flowed like a babbling brook and made no sense to me whatsoever, but their English teacher would have given each of them high marks for effort.

Unfortunately, there was no sign of a shop in the village. Using my limited Urdu, I asked the oldest boy, who looked about twelve, if there was a shop where I could get some food and something to drink.

When he finally understood me, he led me though the village trailed by the other children and took me to his mother who greeted me with a warm smile. The look on her face filled me with joy and told me that she could see that I was exhausted and hungry. Somehow, I knew that she would feed me and give me something to drink.

The boy led me into a darkened room with a *charpoi* and a small table. When an old man appeared out of the darkness as if from nowhere and sat down beside me, I tried not to appear to be too surprised. He spoke neither Urdu nor English, but seemed happy to stay and watch me. The boy and I talked in a mix of English and Urdu and shared jokes about the children outside who were trying to peer into the gloom.

When food arrived, I ate with care, tasting and enjoying every mouthful. The woman produced fresh *puri* (fried dough), *chapatti* and salted milk-tea. As I ate, I told them of my night on the mountain and of my home in England. The boy grinned and told the old man who clasped my hand. When I tried to pay for my hospitality, the woman smiled and shook her head. As she left, her woven cap flashed in the shafts of light from the half open door. The boy accepted my gift of pens with a shy grin.

As I waved goodbye, I wondered what kind of reception their son would have faced if he had appeared in a village in England with a request for help.

The children followed me out of the village and waved as I left them behind. Beyond the village, the land was dry but fertile. Beside the road, the river flowed slowly, filling the air with gurgles of Spring happiness.

After an hour or so, the pain from a large, deep blister on my heel forced me to stop. The blister had become infected and was swollen with pus. There was nothing for me to do except try to use my knife to release the pressure. The skin on my heel was tough, forcing me to dig hard to make a hole deep enough to release the bubble of pus-laden fluid that had built up, but it was worth the trouble.

With no more discomfort in my feet, I tried to make up some of the lost time and pushed on. The track took me though leafy glades of willow trees growing on the riverbank. Deep in the still waters, brown trout flitted in and out of the shadows. The trout had been introduced to the river by the British at the turn of the century to give anglers far from home the chance to do a little fly-fishing.

The hours passed and there was still no sign of either Phandur or the rest house. The track stretched out before me into the fading light and a feeling of hopelessness started to gnaw at my self-confidence.

As nightfall approached, Phandur finally appeared. The bad news was that the government rest house was closed for the winter. A kindly man told me that there was another option. This turned out to be a rest house that was little more than a shack on a ridge three miles beyond Phandur, which added yet another hour to what had been a very long day.

The rest house *chowchidar* (night watchman) grumbled as he let me in and then spent his time trying, but failing to extract additional rupees from me for services he was not able or willing to offer. There was no bed, just a pile of musty quilts on a concrete floor.

Dinner was an unpleasant tasting mess of boiled mustard leaves, rotten potatoes and stale *chapatti*. I ate and ended up wishing that I had not been so hungry. Despite his brusque manner, he did know when the next jeep to Gilgit would pass by and even passed a message to the driver asking him to stop and pick me up.

When I turned in, I discovered that after thirteen hours of hard walking on rocky tracks, my joints ached so badly that I could not sleep for most of the night. When my alarm woke me at five in the morning, it was a welcome relief from the discomfort and pain.

To my surprise, the Gilgit jeep arrived on time and stopped to pick me up just after dawn. Better still; the driver was sure that he had enough fuel to go the whole way. At first, the driver let me share the cabin, but as we picked up more passengers, I was relegated to the metal bench over the wheel arch in the back of the jeep. As the jeep was nearly empty, we bounced over the rocks like a cork in a storm. The bruising effect of the pounding of metal on flesh soon prompted me to sit on my bag in the middle of the cargo bay.

As we moved through villages and passed isolated farms, the driver stopped to pick up more and more people, all men or boys. Most people were only looking to be taken from one village to the next. The more people we had on board, the better the ride as the jeep tended to bounce less over the rocky track.

The track climbed up over steep fields of scree and in places was several thousand feet above the river. If we came off the road, we would not have had much of a chance as the rusted remains of shattered jeeps below testified. The driver hurtled on, seemingly oblivious to the danger.

After a couple of hours of living on the edge, we descended into a village and promptly crashed headlong into a dry-stone wall. Berated by a horde of angry, bruised passengers, the driver showed us that the steering wheel was no longer connected to the steering gear and span freely.

"Shit," I thought and wondered when the next jeep would be passing through.

The driver was not so easily dismayed and dived under the jeep with a spanner. After a few minutes, he reappeared with the news that the ball and socket joint connecting the shaft of the steering wheel to the steering rack had come apart. The "ball" part of the joint had become elongated and had been pulled out of place. As far as I could tell, it was not repairable and the nearest spare parts shop was in Chitral.

Despite the gloomy looks on the faces of the passengers, the driver was sure that he could fix the damage. We watched in astonishment as he used a hammer, a large rock and a rusty metal file to coax the metal back into shape. The problem was that when he had finished, the ball was too small and no matter how tight he made the joint, it refused to stay in the socket.

Once again, he remained calm and after a few moments thought, he came up with a solution. He tied a sheet of greased inner tube around the ball with wire and this time it seemed to hold tight in the socket. He took the jeep for a test drive around the village, watched carefully by the waiting passengers.

When we eventually left, we all prayed that the repair would hold. The sight of a Mullah climbing aboard gave everyone hope that God would look out for us. With some trepidation, we headed out of the village and climbed back up the steep valley sides to where the track had been cut into a relatively stable part of the scree fields, several thousand feet above the valley floor.

The repair to the steering seemed to hold and we continued towards Gilgit with a growing sense of confidence. Under a clear sky, we made good progress, until there was a large bang that coincided with the rear end of the jeep bucking three feet into the air as we came to an abrupt halt. The Mullah and I were thrown into the air and landed on each other in a tangle of arms and legs. He roared with laughter and clapped me on the back.

The driver turned off the engine and the extent of the damage soon became clear. A bolt joining the leaf spring to the jeep had sheared, pulling the drive shaft out of its socket. With a collapsed axle, the jeep was in a sorry state and we were several hours from the nearest village in any direction.

The driver was not easily dismayed and was confident that everything would be all right. He pulled out a cloth bag filled with rusting screws and bolts and found a bolt that looked as if it might fit. The problem was that he did not have a nut that would fit the bolt. The Mullah and I were deputised to walk back along the track to search for the broken bolt, which might have had a nut that would be a match for the spare bolt.

The others went on a search for something that could be used to lever the leaf spring back into place. Unbelievably, the Mullah and I not only found the half of the sheared bolt with the nut, but the nut also fitted the replacement bolt.

Working as a team, we used brute force to lift the jeep up and with the help of a sapling, lever the leaf spring back into place. The driver eased in the bolt and tightened up the nut. The repair had taken just over half an hour and was a tribute to the driver's perseverance and technical expertise.

Luckily for me, travellers are exempt from fasting during the month of Ramadan and as a reward for our good fortune, the driver stopped for lunch in a roadside eating-house. We ate cold *dhal* with congealed *ghee*, sitting on a floor littered with rotting onion skins and vegetable peelings.

On the road again, the monotony of the journey took over and my perception of time started to become distorted. Isolated villages started flashing by as splashes of colour in an otherwise desolate landscape. My mind was numbed by the pounding of the jeep on the track and by the emptiness of the mountains of grey rock. The strain of holding on to the sides of the jeep as we bounced along the track filled my fingers, arms and shoulders with pain. There was no alternative.

Eventually, I was the only passenger in the cargo bay. The driver and his friends in the cab talked and laughed as the sun set. The world closed in on me and I drifted into a state of torpor.

Thirteen hours after leaving Phandur, Gilgit appeared out of the darkness. With great difficulty, I clambered out of the jeep and paid the driver. Our eyes met in the glare of the headlights and I could see the strain of the journey etched all over his face. Money passed between us without a word and he drove off into the darkness, leaving me alone by the side of the road. It was only when I tried to walk that I discovered that my backside was so badly bruised from the pounding metal seat that I could barely move.

My head was throbbing with exhaustion and the walk from the jeep depot into the centre of Gilgit to find somewhere to stay was less than pleasant. A light drew me to a hotel in Rajah Bazar, one of the main streets. With a feeling of relief, I was soon being escorted to my room, only to discover that I had to share with a young man. He smiled and greeted me as I dumped my bag on the floor.

"G'day! My name is Gus."

His Australian accent was unmistakable.

"I got here two days ago from Chitral, over Shandur Pass. Where have you come from?"

This was a wonderful coincidence and one that gave me great pleasure. There are few things better in life than sharing travel tales, particularly when the travelling had involved some level of hardship. Gus told me that he had managed to ride in jeeps for most of the journey. In Mastuj, he had also been asked to help the sergeant with his English homework.

We talked for a while, but eventually, sleep came all too easily. The soft mattress and cotton duvet embraced my aching bones and I slept like a baby.

Chapter 10

Gilgit during Ramadan was not quite as I had expected. During the day, all the restaurants were closed and the hotels would not serve either food or drinks. Rajah Bazaar, on the other hand, was filled with stalls selling delicious snacks. In a darkened shack off Rajah Bazaar, I discovered a makeshift café in a tent that served both food and drinks.

If I looked carefully, I noticed men with guilty looks on their faces sneaking off to eat freshly fried *pakoras* in the narrow alleys leading off the main street. For some, Ramadan was not a time of fasting; it was a time of snacking.

As the hotel was not to my liking, I moved to the Tourist Cottage just outside the main town centre for a period of rest and recuperation. Due to the combined effects of exertion and dysentery, my weight had plummeted by over forty pounds in just two months. I did not need a doctor to tell me that I had to build up my strength for the next leg of my journey.

Gilgit was a good place for both rest and food, despite the obligatory fasting that came with the observance of Ramadan. The Chinese noodle soup with fresh coriander leaves served in the Tourist Cottage was unforgettable. As each day passed, I put on more weight and gradually returned to a state of good health.

Four days passed before I felt ready to move any further than the grounds of the Tourist Cottage. Most of the other guests were Westerners, but for the most part, I kept myself to myself. Javeed, the young manager of the Tourist Cottage and his friends on the other hand, were good company and happy to sit and chat. Javeed explained why the Tourist Cottage did not encourage Pakistani guests.

"They pester the other guests and make a nuisance of themselves. They are nothing but trouble."

When asked how he felt about discriminating against his countrymen, he grinned.

"We are border people here, not really Pakistani. Some Chinese, some Indian and some Pakistani. But in general, we do not like Pakistanis."

Having not phoned home for several weeks, I visited the Post Office only to discover that no one could make long distance calls from Gilgit. The Post Office clerk told me that the line had been damaged in a storm that had also washed away fifteen kilometres of the only road between Gilgit and Rawalpindi.

The other people waiting to make a phone call told me that all outside lines had been reserved for the planners of the coming visit of Pakistan's Prime Minister. To all intents and purposes, Gilgit was cut off from the rest of the world.

The visit of the Prime Minister was heralded by feverish activity all over Gilgit. Rocks by the side of the road were white washed, post boxes repainted, holes in the road repaired and flags strung up along the streets. The smell of fresh paint rose with the heat of the afternoon sun.

At the airport, the Prime Minister's face was calm and impassive. Staring ahead, he was oblivious to the noise and excitement around him. Followed by the sound of wailing pipes and a clatter of drums, his cavalcade forged through Gilgit's narrow streets and came to a halt outside the polo ground.

Despite the best efforts of his security forces, I was invited to the Press Enclosure and watched the polo match from a VIP seat just a few yards away from the Prime Minister. Young men on perfectly turned-out ponies chased a white ball from one end of the field to the other. The crowd cheered as if they knew who was winning and the stadium echoed to the thunder of hooves, wailing pipes and the rhythmic beat of drums. In the old days, they would have played with a prisoner's head and the crowd would have been just as excited.

Between chukkas, soldiers wearing purple tartan uniforms paraded up and down the field in formation beating drums and playing bagpipes. As the ceremonies concluded, the Prime Minster was given a Gilgiti hat and coat to remind him of his visit. In return, he delivered a rousing speech. To tremendous applause, he promised that the Government of Pakistan would provide funding to renovate the polo stadium and to build a polytechnic for the young men in the region. My neighbour, a local journalist was not easily impressed.

"If the Government really wanted to help here, they would provide funding when it was needed, not just when a Prime Minster visits. Anyhow, Prime Ministers always make these promises when they come here and the result is always the same. No funding."

Staying in the Tourist Cottage was like staying in someone's home as a member of the family. The other guests included a recently-widowed English nurse in her fifties travelling in Asia for the first time; a young Japanese women recovering from malaria; and an assortment of young backpackers who made me feel middle-aged.

The lure of distant mountains and new horizons to explore brought my time in Gilgit to an end. Two weeks of eating, resting and relaxing had added three inches to my waist and I was healthier than I had been for weeks. China was there on the other side of the Karakoram Mountains and the Karakoram Highway was now open. I checked the Post Restante for letters one last time and found there was still nothing for me. I knew that it was time to get back on the road.

The Zephyr's letter had also been travelling and as I prepared to leave Gilgit, was making its way up through the towns that lay along the Karakoram Highway: Haripur, Abbottabad, Mansehra, Besham, Dasu and Chilas along the road that had been damaged by floods.

As the depot was only a short distance from the Tourist Cottage, Javeed walked with me and made sure that I got on the right bus. As I prepared to climb aboard, he said goodbye and shook my hand.

"Take care and be safe. May God be with you."

He turned and left with a wave. As I left Gilgit, the Zephyr's letter was delivered to the Gilgit Post Office Sorting Room. Later that day, a clerk placed the letter in the Poste Restante, where it rested after its long journey in the company of hundreds of other uncollected letters.

Despite being nearly empty, the minibus to Karimabad left more or less on time. The only other passenger was a young man who greeted me with a toothy smile. His name was Abdul.

"I am a Palestinian student who lives in Syria, studies in Pakistan and dreams of making his home in the piece of land now known as Israel".

Abdul was studying to be a civil engineer and was a devout Muslim with his own perspective on Islam.

"You are a Christian?"

"I suppose so."

I answered cautiously, half expecting another lecture about the dangers of drink.

"I am Muslim. You are Christian, but there is no problem. We can be friends anyway."

As the minibus headed up into the mountains, he was keen to explain why he did not mind my company.

"The problem with Islam is that there are many Muslims who are not truly followers of Islam. They fight each other and fight peoples of other religions, for what? There is really no point in this fighting."

As the bus pulled away from Gilgit, the scenery became increasingly rugged. The metalled road gave way to a rough track climbing up into the fields of scree. In several places, the bus had to slow down over sections of road damaged by recent landslides. Progress was only possible because of the heavy earth-moving equipment that had been brought in by the construction workers to clear away the tons of mud and rock blocking the road. Some of the repairs to the road were clearly only temporary, but were good enough to let us pass.

The landslides served as a reminder that the scree slopes were in a state of constant flux. It was nothing short of a miracle that there was a road surface at all. Abdul braced himself as the bus lurched over yet another pile of debris and answered his own question.

"I will tell you, these people fight because of politics and because of power. I tell you that for them Islam means nothing."

Abdul was not married and planned to marry when he was older. Half-jokingly, I asked him if he planned to take more than one wife.

"I will only take one wife. Having more than one wife is very expensive and very difficult. The Qur'an is very clear about a husband's duties to his wives, what he gives one wife, he must give the other. If I buy one wife a new dress, I have to buy the other a new dress. If I sleep with one wife, I have to sleep with the other. The first wife usually fights with the second wife and there would be too many problems. Also, I would get two mothers-in-law…"

As the bus made its way through the narrow gorges of the lower Hunza valley, we fell silent, absorbed by the intensity of the scenery, until the driver was forced to pull off the road to change a flat tyre. As he worked, Abdul and I sat on a rock beside the Karakoram Highway, basking in the warmth of the sun. In the shade, there was a distinct chill in the air, a reminder that we were already a mile above sea level. In the distance, ice-capped mountains rose up into a blue sky.

Abdul was more worried about his own future.

"Anyway, I cannot get married until I can support my wife and can afford to buy a house. This will be a long time from now. I have to finish my studies and get a job to earn enough money so we can live comfortably."

With these words, Abdul lapsed into a subdued silence. Overhead, a bird of prey soared on a rising column of air. The driver eventually replaced the deflated tyre, put away his tools and called us back to the bus. He was keen to get moving and waited impatiently as we clambered back into our respective seats.

As the bus ground its way up the gorge, Abdul grinned and revealed a well-kept secret.

"By the way, I do have a girl in mind, but I have not yet mentioned her name to my mother."

Like many Palestinians, Abdul did not have a passport. Instead, he travelled on papers issued by the Syrian government. I could not imagine what it must be like to have no place to call home.

"The Syrians will not give me a passport, but will conscript me into the army and probably send me to Beirut to fight against Palestinians."

The narrow gorge eventually opened out into a broad valley encircled by mountains. Rising out of the valley floor was Karimabad, a town of mud-walled houses dominated by a 700-year-old fortress, set in a tapestry of green terraced fields.

Here, the Hunza valley is a fertile plain enclosed by towering slopes of grey scree that rise 3000-feet above the valley floor in a sombre contrast to the emerald fields below. Above the lifeless fields of scree was another world dominated by walls of bare rock, snow-capped peaks and the majesty of the Ultar Glacier.

The driver headed into the centre of Karimabad and stopped in the shade of a willow tree grove. Here, the air was warm and perfumed with the scent of wild flowers and aromatic herbs.

The guest house that Javeed had recommended was built into the valley side high above the road and was reached by a narrow path that meandered upwards between terraced gardens. Irrigation channels running either side of the path carried water rich in micaceous sediments that glistened in the dappled sunlight.

Having signed the guesthouse register, I sat back in an armchair on the veranda and sipped a cup of sweet milk-tea. Looking out over the fertile fields of Karimabad valley, I reflected on the generations of farmers who had toiled to turn the valley floor and the lower margins of the shifting slopes of scree into productive land. These ancient terraces still produced crops of cereals, apricots, walnuts, mulberries, apples and golden honey. When the farmers were not working in the fields, they were at work in their gardens growing roses, fruit trees and even vines.

Willows and poplars brought here by the Moghuls enclosed fields of ripening barley and winter wheat. The terraced fields were held in place by carefully constructed retaining walls built using rounded rocks carried from the mountains by the Hunza River.

Javeed had told me that if I looked closely at the stones in the irrigation channels, there was a good chance that I would find garnets and even rubies. It did not take me long to find garnets, but they were low grade and crumbled between my fingers. Apparently, there was even a ruby mine near Karimabad. The water in the streams not only hid the odd ruby, but also according to some, contained the secret to long life.

The Hunza valley leads to the Khunjerab Pass, one of a small number of crossing points over the mountains separating China from the Indian sub-continent. The Baltit Fort's commanding position over the valley had given the Mirs of Hunza effective control over trade moving up and down the Hunza valley, as well as a constant source of revenue. When the importance of the Silk Road declined, the Hunza valley sank into obscurity.

Until 1974, when work on the Karakoram Highway started, the Hunza valley was a self-governed federal kingdom ruled by the Mirs. The Karakoram Highway brought the modern world into the Hunza, transforming a way of life that had remained unchanged over the centuries.

Central government funding would appear and better roads would be constructed. A reliable electricity supply would arrive and hotels would be built. The men and women who worked in the fields would turn their hands to making beds and waiting at tables.

Little by little, the men and women who tended the fields would be altered by the people that they welcomed into their lives. Whether they had the strength to cope with this change remained to be seen.

As the sun faded, darkness engulfed the valley and I turned in to sleep. The sound of running water lulled me into a deep, dreamless sleep.

In the morning, I explored the fortress overlooking the valley. Despite the rain and earthquake damage to its mud-walls, the Baltic Fort had a presence that helped me see beyond the dilapidation to the history that it represented.

The fortress was over 700 years old and had been built to protect the ancient capital of the Hunza kingdom. In 1891, the British took residence in the fortress after a successful military campaign. Shortly afterwards, they installed one of the members of the ruling Mir's family in the fort.

A short distance from the fortress was a track that led up to the Ultar Glacier. With resolution in every stride, I set out with every intention of getting there, but after an hour spent walking up a narrow gorge filled with waterfalls, I met a Frenchman coming down from the Glacier and stopped to talk for a while. Sitting on a rock by a waterfall, with the sounds of running water and wild birds singing, time passed without me noticing and eventually, the idea of walking on to the Glacier seemed like something for another day, so I joined the Frenchman for lunch in Karimabad instead.

In the morning, I decided to move on as I was running out of time on my Pakistan visa and China was so close. Waiting for the bus to Sust, I ended up talking to Jamail Abdullah, who was waiting for a ride to Gilgit. The minibus was there, but he could not get anyone to tell him when it would leave. When the driver finally appeared, Jamail caught his eye and beckoned him over to us.

"Salaam, tell me will the bus leave soon?"

Jamail was a very patient man and managed to keep any trace of irony out of his voice.

"When I have passengers, I will leave."

"How long will it take to fill the bus?"

"I do not know."

The bus driver was happy to wait for as long as it took. Time was not important to him. He would rather have a full load than leave "on time".

It was not yet nine o'clock in the morning and already the sun was hot. Sitting in the perfumed air under an apricot tree in the garden of a teashop, we asked for some green tea, having had our fill of milk-tea. The teashop owner shook his head and vanished back into the gloom of his kitchen. A moment later, he reappeared with a battered tin.

"I had no green tea. I have this tea if you like?"

The tin was filled with a sweet smelling brown powder. Gingerly, I tasted it and discovered that it was drinking chocolate, which was an unexpected delight.

With a mug of chocolate in my hand, I felt confident enough to ask when the bus to Sust would leave.

"In a few minutes."

This probably meant that the bus could leave before nightfall. Sure enough, a minibus turned up eventually, just a few hours later.

The section of the Karakoram Highway between Karimabad and Sust was in reasonably good condition and in places, wide enough to allow two trucks to pass each other. Either side of the road were villages, homes to a mountain people who had settled in the valley centuries before. Until the 1960's, the only access to these valleys was along precipitous goat tracks. Looking at the metalled surface of the highway, I could only imagine how much their lives must have changed in just a few years.

Eventually, the minibus stopped in Sust, a dismal collection of half-built hotels, UNHCR tents and mud huts, looking more like a refugee camp than a border town. On some of the UNHCR tents, an attempt had been made to paint out the word "Afghan". Elsewhere, there was every sign that Sust was not ready for business. The Northern Areas Transportation Corporation (NATCO) ticket office was a tent hidden behind a half-finished building.

The pole that marked the symbolic border was a crudely painted branch perched on cairns built on either side of the road. The actual border was much higher in the mountains and would take several hours of hard driving to reach. The hinge was made of twisted wire and the counterweights were rocks held in place with string. Standing beside the checkpoint was a green board with white-painted letters that welcomed visitors with the words:

"GOVERNMENT OF PAKISTAN"

"IMMIGRATION/ANTISMUGGLING"

"CHECK POST SUST"

The manager of the NATCO ticket office was not a happy man, as there were only seven people waiting to cross into China. The daily service to Pirali was thus "on hold". There was nothing to do but wait in the hope that more people would eventually turn up.

The most interesting hotel was little more than a couple of Western-style frame tents with a hand-painted sign telling the world that this was the Tabaq Hotel. The owner came out to meet me.

"Hello there! I am Sher Khan."

He had a kind face and a welcoming smile.

"This is the best hotel in town. You must stay here if you are going to China. The bus will most likely not leave until tomorrow. I can cook you the best food."

Compared with a modern five-star hotel, the Tabaq Hotel had little to offer. The only room was in a frame tent furnished with a couple of camp beds and a dirt floor. On the other hand, the view of the Karakoram Range from that room was something that no big city hotel could ever match. When I agreed to stay, not that I needed much convincing, Sher Khan invited me into the second tent that also served as main reception, concierge, kitchen and dining room.

From the depths of his kitchen, he produced a plate of perfect curried chicken with fluffy rice and we talked as I ate. At first, his main aim was to tempt me with food that he thought would appeal to my European tastes.

"I am a certified expedition cook and will cook whatever you want. What can I cook you tomorrow? I can cook you the best fried egg and chips in the whole of Pakistan."

His smile lit up the tent and made me feel very much at home.

"That does not sound like typical Pakistani food? Where did you learn to cook this kind of food?"

Sher Khan smiled and rubbed his hands together.

"I cooked for a British expedition in 1980."

The frame tents really stood out. All the other tents in Sust were simpler in design and had at one time been supplied for refugees by aid agencies.

"When the climbers left, they gave me these tents, which was how I started in the hotel business. They were very good people and even invited me to England to see their families."

"Did you go?"

"Oh yes, I went to England not long ago now."

As he continued, there were aspects of his story that seemed very familiar and I had a curious sense that I knew what he was about to tell me.

"Which part of England did you visit?"

"The Lake District, in your Cumbrian mountains."

"Where did you stay?"

"In Kendal, with the family of one of the climbers, a very good man called Phil."

As his words tumbled out, I had a strange feeling that I knew Phil and his family, but this would have been too much of a coincidence. I decided to test whether my intuition had been leading me down a cul de sac.

"Do the names Beth and Lucy mean anything to you?"

Sher Khan looked at me in astonishment. "Yes. Oh, yes! You know them?"

This was an incredible coincidence and I was dumbfounded. The expedition on which he had been the cook had been organised by a friend of an old friend of mine, who lived in England. With great excitement, Sher Khan opened up his metal trunk and produced a letter of introduction signed by Jess Stock, the expedition leader.

"If you see them again, tell them I have married a woman from Gulmit who lives in Texas. If all goes well, I will be joining her next year as an immigrant."

During the night, the sickness returned and I spent the following day shivering and shaking in the pale green light of the frame tent. Late in the afternoon, as I lay in a state of near delirium, the sound of BBC World Service news filtered into my mind. Apparently, Margaret Thatcher had been re-elected, but I could just have been dreaming.

Sher Khan coughed politely and peered through the tent flap to see if I needed any help. When he realised that I was sick, he told me not to worry. He soon reappeared with a mug of steaming milk-tea.

The fever subsided as evening approached, leaving me with a nasty headache and a general sense of weakness. Feeling refreshed by another cup of Sher Khan's tea, I took a short walk up into the mountains in search of a hot spring that was supposed to be in a stream close to the road.

The spring was hard to find and only slightly warm. The pounding beat of my headache dragged me away and back to the relative comfort of the Tabaq Hotel., Sher Khan greeted me with a refreshing cup of milk-tea, leaving me to rest and recuperate.

Overhead, an eagle watched crows circling in front of the glacial cliffs in which they nested. The chicks in the nests kept down to avoid the eagles' piercing eyes. The rest of the day passed slowly and I tried to get back to health by resting as much as I could. The road into China was reputed to be hard going and I thought that I would need all the strength I could muster.

Sher Khan had promised to send me off with a good meal and was true to his word. Somehow, he managed to rustle up a plate of fried eggs with chips, nursery food that reminded me of home. He was happy to see a little colour back in my cheeks and to see me on my feet.

Part 3 - Into the Middle kingdom

中國

Chapter 1

Saturday morning dawned, bringing the news that the bus to China would be leaving. As if from nowhere, the passengers began to arrive and gathered around the NATCO ticket office. There were a few people like me, but most of the passengers were Pakistani traders. There was a scramble to buy tickets and clear both immigration and Customs. There were enough of us to fill two minibuses and we were all impatient to get on our way.

At first, the road was well metalled and oddly suburban. At around ten thousand feet, some thirty-six kilometres before the Khunjerab Pass, there was a change in mood and an increasing sense of anticipation as the landscape became wilder and increasingly barren. The mountains of the Karakoram Range crowded around the road, blocking out the sky with an almost sinister presence. There were signs of great landslides around every corner and of the construction work that had been needed to re-open the Highway after the ravages of winter.

As we climbed higher, my nagging headache turned into a nasty headache. At least some of the pain was being caused by mild altitude sickness. It was comforting to be able to look at myself with a sense of detachment and wonder about the sanity of continuing. Instead, insanity ruled and I let the minibus carry me onwards towards China.

Finally, the driver pulled over and announced that we had reached the highest point on the Karakoram Highway. At nearly fifteen thousand feet, this was one of the highest metalled passes in the world. A concrete sign by the side of the road recorded that the official opening of the Khunjerab Pass to traffic took place on 27 August 1982.

The Pakistanis rushed off the bus to celebrate our safe arrival with a snowball fight. The rest of us stood around watching. Young Pakistani men squatting in the snow to urinate for the last time in their own country reminded Fiona, one of the two English women on the bus, that life could be very difficult for a woman. There were no trees or bushes to give them any privacy. She confided to me that she had decided to wait and see if the facilities at Pirali were any better.

Everyone was keen to press on and the minibuses were soon trundling down the pass and towards the Chinese border post at Pirali. On the Chinese side of the pass, the road emerged from a landscape of claustrophobic gorges and gullies into a world of vast plains of dust flanked by distant ranges of ice-capped peaks. The sheer scale of the landscape dwarfed the minibuses and filled our spirits with a growing sense of anticipation. Over the next two days, our journey would take us deep into those empty plains along the trails made by the ancient traders and merchants who made their living on the Silk Road.

A figure appeared by the side of the road and waved us to a halt. He was a Chinese soldier with baleful eyes, dressed in a cheap-looking green uniform, with an AK47 cradled in his arms. From a distance, he looked forbidding, positively threatening. As we drew nearer, details of his uniform caught my eye. His face was hidden under a massive peaked cap of the style popular in totalitarian states. He also sported sunglasses; an ill-fitting green jacket with matching flared trousers; and pointed high-heeled shoes. Another soldier dragging a freshly-killed marmot joined him. The overall impression was surreal. They both climbed aboard the minibus and checked our passports. Judging from the fact that they held some documents upside down, I suspect that neither of them could read. The marmot stayed outside.

The minibuses took us as far as the frontier town of Pirali, where we were all processed through immigration and customs and transferred to a Chinese bus. The driver waited by his bus and watched as we gathered our possessions together. A burly man in his mid-forties, with jet-black hair, a malevolent scowl and a cigarette hanging between unshaven lips, he looked like a man who had seen it all.

There was the usual bedlam as we all tried to get on board at the same time. Some of the Pakistani traders had brought a great deal of luggage and were taking a long time to organise themselves.

Eventually, the bus driver could stand no more and dived into the throng, cursing and swearing in Mandarin. He knew how far we would have to travel and was keen to avoid having to travel after nightfall. He quickly organised the latecomers and finally everything was packed on board and tied down to his satisfaction.

Without ceremony, we set out along a road that headed north towards the distant Tianshan Mountains. There was nothing between us and the oasis town of Taxgorgan, except several hundred miles of sand, rock and scrub. For the most part, the only living creatures to witness our passing would be snakes, wild horses, camels and marmots.

The Pamirs and the Hindu Kush were now to the west and to the east were the Kunlun Mountains. Sandwiched between the peaks were immense glaciers that swept down to the desert. Beyond the Kunlun Mountains lay the vast Takla Makan desert. Behind us were the Karakoram Mountains and Pakistan. Stretching ahead was a half-finished road and a vast empty plain.

The bus was built for this kind of travel and was a true off-roader capable of carrying thirty people at a time. At least a third of the seats had been taken out to make room for lockers filled with tools and spare parts. There was even a spare drive shaft strapped to the floor of the bus. It was clear that the driver was prepared for the worst.

At first, the condition of the road was not too bad, but the metalled surface soon petered out, leaving the driver with no choice but to pick his way across the desert. From time to time, our route took us close to work camps housing engineers and construction workers. They were working both on the road that had not yet been finished and on repairing sections of the road that had been built but had been washed away by the spring snowmelt floods.

From time to time, our driver turned the bus into one of the many shallow rivers that criss-crossed the desert. As the tyres bounced over the rocky river bed, the bus pitched and tossed like flat-bottomed ferryboat in a gale. The view out of the window made me wonder if this was the modern ship of the desert.

In a few weeks, most of the melt water streams would have dried up, leaving behind nothing but a network of empty channels. In one particularly deep section, the water rose ominously around the wheels and up into the engine compartment. With a sad cough, the engine stopped, leaving the bus stranded mid-stream. The driver cursed, pulled open the access plate behind his chair and removed a part from the engine. With a cigarette in one hand, he dried the part on a rag and put it back. After a few attempts, the engine eventually restarted and the driver steered the bus back on to dry land. He was indomitable, confident in his ability to overcome any of the challenges that the desert could place before him.

For the most part, we made steady progress. The desert was rocky and I had to hold on tight to stay on my seat. It was a white-knuckle ride that went on and on … and on. When my grip on the handrail slipped for an instant as the bus crashed into a gully, my head met the ceiling with a sickening thud and I was knocked unconscious for a moment. As the bus started to clamber back out of the gully an instant later, I crashed back onto my seat as it rose to meet me. The headache that had started at 10,000 feet was now almost unbearable. Ahead of us lay another six hours of torment.

The savagery of the landscape was all that kept me sane. Every now and again, the sight of a village of mud huts in the middle of nowhere or a solitary domed nomad's tent made me realise that this barren landscape was capable of supporting human life. Wild life abounded: marmots sitting by the road that watched us pass before ducking down into their burrows; small groups of Bactrian camels; and vast herds of wild horses.

The sight of the occasional group of horsemen wearing long quilted coats and long boots was a reminder of the days when the old Silk Road was in its prime and started a train of thought that helped me forget the pain in my brain.

The Silk Road was in fact a network of trails that swept over the mountain ranges linking the East with Central Asia and Europe. The development of these trade routes across Central Asia supported the trade of precious metals, ivory, precious stones and glass into China. From China came furs, ceramics, jade, bronze objects, lacquered goods and silk. The trade routes also served as a network along which flowed new technologies and ideas. In some ways, the Silk Road was the Information Highway of its day.

The inventions that came out of China must have astounded the rest of the world: papermaking, printing, gunpowder, matches, astronomical observatories, decimal mathematics, paper money, umbrellas, wheelbarrows, flamethrowers, multi-stage rockets, spirits and the game of chess.

The merchants who ventured across the great western wastelands in search of new technologies and manufactured goods carried with them ideologies and religious beliefs. Buddhism travelled to China from India, arriving in the fourth and fifth centuries AD during the Ting dynasty. Christianity appeared in Changan at the start of the

Silk Road, in the seventh century carried by Nestorians from northern Persia, who had been outlawed in Europe by the Roman church in the fifth century. Islam was first brought to western China in the middle of the seventh century under the Tang Dynasty.

In the 13th century, the Mongols united under the leadership of Genghis Khan conquered a large swathe of Central Asia creating a vast Empire that cut deeply into the Islamic Empire. Major cities on the Silk Road were sacked as the Mongols advanced westwards into Persia and towards the Mediterranean. During periods of political stability, conditions for trade improved along the length of the Silk Road. Under the protection of the Mongols, the merchants on the Silk Road prospered.

When the Mongol Empire began to collapse in the fourteenth century, the expansion of the influence of Islam into the towns and cities around the Takla Makan began in earnest. After nearly a thousand years, Buddhism retreated as Islam encroached ever deeper into China.

Even as Islam was carried into China, European merchant seamen were perfecting the navigation skills that one day would put the Silk Road traders and their intermediaries out of business.

A sudden jolt brought me out of my reverie and back to the noisy, dusty, stomach-churning nightmare, that was reality on the bus. Just sitting on my seat was an effort. As the hours passed, my eyes, nostrils and mouth became encrusted with a layer of fine sand. The taste of the desert coated my tongue and its dryness sucked the moisture from my nostrils.

From time to time, the bus rose into the air and crashed back down to earth with a sickening shudder that filled the air with a thin film of fine dust. Aching muscles and weary joints now compounded the pain in my head. An aspirin washed down with a mouthful of sweet

Chinese wine offered by one of the Pakistani traders helped, but there was still a long way to go.

The day began to fade and my head felt as though it was about to split. The only good news was that the road was better and it seemed that our destination, Taxgorgan was not far away. Just as the sun began to sink behind the mountains to the west, lights appeared in the distance and Taxgorgan came into sight. From a distance, I could see nothing but the walls of a large compound surrounded by desert.

Almost without warning, the bus turned off the road into the walled compound that looked suspiciously like a prison. Somewhere beyond the compound was the oasis town of Taxgorgan. Behind us, the outer door was ceremoniously closed and locked. One of the Pakistanis told me that this was the only hotel in Taxgorgan. Were the Chinese keeping the people of Taxgorgan safe from foreign influences or was it that it was the foreigners who were in need of protection?

Alternatively, was it just that the oasis town of Taxgorgan did not have much nightlife? After a gruelling day on the road, I was past caring. All I could think about was finding somewhere to lay my aching head and to get to sleep. At first there seemed to be no easy way of getting a bed. The hotel manager was not interested in letting out any of his rooms.

In the end, I teamed up with the two English women. With patience and the help of a Japanese student travelling on the bus who spoke some Manadarin, we managed to argue our way into one of the three dormitories.

Fiona convinced me that I should eat something. A quick tour of the compound revealed that the only food on offer was boiled mutton and vegetable noodles. We ate in near silence and stumbled off to our beds knowing that we had an early start in the morning.

On the beds were thick quilts with clean cotton covers, which helped ward off the chill night air. The pillows felt and sounded as if they had been filled with chopped-up paper and rustled whenever I moved my head. The mattress was very hard and despite being exhausted, my need to escape into the world of sleep was for the most part unfulfilled.

It was still dark when I crawled out of bed and stumbled back onto the bus. The driver had been keen to make an early start, because he knew that the journey from Taxgorgan to Kashgar would take the best part of fifteen hours.

Fifteen hours is a long time to spend sitting in one seat, even when the time is spent in one of the greatest landscapes on the planet. The scenery passed in a magnificent, stunning, awe-inspiring blur that numbed the mind.

The road twisted through wild and rugged mountains. One straw-coloured mountain caught my eye because it was different from all the others. From a distance, it seemed to have a magic quality that stopped my eyes focusing on its surface. No matter how hard I tried, I could not see anything, but a featureless mass. It towered over the road and had an almost ethereal, fluid look. For a long time, my mind tried to grapple with the sight of a mountain that was not a mountain.

Only as we drew closer, did the mountain surrender its secret. It was a sand dune of immense proportions. There were no outcrops of rock or gullies on which my eyes could have settled, only curving contours, soft shadows and shifting sands.

Scattered along the route were more work camps for the construction gangs building the remaining sections of the Karakoram Highway. They could be seen at a distance building bridges, blasting rock, clearing landslides and rebuilding sections of damaged road. Against the backdrop of this never-ending landscape, they looked like ants.

Some of the camps were the size of small villages that reminded me of old photographs of the Klondike during the Gold Rush. The workmen I had seen seemed to be mostly Han Chinese. Very few had Uygur-looking faces. Were they conscripts? Or convicts? Perhaps they were volunteers, men who chose to live on the edge and were paid that little bit more as compensation for the rigour of their lives?

As the bus headed north, the state of the road deteriorated and eventually petered out into the desert. The driver stopped to light a cigarette and then headed out into the unspoilt desert, seemingly oblivious to the motion of the bus on the uneven surface. Every few hours, he pulled into a small settlement and allowed us a few moments to rest and find food. Mostly, the fare was plain, peasant food: fried meat and vegetables, served with steamed dough dumplings. We were encouraged to bolt our food and were soon on the move again.

As the hours passed, I tried to size up some of my fellow travellers. The Pakistani traders, who were friendly enough, but kept to themselves when we were on the move. Sitting together at the back of the bus were two silent Swiss couples; the two young English women; and the Japanese student. In front of me was a beautiful young African American woman, who sat next to her sour-faced, white American travelling companion.

During one of the rest breaks, the American man cornered me and fixed me with a smile that looked out of place on his face. At first, he tried to put me at my ease with pleasantries, which in fact had the opposite effect. Leaving behind the niceties, he got down to business and told me that he had decided that the time was right for me to be shown the way to Jesus.

I was not really in the mood to be converted, but the challenge of an argument to while away the hours was one that I could not resist, at least until I got bored. The conversation served to distract me from the pain in my head. He was very well prepared, but seemed to be oblivious of his failure to make any headway.

The more we talked, the more it was clear to me that he had been trained to a very high standard. Every time I questioned his hard-line views, I was countered by a rehearsed answer and a quotation from the New Testament. Every one of my questions was treated with barely disguised scorn. His overwhelming belief in his rightness was almost overpowering. Eventually, I resorted to irony, which he did not understand, but made me feel better.

He lived in a world without doubt. His world was one in which reason had been cast aside and replaced by blind acceptance of a belief system based on ancient fables.

He was but a foot soldier in an ideological battle that was being fought for the hearts of the poorly-educated people who lived in the mountains. He was a dangerous man, because he was ruthless and driven by the certainty that he was right. There were too many men like him sweeping through the North West Frontier seducing illiterate men with perverse versions of Islam and Christianity.

When I finally had had enough of his righteousness, I turned my attention to his stunningly beautiful travelling companion. The American turned away, perhaps frustrated by his lack of headway, or perhaps he had an idea that his companion might have had a better chance.

"Where are you from?"

"Idaho."

Of course.

"What were you doing in Pakistan?"

"Teaching and preaching. Evangelising in the Hindu Kush."

This was impressive enough. I suspect that Pakistan would not be my first choice if I were in an evangelist. She was keen to share her past with me and managed to make me smile, which was more than I could say for her companion.

"I used to be a stripper."

This was a surprise and she suddenly became even more interesting. I had never met an evangelising stripper before. Seeing my evident confusion, she explained.

"I was living in a trailer park and was watching television one day, when the Lord spoke to me. I just knew that I had to spread his word from that moment. I gave up stripping and became an Evangelist right then."

"How did he speak to you?"

"Through the television. Clear as a bell. I turned to Jesus on that very day."

Her broad smile, long vowels and glittering eyes seem to challenge me to mock her, but who was I to say that God would not use a television to talk to people?

She saw into me, smiled and turned back to her friend.

Fiona, who was in the seat behind me had been listening to my juvenile word games with the Evangelists and leaned forward to talk to me with a conspiratorial grin all over her face.

"You were very rude to those Americans, but I think that they deserved everything that they got. What right have they to come here and spread their weird ideas? Hasn't the world got enough problems without them stirring things up and creating more trouble?"

She told me that they had been travelling together for nine months and were near to the end of their trip. They were also the first English women I had had any contact with for nearly three months.

"After Kashgar, we will fly to Urumqi where we will connect with a flight to Beijing. We are going to stay with a friend of my parents and his wife. He is a senior diplomat at the British Embassy."

Having been on the road for so long, they were clearly looking forward to a spell of civilised living.

The journey continued and we sat absorbed in our separate thoughts, watching as the desert slipped past and the sun crept across the sky. The driver sat hunched over his steering wheel, his brows furrowed with concentration and a cigarette permanently in his hand.

Eventually, as evening approached, lines of poplar trees in the distance were the first indications that the end of the journey was near. Almost imperceptibly, the rocky desert gave way to green fields criss-crossed with irrigation channels.

Even the road surface improved and there was a respite from the bone-crunching, tooth-rattling, brain-addling torment of the open desert. A sense of relief descended on the bus as we all realised that Kashgar was not far away. The driver had to slow down because of the volume of traffic coming out of Kashgar. The road was packed with trucks, bicycles and men on horseback. Children on two-wheeled pony carts waved as we passed, safe in the arms of their mothers and fathers.

Just as we all began to relax, the engine spluttered and died, bringing the bus to a silent halt. The driver swore and threw us off the bus in a rage. After a few moments of confusion, the driver calmed down and was able to explain why we had stopped with only four kilometres to go. The bus had run out of fuel.

There was nothing to do but wait in the shade of a poplar tree and hope that the driver could somehow get hold of some fuel.

As we waited, a stream of trucks, bicycles and horse-drawn carts taking people back from the famous Kashgar Sunday market to their villages in the surrounding countryside passed before us.

Eventually, the driver managed to buy enough fuel from a passing Army truck to get us to the central bus station. As we unloaded our luggage from the bus, two-wheeled horse and donkey-carts appeared. Their drivers grabbed as many bags as they could and started loading them on to their carts.

They were all Uygur men with shaven heads, four-sided Gaba embroidered caps and well-worn woollen two or three-piece suits. Some of them had rolled their trousers up to the knee, revealing leggings down to their ankles.

After a few moments of chaos, all the passengers had a seat and every piece of luggage was loaded on the right cart. When those of us going to the Qinnabar hotel had all agreed the price of the fare, we were ready to leave.

Fiona and I shared a cart driven by a middle-aged Uygur man with a thin face, a naughty schoolboy's grin and an ancient threadbare two-piece suit. Belinda was perched on one of the other carts with the Japanese student.

The drivers were eager to depart and lined up across the road. It was clear that they planned a race to the Qinnabar Hotel. With a shout, the drivers set off at a canter, raising clouds of dust. Sitting next to the driver, Fiona soon noticed that he was using a thin, pointed stick to prod a sore in the donkey's back to make him go faster, with great effect.

Fiona began by making it clear to him that she did not want to see him using the stick to torment the animal and rebuked him in English.

"You are not going to do that when I am around."

He may not have understood her words, but the tone of her voice left him with no doubt about her meaning. The driver grinned and proceeded to prod the sore with renewed vigour. Eventually, Fiona could stand no more of his cruelty and confiscated his stick.

Meanwhile, the five heavily-laden carts continued their madcap chase through the backstreets of Kashgar to the Qinnabar Hotel. All was well, until Fiona spotted the driver surreptitiously digging a rusty nail into the donkey's anus when it looked as though he would be beaten. She grabbed his hand and prised the nail from between his fingers. He began to giggle like a schoolboy caught smoking behind the bicycle sheds and whipped the donkey with the reins. The race was over all too soon with each driver claiming victory in the hope of a tip. As soon as our bags were off loaded, the pony carts turned and ambled back towards the bus-station.

Little more than a collection of barrack-like buildings, the remains of the old British Consulate were not as impressive as I had hoped. A group of young Pakistani men came out to greet their newly-arrived friends and to look at the other newcomers. The sight of the women in our midst generated a great deal of barely-disguised attention. As Fiona's hackles rose menacingly, most of the wide-eyed young men stayed at a discrete distance.

The main problem was that the hotel booking clerks were overwhelmed by the new arrivals. Unable to get to the check in desk, Fiona and Belinda were surrounded by a handful of the more persistent Pakistani men trying to get them to share their dormitory. Fiona was not impressed with their efforts and told them to go away in no uncertain terms. They seemed more like oversexed adolescents than devout Muslims. When they finally realised that the three of us planned to share a room, a spokesman from within the group insisted that the check-in-clerk had told him that there were no more rooms for three people.

"You come with me and I will fix you all beds in my room."

Fiona smiled politely and muttered "fuck off" under her breath. After a struggle to get to the reception desk, I booked the three of us into a room for four people. An old lady showed us to the room, which was clean and perfectly acceptable. She then rented us a key. Our second priority was food. Not far from the hotel, we found pavement stalls selling lamb kebabs and bottles of local beer, my first since Egypt. Sleep came easily to us all.

Chapter 2

By morning, the aches and pains of the journey were gone and my desire to explore Kashgar was sufficient to get me out of bed shortly after dawn. The other reason was a demand of nature that had become such a key part of my existence in the last couple of months.

The facilities at the Qinnabar Hotel were very different from anything I had previously experienced. The fact that the lavatory block was unisex was the first surprise. The second surprise was that the lavatories could only be reached by climbing a flight of stairs. The upper floor was set out in stalls, perhaps twenty or thirty in total. The dividing walls between the stalls were waist height and there were no doors. Inside each stall was a rectangular hole cut through the floor to the room below, in the middle of which a pyramid of excrement was just visible in the gloom.

There was no alternative and I faced up to the challenge as best as I could. Squatting over the hole, I was surrounded by other people doing the same thing. The Romans would have recognised this shared lavatorial experience. Archaeological work in Pompeii and elsewhere had found evidence of communal lavatories in which Romans sat cheek-to-cheek as they defecated. In the world in which I grew up, this was one aspect of life that had always been strictly private. The sight of Fiona and Belinda coming up the stairs was a reminder of that very fact.

A movement below me caught my eye. Looking down through the slot into the room below, I could see a shovel being forced into the pyramid. Someone was shovelling the shit into a wheelbarrow, even as I added to its apex. With as much dignity as I could muster, I escaped and returned to the relative sanity of our room to wait for Fiona and Belinda. As soon as they got back, we took a pony cart into the centre of Kashgar.

Architecturally, Kashgar was a bit of a muddle. Much of the ancient town centre had been torn down and replaced by modern buildings, most of which were rather dull concrete structures. Many of these buildings had been painted in a vain attempt to make them aesthetically pleasing. The older buildings were either rather shabby affairs constructed using mud bricks, or more rarely, beautiful structures with verandas, walls covered in patterned ceramic tiles and elegantly tiled roofs. Some of the older buildings had elaborately carved front doors, often showing signs of faded paintwork.

Perhaps it was deliberate, but the modernisers were destroying a large part of the architectural history of Kashgar.

The Uygur people were mostly Muslim and used an Arabic script. Their language was an ancient Turkish dialect that could be understood by modern-day Turks. In an attempt to bring the Uygur into their culture, the Chinese were taking steps to introduce both spoken and written Mandarin. They were also trying to limit the power of the Mullahs, who had stirred up unrest in the region in the recent past. The real issue was that Uygur people were struggling to come to terms with an ever growing population of Han Chinese immigrants in their midst.

Having changed very little money at Pirali, the girls and I needed to find the only bank that would change travellers cheques. What should have been a simple task turned into a major exercise and after six hours, we were still no closer to finding the bank. No one seemed to know where it was, even the normally helpful Pakistani traders seemed unable or unwilling to give us directions. Some of them were still sulking because the girls turned down their impassioned offers of friendship.

Finally, we found a young Turkish woman who spoke English and knew how to get to the foreign exchange bank. She was even prepared to take us there and set off on her bicycle with Fiona balanced on the pannier. Belinda and I followed closely behind on a rickety donkey-cart taxi.

The bank was crowded with other foreigners, but there were plenty of sofas and armchairs, so we were able to wait in comfort. The staff were polite and efficient. They even had a device to test for forged US dollar notes.

As soon as they had exchanged their travellers' cheques, Fiona and Belinda rushed off to book their flight to Urümqi at the China Airlines Adminstration of China (CAAC) Ticket Office. Feeling lazy, I was quite happy to wait for them in a well-padded armchair in the bank's lobby. When they finally returned with tickets in their hands and grins all over their faces, I knew that we had something to celebrate.

In the evening, the Oasis Restaurant provided a surreal setting for our first dinner in Communist China. This iconic eating establishment offered western-style pizzas and beer served with an ancient tape of The Doors playing in the background. The sad thing was that the owner was blissfully unaware of the interest that his success had generated in the corridors of power. He was seen as being too successful and there were people close to him planning to close down his magical pizza house.

By the time we got back to the hotel, we were ready to crawl into our respective beds. As the sounds of the night faded into our dreams, we exchanged our last touching words of the day. One of the girls sighed and asked me one last question as we settled down for the night.

"When did you last have sex?"

Pause.

"Months ago. And you?"

Longer pause.

"At least nine months ago."

For a brief moment, there was silence as we each relived our last encounter. Reality returned, bringing the realisation that it was time for sleep.

"Good night. Sleep well."

"You too. Good night."

Sleep came easily, but at seven in the morning, there was a resounding knock on the door. After a brief pause, our door was unlocked from the outside and in marched a stout, flat faced woman with a large kettle of hot water. Without a word, she refilled the vacuum flask and left, locking the door behind her. Half an hour later, there was another knock on the door. This time, it was a gentle-faced woman in her fifties or sixties selling bowls of yoghurt. She carried two stacks of bowls; each wrapped in a cloth, with sheets of hardboard separating each bowl. The yoghurt was delicious.

As the two girls got ready for the day, I read and half-listened to their chatter, which was full of nostalgic references to their schooldays. They giggled as they relived encounters with past matrons. They remembered secrets that had been shared in their dormitories and laughed about spending time in the "san." Their stories made me realise how far I had travelled from the comforts of home in just a few months.

After breakfast, we explored the outskirts of Kashgar. After wandering through a maze of narrow streets and alleyways for several hours, we eventually got to a point where we were not sure of the quickest way back to the centre. As we tried to work out the best route, a European couple strolled down the street towards us. The man was English, tall, silver-haired and had a distinguished air. His wife was American and had a certain aura of confidence. As the man had a Kashgar guidebook, I approached him and asked if I could look at his map.

As the two of us tried to work out the quickest way back to the centre of town, Fiona and Belinda chatted with his wife on the other side of the street. After a minute or two, the man glanced over to his wife, who was deep in conversation with the two girls. A wry grin crossed his face and he turned to face me.

"Those girls are not called Fiona and Bindy by any chance?"

This was a very strange question. After all, it would have been too much of a coincidence that he could possibly know them.

"Yes. Do you know them?"

"Not really, but I think that they are coming to visit us in Beijing. We know their parents."

Kashgar seemed to be the place for coincidences. Fiona rushed over to us and shook him by the hand.

"This is Mr Thompson and his wife. We are going to see them when we get to Beijing, can you believe it?"

Mr Thompson turned out to be an "important person" at the British Embassy and was in Kashgar for a short break.

"We are on our way to visit the old Russian Consulate. Would you care to join us?"

Mr Thompson was an avid historian and was able to describe in detail how the Russians and the British had competed to establish a presence in Kashgar because of its strategic position and its proximity to India.

While the Qinnabar Hotel was once the British Consulate, the Seman Hotel had been the Russian Consulate. Both Consulates had been established during the time of the Great Game played between the British and Russian Empires at the end of the nineteenth century. It did not take long to see that the Seman Hotel was a better class of hotel than the Qinnabar Hotel.

After tea, it was time for me to leave and say farewell to the girls. As I shook Mr Thompson's hand, he whispered to me.

"I cannot understand why they want to fly to Beijing. I would much rather travel overland than fly. The west of China is fascinating and so different from the rest of the country."

On my way back from the old Russian Consulate, two small girls around eight years old joined me. At first, I tried hard to ignore them, but they followed close on my heels and started chanting the alphabet in English.

"ABCDEFG,HIJKLMNOP, QRST..."

After a while, I quietly joined in and our chanting began to sound more like a song, with my toneless drone given life by their shrill melodies.

"HIJKLMNOP,QRSTUVWXY..."

After a couple of refrains, one of the girls stopped me and asked me to write out the alphabet in her notebook. Out came a pencil from a pretty, pink plastic pencil case and in the quiet of a tiny back street, I carefully wrote out the letters in my best handwriting. As I wrote, a crowd of small boys gathered around us. One of the bigger boys reached forward and took the pencil and the notebook from me. With great care, he began to write in English. As he wrote, the children fell silent. His words were misspelled and barely legible, but I was sure that I could understand what he was trying to say.

"DOŚ MŰSEMAN MINING ISIM" *"Does Muslim mean Islam?"*

Looking at the little girl, I could tell that she was getting very nervous and took the book back from the boy, placing it gently back in her hands. My reward, albeit unearned, was the most wondrous smile of gratitude. Leaving the bigger boys behind, we continued walking and chanting the alphabet until it was time for them to leave.

"Bye bye."

They both waved and blew me kisses. Perhaps one day, I would be lucky enough to have a daughter as charming as those girls.

Back at the hotel, I was in time to see Fiona and Belinda as they left to catch their flight from Kashgar to Urümqi. From there, they would take the four-hour flight to Beijing, missing most of western China. I was sad to see them leave, but would not have given up the chance to travel across China for the world.

As I wandered through the streets of Kashgar in search of something to eat, I bumped into David and Linda, my hippie friends last seen in the valleys of the Kalash. They had been looking for interesting objects in the bazaar to take back to their shop in Goa and were now keen to party.

Linda had some old friends whom she wanted to meet, because she had something for them that they needed. She led me to a local bar that doubled up as a kind of a truckers' brothel. I should have guessed from the fact that all the serving staff were women, which was unusual in a town as Muslim as Kashgar. Apparently, the girls met the truckers in the bar and did their business elsewhere.

Linda had a collection of Western padded bras to show the girls. She had met the girls a year before and promised to bring them better bras than they could get in the bazaar or in any of the local shops.

As soon as Linda brought out her collection of padded bras, the girls clustered around, giggling and laughing at the sight of the padding. The Western bras were delicate structures of lace with elastic webbing; pink ribbons; and embroidered roses, very different from the heavy duty, utilitarian bras on sale in the bazaar. The more adventurous girls held the lacy bras to their chests and danced around the bar, giggling and laughing.

The lady of the house took us to a table covered in a plastic tablecloth and brought us bottles of chilled beer. There was no one else in the bar, so we sat and chatted, until a very drunken trucker arrived and sat down at a table next to us. He bought us a beer each and at first seemed friendly. His attention was slowly drawn to my height and then to David's beard, both of which seemed to annoy him. His mood became increasingly dark and when the lady of the house moved us to another table at the other end of the room, something deep within him gave way.

With a mighty effort, he staggered to his feet and stood in the middle of the room, swaying ever so slightly and started to shout, filling the bar with the heat of his anger. Judging from the way he was looking at David and me, I was sure we were the object of his spleen. He was clearly very angry. Out of the corner of my eye, I could see that one of the girls was holding a short steel cosh on the end of a chain, the weapon was half hidden in her hand.

He then grasped two full pint bottles of beer and held them in his outstretched arms. Standing there in his ill-fitting grey suit, he froze for an instant, looking as though he was begging to be nailed to a cross. There was something in his eyes that told of an anger that raged within. I half expected him to attack us at any moment. Instead, he made a long and impassioned speech.

As he talked, we were all frozen in our seats. At the end of his speech, he brought his arms together in front of him in one swift, violent movement. The bottles crashed together, showering the room with beer and shattered glass. He then apologised profusely and staggered out into the night. The owner of bar was very upset and made sure that the barmaids kept the beer flowing. I did not get back to my room until early in the morning.

Chapter 3

In the morning, I got up late and missed the bus to Korla by two hours. In fact, I had arrived at the bus station at what I thought was the right time, but discovered that I should have established which time had been used to compile the bus timetable. A friendly shopkeeper explained that I could have chosen from one of four times. The timetable turned out to have been based on Beijing Standard Time, rather than Urumqi Standard Time, which was two hours behind. Clocks owned by Uygurs tended to show local time, unless they were official clocks in which they showed Beijing Standard Time. Some Uygur clocks had been set to local time with a daylight saving adjustment of one hour. Some official clocks showed Beijing time with a daylight saving adjustment. No wonder I had no idea of the time of day.

To compensate for missing the bus, I set out to find some breakfast. On the way, I bumped into a Dutch couple whom I last seen in the valleys of the Kalash. They had been looking for me to tell me that an Australian who I met there had seen two letters waiting for me at the Post Office in Gilgit. He had been trying to get the Post Office to release the letters to him so that he could bring them to me in Kashgar. If Linda and David had not kept me from my bed, I would have left for Korla and never known about the letters.

I was eager to get back on the road, but it would have been churlish of me not to wait for the Australian to cross the Karakoram Range and deliver my mail. I could only hope that he would not take too long to cross the desert. As he was coming from Pakistan, he had to pass through Kashgar. All I had to do was make sure that I could find him when he arrived.

In the meanwhile, I had the time to explore the delights of the food stalls in the bazaar next to the Idkah mosque. The choice of dishes was mouth-watering: lamb kebabs; breaded intestine kebabs; bowls of steamed sheep lung and intestine stuffed with rice; mutton kebabs; chicken liver kebabs; barbecued sheep's tail; mutton stew with Chinese naan breads; noodles with meat and vegetables; and even boiled pig face. There were *"samas,"* patties stuffed with mutton, onion and tail fat, cooked in a *tandoori* style oven; dumplings filled with mutton; chunks of deep fried fish; and cold rice noodles with tofu and chilli sauces.

For the sweet-toothed, there was a choice of homemade ice cream; fresh yoghurt with honey; doughnuts coated in sugar; and even neat little steamed sachets of honeyed rice packed on top of a cherry and wrapped in lily leaves. The best cold drink on offer was a honey-yoghurt lassi served with chips of ice. The ice chips had been hacked out of a block carved from a distant glacier. I was forced to conclude that while some Pakistanis ate to live, most Uygur and Chinese lived to eat.

There was also a thriving black market for foreign currency, with one hundred Foreign Exchange Certificates (FEC) selling for one hundred and sixty *reminbi*. In the bazaar, several black market moneychangers approached me. Based on the wads of cash they showed me, I estimated that there must have been at least £50,000 worth of *reminbi* on sale in the central market area alone. This was big business in a country where a monthly wage of one hundred *reminbi* was considered acceptable.

The FEC could be used to buy foreign goods in the Friendship Stores and to buy foreign currency, but the amount of cash on sale in the bazaar suggested to me that there was probably more behind this market than met the eye. Someone had an excess of *reminbi* and needed to convert that excess into something more useful and was prepared to pay a hefty fee for that conversion. The phrase "money laundering" sprang to mind and I could only assume that there were some connections with the illegal drug trade in China. Given that Afghanistan and Pakistan were both major producers of heroin and opium, was it possible that none of these drugs passed into China via Kashgar? If there was such a trade, was it possible that illicit traders in Kashgar played no part?

I could imagine Uygur traders paying Pakistani middlemen hard currency for drugs grown in Pakistan and Afghanistan. They sold drugs across China and were paid in *reminbi,* some of which were laundered back into hard currency by black marketeers to pay for luxury goods and the next cargo of drugs from Pakistan.

In the evening, I returned to the hotel to find the manager waiting for me. It turned out that she needed my help.

"Will you write a sign for me...in English?"

She took me back to her office and explained that she needed a poster telling guests that the hotel had started selling both bus and airline tickets. She then gave me a Chinese writing brush, a pot of ink and a poster-size sheet of low-grade paper. Perhaps someone with some artistic talent could have used the brush to write words, but painting never really was my forte. After a few failed experiments with the brush, I gave up and traced the words on the paper using a pencil. Using a fountain pen, I painstakingly filled in each of the letters. The manager seemed pleased with my efforts and rewarded me with a smile.

Outside, a group of Pakistani men playing soccer asked me to join them. After a few minutes, I decided that it would be a good idea to introduce them to touch rugby. The result was chaotic and hilarious. The ball vanished into a swirling cloud of dust, white teeth and flapping *shalwars*. They played with great enthusiasm and for a moment, I was back in Luxembourg playing with my old teammates in the Rugby Club de Luxembourg. For the first time since leaving Luxembourg, I was hit by a wave of longing to be back in the world that I had left behind.

Four days later, the Australian arrived with my letters and somehow managed to track me down. He handed me two battered envelopes covered in stamps from post offices across northern Pakistan. I recognised the handwriting on the envelopes and was thrilled. One was from a very good friend in Luxembourg and the other was from the Zephyr. The sight of the letters filled me with a rush of happiness, because I had not heard from either of them for many months.

My mood changed as I opened and read each letter, absorbing every word in silence. Both letters contained news of personal distress and trauma. The letter from the Zephyr began with the words "if this letter is meant to reach you, it will."

One had lost a baby and the other had been taken into hospital, having been taken very ill. The postmarks on the letter from the Zephyr told of its incredible journey from Wisconsin to Kashgar. Just as I had started to miss my distant friends, they had somehow managed to reach out and touch me. Reading their words I felt the distance between us and at the same time, felt very close to them.

As I tried to sense their feelings of sorrow and sadness through the veil of paper, ink and words, tears welled out of my eyes and rolled down my face. All I could do was write back, hoping that my words of solace would reach them one day. I posted the letters and decided that it was time to move on.

The bus-ride from Kashgar to Kuqa took a day and half, with an overnight stop in Aksu. This time, the road was better and ran parallel with the Tianshan Mountains to the north. To the south was the Takla Makan desert, one of the most hostile of the world's deserts, known as the "Land of Death" by local people. As in the past, the road skirted the desert, where sand storms, extremes of heat and cold and the scarcity of drinking water made life impossible for all but the most highly adapted species. Where water did flow, it was salty, leaving white deposits of salt on the surface of the desert. Out of the corner of my eye, the deposits looked like reflections of the distant mountains in pools of still water.

For hour after hour, the bus slid over a good metalled surface. The noise of the engine made talking impossible, so I sat with my head against the window watching the desert roll past. After a few hours, my eyes began to tire from focusing on the endless expanse of nothingness and my mind started to drift inwards. This was a time for contemplation and time to remember good times with friends in faraway lands and to wish them both speedy recoveries.

The Zephyr had travelled to Luxembourg from Wisconsin and when we first met had been staying with distant Norwegian relatives. I had been invited to a dinner party given in her honour to "make up the numbers." From the first moment, the Zephyr had captured me with her gentle eyes. What started as friendship developed into a passionate relationship and before long we found ourselves living together.

As the bus rumbled across the desert, fragments of the past slipped into my thoughts bringing back memories of that time. In Paris, she had shaken me awake to tell me that a bomb had exploded outside our hotel room. I tried at first to tell her that it could not have been a bomb, but when I replayed the incident in my mind seconds later, I remembered hearing a loud bang; the sight of our French windows opening wide; the sound of breaking glass; and the sound of people screaming in the street below. Yes. It was a bomb.

The Zephyr and I had spent the day visiting the sights of Paris, before returning to our hotel next to the famous Gilbert bookshop. Shortly afterwards, the bookshop and our hotel were rocked by a bomb that injured at least three people.

Next day, we read that the French police had evacuated tourists from the Eiffel Tower after a bomb had been discovered in a public lavatory on the third level and was defused just ninety minutes before it was due to go off. We also read that a bomb had exploded in the Champs-Elysées, wounding eight people.

What was most sobering was that we had visited both the Eifel Tower and the Champs-Elysées on that day.

The following day, an Islamic terrorist group calling itself the "Committee of Solidarity with the Arab and Middle East Political Prisoners" claimed responsibility for the bombing in a letter to Agence France-Presse.

Sitting on my own in a bus travelling across the northern margins of the Takla Makan desert, I could only hope that the Zephyr was on the road to recovery.

Several hours later, the desert finally gave way to Aksu, an oasis town nourished by a river and surrounded by green fields kept alive by an intricate web of irrigation channels just visible in the headlights of the bus. The bus came to a halt in the courtyard of a roadside hotel a few minutes before midnight, Beijing time.

The hotel manager found me a bed in a dormitory with two middle-aged Chinese men. As the dormitory was locked, he had to bang on the door to get them to wake up and let me in. The manager switched on the light and made sure that they were awake. Both men looked very dismayed when I left my bags on my bed and set off into the darkness in search of food.

Tiny roadside cafés lined both sides of the road. Their electric lights and blazing cooking fires were a welcome sight and I chose the busiest in the belief that the locals knew best. As I approached, a group of Uygur travellers from the bus called me over to sit with them.

The food was plain but wholesome. The café only served noodles with stir-fried vegetables and meat, which I washed down with a cup of scalding hot tea. My lack of Mandarin was a partial barrier to conversation, but with an effort on both sides, we could communicate. It was here that my first Mandarin lessons began. My hosts started by teaching me how to count from one to ten. With a little extra effort, they showed me how to use these numbers to count to ninety-nine. Whether I would still remember in the morning was another matter.

At last, I could start to communicate with my new-found friends. They soon discovered that I was not married. They wanted to know my age and my nationality, which I was able to tell them.

The news that I did not have children at the ripe old age of thirty-one was passed around the group. One old lady took me by the hand and looked at me with dark, expressive eyes filled with tenderness. In a country in which children are so precious, the assumed pain of my lack of children was felt by all. Their compassion was very moving and tears welled up in my eyes.

Back at the room, my roommates grumbled as I woke them up to get back into the room. I slipped between ancient, but spotless sheets and fell into a deep, haunted dream.

Rising before dawn, I set out in search of breakfast. All the roadside eating-houses were still closed. Two of the cooks were asleep on one of the tandoori-style ovens. One had his feet in the oven and his face was pressed against the clay on top. Eventually, I found a bread seller and a group of old women selling red-coloured hard-boiled eggs.

Back on the bus, I ate my breakfast and then slept most of the way to Kuqa. From the bus station, a horse-drawn cart took a young couple from Hong Kong and me to the courtyard of an elegant hotel in the old city. Their room rate was twenty percent less than mine because of their Chinese ancestry.

Kuqa used to be a major centre of Buddhism in China. The great monasteries of Kuqa flourished, nourished as they were by the wealth that came with the trade caravans. Islam arrived in Kuqa in the ninth century and in a relatively short period, the power of the monasteries waned and Kuqa lost one its key reasons for existence.

Francis Younghusband, who passed through Kuqa in 1887 on his journey from Beijing to India, would have been treated with deep suspicion. He was one of the first Englishmen to visit Kuqa and described it as being a small walled town full of houses and "a few bad shops." A century later, Kuqa was one of the poorest cities in China.

My reason for coming to Kuqa was its proximity to the Kizil Buddhist caves. In the hotel reception, I bumped into a group of Hong Kong students haggling over the price of a minibus to take them to the caves. As there was a spare seat on the bus, they invited me join them.

It soon became clear that the driver was not keen to take me, so they appealed to the hotel manager, who also happened to be the local tourist officer. One of the students explained why there was a problem.

"He says you can't travel with us because you are not Chinese. Apparently, Chinese people cannot travel with Westerners like you. This is just bizarre."

An argument ensued, but I sensed that progress was being made on my behalf.

"He says that you cannot go to the caves because you do not have a permit."

"Could you ask him where I could get one?"

The argument continued and then it became clear that the hotel manager was also responsible for issuing the permits, which was why he knew I did not have one. The students eventually convinced him to issue me with an "Alien Travel Permit" and to let me travel with them.

As we set out, I had no real idea that we were in for a two hundred-kilometre journey deep into the desert. At first, the students left me alone, but as we moved deeper into the desert, they started to open up a little.

"We were all waiting for the examination results that will determine whether we will go on to university."

When asked about Hong Kong returning to China, they were all optimistic, but showed signs of apprehension.

"It had better be good, because it is the only future we have. We have nowhere else to go."

After an hour or so, the bus stopped at the Kizil Thousand Buddha Caves, on the banks of the river Muzat. Altogether, there were only 236 caves, which had been abandoned in the 8th century after the arrival of Islam, of which only 135 remained relatively intact.

The custodian of the caves looked at my Caucasian features and charged me four times as much as the students from Hong Kong. A major conservation project was in progress and the visible extent of the damage inside the caves was evidence of the scale of their challenge. Most of the hundreds of wall paintings had been vandalised. Many of the images of Buddha had been defaced. Some of the images had been had been cut out and taken away. Those remaining paintings that had not been vandalised were decaying.

On one wall was a poignant inscription made by a Chinese archaeologist stating that foreigners had looted the caves during the nineteenth century. The writer even named the culprits: Albert von Le Coq, a Prussian; and Sir Aurel Stein, an Englishman. They had arrived here with a caravan of camels and donkeys, having been guided here by local Muslims. They packed the stolen wall paintings and statues in straw and cotton, lashed them to donkeys and carried them out of China. Some of the statues that they stole then can be seen today in the British Museum in London. Those murals that were taken to Berlin were destroyed during World War II.

The driver hurried us out of the caves and drove us to a roadside noodle bar. When I was charged twice as much as the students for a frugal meal of noodles and stir-fired vegetables, they were outraged and tried to force the eating-house owner to accept the same amount from me as they were being asked to pay. When he refused, they offered to pay for my meal, which confused the poor man so much that he gave in, albeit ungraciously.

The driver chased us back into the bus and we set off once more into the desert. The landscape became wild and rugged, with vertical slabs of exposed strata snarling at an indifferent sky. Stopping by a stream, the driver told us to taste the muddy water. It was very salty and disgusting.

Onwards to the next set of caves. This time a Uygur guide attached himself to us and proceeded to baffle us all with his total ignorance of either the caves or the wall paintings. Picking out a scene with beautifully painted dancers, he giggled and spoke his only word of English.

"Disco!"

For the rest of the visit, he spoke nothing but Mandarin, but with a strong accent that was barely comprehensible to my student friends. After a while, we gave up and moved on.

The day ended in the ruins of Subashi, a great city abandoned in the 13th century. Here as in Multan, hundreds of thousands of people had lived and died, returning to the land from which they had risen. As the winds and rains swept over their buildings, even their monuments were being taken back into the soul of the desert. These ruins marked the end of a race of people who grew rich on the trade that flowed up and down the Silk Road. As the wealth of the Silk Road traders began to wane, their way of life shrivelled and died.

Kuqa was no more than a staging point on my journey and I was soon itching to get moving once more. A motorcycle-drawn rickshaw sped me to the bus station in the new city, where a bus to Korla was waiting to leave. The only remaining seat was at the back of the bus and with minutes to spare, I managed to buy a ticket and clamber aboard. The locals watched me with great interest and did their best to make me feel welcome.

The bus pulled away from the city and headed out into the Takla Makan desert. The monotony of the unchanging landscape soon put me into a trance-like state in which my eyes started playing tricks with me. In the distance, the sight of white horses flitting over the surface of a great body of water filled me with excitement for an instant. A second later, the water turned back into sand, scrub and rock. I felt strangely cheated.

The hours passed and my mind began to seek solace elsewhere. Almost without noticing any change, I become oblivious to the noise, the shaking and the discomfort. The desert stretched out as far as the eye could see. It was as flat as a lake, but reddish in colour, with a scattering of rocks and scrub across its surface. It was a mirage of arid savagery, more like Mars than Earth.

The hours passed and gradually, the shadows lengthened, bringing a long day towards its end in the outskirts of Korla.

Korla, a small industrial town, had an orderly, even planned look that was in stark contrast with the entrepreneurial, seemingly unplanned industrial developments I saw in Pakistan. This was a town laid out with rectangular concrete forms, straight lines and conformity.

Chinese architecture of the 1960s and 1970s was all too often austere, functional and had few obvious roots in China's past. Whatever had existed had here in the past had been torn down and replaced with Mao's vision of an architectural style fit for a new united China. Whether the same degree of change had been effected in the minds of the Chinese people was another matter.

Outside the bus-station, chance brought me into the sight of the driver of a passing van. He stopped and pulled up beside me. He was a young man with rotten teeth and an open, friendly smile. Without a word, he took me to a modern hotel, where I was given a room furnished with armchairs, a lockable cupboard, a writing desk, a small table with a washing bowl and three empty single beds. The view from the window was of the town of Korla and in the distance, the Tianshan Mountains. As I settled down in an armchair to enjoy the comfort and privacy, the hotel manager arrived with a vacuum flask filled with piping hot water. With mug of tea in one hand and my feet resting on the small table, I felt I was truly a king.

The humble vacuum flask is a technological innovation that had done more to improve public health in China than most of the expensive water-treatment projects that I came across in Pakistan. For me, amoebic dysentery was now little more than a distant memory. Every room, no matter how basic, had a supply of boiled water in a vacuum flask.

As evening approached, I set out to explore Korla. The wide, open avenues were packed with groups of young men and women dressed in their best clothes; couples walking hand-in-hand; and families out for an evening stroll. After a minute or two, I started to notice that people were stopping dead in their tracks as soon as they saw me. Some of them even turned and kept pace with me. Drunken young men called out to me and before long, I had a crowd of two hundred people following me at a discrete distance. It was clear to me that very few foreigners had visited Korla in recent times.

I sought refuge in a restaurant, where the waiter handed me a menu that naturally enough was printed in Chinese characters, which I could not read. Realising that I could not read his carefully prepared menu, the manager invited me into the kitchen and asked me to show him what I wanted to eat. His patience was unbounded and eventually, a bowl of fried noodles with vegetables arrived at my table. The crowd peering through the window soon dispersed and I was left to eat in peace.

Back at the hotel, I had a long discussion with the manager about getting to Turpan, an oasis town built in one of the deepest depressions on Earth. As we had no common language, we communicated using simple drawings. Had we been able to communicate using the spoken word, the conversation would have been something like this:

"When does the next bus to Turpan leave?"

"I wouldn't take the bus if I were you. Why don't you take the train, it would be much quicker."

"When does the next train leave?"

Using a drawing of a clock face on a scrap of paper, he showed me when the train was due to leave and told me when and where to catch the bus that would take me to the railway station.

At the station, an old man helped me buy my ticket for the eight-hour journey to Turpan travelling "hard" seat class. A foraging trip around the station produced five hard-boiled eggs and four small loaves of sweet bread.

The train was slow, but clean and headed north out of Korla into the Tianshan Mountains. The track corkscrewed its way up a narrow valley, reaching its highest point at 8,858 feet in a small town called Ewirga. The track had been carved into the mountains, with several long tunnels. The quality of the engineering workmanship was evident and the views almost overwhelming. Beyond Ewirga, the track turned east and began the long winding descent to Turpan Zhan station, which stood on the very rim of the Depression.

The Turpan Depression came into sight just as the sun began to set. The track did not descend into the Depression, staying instead just inside the rim. Silhouetted against the sunset were the blue and grey shadows of the Tianshan Mountains. To the east was the flatness of the Depression itself, just visible into the gathering gloom many thousands of feet below. At its lowest point, the Depression is over five hundred feet below sea level.

By the time the train finally pulled into Turpan Zhan, there was no sign of the sun. Despite the darkness and the milling masses at the station, the driver of a luxury coach, which just happened to be headed for Turpan, sought me out and offered me a ride. Within a few minutes, he had located four more Westerners: an Argentinian couple; and an Italian couple.

With our bags loaded on to the bus, we were all ready for the descent into the Turpan Depression. The driver pocketed our money with a flourish and eased the bus into gear. As the bus tipped over the rim of the depression and dropped below sea level, the temperature rose slowly but surely.

Faced with the prospect of having to deal with five foreigners in the early hours of the morning, the hotel receptionist worked hard to make us feel unwelcome, but found us rooms for the night after a brief, but terse discussion. Once again, sleep came easily.

Breakfast was served outside in the hotel's garden. Overhead, a carpet of vines cooled the air and softened the glare into pools of dappled sunlight. The temperature had already climbed to 40°C. After so many hours spent driving through deserts, the prospect of a drive into the Turpan Pendi, a desert of roasting rock and sand that covered the Depression, was surprisingly appealing.

After a morning spent wandering around the bazaar, I returned to the hotel to test the local melon juice and bottles of chilled beer.

The minibus arrived promptly at five o'clock Beijing time with the temperature already at 45°C and the sun high in a cloudless sky. The road into the Turpan Pendi was very straight and metalled. The road surface glistened as though there had been recent rain. In fact, it was already little more than a river of molten tar.

Two hours later, the bus rattled to a halt at the Bizaklik Thousand Buddha Caves in the Moutou valley. This vast complex of Buddhist caves had been a prosperous centre of religious activity up to the 13th century, when it too had been abandoned. In most of the caves, there was ample evidence of the damage inflicted by vandals and Muslim fanatics on these caves over the centuries. Hundreds of the paintings had been desecrated with faces scratched off or daubed in mud because of the Muslim belief that the human countenance should never be represented in art. On one wall was graffiti stating that Voi le Coq had come here and removed whole paintings to Berlin, where they were safe from the Muslims, but not from the bombs dropped by the allied Air Forces during World War II.

Beyond the caves were the ruins of the city of Gaochang, a great centre of trade that was established a thousand years before Jesus Christ and abandoned in the sixteenth century as the economic importance of the Silk Road waned. Although the risks to the merchants that plied their trade along the Silk Road were great, they accepted those risks because the rewards were high. They faced raiders, inhospitable deserts, disease, endless sandstorms, lack of feed for their animals and high passes, but the profits to be gained kept the Silk Road alive.

There were many causes of the decline of the Silk Road, including the disintegration of the Mongol Empire in the 13th century, which was followed by an increase in the number of raids on caravans; the encroachment of the deserts into inhabited land; and the increasingly isolationist policies of the Ming dynasty, which was established in 1368. In the end, it was the economic impact of the development of new navigation aids by Arab and European mathematicians that sealed its fate.

The arrival of the Portuguese explorer Vasco da Gama in Calicut on the Malabar Coast on 21 May 1498, after the first direct sea voyage from Europe to Asia, signalled the end of the Silk Road. In the face of an increasingly isolationist China and fierce competition from Arab and European merchant seafarers, its terminal decline became inevitable.

Improved ships, navigation techniques, weaponry and a pressure to reduce transportation costs led to the disintermediation of the middlemen who earned their living along the Silk Road trade. Without the revenues generated by these traders and intermediaries, the towns and cities that lived off the Silk Road faced total ruin. As Portuguese sailors started to bring increasing quantities of spices back to Europe by sea, the price of pepper in

Lisbon fell to a fifth of that charged by merchants in Venice. The Venetians who had grown rich because of their near monopoly over the European end of the Silk Road and their Arab suppliers were devastated.

There were signs that the Chinese government was funding a major conservation effort. Given the scale of the ruined city, only a few of the more interesting structures, city walls, the grander houses and key official buildings, were being conserved. The work was made more difficult by the nature of the construction materials that the ancient builders had used, mostly mud bricks that crumbled into a muddy paste in the rain. When it was not raining, sand and wind erosion worked together to grind away the very fabric of these ancient buildings.

Our driver surveyed the ruins of the city built by his ancestors with a sanguine look in his eyes. Perhaps he realised that the Silk Road was re-awakening and that he and his peers were now beginning to prosper from a new source of trade that was developing across Central Asia, tourism.

There was no time for deliberation, so we were taken on to the Astanta-Karakhojo tombs, where nobles, officials and others from the fourth to tenth centuries AD were buried. Of the five hundred or so tombs, three were open to the public. In the first, there was a mummified naked couple lying on a sheet of sackcloth. The degree of preservation of the flesh had frozen their bodies in time, revealing fingernails, soft skin and even traces of body hair. I was touched to be so close to these people.

In the other caves, there were wall paintings untouched by the desecrators. One wall was covered with delicate paintings of wild birds, including ducks and geese. The other paintings were of Buddha sitting in different poses.

Outside, the heat was now even more intense and sucked at the moisture in my mouth, eyes and nostrils. This was the heat of an oven and it was unrelenting. The driver was keen to push on again, this time towards the Flaming Mountains, a sixty-mile long sprawl of red and orange sandstone criss-crossed by ravines and gullies. The mountains rose out of the desert like a wall of petrified fire. In places, the temperature of the bare rocks exceeded fifty degrees Celsius. Above the mountains, updrafts of superheated air shimmered against the backdrop of an empty sky. Finally, the driver turned back towards Turpan along a road that glistened in the light of the setting sun.

Under the vines in the hotel's garden, the ice-cold beer tasted good and the food was excellent. Tomorrow awaited and there was still a long way to go.

Turpan Zhan railway station at first light was a hive of activity. Groups of men in grey woollen suits with their trousers rolled up to their knees stood half-hidden in permanent clouds of cigarette smoke. Quite a few of them wore brightly-coloured leggings under their trousers. Beneath hairless calves were narrow, high-heeled sandals and dark socks. The less well-off smoked cigarettes made from sheets of newspaper, which were on sale in a stall outside the station. Wealthy smokers held filtered cigarettes between yellowed fingers.

Both smoking and spitting seemed to be fashionable activities. Perhaps 'spitting' was not quite the right word to describe how local men dealt with a build-up of spittle and phlegm coughed out of their lungs. I watched as one man dressed in a three-piece suit formed a gob of spittle and phlegm in his mouth after a bout of heavy throat clearing and coughing, which he then dribbled on to the ground by his feet. He then used the ball of his foot to drive the spittle into the ground. He was not alone.

The majority of the women wore trousers. Compared with the men with their badly-tailored suits, Mao caps and beards, the women were generally smartly dressed with brightly-coloured headscarves, cotton blouses and perfectly ironed flared trousers or skirts.

Chapter 4

Compared with the orderliness of the train from Korla, the Urümqi to Xi'an train was crowded, chaotic and disorganised. It was a struggle just to get on to the train and to get a seat. I was an object of great interest to my Chinese travelling companions who stared at me with unflinching eyes. For some, I was the first Westerner that they had encountered in the flesh and they were naturally curious. The train was so full that I had to push and shove my way to the boiler at the end of the carriage to fill my enamelled mug with hot water. Approving glances watched me make a brew with dried tea leaves.

As night fell, sleep overcame most of the people around me. No matter how hard I tried, I could not sleep sitting upright on a hard seat. As I took refuge on the floor under the seats, the train steamed out across the desert under the stars.

Travel by train in China tends to be measured by the brief stops in isolated railway stations and by the appearance of a uniformed attendant pushing a trolley laden with meals and snacks. Breakfast arrived at seven in the morning, a hearty meal of noodles with mutton served in polystyrene dishes. Up and down the length of the train, empty bellies warmed to the arrival of fresh food. Moments later, a harvest of empty polystyrene cartons floated out into the countryside from every carriage like grotesque flakes of snow.

Several hours later, the train pulled in to Luiyang in time for lunch. The choice of food was surprisingly good and I was invited to eat with some of my fellow travellers. Following their lead, I used my chopsticks to pack the food into my mouth as the train headed southwards across the Gobi desert towards Dunhuang.

Dunhuang, an oasis town on the Silk Road, was built in the heart of the Gansu corridor. Flanked by the Gobi desert on one side and the edge of the Qinghai plateau on the other, Dunhuang was an important stopping place for the caravans that travelled the Silk Road, not just for trade, but also for Buddhism.

Buddhist monks started work in 366 AD on a monastic centre by carving caves into a cliff overlooking the River Da, fifteen miles from Dunhuang. Over the next six hundred years, the Magao caves developed into one of the most important centres of Buddhist art.

In the eighth century AD, Tibetans occupied Dunhuang and brought with them their combination of Buddhism and the older animist Bon religion. Theirs was a form of Buddhism strong in art, witchcraft and magic.

A Tang general forced the Tibetans out after less than a century. In the eleventh century, Dunhuang was invaded once again, this time by the Tangut from Tibet, bringing the monastic system to the end. It was at that time that caves were sealed and not rediscovered until 1899 by a Taoist monk.

The day began on a bus heading out across the desert towards Anxi. There were high dunes to the west and menacing rocky outcrops sliced open by deep ravines and gullies to the east. Compared with Buddhist caves seen over the past month, the Magao caves seemed untouched by either time, desecrators or European adventurers. Despite the fact that so many non-Buddhists had lived here over the centuries, more than two thousand statues and over a half million square feet of delicately painted frescoes survived.

A well-informed English-speaking guide collected a motley crowd of visitors and led us though 20 of the 495 caves. The tour was a blur of colour, form and history. Thousands of representations of Buddha and bodhisattva figures blended into mountain landscapes filled with noblemen, farmers, traders and musicians.

As the tour progressed, a Belgian who taught French in a Beijing primary school introduced himself to me and immediately started to get on my nerves. As we moved deeper into the caves, he seemed to have been taken in by the delusion that I was one of his primary school pupils. I tried keeping out of his way, but he noticed and took me to one side.

"If you do not keep with the group, you will not hear our guide. He will not want to see you wandering out of his sight."

"Thanks,"

I smiled back at him though gritted teeth. His tone was at exactly the right pitch to set my teeth on edge. For a moment or two, I made an effort to keep up and then slipped back to my natural position at the back of the group. Out of the corner of one eye, I could see him glowering at me.

Away from the rest of the group, I started to imagine what this place might have been like at its apogee. The empty caves started to fill with pilgrims, traders, camel drivers, leather-workers, merchants, peasants, entertainers, soldiers and travellers, all seeking protection from the dangers that lay before them. Their fears were of raiders, sickness, starvation, thirst and the merciless torment of the desert. This was a womb-like space in which they could feel safe and closer to the gods that would keep watch over them on their way.

I imagined the members of each ethnic group dressed slightly differently from the other groups, creating a rich tapestry of styles and fabrics. Flat faced Tibetans pushed past fat Uygur merchants standing shoulder to shoulder with lean faced Han Chinese bureaucrats. This crowd of motley travellers from all over Asia shuffled through the labyrinth of caves in an endless stream. The sound of murmured prayers echoed though the caves as if spoken by a swarm of a thousand bees. Despite the crowds, the temperature was cool and pleasant. Flickering oil lamps provided the only light in a musty atmosphere thick with the scent of soot, burning incense and unwashed bodies.

"Hurry up! You must keep up. It is time to eat."

The sound of a harsh Flemish accent broke into my reverie, bringing me back into the present with a jolt. I resisted my desire to teach him some manners.

In the restaurant, the Italians and Argentinians asked me to join them for lunch. After a brief discussion, we decided what we wanted to eat. As we were all starving, we ordered one dish each and even ordered one for Willy, the Belgian. When Willy arrived and discovered that we had already ordered, he was furious.

"I am sorry, but that will be too much food for six people."

Using his near fluent Mandarin, he cancelled one of the main courses, despite our protestations.

"There was no use in wasting good food. There will be plenty of food for everyone."

The waiter scowled and crossed out one of our orders. Willy ignored our attempts to change his mind. There was an uncomfortable silence.

By the time the food finally arrived, we were even hungrier and cleared the table in a matter of moments. There was clearly not enough food for six people and in the stony silence that followed, Willy tried to apologise.

"I thought that the helpings would be bigger."

He felt the need to move on and away from the sight of five still hungry people.

"Never mind, let's continue with the tour. I will bring the guide."

There was no alternative, so we all grudgingly got ready to move on. As the Italians had to visit the lavatory, I decided to buy a soft drink to take with me and practise the Mandarin that I had been taught. Feeling quite proud of my ability to ask for the price of a drink, I approached a man standing behind the counter with a bored expression on his face.

Before I could get out the words that I had been rehearsing in my mind, Willy reappeared and noticed that I had left the table. With almost indecent haste, he darted across the room to join me at the counter. He was furious with me.

"What are you doing? What are you asking him?"

His tone was accusatory and his manner overbearing. I resisted my inner desire to smack him on the nose.

"I was just asking how they charge for soft drinks. Why do you want to know?"

"He will not understand you. I will ask for you."

The teacher in Willy was keen to take charge and help me talk to the man behind the counter.

"No thanks. I want to ask him myself so I can practise my Mandarin. I do not need any help. I can manage. Thanks anyway."

Willy ignored my protestations.

"How many drinks do you want?"

"Thanks, but I do not need your help."

I could felt the irritation building inside me, but as we continued arguing, the man behind the counter wandered off. At that moment, the guide turned up and we had to leave.

Willy realised at the last moment that his attempt to help me had once again backfired and apologised for a second time. I smiled and tried to hide the feelings of antipathy that were welling up inside me. The soft drinks stayed in the cooler and we stepped out into the heat once again.

The guide took us through twenty more caves filled with more undamaged frescoes and statues. This was like walking into a lost world of colour and beauty. As most of the caves were closed to visitors, I felt privileged to have been able to witness those caves that were open.

As soon as I could, I left Willy and Dunhuang behind and escaped to Jiuquan by bus. Only eight hours away across the Gobi desert, Jiuquan was at the westernmost end of the Great Wall of China and marked the entrance to ancient China.

Halfway through the journey, the driver stopped for lunch and I found myself sitting next to a Japanese student who was studying in Xi'an. He spoke good English and was keen to know why I was travelling on my own.

"Why do you not travel in a group?"

"I like travelling like this. I meet more people when I travel on my own."

"But how can you travel in China when you do not speak the language? You cannot even read any of the signs."

"I am learning to speak some Mandarin and can even read some basic characters. It is difficult, but I like a challenge. Also, I have been travelling across China for a few weeks already and so far, I have had no problems."

In the end, I think that he accepted that there were certain things in life that he did not need to understand.

In Jiuquan, we splashed through the rain together in search of a hotel. When we found a suitable hotel and checked in, he was alarmed to see that I had booked myself into one of the dormitories.

"You know you will have to share this room with Hong Kong Chinese students?"

He looked very worried.

"They will be very noisy."

The dormitory turned out to be half-full and the students were not noisy. As arranged, I joined Ichiri, the Japanese student, for dinner. The food was excellent and just kept on coming: noodle soup; stir-fried aubergines; egg and tomato foo yung; stir-fried dried Chinese black fungi; stir-fried red and green peppers; stir-fried green beans; local bread and white rice, all washed down with a large bottle of local beer.

Walking back to the hotel through the dimly-lit streets, we witnessed groups of drunken young men brawling. They ignored us and staggered off into the night, laughing, singing and shouting. There was something about them that reminded me of English drunkards on their way home from the pub.

In the morning, the students from Hong Kong invited me to join them on a visit to the fortress at the end of the Great Wall of China. They waited patiently for me to wash and get dressed. We then set off by bus to Jiayuguan, which is to the west of Jiuquan. After a brief discussion with some locals, we caught a second bus on to the fortress.

Built in 1540 during the Ming dynasty, the fortress had been built with a rectangular curtain of crenelated battlements. Inside were two keeps, each with three layers of green glazed tiled roofs. The fortress had been restored in 1949 and looked as good as new.

A Japanese film company had been filming a military epic at the fort earlier in the morning. Workmen were in the process of clearing away piles of foam rubber, used by stuntmen, from under the battlements.

The fort was surrounded by vast deserts, the remains of the last few miles of the Great Wall of China and in the distance, the snow-capped peaks of the Tianshan. No wonder it was popular with filmmakers.

Lunch was a picnic provided by the students. Sitting on the sand on the edge of the desert around a discarded three-legged stool, we ate in style: sweet bread rolls, tinned luncheon meat and a tin of stewed pork fat, washed down with orange soda. Behind us, the fortress stood before a blue backdrop flecked with white. Beyond the fort lay the Middle Kingdom of ancient times and the true heart of China.

Back in Jiuquan, there was little of the ancient town remaining. Instead, modern streets lined with avenues of poplars stood to remind me of the changes that were sweeping through China. As ever, there were reminders of an older way of life. In a shaded corner, a traditional medicine man sat on the pavement with his wares spread out beside him on a sheet of red plastic. Among the bones and horns in his collection, I recognised the skull of a bear; the dried head of a monkey with its mouth wide open; and a single horn from the rare Saiga antelope. There were many other bones and dried remains that I could not identify.

At the request of my Hong Kong friends, I joined them on a visit to a jade factory in Jiuquan. They had come prepared to profit from the price differential between Jiuquan and Hong Kong. The factory was small and made wine cups and glasses from a particularly dark jade. In the yard outside the factory were two men using carborundum wheels to grind shapeless lumps of jade to the approximate shape of a wine cup. Upstairs was a small army of young girls who used a paste of fine carborundum powder to grind and polish the rough forms into delicate jade cups. Each girl used an electric light to test whether the jade was thin enough.

The sight of comfortable armchairs with fine lace covers in the factory shop was a surprise and a good place to sit as the students bought a sack-load of polished jade pieces. In many ways, this was a confusing country, staunchly communist on one hand and openly capitalist on the other.

Once again, I felt the need to move on and bought a train ticket that would take me as far as Xi'an. The scheduled time for the journey from Jiuquan to Xi'an by train was thirty-six hours. For all of the first day, the train snaked its way across the desert like a green reptile running from the heat of the sun. The sun set on the desert and the train continued through the night into the world beyond the desert. I woke up to find that the Takla Makan and Gobi deserts had given way to a cultivated landscape with fields of rich orange soil nourishing crops of maize, wheat and rice. This was a landscape bursting with life, with water in abundance and fertile terraces covering every inch of tillable land.

The track turned south towards Xi'an. Almost imperceptibly, the temperature and humidity began to rise. After Lanzhou, capital of

Gansu province, the transition from the arid conditions in the west of China to a climate better suited to farming was very noticeable, as the crops had already been harvested. Peasant farmers used every flat surface to lay out the grain for threshing and drying on roads, railway platforms, pavements and flat rooftops. This was a form of communal farming recognisable to peasant farmers all over the world.

In a rural station, a beautiful young Chinese woman came aboard and found a seat facing me. She smiled at me, before settling down to sleep. On the seats on the other side of the carriage were two young men, the "Artful Dodgers" of the carriage. They were rogues of the finest kind. Whenever the train pulled into a station, they immediately lay flat out on their seats and pretended to be asleep. Every now and again, a brave soul looking for somewhere to sit woke them up and demanded a seat. This brought out the next stage of their plan.

"My girlfriend is looking for a friend and will be back in a minute."

Or, perhaps.

"My wife is pregnant and is being sick. She will be back in a minute. I have to stay here to look after her seat."

They soon realised that I had spotted their game and winked at me whenever they succeeded in conning yet another hapless passenger into looking somewhere else to sit.

Most people were taken in by their tomfoolery. The only people who did not believe them were young men of their age who were not taken in by their glowering faces. The funny thing was that as soon as their bluff was called, the rogues welcomed the newcomers as if they were long-lost friends and introduced them to their favourite drinking game, which turned out to be a version of Spoof. Each round began as the three of them called out a number between one and thirty and simultaneously used their hand to indicate a number between one and ten. If anyone was unfortunate enough to call out a number that equalled the sum of the numbers revealed in their hand-signals, they had to drink a slug of shaojiu, a Chinese spirit, which is a distilled liquor rather like vodka.

Between shots, they consumed vast quantities of bottled beer. Empty bottles were flung out of the open windows, vanishing into the countryside. From time to time, they all fell into a drunken stupor, waking only when we slowed down.

They even devised a ritual for my benefit. Whenever the train left a station, they opened their window and yelled out as many English phrases as they knew to anyone foolish enough to listen.

"Helloo!"

"What is this?"

"What is then?"

The startled looks of the passengers waiting on the platform were greeted with raucous laughs. With their trousers fashionably rolled up to their knees, their broken, blackened and rotting teeth and their drunken antics, they made great travelling companions.

When Wei Hua joined the train and sat next to the angel sitting opposite me, my day was made complete. He spoke good English and was keen to help me improve my Mandarin.

When I complimented his spoken English, Wei Hua smiled.

"Do you know who said that *'a foreign language is a weapon in the struggle for life'*?"

"I have no idea."

"Karl Marx." His smile turned into a broad grin.

Thirty-six hours after leaving Turpan Zhan station, the train pulled into Xi'an on time. As I stood up to collect my bag, the beautiful Chinese girl gave me a tantalising half-smile and placed one hand around her chin, curling her fingers as she waved good-bye. The reprobates jumped up to help me fight my way through the melee to get off the train and waved furiously as I left the platform. When at last installed in a modest hotel, I ate an indifferent dinner and surrendered to the seductive powers of a comfortable bed with clean sheets

Chapter 5

The region in which Xi'an stands today was first home to a capital in the eleventh century BC, when the Zhou dynasty established its centre of government on the banks of Fen River, west of present day Xi'an. Because of its location at the head of the Silk Road, the city became the richest city in China.

The prosperity of Xi'an was to reflect the ebb and flow of political power in China over two millennia. Between the fifth and third centuries BC, China was divided into five separate states, until Qin Shi Huang conquered all of them. He united China and became the the first Emperor. He established his capital at Xi'anyang, near present-day Xi'an. His army of terracotta warriors still stands in his tomb in Xi'anyang. Qin had replaced the feudalistic system of the Zhou Dynasty with a centralised, almost bureaucratic system that was imposed with a rod of iron. He also developed a centralised legal system and common forms of writing that reached across the empire. Qin started the construction of what was to become the Great Wall of China.

After his death, a commoner, Liu Pan, led a successful revolt in 206 BC that gave rise to the establishment of the Han dynasty. Four hundred years later, the Han dynasty collapsed and was followed by three more centuries of upheaval.

Xi'an, then known as Chang'an, was built in 582 AD by Wen Ti, first Emperor of the Sui dynasty. The Sui dynasty was replaced by the Tang dynasty in 618 AD. Under the Tang dynasty, Xi'an grew to become the greatest city in Asia, if not the world. Xi'an became a centre of international trade with links to seaports and the main caravan routes. All roads led to Xi'an. The city flourished and developed into a multicultural melting pot of many different languages, religions and ideas.

By the end of the eighth century, Xi'an had a population of two million. When the Tang dynasty finally began its decline, the unified China once again fell apart as warlords and foreign invaders broke up the Empire, disrupting transport networks and tax collection systems.

Xi'an became a regional centre of power and never recovered its former supremacy. It was not until 1930, when a rail link with Zhengzhou was completed, that Xi'an started to expand beyond its position as a minor provincial centre.

Despite this great history, I had no real desire spend time in Xi'an, which after my experiences in the west of China seemed very commercialised and too geared for tourists. I did make the time to visit the Great Mosque, founded in 742, during the Tang Dynasty. Islam had been brought to China along the Silk Road and is believed to have been first introduced in the 7th century AD.

Muslim traders had reached Xi'an and settled, bringing with them ideas and beliefs that challenged the local beliefs based on the nontheistic religions and philosophies such as Buddhism, Taoism and Confucianism. The Silk Road had played its part in the great network of highways that had carried Islam around the world.

In my rush to get to see the Terracotta army, I inadvertently found myself on a local Chinese tour bus. I was the only non-Chinese and was soon adopted by a couple of intellectuals, Yang and Lee, who took me under their wings and acted as my interpreters for the day. Yang was a gynaecologist and Lee a civil engineer.

Half an hour from Xi'an, the soldiers of the Terracotta army stood in an excavated pit as silent witnesses to the passing of the centuries. Protected from the elements inside a hangar-like shed, they faced the visiting masses, who peered at them from a walkway. Guards in green uniforms watched for signs of illegal camera use.

My newfound Chinese friends asked me to join them for lunch. As the food arrived, I pulled out my chopsticks, having been warned of the dangers of catching hepatitis from the wooden, reusable chopsticks provided by most restaurants. Lee started to laugh uncontrollably and grinned at her husband. Seeing my confusion, Lee reached out and held my hand.

"I am sorry; we are not laughing at you, look here."

Lee opened her handbag and extracted a pair of spoons and forks.

"This is the first time that we have eaten with a foreigner. You have chopsticks and we have foreigner spoons and forks. We do not want to get sick either, so we bring our own cutlery. How did you know it was not safe to use these wooden chopsticks?"

She pointed to a pot of used chopsticks in the middle of the table. Never sterilised and shared by many, these chopsticks were the source of many communicable diseases. When we started to eat, Lee told me that she had been worried that I would try to share out the food at the beginning of the meal in European style and was relieved to see me using chopsticks in accordance with Chinese custom.

The conversation moved on to healthcare in China.

"Government workers, including soldiers and factory workers are entitled to free healthcare, but peasants usually have to pay for their healthcare."

We talked about the National Health Service in the United Kingdom. Lee was sceptical that we had a system that was free to all and I suspect that she did not really believe my strange tales of state-funded healthcare in a capitalist country.

The heat rose to around 37°C with almost one hundred per cent humidity. By the end of the day, my clothes glistened with salt crystals and chafed my skin until I could barely walk.

Chapter 6

Having had enough of Xi'an, I decided to leave and take the train to Beijing, a relatively short journey of twenty hours. The booking office clerk told me that I could only get a hard seat, as all other classes of travel were fully booked. Mentally, I tried to prepare myself for a long, uncomfortable ride. Covered in plastic, the hard backed seats were as comfortable as church pews. There were 120 seats in the carriage and they were all occupied. Thirty more people were standing or squatting in the narrow passage between the seats. Two middle-aged Chinese women caught my eye and made enough space for me to sit down next to them. I could not have thanked them enough.

As the train waited to leave the station, I was almost suffocated by the rank, still atmosphere of the carriage. The smell of unwashed bodies, cigarette smoke and soot made the air taste like a warm, rancid soup that almost made me choke. Looking around at the placid, almost resigned faces of my newfound travelling companions, I appeared to have been alone in noticing the stench.

The reality was that most of them were just grateful to be on a train heading for Beijing. Once I realised this, I was equally thankful, so I put my sensibilities to one side and settled down to enjoy the journey.

Even when the train was moving, the heat and humidity inside the carriage formed a sauna-like atmosphere and my skin began to leak water like a sponge. Rivulets of sweat ran down my face and dripped off the end of my nose. I tried writing, but had to stop, as I could not stop the rivers of perspiration from dripping onto my notebook.

Around me, the sight of seasoned Chinese travellers sipping mugs of steaming hot tea reminded me of the need to keep my fluid balance under control.

As I produced my enamelled tea mug and a pack of dried tea, my neighbours gave me approving glances. After filling my mug from the boiler at the end of the corridor, I brewed up and when my tea had cooled slightly, began to drink.

With experimentation, I realised that I could tell when I was getting dehydrated. I stopped sweating, my skin began to feel dry and I started to feel unwell. Fifteen minutes after drinking a half a pint of tepid tea, I started to feel better and my skin started leaking again.

I had read that the Chinese say that Europeans smell of milk and had never really understood why they would think this. After eight hours of sitting in the unrelenting heat and fetid air, I began to smell of sour milk. The smell emanated from every pore and even washing would not make it go away. The smell could not have been caused by my diet as I had eaten only Chinese food since leaving the Pakistan border town of Sust.

Above our heads was a rail on which the experienced travellers hung their flannels. Some also had wash bags containing toothbrushes, toothpaste and soap that they tied to the rail. They also had enamel mugs with lids in which they brewed tea and a fistful of small change to buy snacks from the hawkers who came to the carriage windows at every stop offering hard-boiled eggs, newspaper twists packed with sunflower seeds, fruit, cigarettes, soft drinks, cakes and bottles of warm beer. I watched and learned.

Each carriage was supervised by an attendant who monitored the behaviour of the passengers and kept the floor clean with regular brushing and mopping. When the carriage was not too full, he cleaned the floor on the hour. This was a thankless task as most travellers thought nothing of dropping their rubbish, spittle and sunflower seed cases onto the floor as soon as his back was turned.

A complaints book hung on a string at the end of the carriage, but no one paid it any attention. Every now and again, a grim-faced attendant forced a trolley along the passage between the seats selling cigarettes, books, soft and alcoholic drinks and even rice-based meals in polystyrene trays.

As all the electric fans in the carriage were broken, most of the windows were opened as far as possible. This forced some fresh air into the carriage. There was one downside. Smoke from the coal-fired steam engine was drawn into the carriage and after a few hours, my sodden shirt was covered in specks of soot.

When night fell, I tried to sleep sitting upright, but could not find a comfortable position despite being exhausted and the gentle rocking movement of the train. The people standing in the passage between the rows of seat were packed in so tightly that there was no room for me to lie down. Even the luggage racks were full.

In desperation, I wrapped myself in a blanket and lay down on the floor under the seats. For a few hours, I slept like a baby. The other occupants of the carriage thought I was just a crazy foreigner and perhaps, they were right. When the train screeched to a juddering halt in a station, one of my friendly middle-aged women woke me up and chastised me for not keeping a closer eye on my bags in the luggage rack. Suitably chastened, I crawled back into my seat.

Little, by little, the rivulets of sweat trickling down my body seeped into the fabric of my shorts. Before long, I could feel the movement of the train driving the salt-encrusted cloth into the soggy mess that had been my skin. The more I poured fluid down my throat, the more it seeped out of my pores and soaked into my shorts. What started as a feeling of discomfort slowly developed into pain. The lack of space meant that I could not shift my body position at all, which might have eased the misery a little.

Twenty hours after leaving Xi'an, the train pulled into Beijing on time at exactly 11:28. I had never been so happy to see the end of a train journey and escape the claustrophobic, steamy atmosphere of the carriage as quickly as I could.

Beijing station was vast and crowded with travellers from all over China. Most were weighed down by bulging suitcases, packing cases and bundles wrapped in cloth. Men, women and children lay in exhausted heaps all over the concourse, waiting patiently for trains that would transport them to a new life.

Every train arriving disgorged another wave of country folk and their families looking for a better life somewhere else. Most seemed a little intimidated by the strident announcements coming from the public address system and the sheer scale of the building.

This movement of Mao's army of workers and peasants from the rural areas towards the cities and the promise of future prosperity was part of the greatest rural-urban migrations in human history. In the thirty years following 1979, China's urban population grew by 440 million. Around 340 million of this growth was attributable to migration. This was urbanisation on an unprecedented scale.

Many were to migrate to the Special Economic Zones set up by Deng Xiaoping. In these Zones, foreign investment flowed without the restraints of the past. Little by little, capitalism was beginning to develop and thrive in what had been one of the greatest strongholds of communism.

From the railway station, I took a bus and ended up at the Long Tan Hotel, which was not far from the city centre. This was a good place to for me to rest and recuperate after the long journey across China.

In the privacy of my room, I undressed and inspected the damage. The skin on my backside and upper thighs was red, blotchy, blistered and in places, chafed raw. Essentially, I was suffering from what looked just like nappy rash.

I slept like a baby for the rest of the day, face down, to give the tattered skin on my buttocks a chance to dry out and heal. That night, I took a bus into the centre of Beijing and failed to find anywhere to eat in a sterile jungle of concrete and glass edifices. I hobbled back and found somewhere to eat near the hotel. As soon as I could, I went straight back to bed. For two days, I stayed in the hotel and let my skin recover. Only then did I feel that I was ready to explore Beijing.

I soon discovered that the best way to get around Beijing was by bicycle, which was also a good way to get a little cool breeze across my face. The only bicycle to be seen in Beijing was the famous Flying Pigeon, made by the Tianjin Flying Pigeon Bicycle Company. The sturdy tubular frame with rim brakes, a full chain cover, a double stand and a carrier over the rear wheel was just like my mother's old bicycle, which had been made in England in the 1940's.

The hotel was happy to rent me a Flying Pigeon and I was soon en route for Tiananmen Square. Not far from the hotel, I discovered that the bicycle had an annoying fault. The steel used to make the cotter pins was too soft. Consequently, the crank arm was not fixed properly to the bottom bracket. Every turn of the pedal included a slight jump as the slack was taken up. The more I pedalled, the more the cotter pin gave way and the greater the slack. This made cycling more difficult than it should have been.

At most street corners, I noticed groups of bicycle repairmen waiting for cyclists needing someone to mend punctures, replace worn-out cotter pins or fix any other mechanical problem. This was a good business, as punctures were commonplace and the cotter pins were so badly made that they wore out in a matter of hours. Stopping at one of these roadside workshops, I asked them to replace my worn-out cotter pins. They hammered out the old pins and replaced them with new pins in a matter of minutes, sending me on my way with a wave and a smile.

Joining the throng of riders in the cycle-lanes running parallel to the almost empty boulevards, I pedalled past the Temple of Heaven and soon found myself in a vast open space in front of the Forbidden City. This was Tiananmen Square.

To the south was the Zhengyangmen Gatehouse, which once guarded the southern entry into the Inner City, a solid pagoda-like structure with a tiled roof first built in 1419 during the Ming dynasty.

Not far from the gatehouse, in the centre of Tiananmen Square, a long line of pilgrims stood in the sun outside Mao Zedong's mausoleum, waiting patiently in silence to see his embalmed remains.

To the west, the Great Hall of the People, used as the meeting place of the People's National Congress, was a massive structure that occupied more land than the Forbidden City. Built in ten months by volunteers, it was then one of modern China's most impressive buildings.

To the North, the Tiananmen Gate, or Gate of Heavenly Peace, stood guard over the entrance to the Imperial City, serving as a reminder of the Emperors of the past.

Above the main entrance, a large picture of Chairman Mao looked out across Tiananmen Square, leaving visitors with no doubt that China belonged to a new generation of leaders.

Beyond this entrance, I found myself facing the Meridian Gate, which guards the entrance to the Forbidden City. For centuries, this gate concealed the lives of the Emperors from the people of China.

As I stood before the Meridian Gate, I paused to reflect on the last of these Emperors, "Henry" P'u Yi.

In his lifetime, China abandoned the monarchy, became a Republic governed by warlords, was invaded by the Japanese and then after a bloody civil war, became a People's Republic, governed by the Communist Party of China.

Imprisoned for much of his early life in the Forbidden City, the last Emperor of China, P'u Yi was never in a position to stop China from ending two thousand years of monarchy. He had been born on the wrong side of history.

P'u Yi became Emperor of China in 1908 at the age of two years and ten months. His father, Prince Chun became Prince Regent and in three years tried to implement economic and political reforms in response to the Boxer Rebellion. He was only partly successful and in the end was not strong enough to drive through the changes that were needed. After three years, he stepped down. He was replaced by his sister-in-law, Empress Dowager Longyu.

P'u Yi was too young to be concerned by any of this and was anyway more interested in toys, games and the affections of his nursemaid. Despite being a child, he was treated as a god and everywhere he went grown men kowtowed to him and averted their eyes. Neglected by his mother, he was waited on by over a thousand eunuchs, who he later described as his "slaves and teachers."

Isolated from the rest of China in the Forbidden City, P'u Yi knew nothing of the wind of change that was sweeping across the country. He was Emperor in name only.

In 1911, eighteen provinces rebelled against the monarchy and a Republic was declared. As many of generals had allied themselves with the rebellion, the government was unable to react. P'u Yi was forced to abdicate at the age of six, but was allowed to remain in the Forbidden City.

Unseen by the rest of the Republic of China, the pomp and ceremony of the Imperial Court was maintained and he continued to live in ignorance of the real world. He briefly became Emperor again in 1917, when the warlord Zhang Xun occupied Beijing. This time P'u Yi was forced to abdicate after just twelve days.

Reginald Johnston, a Scotsman, was appointed tutor to P'u Yi in 1919, when P'u Yi was thirteen years old. Johnston was one of only two foreigners allowed in the Inner Court of the Forbidden City.

Johnston was to become a firm friend of P'u Yi and helped him choose the nickname "Henry," which he selected from a list of English kings. For the rest of his life, the child who became an Emperor was known as Henry P'u Yi in the West.

A year after his first marriage in 1922, he began to take control of the palace. The eunuchs resented this attempt to reduce their power and began to plot against P'u Yi. In revenge, he expelled them from the Forbidden City.

When Feng Yuxiang, a warlord, forced P'u Yi to leave the Forbidden City in 1924, he sought refuge in the Japanese Embassy and in 1925, moved to the Japanese Concession in Tianjin. Over the years that followed, he tried to cajole the Japanese into helping him win back the throne. Instead of helping him, they sought to use him to their advantage.

This was the Warlord Era, during which China was divided into regions by warring factions and cliques. Chiang Kai-shek, leader of the Kuomintang (KMT) or Nationalist Party emerged as China's nominal leader in 1926. A year later, the Nationalist Party split from the Communist Party of China and yet another civil war broke out.

In 1932, the Japanese saw how they could make use of P'u Yi and installed him as ruler of Manchukuo, which served as a puppet state of the Empire of Japan in modern northeast China and Inner Mongolia.

When the Japanese invaded China five years later, the Nationalist Party and the Communist Party of China agreed a truce so that they could join forces against the Japanese. The reality was that neither side trusted the other and when world war II ended, the civil war resumed.

At end of WWII, P'u Yi was captured by the Soviet Red Army and taken to a sanatorium in the Siberian town of Chita. Eventually, he was moved to Khabarovsk, just 19 miles from the Chinese border. In 1946, he was called testify in Tokyo against Japanese war criminals at the International Military Tribunal for the Far East. His testimony revealed a man who believed that he had been treated as a puppet by the Japanese. In later life, he would admit that he had supported the Japanese in their quest to dominate China.

With hindsight, it is hard to see any time in his life up to that point when he had not been someone's puppet. His eviction of the eunuchs from the Forbidden City may have been the only decision he made there for his own benefit.

In 1948, the Communist Party of China defeated the Nationalist party and Chiang fled to Taiwan. A few months later, in 1949, Mao Zedong proclaimed the foundation of the People's Republic of China, a one-party socialist state controlled by the Communist Party. The land reforms that he enacted took land from feudal landowners and divided it into people's communes.

P'u Yi was not to return to China until 1949. His repatriation was the result of delicate negotiations between the Chinese and Soviet governments. P'u Yi then spent ten years in the Fushun War Criminals Management Centre undergoing re-education that continued until the authorities thought that he had been reformed. In 1960, P'u Yi was pardoned by Mao and made a citizen of the state.

His journey from riches to rags had been long and hard. The fact that he had survived at all may have been a reflection of Mao's unshakeable belief in the ideals underlying China's Revolution of the People. He believed that any reactionary could be reformed, even a man who had been an Emperor.

On his release, P'u Yi worked as a gardener in the Beijing Botanical Gardens and openly supported the Communists. He survived the Cultural Revolution with the help of the Public Security Bureau, which had been instructed by Mao to protect him from those who wished him harm.

P'u Yi had survived one of the most tumultuous periods in Chinese history. In one lifetime, he had lived as the Emperor, been accused of treason, made ruler of a puppet state by the Japanese, become a gardener and ended his life as editor of the literary department of Chinese People's Political Consultative Conference. He died in 1967 at the age of 61.

As an old man, he must have understood that the Forbidden City had to be preserved as a reminder of the gulf that had existed between the Emperors and the workers. It is also a testament to the architects, craftsmen and workers who built what is now recognised as one of the wonders of the world.

Passing through the Meridian Gate, I entered the Inner Court, which was packed with hundreds of Chinese citizens and a handful of foreign tourists. Tour groups scurried from palace to palace, chasing after their flag-waving uniformed guides armed with megaphones. Like an army of manic Pied Pipers, the guides rushed their followers around the Inner Court leaving behind nothing but litter and the fading echoes of their passing.

One guide trotted past me with a loudspeaker that played "God Save the Queen" in double time. He was being chased across the Inner Court by a group of flustered Chinese tourists.

For an hour or so, I explored the Forbidden City and soon realised that it was just too vast for me to explore in a single visit. I decided to try again in the morning, when it would be cooler and perhaps less crowded.

Back in Tiananmen Square, I joined the Chinese tourists milling around aimlessly in the humid air. A few wore Mao suits, many more were dressed in Western-style clothes. White shirts and blue trousers were worn by the more fashionable women, who shaded their delicate pale skins under coloured umbrellas. The fashionable young men wore flared trousers, shoes with high heels and smoked endlessly. The atmosphere was peaceful and relaxed, perhaps even a little sleepy. It was time to find something to do that did not take much effort.

The straggly beard that I had grown in Pakistan had become increasingly uncomfortable in the heat and humidity of Beijing, so I decided that it was time for me to get a proper shave in a Chinese barber-shop.

I found one close to the railway station. The barber was a bald, thickset man with a serious expression. He started by lathering my face with shaving cream and after letting it soften my beard for a few minutes, began to shave me with a cut-throat razor. He started with my chin and cheeks, which was fine. He then shaved my nose. This was a surprise.

Next, he shaved my forehead, ears and between my eyebrows. My eyes then widened in horror as he moved the razor towards my right eyeball and shaved my eyelid. The shock of seeing the edge of the blade so close to my eye was enough to stop me breathing. Time froze as he expertly scraped away whatever hair grew on my eyelids.

With a final flourish, he scraped off the last remnants of shaving cream and wrapped my face in a scalding hot towel to open up my pores. After a few minutes inside the hot towel, he massaged scented lotions and oils into my face. He then washed my hair and then kept on cutting until I thought that he had done enough. He rubbed more lotions into my scalp and then massaged my head, neck and shoulders. By the time he had finished I was so relaxed that I did not want to move.

Back on my bicycle, I observed signs of the growing influence of Western culture in China. The most intriguing was the Kentucky Fried Chicken outlet not far from Tiananmen Square. The juxtaposition of the pictures of Colonel Saunders and Chairman Mao was perhaps the most poignant symbol of the changes that were taking place in China in 1987.

The sight of Colonel Saunders made me think of food, but not Kentucky Fried Chicken. As most of the food that I had seen on my journey to Beijing had been basic country-fare, made to satisfy the needs of hungry people rather than the sophisticated palates of the diners of the capital of China, I was looking forward to the culinary delights of Beijing. It did not take me long to discover that the "North capital" had some excellent restaurants serving every style of Chinese cuisine.

A recommendation from the hotel manager led me to the Quanjude restaurant, which had been serving Peking duck for centuries. The delicacy of the meat was complemented by the personal service provided by the waitress, who shredded the duck at the table and then used her chopsticks to keep me supplied throughout the meal with shredded duck, sliced spring onion, cucumber and hoisin sauce rolled up in a wafer thin rice pancake. This was a meal to remember.

After eating, I cycled back to Tiananmen Square to watch the Chinese national flag being taken down in a simple ceremony as the sun slid into the haze to the west.

Three soldiers marched out of their barracks in the Forbidden City, through the unbroken stream of bicycles on Dongchan'au Jie and onto Tiananmen Square, where they took the flag down with a minimum of formality and then marched back to their barracks.

As soon as the ceremony had finished, I bumped into an Englishman who introduced himself as William Lyndsay. Coincidently, he was also staying at the Long Tan hotel. He recommended a visit to the Bell pub at the British Embassy.

We made for the bar and ordered two beers. As fast as I poured cold Beijing beer down my throat, it seeped out again through my pores, but it was like nectar of the Gods.

After a few more beers, William shared his plans with me.

"I am trying to run the length of the Great Wall of China. A few years ago, I ran the length of Hadrian's Wall, so the Great Wall of China seemed like the next thing to do. The problem is that most of the Wall is in territory that is still closed."

He explained that after he had been running for about six months, he the PSB had arrested him and thrown him out of China for trespassing in an area closed to foreigners without a permit. He had taken a flight to Hong Kong, picked up another visa and flown straight back.

"This time," he explained, "I am going to try to get the British Embassy to help me get permission to finish the run. I am off to meet someone senior from the Embassy tomorrow at the Jiangou hotel. Why don't you come with me?"

I could not refuse this offer. It was also an opportunity to see what five-star luxury looked like in communist China.

The British Embassy Bell pub staff asked us to leave at 01:30 in the morning. Cycling back to the hotel through the near-deserted streets of Beijing in the early hours of the morning was an experience that made me realise that I was a lucky man. While the main boulevards were deserted, the pavements of the smaller streets were crowded with thousands of people, many sleeping on beds that they had carried down from their apartments. These were not homeless people, but people driven out of their homes by the heat and humidity.

In the morning, I cycled to the Zhongsan Park just southwest of the Forbidden City. Among the gardens, pavilions and bamboo groves, I found a group of people practising Wushu. They were being coached by a teacher who quietly, but firmly corrected their errors with the occasional grunt or nod of encouragement.

Two young women were being taught a series of movements using a Jian, a double-edged straight sword. I watched them from the XiLi Ting pavilion for half an hour bewitched by the controlled power and grace of their stabbing, slashing and percussive cuts.

The following day, William and I cycled back into the centre of Beijing to meet the "important man" from the British Embassy who had offered to help and advise him.

"Apparently he is both Counsellor and Head of Chancery. This means that he is a senior diplomat ranking just behind the Ambassador."

After the steamy heat of Beijing, it was a pleasure to step into the cool, air-conditioned lobby of the five star Jiangou hotel, a joint-venture hotel built in 1982 and managed by the British Peninsula Group. The service was impeccable.

William and I sat in the Greenery coffee lounge to wait for William's "man from the embassy." A few minutes later, a tall, distinguished English man arrived and came straight over to where we were sitting. I recognised him straightway. He smiled and shook my hand.

"Hello Chris! Good to see you again. How are you?" He turned to William and explained that we had to talk about my journey from Kashgar before we could start discussing his run along the Great Wall of China.

It was Peter Thompson, last seen at the old Russian Consulate in Kashgar. William looked at us in astonishment.

"You know each other?"

Before we could talk about William's plans, we discussed my overland journey from Kashgar to Beijing and western China in general. Peter also gave me an update on Fiona and Bindy. After flying directly to Beijing from Urumqi, they had stayed with the Thompsons for a while and had then left to fly back to England. We agreed that they had flown over one of the most interesting regions in China.

William coughed gently to remind us both that he was keen to talk about his plans to complete his journey along the Great Wall of China and that he knew that Peter would have to get back to the Embassy before too long. Peter was very happy to offer his advice and promised to see what could be done to help William complete his run.

Before he left, Peter invited us to visit the Embassy and join the Beijing Hash House Harriers on their weekly run.

William at least could run. I have never really enjoyed running, but as the invitation included joining the Hash House Harriers for a beer in the Bell after the run, I was forced to promise to come along and do my pathetic best.

The Hash House Harriers started in what was then the Federated Malay States in 1938, when a group of British colonial officers and expatriates began meeting on Monday evenings for a run to help them recover from the excesses of the weekend. Traditionally, Hares set a trail for the Pack of Hounds. Ironically, the culmination of a run was typically another session of beer drinking. Hash House Harriers are now found all over the world and the sport of Hashing is always open to all comers.

Our Hares set a trail that took us out of the Embassy and straight into the unpaved back streets of Beijing. The rain had been falling all day long, leaving muddy puddles through which we splashed with enthusiasm.

The downpour had turned the road surface into a sticky morass that sucked the strength out of my legs. The muscles in my thighs and calves ached and every step became harder than the last. At this point, I began to struggle to breathe and found the heat and humidity almost overpowering. This was why I had never enjoyed running.

Just as I was about to stop to catch my breath, I looked up and saw that the street was lined by hundreds of local people who cheered and clapped as we passed. The sound of their encouragement gave me the strength needed to keep running. The trail eventually led us across Tiananmen Square.

I still cannot imagine what the Chinese tourists made of the sudden appearance of some very bedraggled, muddy Westerners running through the very heart of Beijing.

The trail led us back to the Bell pub, where I eventually caught up with William. Unlike me, he did not look as if he felt that he was about to die.

With the last of my remaining energy, I crawled into the bar where some kind soul placed a glass of cold beer into my hand. The glass emptied itself in an instant. I completed my return to the world of the living by slipping into the swimming pool. The rain stopped and the sun began to shine.

Later, William and I sat in the sun and talked about adventure.

"Why are you running along the Great Wall of China?"

"Because no one else has done it. I want to be the first person to run the whole length of the Great Wall of China. What are your plans?"

"I am heading for Tibet and plan to explore the route that Francis Younghusband took when he led the British Mission to Lhasa in 1903-1904. The Mission marched into Tibet through the Chumbi valley from what is now Sikkim."

He handed me another beer and I continued.

"The Chumbi valley also has a reputation as being a place where the yeti has been seen. As a biologist, I thought that it would also be interesting to see what kind of place the yeti is supposed to live."

"So you are going to be a yeti hunter?" He laughed and drank some more beer.

"Well, I am looking for some adventure and I want to visit a part of the Tibet that has not really been seen by Westerners since the Chinese moved into Tibet. But I do like the idea of being a Yeti hunter! Why not?"

The matter was decided.

In my father's time, most young men were exposed to more excitement than they needed in the battlefields of Europe and the Far East. My generation was lucky enough not have had to fight in a world war, but the downside of this was that our lives lacked adventure and challenge.

One small adventure to the edge of the Tibetan plateau paled in to insignificance when compared with the challenges faced by my father's generation, but some adventure is always better than no adventure.

Through William, I met Stephen Nisbet, a Reuter's correspondent based in Beijing. Over a beer, we talked about the idea of me looking for signs of the Younghusband Mission and going to the edge of the Tibet plateau. In the end, he agreed that it was an interesting idea, made more interesting to him by the "Yeti" angle, which had been dreamed up over a couple of beers.

He wrote a short article about my plans that was picked up by the local newspaper in Gloucester, where my parents lived. The article that they printed must have brought a smile to many of my old school friends. The Mirror newspaper also dedicated a column inch of newsprint to an article that described me as an explorer facing the risk of seduction by saggy breasted, sex mad female Yetis. My mother must have been so proud of me.

Once I had decided that I was going to be a Yeti hunter, I felt that it was time to explore more of Beijing before I left. Each day I hired a bicycle and set out on to see the sights. Cycling was easy as the roads were good and there was very little traffic. On some major roads, cyclists had a dedicated lane that kept them safe from other road users. While the bicycle lanes were full of cyclists, the other lanes were mostly empty. The traffic that there was consisted of buses; taxis; shiny black government saloon cars for the high-ranking cadre; and the occasional police vehicle. I saw almost no private cars.

Joining the many thousands of local cyclists on my hired Flying Pigeon, I made full use of the opportunity to explore the older quarters of Beijing. Each one served as a stage on which so much of the lives of the people of Beijing were played out. There were street markets selling all kinds of goods: plastic toys; tomatoes; watermelons; preserved eggs; hawkers selling crickets in baskets woven from bamboo; food stalls and even one old man in a straw-hat "fishing" for crickets in a tree lined avenue There were more market stalls than shops.

The sight of beautifully dressed children being cared for by their adoring grandparents, while their parents worked, was a reminder that the one child per family law was creating a generation of spoilt Little Emperors and Empresses.

Given the heat and humidity, those who could, escaped the sweltering heat of their homes and moved on to the pavements where they cooked on charcoal stoves, ate, talked and played cards or mah-jong. Most homes lacked air conditioning and in any case, the electricity supply was so unreliable that even those who could afford air conditioning suffered as much as anyone else did.

Men in flared trousers or shorts, high-heeled sandals, string vests, blue cotton shorts and dark silk socks sat on the curb smoking homemade cigarettes, drinking beer and playing cards. Some of the younger men quarrelled and some just slept. Grandparents lay on bedsteads, with their grandchildren, babies and young children, curled up beside them. Most of the women sat together in groups and gossiped. As night fell, families slept together in a tangled web of string vests, shorts and frilly dresses. The sense of community spirit was tangible. The atmosphere was that of a vast, unplanned street party.

When I explored the Forbidden City again, I was fascinated by the sense of space created by this world within a world. This was a miniature city, hidden behind massive walls, which in turn were hidden by inner walls, all of which had been built to keep the Imperial Emperors and their people apart.

Living behind walls seems to have played a big part in the psyche of the Chinese, from the sprawling walled compounds of the western deserts and the Great Wall of China, built to keep China safe from the Mongolian armies of Genghis Khan.

Construction of the Great Wall started nearly two and a half thousand years ago when Qin Shi Huang unified China. He constructed a wall designed to protect China against the nomadic Xiongnu people from the North. Over the centuries, the wall was variously extended, left to decay and renovated by the Han, Sui and Northern dynasties.

In the 13th century, the Ming Dynasty perfected the art of wall building, using bricks and stone instead of packed earth and board frames. The Great Wall of China became a complex network that stretched as far the Jiayuguan Pass to the West and Shanhaiguan in the East. According to some researchers, over 21,000 kilometres of wall sections were built.

William Lyndsay's run along the length of the main sections of the wall was to cover a distance of some 2,470 kilometres, a feat that no other foreigner had accomplished.

Leaving William to continue his run along the wall, I took a train south to Wuhan, capital of the Hubei province. Knowing that

Wuhan was located at the intersection of the middle reaches of the Yangtze and Han rivers, I was sure that I would be able to find a boat to take me down the Yangtze River to Shanghai. This would take me along the route travelled by my dear Uncle Lawrence in 1949 in very different circumstances.

He had been a signaller in the Royal Navy and in 1949 was serving on HMS Amethyst, a WWII vintage frigate. On 20 April, HMS Amethyst sailed from Shanghai to Nanking to rescue British and Commonwealth families from the fighting between nationalist and communist forces. En route, the Amethyst was attacked by the guns of the People's Liberation Army and trapped for just over three two months. Despite being hit by over fifty shells, HMS Amethyst managed to survive and slipped away from the Chinese batteries at night in a daring escape that ended in a 104-mile dash for freedom.

Lawrence was proud of the fact that he had been baptised twice. He had been christened when he was in the Royal Navy. Years later, he discovered that he had also been baptised as child by his foster parents. He always maintained that he thought that he probably needed two baptisms given the life that he had lived. The man I knew was one who could do no wrong. He was kind, had a great sense of humour and always lived life to the full.

Chapter 7

Having learned my lesson the hard way on the journey from Xi'an to Beijing, I booked myself into a hard sleeper for the overnight journey to Wuhan. Following the details printed on my ticket, I headed down the platform and found my carriage.

The carriage was divided into eleven open compartments, each of which had six bunks, with three bunks on each side. A narrow corridor ran down one side of the carriage, with single fold down seats that could not be used until people stopped searching for their berths.

Luckily, I had been booked in one of the middle bunks. This was the best place to be as the top bunks had very little headroom and the bottom bunks tended to be used by everyone as a seat.

As I found my compartment, I was greeted by two balding middle-aged men with paunches, who were sitting on the bottom bunk. With broad grins and dressed in matching faded blue shorts, string vests and open toed sandals, they looked like a pair of migrating farm workers.

Despite having been engaged in an animated conversation when I turned up, they were both eager to help me check my ticket and confirmed that I was indeed booked in the middle bunk. They both spoke excellent English, which surprised me. The tallest helped me lift my bag onto my bunk. They then invited me to join them on the lower bunk. A tall man with a thin face, who I later discovered was a doctor, claimed the other bottom bunk and stretched out so that he could read his newspaper.

I asked the other two what they did for a living. This caused them both to giggle uncontrollably and for a moment, neither of them could speak. The shorter of the two managed to stop giggling long enough to catch his breath and speak.

"We are professors!"

They both roared with laughter again. Neither the doctor nor I could see what was so funny. They eventually were able to explain that they were leading a project to compile a dictionary of technical Chinese and Japanese hydraulic terms and it became clear that this was why they had been laughing.

"How long have you been working on this?"

My question triggered another fit of giggles.

"Ten years!"

They tried hard to be serious for a moment and took a second or two to wipe the tears out of their eyes. The smaller professor told me a little more about their work.

"We have a team of three hundred working on the project. We are now also working on a three-way translation of Chinese, Japanese and English scientific words and terms for another dictionary."

He paused and a look of despair clouded his eyes.

"The trouble is that we have now been given a finishing date. We have to finish in two years."

His colleague explained that as fast they translated words, new words appeared and they needed to find out what these words meant, which was a time-consuming task at the best of times.

"We have no computers, just thirty metres of filing cards full of technical terms that we have translated and cross referenced to other technical terms."

Our conversation rambled on through the evening and I soon understood that their sponsors were keen to see the end of their project. In fact, they were getting increasingly impatient. I soon gathered that the word 'urgency' was one that the team had not yet discovered.

Night fell and it was soon time to turn in. I clambered into my bunk and slipped into a deep, dreamless sleep. The motion of the train rocked me gently and carried me southwards to the great Yangtze River.

As we neared Wuhan, my fellow passengers started to get ready to leave the train. The commotion woke me up and gave me just enough time to drink a mug of green tea with the professors. Around us, I could see towels and flannels being repacked and the lower bunks filling up with passengers impatient for the journey to end.

Again, the train arrived on time and all too soon, it was time to say goodbye to my new friends. I gave them my best wishes for a successful end to their project. Their grins gave me the impression that their plan was to find new ways of delaying the completion of their work for as long as they possibly could. I shook their hands and we parted company in the melee of passengers disembarking in Wuhan.

Within seconds of leaving Wuhan station with my luggage hanging off my shoulder, I was again drenched in sweat. Trickles of perspiration ran down my cheeks, dripped off the end of my nose and chin, ran down my chest and collected in the small of my back.

With the help of a crude map drawn by the professors, I headed towards the centre of Wuhan in search of the Aiguo hotel.

The further I walked, the more I began to believe that my skin would never stop leaking and that I would never again be able to move without getting soaked. The heat drained the energy from my legs and made each breath harder than the last. Wandering through the back streets, I came across a hawker selling fizzy drinks from a stall he had laid out on the pavement.

When he saw me, he waved me over to join him. I could see that he was standing with a small crowd in front of a barred window. Inside, I could just make out the shadowy figure of a balding, sorry-looking man in his fifties. Intrigued, I crossed the road to see what had attracted this crowd of onlookers.

The hawker took me by the arm and pointed to what I first took to be a political poster with a large official seal on the wall next to the window. A passer-by who spoke English explained that the prisoner was a criminal who was soon to be executed.

When the condemned man realised that I knew who he was, he once again mimed being shot in the head and grinned at me. He was taking it all very well and seemed to be enjoying his celebrity status.

The hawker had realised that he could use my arrival to boost his sales. His aim seemed to be to keep the bystanders lingering in the heat of the sun long enough to develop a thirst and buy his sugary drinks.

With great theatre, he introduced me to the gathering crowd as if we were lifelong friends. Although I could not speak Mandarin, it was easy for me to guess what he was saying. I had become his stooge.

"Ladies and gentlemen, I would like you to meet my new friend, this giant of a foreigner. As you can see, he is not only tall, but also has an enormous nose."

He pointed to my nose and compared it with his more refined Chinese nose. The crowd gave a murmur of approval. The drink seller paused to sell a few more drinks and started again.

"The thing about foreign devils is that they all very hairy. Just look his legs."

He pulled at the hairs on my thigh and invited the people in the crowd to do the same. They were inquisitive but gentle. He then turned his attention to my size twelve feet and showed how they dwarfed his tiny feet.

"You see how big his feet are? See how much bigger they are than Chinese feet?"

Several members of the crowd measured their feet against mine, creating a ripple of laughter that ran through the crowd.

He held up one of my hands against his to show that I was indeed a freak of nature.

"Look at his hands! They are enormous and you all know what that means…"

He pointed at my groin and drew a murmur of approval from his audience.

Continuing in a more vulgar vein, he drew guffaws of laughter from the crowd at my expense and sold more drinks. As it was just good-hearted ribbing, I did not mind.

The hawker was making the best of the opportunity to make a profit provided by the sight of a condemned man and a Westerner in the same place. The drinks sold well and after half an hour, he had almost nothing left to sell.

With the performance at an end, the crowd gradually melted away. To celebrate his good fortune, the hawker gave me his last bottle of green sugar water and thanked me for helping him have a very successful morning.

I said goodbye to the doomed man who grinned and waved again as I turned away, leaving him to his fate.

Due to what must have been a misunderstanding on my part, I ended up walking around Wuhan for three hours. The hotel was close to a railway station, but one on the other side of the Yangtze. By the time I found a bus to take me over the river, found the Aiguo hotel and checked in, I was exhausted and a sodden mess.

Even though the hotel had seen better times, my room was well equipped. I had an en suite bathroom with a bath and a shower. For once, both hot and cold-water taps worked and there was even a plug in the hand basin. The ceiling fan worked and turned languidly in the thick, humid air, creating just a hint of a breeze. The bed was comfortable and sheets were white and clean. There was even a television.

A smell of damp hung in the air and the tiled floor sweated profusely, but after another night on a train, the room was just perfect

After a refreshing cold shower and a few cups of green tea, I began to feel to start to feel human again.

The professor and his colleague had shown me more of a side of China that I had not really seen in my travels across the west of the country. They represented the educated classes who had suffered during the Cultural Revolution. This was a time when scientists and academics had been subject to purges and long periods of "re-education" designed to awaken their political awareness.

During this period, the number of papers published in scientific journals fell dramatically. Instead of working on the development of knowledge, many scientists and academics had been forced to work in the fields.

I had read an article in an English language paper reporting that the generation of scientists and academics who had survived that period were dying much younger than workers of the same age. The Chinese researchers had suggested that this was because of the depredations that they had endured in their youth.

Leaving the hotel early enough in the morning to miss the heat of the day, I found a small café in a side street in the old centre of Wuhan. Breakfast was being cooked in a large wok by a round-faced cook toiling in the gloom of a grimy kitchen. He started by covering the inside of the wok with a rice flour and mung bean batter. A cupful of beaten eggs was added next and spread in a thin layer over the batter. The cook then added cubes of fried tofu. On top of this, he dribbled a generous portion of fried chopped ginger, garlic and chives. Next was a thick layer of glutinous rice, spread evenly over the batter and egg base.

With great care, he trickled cooking oil under the batter and cooked the pancake until it was crispy. He then turned it over and cooked it on the other side.

The cook divided the pancake into bite-sized blocks and then placed four blocks in my bowl. The outer layer was crispy and the inside soft. This was the famous Wuhan "doupi" breakfast. I could not have had a better start to the day.

The cook watched me eat and grinned when he saw that I was enjoying my breakfast. I thanked him in Mandarin and set out to explore Wuhan. Before long, I found myself in a farmers' market where people from the countryside came to sell their produce.

One man had marked out his stall with an old sack that he had laid out on the pavement. He was selling bags stuffed with live green and buff coloured frogs. They looked delicious and he was doing a roaring trade.

Nearby, two young couples had set up a stall selling five different types of preserved eggs. Each batch of eggs was encased in a mixture of clay, ash, quicklime and rice husks. The colour of each coating of each batch was different and buyers could choose their flavour of choice.

A woman at another stall squatted on a low stool and was filleting an eel that she had just killed. In front of her was an ever-widening pool of eel blood and entrails. Beyond that were plastic bowls full of live eels. Her foot held down a short, bloody plank with a six inch nail protruding from the end furthest away from her.

I watched as she grabbed an eel out of the bowl and then impaled its head on the spike. In one motion, she slit the eel from head to tail and scraped out both the innards and its backbone, which she dropped onto a bloody heap between her feet. She threw the still writhing fillets into an enamel bowl. As far as I could tell, she was preparing the fillets to order, which helped ensure that they were fresh.

Food stalls offered snacks to feed both stallholders and shoppers. Trays of boiled chickens and their internal organs were waiting to be served with a spicy sauce with beans and fresh tomatoes. Elsewhere, bowls of Wuhan's hot dry noodles were being prepared. Cooked noodles had been mixed with oil and then dried. When a customer appeared, the noodles were scalded in boiling water and then covered in a sauce made with chopped chilli, sesame paste, garlic and chives. The dish was topped off with a generous helping of pickled vegetables.

I was also tempted by the stalls offering dishes of spicy, red-brown duck parts; some of which I recognised. Duck neck seemed to be a local delicacy.

For the first time in many years, the government was actively encouraging the growth of private enterprise in a country that had been a dominated by Mao's version of communism. Reforms had liberalised of the rights of individuals so that they could build their own businesses. The leadership under Deng had understood that the world was changing and that the time would come when China would rise to be an economic power in its own right. The enterprising young men and women running the stalls in the market were playing their part in the development of a private sector economy that was starting to make a difference.

In one corner of the market, I came across an elderly man operating a strange looking contraption on a handcart. Using a hand-crank, he rotated an urn-like steel vessel over a charcoal brazier. With his free hand, he operated a set of primitive bellows that forced air up through the red-hot coals to raise the temperature of the flames.

The container had a pressure gauge and a complex locking mechanism with a quick release lever. As the temperature inside climbed, he monitored the pressure with great care.

Bolted to the other side of the handcart was what looked like a chimney set at a 45-degree angle, made with a rusting steel drum, capped off with a battered basket of woven bamboo. Having no idea of what he was doing, I decided to wait and see what would happen. I did not have to wait long.

When the pressure inside the container was right, he pointed the end of the vessel up the chimney and operated the quick release lever using a short length of steel pipe to protect his hand from the heat. With a loud boom and cloud of steam, the contents of the steel container exploded out up the chimney. When I looked closely, I saw that he had half-filled the steel drum with puffed rice.

Drawn by the sound of the "explosion," children and adults alike queued up to buy paper cones of puffed rice.

The temperature of the water in the rice grains in the pressurised container must have increased above the boiling point of the water. When he released the safety catch, the pressure release was almost instantaneous and the water in the grains turned into vapour, exploding each grain of rice so that it looked like puffed wheat.

Little by little, I drifted downhill though the backstreets towards the river. Turning a corner, I caught my first proper glimpse of the Yangtze River, which appeared as a broad expanse of ochre coloured water around half a mile wide.

The Yangtze is no ordinary river; it is part of the lifeblood of China. The word "Yangtze" literally means Long River and at over 6,400 km long, it is the longest river is Asia.

The Yangtze drains almost a fifth of the land area of China and runs from the high Tibetan plateau down to Shanghai, where it spills out into the South China Sea.

Over the whole history of mankind in China, the Yangtze has provided water for drinking and cooking; supported the production of food; served as a means for disposal of waste; acted as a conduit for trade; and as a thoroughfare for the transportation of people. In times of war, the Yangtze has acted as a both as barrier and as a highway along which armies could move men and material.

The first bridge across the Yangtze was the great Wuhan Yangtze Bridge, which was completed in 1957. Built with the help of the Soviets to carry both road and rail traffic, the bridge brought the cities of Wuchang, Hankou and Hanyang together into what has become Wuhan. From where I stood, the delicate latticework of the span belied the solidity and strength of the thousands of tons of steel girders with which it had been constructed.

Beneath the bridge, the heaving, ever-swirling surface of the water was dotted with junks, long columns of junk-rigged river barges being towed by tugs, sampans, rusting freighters, ferries and passenger ships.

The jetties and quays along the riverbank marked out the boundaries of the port of Wuhan. This was where I planned to search for a riverboat to take me to Shanghai.

Above all of this activity, pollution had stained the sky with streaks of grey that complemented the florid tones of the river, making it seem that the port of Wuhan was flattened between two sides of ageing and rotting beef. The distant horizon was hidden behind veils of man-made haze.

Pressed by the need to keep moving and the excitement of seeing the Yangtze River, I soon felt that the time had come for me to move on again. A short walk to the quayside took me to a ticket office, where I bought a ticket for a berth on a riverboat bound for Shanghai.

One reason for choosing to take a riverboat down the Yangtze River was that it would take me along the route that the crippled HMS Amethyst had taken on her daring escape from the artillery of the People's Liberation Army. Sailing under the cover of darkness, HMS Amethyst sailed all the way to the sea, a journey of a hundred and four miles. The very fact that I was able to make this trip in a

Chinese ship was a measure of how much progress has been made by China since July 1949.

After the rigours of travel by train on hard seats, I had decided that it was time for a touch of luxury. I had hoped to travel in first class, but could only get a second-class ticket, which at least gave me a private cabin and access to the second-class lounge.

Mentally, I was exhausted having travelled overland across China from Pakistan, a journey of three and a half thousand miles, travelling on buses, trains and even donkey carts. The time had come, I had decided, for me to relax and live life at a gentler pace for a few days.

Chapter 8

Early in the morning on the following day, I made my way back to the quayside to find the riverboat that would take me to Shanghai. Painted in green and white, the superstructure rose from the deck like a mint-flavoured layer cake. The vessel was bigger than I had expected and looked well maintained.

A member of the crew showed me where to find my cabin, which was clean and comfortable. Although my ticket stated very clearly that I would be travelling in a Second-Class cabin, it was first class in terms of accommodation and facilities. Curiously, there was no First Class accommodation on the ship.

I stowed my luggage, locked my cabin and set off to explore the rest of the boat. As I walked towards the stern, I could see that the lower decks in the aft section of the boat were reserved for third class passengers. Their accommodation was very basic, in places little more than a cargo hold with hard seating. Men, women and children sprawled over the deck so that every available space was taken. Compared with this, my cabin was a palace.

The view from river-facing side justified my decision to travel to Shanghai by boat. The Yangtze River appeared as a brooding sweep of liquid mud, churning in eddies and whirlpools. Above, the sun shone in a blue sky flecked with white clouds. The haze and smog of the previous day had been blown away, revealing the beauty of Wuhan and its Long River.

I was elated at the prospect of following this great waterway to the sea. Beneath my feet, I could feel the river tugging at the boat as if anxious for us to be on our way. On the quayside, the mooring party released us from the quayside and the boat leapt out into the main flow of the river with a shiver of delight.

In the second-class lounge overlooking the bow, I found a group of Chinese professors of marine engineering relaxing in armchairs. They were all in their mid-fifties and dressed in battered shorts and vests. Between them was a coffee table covered with a lace edged tablecloth. Pots of plastic flowers and fading prints gave the lounge a cheerful splash of colour. The lounge was like a faded gentlemen's club from the fifties, with the air thick with cigarette smoke.

The professors welcomed me warmly and insisted that I joined them. We passed our time watching the traffic on the river and chatting about life in China in bygone years, the present and the future.

One thing was clear. The past had not always treated them well, but they were reluctant to talk about the trials and tribulations that they had faced during the Cultural Revolution. Their perspective on the future of China, on the other hand was uniformly positive.

The boat carried on downstream, stopping from time to time to pick up and drop off passengers. The sight of farm workers toiling in the fields was a reminder of the importance of agriculture to China. There were few signs of automation or the heavy tractors seen on European farms. Instead, much of the work was done by hand.

When we were not talking, the professors and I read, enjoying the tranquillity of life on the river. We all drank a lot of tea and in the evenings, enjoyed a few glasses of tepid bottled beer. This was a good time to relax and let the river take me down to the South China Sea.

When the boat stopped in Nanjing at midnight on the second day, I made my way to the bow and leaned against the rail in the hope of finding some hint of a breeze. The Yangtze gurgled below me, hidden by a blanket of darkness, which in turn was tucked in by the bright lights of the city. Every now and again, I thought I heard the river give out a deep sigh of contentment.

The air was thick, hot and humid and enveloped me with its cloying embrace. A gentle breeze carried by the current provided some relief from the heat, but it too was struggling.

In the distance, the streetlights on the Nanking Bridge, nearly half a kilometre long, glittered like jewels in the night. One of the professors had told me with pride that the bridge had been completed in 1968 and that this massive structure was the first of its kind to be built without the help of Soviet technical assistance. The project had been a triumph for Mao and his People's Republic of China. For the first time, the Chinese had taken on the might of the Long River on their own and succeeded.

As I listened to the splashing of the waves on the hull, I realised that from the moment I crossed the border from Pakistan, I had been witnessing some of the early steps of China's journey away from Mao's communist dream towards what was becoming China's take on capitalism.

It was in this moment of reflection, that I thought I heard music in the wind. At first, I thought it came from the ship's public address system, but as I listened more carefully, I realised that someone on the boat was singing a Christmas carol. It was "Silent Night," a song that I knew from my childhood. The mysterious singer sang with the graceful, crystal-clear voice of a tenor.

In the torrid heat of the night, each note was like a blast of fresh, cold air that ran down my spine. Leaving the bow, I turned to see who was singing so beautifully and found one of the professors standing by the port rail in his shorts and string vest. He was singing for joy and perhaps, for me.

The song, an old German carol, so incongruous in this setting, evoked vivid memories of my childhood. In an instant, I was transported back to a time when I was the schoolboy with grubby knees who sang in the church choir. We sang this carol year after year. It was part of the very essence of Christmas.

This memory faded only to be replaced by another. Safe and snug in our home, my father, mother, brothers, sister and I were sitting around our Christmas tree, opening our presents. The coals blazing in the grate, kept us warm. Outside, a winter chill hung in the air like a shroud, but inside was the warmth of a close-knit family.

I had sung this song so many times over the years that each note was now like an old friend, but at that moment, I felt very alone and very far from home.

The professor smiled when he saw me watching and carried on singing, the music of his voice flooding out into the still of the night.

I listened to him until the last notes faded into the darkness and asked:

"Do you know where that song comes from?"

He grinned. "It is American."

"Where did you learn it?"

"From Bing Crosby. We used to listen to him on the radio during World War II, when I was ten years old."

With a smile, he sat down beside me and we looked out across the lights of Nanking. Being out of earshot of his fellow professors, he was more open that he had been in the lounge and spoke freely about his life.

He was born in 1933 as the Chinese Civil war between the Nationalist forces led by Chiang Kai-Shek and the insurgent Communist party grumbled on in a series of bloody clashes.

He had seen the fall of the Last Emperor and lived through the Japanese invasion of Manchuria. He had survived World War II and the return to civil war that led to the ascendency of Mao Zedong's Communist Party and the subsequent rout of Chiang Kai Shek's Nationalist Party.

He had watched as the People's Republic of China was created on 1 October 1949 and experienced the turbulence of the Cultural Revolution for which the Gang of Four was blamed.

"There has been turmoil all though my life. Now, for the first time we have peace. There is a new feeling of hope for our future. China is moving away from the violence of the past."

The professor was a good, kind man and I could only hope that his hopes for the future would be fulfilled.

As we talked, the boat left Nanking, steaming down the Yangtze in darkness. As each hour passed, the river carried us onwards towards the South China Sea.

Morning revealed a landscape of paddy fields and tidy villages that eventually gave way to towns, cities, factories, belching chimneystacks and industrial wastelands. Out of this urban desolation, the city of Shanghai appeared, half-veiled in air thick with pollution.

As the boat headed towards the quayside, I could see a skyline dominated by the buildings of the Bund, which stood as a reminder that Shanghai had once been the third largest financial centre in the world. It had also been the powerhouse of the Chinese economy in the late nineteenth and early twentieth centuries, in the days before Communism had made its mark.

The Bund was built by men of vision from the West, who invested in Shanghai in the 1920's and 1930's.

They also highlighted the lack of investment in Shanghai since the 1930's by either Nationalist or Communist governments.

These towering blocks of stone and glass dominated almost everything that had been built in Shanghai since the 1930's. Other than a couple of non-descript tower blocks and a sprawl of concrete low-rise buildings, there was little evidence that the People's Republic of China had had any impact on the architecture of Shanghai.

As the boat docked, I thought that Shanghai looked like a port that had become a forgotten backwater. Compared to the skyscrapers and energy of Hong Kong, Shanghai's low-rise landscape seemed tired and unloved.

After a few hours in Shanghai, I realised that my first impression was wrong and that change was in the air. The signs of Shanghai's growing wealth were everywhere. In the commercial district, the roads were packed with private cars; there were shops selling expensive electrical goods; and even the Friendship Store was modern and well stocked.

Appearances had been deceptive, far from being a forgotten backwater, Shanghai was in the process of rediscovering its potential. Perhaps, the people of Hong Kong needed to worry about the growing economic strength of Shanghai, given its strategic position at the mouth of the Yangtze River and undoubted plans for growth.

In my hurry to get to Hong Kong, I spent too little time in Shanghai, just long enough to explore the Nanking Road and buy my ticket for the next stage in my journey, which would involve steaming across the South China Sea in a luxury liner.

On the day of sailing, I visited the jazz bar in the Peace Hotel on the Bund. Overlooking the Huangpu River, the hotel had been built by a

British businessman with Iraqi Jewish origins and had somehow survived the destructive forces of civil war, the Japanese invasion and the Cultural Revolution,

The purpose of my visit was to spend half an hour enjoying a drink in the most bizarre half-timbered jazz bar in China. Established in the 1930's, the bar had entertained guests with a fine selection of cigars, gins, malt whiskies, art deco surroundings and fine jazz for nearly half a century. I had only left myself the time to sip a single ice-cold beer in an empty bar.

The members of the original Jazz Band had all since died, but some of the artists who had played in the Jazz Band when it was disbanded during the Cultural Revolution had regrouped and returned to the Peace Hotel. Most of them had been born in the 1930s and lived through the same turmoil as my professor friend. Like him, they had endured years of re-education, but had remained true to their love of Western music.

The hotel first opened in 1929 and over the years has served as a base for Western entrepreneurs, Sun Yat-sen, the founding father of the Republic of China in 1911 and the Japanese army during World War II.

The Cathay Hotel, as it was known then, was taken over by the Communist municipal government in 1952 and used by the Municipal Construction Department. It was not until 1956 that the hotel was renamed the Peace Hotel and reopened.

Although there was no one to play the grand piano opposite the bar, I could almost hear echoes of those long-dead musicians who had made this bar such a special place. After finishing my beer, I took a taxi to the docks and found the quay where the Jin Jiang was moored with just minutes to spare.

From a distance, the Jin Jiang was a modern-looking ship with a fresh coat of white paint and an air of luxury. As I got closer, I saw that the white paint was mottled with streaks of rust and that my 'luxury' liner was in fact a converted freighter that had seen better days. The ship had been built before I was born.

The Jin Jiang had been built as a cargo carrier named Pine Tree Mariner for the U.S. Maritime Commission by Bethlehem Steel Co., Quincy, Massachusetts. The Pine Tree Mariner was launched in November 1952 and entered service in 1953.

In 1956, the ship was sold to Matson Navigation Co, converted into a passenger ship at Willamette Iron and Steel Corp., Portland, Oregon and renamed Mariposa. Her maiden voyage for Matson was from San Francisco to Sydney, by way of Honolulu and Auckland, and started on 27 October 1956.

In 1971, the Mariposa was sold to Pacific Far East Line, Inc., which used her for Pacific Ocean cruises. Laid up in 1978, she was sold to World Airways, Inc., in 1979 and was towed to Japan in November 1980. After her arrival in Japan, she was again laid up and later the same year was returned to Pacific Far East Line.

In 1983, she was sold to China Ocean Shipping Co., renamed Jin Jiang and placed on the Shanghai-Hong Kong service.

This was my luxury liner. Not quite the luxury liner that I had hoped for, but perhaps that should not have been a total surprise given the cost of my ticket.

Once on board, I made my way to my cabin where I settled into my berth and spent a few moments enjoying some peace and quiet before we sailed. As soon as we were under way, I went on deck to watch Shanghai slip below the horizon.

When we were no longer in sight of land, I explored the ship, I noticed signs of the Jin Jiang's previous life as a luxury liner: an empty swimming pool; a ballroom; and a deserted shuffleboard court.

The open sea soon welcomed us with a storm that kept all but the most intrepid passengers inside. The rain clattered into the decks and was whipped away by the wind in clouds of spray. The deck pitched and rolled as the ship ploughed its way through heavy seas. Many of the passengers had retired to their cabins, leaving the rest of the ship eerily empty. With little else to do, I retreated to the bar and ordered a beer.

The barmaid spoke some English and was happy to practise with me until we were joined by two English men, who started to drink beer after beer. From their conversation, which grew louder by the glass, I gathered that they worked in the fruit machine business and were based in Hong Kong. As they became more garrulous, I sank deeper into my book and pretended to read.

The more they drank, the more they picked on the barmaid, taunting her with comments that became increasing suggestive. The barmaid continued to serve them, but was visibly upset by their rudeness and lewd comments. As I watched this scenario develop, I realised that I could not just sit back and not intervene.

To start with, I suggested politely that they stopped baiting the barmaid. The shorter of the two told me to mind my own business.

I tried again and this time the other man told me to "fuck off." They sat hunched over their drinks, creating an atmosphere tainted with malice and menace. They could easily have just stepped out of the set of the film Clockwork Orange.

Asking them to leave the barmaid alone for the third time was not the most sensible course of action, but seemed to be the right thing to do at the time. Casting common-sense to the wind, I tried one more time.

"I really think that it would be good if you left her alone. You can see that she is not happy."

The taller man stood up and squared up to me. "Are you going to make us?"

Without thinking, I gave him the answer that he had hoped I would give.

"If I have to…"

As he lunged at me, I ducked under his flailing fists, grasped him by the throat and ran him backwards against the far bulkhead. As I had not released my grip on his throat, this set up a stalemate and he growled at me.

"What are you going to do now?"

I had no idea. His friend came up behind me and started to punch and kick me. In the ensuing scuffle, I ended up facing the two of them. They both raised their fists and I began to wonder why I had been foolish enough to intervene. Just as I was considering what to do next, I heard a sound behind me and turned to see four members of the crew lined up behind me. They rushed forward and grabbed the two men.

Moments later, they were gone, leaving me alone with the barmaid in an otherwise empty bar. She smiled shyly, thanked me and offered me a beer. This gave me a few moments to wonder what had induced me to take on these two fine representatives of the gaming industry. Perhaps, I had just had enough of their company.

On the third and last day on the Jin Jiang, I settled down in the main lounge and opened my book again. Budd Brooksieker, an American from Ohio, had heard about my problems in the bar and came to ask if I was all right. He was a jovial man in his late fifties, with a huge smile, glasses, slightly thinning hair and a quiet, but noticeable presence. He was clearly someone who had lived well.

"How are you doing, buddy?"

"Fine thanks. Just a little shocked by my reaction to those guys."

"I guess it will take you a couple of days to get over something like that."

Bud asked what I had been doing in Shanghai, so I told him about my travels across China and my plans to explore a remote corner of the Tibetan plateau. In turn, he explained that he had been in China because he was interested in Taoism.

Bud was one of those people who had found his answer to life's most puzzling questions and had devised a form of Taoism to give some structure to his beliefs.

I had to admit to him that I knew almost nothing about Taoism. Sliding his frame deeper into the armchair, he started to teach me about this ancient system of beliefs.

"Let's start with Wu Wei. This is the Way of following the Tao, which is all about going with the flow and letting things take their natural course. This means that we should place our will in harmony with the natural order of the universe."

He took something out of his bag and flattened it against the palm of his hand so that I could not see what he was holding. He wanted to share something with me, but needed to tell me something first.

"Lao Zi, who some believe is the key author of Tao Te Ching, the key book of Taoism, wrote that a good traveller has no fixed plans and is not intent upon arriving. Your journey has taken you from your birthplace to this lounge in the same way that a river flowing down from the mountains to the sea finds its natural course."

He paused for breath.

"You walked away from a structured life and set out on a journey with no clear idea of where you were going, or when you were going to leave one place for another. From what you have told me, your journey has been taking you along the way of Tao for a long time now."

The more Budd talked, the more I understood about his perspectives on Taoism. He was a good, patient tutor. He reminded me of my teacher from Cairo, Mr Orman. They both had found beliefs that helped them come to terms with the one thing that binds all people, the knowledge that one day our individual journeys will end.

He opened his hand and revealed a square of purple cloth that he gave me as a talisman to keep me safe in Tibet.

"The colour purple is associated with physical and mental healing and spiritual awareness. Purple is also the colour to the North Star, which will give you strength and help guide you on your way."

He reached out and shook my hand, with a reassuring, firm grip.

"I know that you will find what you are looking for, I just know. When you are done, come and look me up and tell me what you found."

As he spoke, the tension that had built up within me because of the incident in the bar ebbed away and I was able to relax and enjoy the last few hours of our passage to Hong Kong.

The storm abated and for the rest of the day the ship made good progress, arriving in Hong Kong more or less on time. As I was preparing to disembark, Budd came to find me to say goodbye and to wish me luck with my travels in Tibet.

I saw no sign of the two men from the fruit machine business. My focus anyway was on getting ready for the mountains of the high Tibetan plateau.

Chapter 9

After the relative austerity of mainland China, Hong Kong was a shock to my system. In the narrow alleyways of Kowloon, neon signs and billboards crowded together like leaves in a tropical rainforest battling for the rays of the sun. The neon lights, the crowds, the smell of Chinese food rising from steaming woks, coupled with the hubbub of traffic and people talking to each other in Cantonese exploded into my senses in a rush.

At night, drips from a myriad of air-conditioning units hung outside high-rise apartment blocks spattered on the pavements, only to evaporate and rise into air already heavy with humidity. Food stalls offered a bewildering selection of snacks, some of which I recognised. Woks cooking over air-driven charcoal stoves that roared in the night churned out countless servings of stir fried chicken, pork and seafood. The sound and smells of crab sizzling in a chilli sauce caught my attention and it tasted as good as it looked.

My godfather's son, Stephen Bourne, was kind enough to offer me the comfort of his spare room. He lived on Lantau Island with his wife and his baby daughter, Jade. She was a delight and made me realise once more that being single and not having my own family had some very real downsides.

Stephen took me racing in Hong Kong harbour in his Flying Fifteen sailing boat. Just over twenty feet in length with a hefty keel, this was a beautiful craft to sail.

Stephen was even foolish enough to ask me to crew for him in a race. This was an exhilarating experience, which involved darting between the many ships, ferries and junks that criss-crossed the harbour. I was not much help to him and even half-fell out at one point, which slowed us down as he hauled me back on board. After the race, we retired to the Royal Hong Kong Yacht Club for an ice-cold beer.

After the delights of the cave on Shandur Pass, the Royal Hong Kong Yacht Club, one of the oldest sports clubs in Hong Kong, seemed like another world. Stephen told me that the club had been founded in 1893 and granted a warrant by the Lords of the Admiralty a year later in 1894.

This reminded me that my grandfather, Austin Frost, then a doctor in the British Army, had been in Hong Kong on 18 September 1906, when a typhoon with winds in excess of 77 miles per hour had killed over ten thousand people. More than 3,500 boats were also lost, including two vessels belonging to the famous Star Ferry company.

A photograph of the aftermath of the typhoon taken by my grandfather shows the Sailing Packet Hitchcock half-sunk against the sea wall of 14 Kowloon Wharf. The SP Hitchcock was a three-masted schooner, a skysail yarder, which had been launched in 13 October 1883 in Bath, Maine (USA). Built for California trade, her original owner was a certain J. F, Chapman of New York.

The photograph also serves as a reminder that at the turn of the twentieth century people travelled all over the globe by ship. By modern standards, travel by sea took a long time, but those who did endured storms, the heat of the Tropics and often-cramped conditions. Life in those days was lived at a very different pace from today. A steamer from Europe could have taken around 25 days to reach Hong Kong. By contrast, a flight in a modern passenger jet from London today takes around 12 hours.

After a few days in Hong Kong, I called the Zephyr. We spoke of many things, but I soon knew that there had been a change in the wind from the West. Something that had been there had slipped away. When finally I put the phone down, I knew that the time had come for me to move on and find my own way.

In my last few days in Hong Kong, I assembled the supplies needed for my trip to Tibet and booked a ticket on a train to Guangzhou. Leaving from Hung Hon station in Kowloon, the train set off on time and a couple of hours later arrived in Guangzhou.

This was a city with modern hotels and an energy that I had not seen elsewhere in China. I bought another watch, which nearly lasted a whole day before it expired. I also bought a ticket for the train to Chengdu.

The distance between Guangzhou and Chengdu is a little over two thousand four hundred kilometres, which is about the same as the distance between London and Istanbul. This was going to be a long journey. Knowing that the ride would take around sixty-five hours, I booked myself into the most luxurious of the carriages and travelled in the "soft sleeper".

In soft sleeper class, I shared a compartment with three other passengers. At night, the compartment was converted into a bedroom with four bunk beds, two lower and two upper. There was a dining car and some of the fans actually worked. This was my most luxurious train journey in China and worth every penny.

For part of the journey, I shared the compartment with Chikato, a Japanese man and Xiao, a Chinese woman. Neither could speak the other's language, but they could communicate by writing to each other using Chinese characters.

Each character carries the same meaning in Chinese hanzi and Japanese kanji, even though the sound of the character in each language is different. Through writing, they forged a relationship that brought two worlds together in harmony.

The train continued through the southeast of China, passing through a constantly changing landscape filled with rivers, mountains and verdant plains. This was an antithesis to the empty deserts of the far west of China.

All too soon, this stage of the journey ended as the train pulled into Chengdu. With a population over eight and a half million people, Chengdu was a great industrial city, more like Manchester than Bath.

The pollution of China's new industrial revolution painted the sky with the florid shades normally found on the face of a heavy drinker. The air had an acrid taste that scoured my lips and left me wanting to get to the Tibetan plateau as quickly as possible.

Chapter 10

After a few days in Chengdu, made memorable by spicy dishes replete with whole dried chillies, cashew nuts and cloves of garlic, I travelled by plane to Lhasa. I had considered trying to hitch a ride on a truck heading for Lhasa, but such travel was against the law and in any case, an overland journey would take too long.

A short flight in a plane was the only way I could be sure get to Lhasa before the winter snows made solo travel by foot impossible. The two-hour flight from Chengdu to Lhasa took me from a vast, polluted city to an airport on top of the world.

Some 93 kilometres to the south-west of Lhasa, the airport is one of the highest in the world at 11,712 feet. As we turned to line up for the landing, the broad expanse of the Brahmaputra River could be seen to the north of the runway.

A shuttle bus took me into the centre of Lhasa and into a world that I recognised from the descriptions in Heinrich Harrer's book "Seven Years in Tibet", which I had read as a child.

As the bus moved off, I stood on the pavement and breathed in deeply. The air did not seem any different, until I started to walk around with the weight of my rucksack pulling down on my shoulders. Only then did I notice how quickly I ran out of breath and started to pant like a puppy.

I needed to rest to acclimatise to the altitude and found myself a room in the Yak Hotel, a stone's throw away from the Jokhang Square in the centre of old Lhasa. Settling down on a chair in front of the hotel, I began to contemplate the next stage of my journey and the history of Tibet's complex relationship with the rest of China.

Part 4 - Land of Bod

Chapter 1

The origins of Tibet, once known as the Land of Bod, have long been the source of the conflict between those who see Tibet as a country in its own right that has been occupied by the Chinese and those who see Tibet as an autonomous region of China. The origins of this conflict are complex and date back to the 7th century AD.

In 600 AD, the warrior king of Yarlung valley, Namri Songsten began the task of unifying the tribes of Tibet. His son, Songsten Gampo ruled c.605-650 AD and moved the base of the kingdom to the Lhasa valley. He also established an interpretation of the Sanskrit alphabet for the Tibetan language and set up the first Code of Tibetan Law. Songsten Gompo married five women: three Tibetans, a Nepali princess called Bhirikuti Devi and a Chinese princess called Wen Cheng. It was to be the last of these marriages that formed the basis for modern China's claim on Tibet.

Songsten also united the Tibetan animist Bon religion with Buddhism and built two temples in Lhasa in honour of his princesses. The Jokhang, the largest of these temples, was built for Wen Cheng in the heart of Lhasa.

By the 7th and 8th centuries AD, Tibet was a vast empire stretching into what is now Kashmir; China proper; Turkestan (Xinjiang province); Sikkim; Bhutan; Nepal and Upper Burma. It was only when the Tibetans began to take control of the Silk Road by taking the oases of Kashgar, Khotan and Kuqa that Emperor Xuanzong finally decided to respond. He sent troops to attack the Tibetans, who responded by sacking the Chinese city of Xi'an in 763 AD.

However, by 842 AD Tibet was again divided. The centres of power were spilt between lay and monastic pockets of influence. Simultaneously, a power struggle between the Bon and Buddhist religions resulted in the kingdom dissolving into chaotic factions, torn asunder by internecine strife.

In the early 13th century AD, the Tibetans submitted to Genghis Khan, who in 1253 appointed Drogön Chögyal Phagpa as Viceroy of Tibet. Kublai Khan himself became a Buddhist convert in 1270. From c.1200-1350 AD, Tibet was welded into a single political unit, with the core area being Yarlung-Lhasa-Shigatse, under the control of the Grand Lamas of Sakya. With the collapse of the Mongols in China in 1368, the power of the Sakya lamas declined.

From the 14th to the 20th centuries AD, Tibet stood still in geopolitical terms. The great monasteries flourished, but Tibet never regained its position as a military power and remained a country ruled by its religious leaders, the Grand Lamas of Tibetan Buddhism.

Tibet was reunified by the fifth Dalai Lama, Lobsang Gyatso (1617-1682), a man of vision who realised that Tibet could not exist in isolation. He visited China and reopened trade routes into India. It was during his reign that the Potala was built. In fact, the Potala was completed after his death, which had been kept from the people to ensure that the massive palace was finished.

Following the death of the fifth Dalai Lama, Tibet became a pawn in a grand series of Asian power plays. In the early eighteenth century, the Mongolians twice occupied Tibet. To counter this threat to China, the Manchurian emperor, Xangxi of the Qing dynasty, sent armies to Tibet to expel the invading Mongolian hordes in 1720. The Imperial troops stayed for three years and acted as "protectors" of the Seventh Dalai Lama. Under the Chinese protection, the Seventh Dalai Lama spent ten years interned in Kumbum. A new government in Tibet was set up, led by a Council of Ministers under the supervision of an Imperial representative, who had no administrative powers.

Following the death of Xangxi, his successor, Yong Zheng (1723-35), moved the major part of his troops back to China. A civilian advisor replaced his military advisor in Tibet. In 1728, the Chinese set up a hospital in Lhasa to cope with an epidemic of smallpox. This marked the end of the first short period of direct and close Manchurian involvement with the Tibetan administration.

As the extent of the Manchurian Emperors' influence in Tibet waned, Tibet became a pawn in the Great Game between the British and Russian Empires. The British government in India began to receive reports of attempts by the Russians to gain influence in Tibet and in 1903, Sir Francis Younghusband invaded Tibet with an expeditionary force of some 10,000 and marched to Lhasa. As the British approached Lhasa, the 13th Dalai Lama fled to Mongolia.

In spring 1908, the 13th Dalai Lama visited Beijing, becoming the second Dalai Lama to do so and was received by the Chinese with disdain. A Chinese Imperial decree stated his position:

"The Dalai Lama already, by the Imperial Commands of former times, bears the title of the Great, Good, Self Existent Buddha of Heaven. We now expressly confer upon him the addition to his title of the Loyally Submissive, Great, Good, Self Existent Buddha of Heaven."

The Dalai Lama left Beijing on 21 December 1908 and arrived back in Lhasa on 25 December 1909. He found the situation in Tibet had not only worsened in his long absence, but that events had reached a critical stage. Chinese troops had sacked the monastery of Litang in retribution for the murder of a Chinese Amban. Stories were circulating in Lhasa that Chinese soldiers were using sacred Buddhist books for making boot-soles. This was seen as a sacrilegious act and made matters even worse.

By 1910, the situation had become desperate and the 13th Dalai Lama fled to the British in India accompanied by six ministers and a small escort, by way of the Chumbi Valley.

The Dalai Lama returned to Tibet two years later, following the fall of the Manchurian dynasty in China. Tibetan armed forces, trained by the British, expelled all Chinese troops and officials. A crude border along the Mekong-Salween divide was established.

The President of the New Republic of China, Yaun Shikai sent a message to the Dalai Lama announcing the restoration of his rank. The 13th Dalai Lama replied that he already had that rank and that he had resumed the normal government of Tibet. This was regarded in Tibet as a statement of independence.

In an attempt to try to clarify the situation, the British set up what became known as the Simla Conference (1913-14) involving Tibetan, British and Chinese delegates. The Convention prepared during the Conference stated clearly that Tibet should be allowed autonomy under a Chinese suzerainty. In the end, the Chinese did not sign the Convention. The British and the Tibetans however, did sign.

The Tibetans knew that as long as the British maintained an influence in Tibet, the Chinese were unlikely to interfere and for a few years, Tibet remained in a state of peace. In 1947, India won independence and the British deterrent to the invasion of Tibet by China was removed.

In October 1950, Chinese forces advanced into Tibet. One army from the east attacked through Sichuan province and one from the west through Xinjiang province. The Tibetan army was woefully ill-equipped and fell back before the advancing armies. In May 1951, the captured governor of Chamdo signed a 17-point agreement for the "peaceful liberation of Tibet".

Between 1954 and 1959, armed resistance to the Chinese took place at various locations in Tibet. In response, Chinese communist forces laid siege to Litang monastery in 1956. The monastery was bombed and strafed by the Chinese air force. People of the Kham region, the Khampa, fled from the Chinese and many joined the "Four Rivers and Six Ranges Rebellion Group."

In March 1959, an armed rebellion broke out in Lhasa. Chinese troops shelled crowds of Tibetans circling the Summer Palace and thousands were killed.

In the following years, until 1979, Chinese policy in Tibet led to the destruction of monasteries, fortresses and historic buildings. According to some estimates, only 250 of the original 2,500 monasteries remained. The worst years lay in the period that has become known as the period of the Cultural Revolution.

During the Cultural Revolution, between 1966 and 1976, all acts of Tibetan custom and religion were banned. Large numbers of Tibetans died in labour camps and prisons. No accurate figures for the number of deaths have been compiled. Some estimates indicate that as many as 1.2 - 2.0 million Tibetans died between 1951 and 1979. Some estimates suggest that 10,000 Tibetans died in Drapchi prison alone, which is situated a few miles east of Lhasa between 1960 and 1965.

Chinese figures reveal a 7% decline in the Tibetan population between 1953 and 1959. Statistics vary, as borders were redefined several times during the period.

In 1979, three years after the death of Mao Zedong, there was a major turnaround in Chinese policy towards Tibet. General Ren Rong, Chinese Communist Party Chief in Tibet (1969-79) was dismissed in disgrace.

The Chinese government began to admit "a number of mistakes in attitude to Tibetans." In the late eighties, the Chinese government blamed "wrong thinking" and "Leftist policies" for the events of the Cultural Revolution in China and in Tibet.

For a while, the introduction of tourism into Tibet was accompanied by a number of policy changes. Some of the larger monasteries were rebuilt and Tibetans were allowed to worship openly again. The Jokhang Temple was opened for worship and the Tibetan language was taught at the University in Lhasa. Civil engineering projects modernised basic infrastructure services. Schools were built and many new roads constructed; a more or less reliable bus service was established; hydroelectric projects were completed; and Tibetan radio and television stations began broadcasting.

In mainland China, economists had expressed their concerns regarding the cost of the occupation of Tibet. Some 53 billion Yuan had been invested by the Chinese in Tibet in the years between 1952-1985 and there was "nothing to show for it" according to an article in the Shanghai Economic Journal in 1985. For every 1.2 Yuan invested during that period, China saw a return of 1.0 Yuan. Economists within China increasingly saw Tibet as being little more than a drain on a struggling economy.

Chapter 2

Jay was a bright, personable Californian who introduced himself as I settled into the dormitory of the Yak Hotel in the centre of Lhasa. He sat down on my bed and asked what seemed to me to be an incomprehensible question.

"Are you here for the Harmonic Convergence too?"

Completely stumped by his question, I wondered if this was something I missed during my time out of circulation in the Hindu Kush and in China. Perhaps it was some kind of music festival? Confused, I shook my head and admitted my ignorance.

"I don't think so...what is the Harmonic Convergence?"

"It is the beginning of the New Age."

Jay was clearly surprised that I had not heard about the New Age, but he was very patient with me and tried to explain.

"You must have heard of José Argüelles?"

"Sadly, not."

"He wrote a book called the Mayan Factor, which describes his researches into the Mayan culture and calendar. He has discovered a 5,052-year cycle, after which a galactic wave will culminate in a New Age. The start of the last twenty-five years of the current cycle began on 17 August 1987. On 21 December 2012, he says that the Earth will enter the Galactic Federation as a member and take its place on the council. Right now, groups are meeting at sacred sites all over the world to channel the energies of the Harmonic Convergence for world peace."

This was all a bit much for me, but Jay was very serious and seemed to believe that something special was about to happen.

One of his friends joined us and was keen to bring me in to the fold, without much success. The Yorkshire blood in me just could not cope with this kind of nonsense. He was eager to explain how he had contributed to peace in South Africa.

"I bought a crystal nearly eight inches long and buried it on a beach for world peace and peace in South Africa in particular."

"But it must have cost a fortune...did you get it back?"

"Couple of thousand dollars. No, I left it there. The energy on the crystal is now being channelled into world peace, so it was worth every cent."

The idea of New Age based on strange quasi-magical ritual and that a quartz crystal placed on a beach in California could help world peace just seemed too far-fetched to me, but then I am a dyed-in-the-wool rationalist. Jay was a good person, but he did have ideas that seemed very odd to me.

When news of my planned trip to the Chumbi valley slipped out, Jay came back to me with a request.

"Could you take a crystal with you and leave it in the forests on the edge of the Tibetan plateau? If you could leave it hanging in the breeze that would be even better."

The crystal was about the size of a walnut and not too heavy, so I agreed to take it with me.

"Thanks, it would be cool to think of it just hanging there."

For the New Age believers, the portents of an important event came thick and fast. For several days, a strange double halo surrounded the moon, looking like a pair of ghostly shrouds. There was an earthquake, not quite as severe as the earthquake that shook me out of bed in Pakistan, but strong enough to damage some buildings and scare the wild dogs. The earthquake was followed by an eclipse of the sun. Jay was certain that a major event was just around the corner and grew increasingly excited. I had other matters to sort out. It did not occur to me that Jay might have been right.

Chapter 3

From the outset, my aim had been to arrive in Lhasa in August, spend a few weeks adjusting to living at altitude and then set out to trace the route of the Younghusband's British Mission, which had marched to Lhasa in 1903 and to photograph the cloud forests on the southern face of the Himalaya.

By the end of September, my body had become quite used to the altitude and I was ready to begin my journey to the closed Chumbi Valley. I knew that winter was not that far away and that I had no more than six to eight weeks to get there and back to Lhasa. This plan did not leave much in the way of a margin for error.

I had chosen the Chumbi valley because of its geographical position and its historical importance. The valley is a narrow cleft cut into a spur thrown off the main Himalayan range on the Bhutan and Sikkim borders and lies along one of the ancient trade routes between India and Tibet. The names of the men who have passed through the valley include eccentrics, explorers, adventurers and great lamas. One of the earliest Europeans to visit the Chumbi valley was Thomas Manning, of the Chinese branch of the East India Company, accompanied by his Chinese servant in 1811. He made his way to Lhasa and lived there for several months until he was arrested by the Chinese and deported back to India.

In 1903, Sir Francis Younghusband, then an officer in the Indian Army, marched into Tibet through the Chumbi Valley with a military force of five thousand troops, supported by five thousand Sherpas, porters and camp followers.

In the Chumbi valley, Younghusband lunched with one Captain Parr, resident of the Chinese Customs post in Yadong. The post had been set up in May 1894 under the Sikkim-Tibet convention of 1890.

Yadong had been given the status of *trade mart* to encourage trade into Tibet. Younghusband and his military mission eventually left the Chumbi valley and after a series of battles, made their way to Lhasa.

In 1910, the 13th Dalai Lama had slipped out of Tibet through the Chumbi valley and sought refuge in Darjeeling. Accompanied by several monks, he was greeted at the border post by a gruff British Sergeant Major who asked, "Which one of you blighters is the Dalai Lama?"

History repeated itself 49 years later when the 14th Dalai Lama left Tibet along the same route, leaving behind a country having to deal with the impact of an occupying Red Army.

In 1987, the border was closed as relations between the governments of China and India were going through a difficult period.

I had done my research and knew that the route was well-guarded. The Chinese had established a series of police and army checkpoints on the road between Lhasa and Yadong to monitor the movement of people in and out of the Chumbi Valley. To avoid these checkpoints, I decided to leave the road and travel south over open country, finding my way using Operational Navigation Charts and American military maps prepared from old British Army maps. My planned route took me over a few high passes and into areas in which no signs of habitation were visible on any of my maps. The distance from Lhasa to Yadong, the main market town of the Chumbi Valley was a little over two hundred miles as the crow flies, but around three hundred miles by road.

The first leg of the journey involved taking a bus to Gyantse over Kamba La, past Yamdok Tso, the Turquoise Lake, up over the Karo La pass and finally over the Simi La pass.

The idea that the British mission could march over these high mountain passes must have seemed unthinkable to the Tibetans in 1904. It was hard enough for me to imagine in 1987, when the road was just about good enough for buses and trucks

The Karo La pass, overlooked by a glacier, was the site of the British mission's highest battle. According to Younghusband's own account, Ghurkha troops climbed to 18,500 feet so that they could fire down on the Tibetan positions on the pass, "concluding the conflict."

No other army had fought at such an altitude. As my bus wheezed over the pass and began the long, winding descent to Gyantse, I had to admire those British, Indian and Tibetan soldiers. The landscape was a barren wilderness haunted by rocky crags and lacking any vegetation. The wind filled the air with dust and the cold seemed to seep into the very fabric of my bones.

The road was mostly a two-lane dirt track that twisted and turned up over the three high passes between Lhasa and Gyantse. Kampo La at 15,725 feet, Karo La at 14,206 feet and finally, Simi La at 16,272 feet. The roughness of the road and the altitude made this a gruelling journey. In places, crude repairs showed where landslides had torn away sections of the road. At the top of every pass, we stopped. I admire the view, while the Tibetans recited mantras at stupas covered in prayer flags. As the narrow road twisted and turned down from the high passes, I could only hope that the bus-driver was sober.

Having seen photographs taken by the Younghusband expedition, my first sight of Gyantse left me with the impression that little had changed since 1904. Many of the streets were still unpaved and the town was still overshadowed by the massive presence of Gyantse Fort. The scars of the battle that had been fought there between the Tibetans and the British in 1904 were still evident.

I was able climb up over the remains of the walls that had been breached by the mission's seven pounder cannon. Fortunately, most of the fort remained intact despite the ravages of the British attack and more recently the Cultural Revolution.

It was in Gyantse that the young Lieutenant Gurdon fought his last battle, killed trying to storm the fort through the breach that had been blasted into the outer wall. Like him, I had made the long journey from England to Chitral and from Chitral to Gyantse. His journey ended in Gyantse. Mine was just about to take me along the road that had taken him into Tibet.

Chapter 4

Rising with the sun, I left the truck stop and headed south on the road to Gala. The road, little more than a dirt track, took me past the building that Younghusband had used as a base in his siege of Gyantse Jong. The Chinese army had moved in and it was being used as a garrison. There was no-one to see me walk past, but ahead of me was a squad of soldiers heading back to the garrison from their morning run. They ran past me, more interested in the breakfast that I assumed was waiting for them.

Leaving Gyantse, my route finally took me into closed territory and I soon began to feel like a fugitive, always on the lookout for checkpoints and army patrols and never totally at ease.

For the first day, I kept off the road, walking a few hundred feet above it most of the time. The only creatures to see me pass were darting Himalayan hares living among the rocks. The road south was not busy, but the little traffic that passed seemed to be either Chinese army trucks or tracks laden with timber, all heading north towards Lhasa.

My first night was spent by a shrine to Buddha erected on an otherwise desolate hillside. A lone goat herder on the other side of the valley watched me set up camp.

In the morning, I started out again as soon as there was enough light. Having seen how little traffic there was, I decided to risk walking on the road. The surface was unmetalled, but in good condition. When I heard vehicles in the distance, I moved off the road and stood by to watch them trundle past. By late afternoon, I had made good progress and felt increasingly confident. From time to time, the sight of a ruined monastery reminded me of the years of destruction that followed the "liberation" of Tibet.

Later in the day, I came across a young man leaning on a fence in front of his house. He stepped into the road to greet me and shook my hand. He was Chinese and had married a Tibetan girl. His official looking Mao cap and jacket made me nervous at first, but then I noticed his sunglasses and American style filter cigarettes. Even though I did not smoke, I carried a pack of real American filter cigarettes just for this kind of encounter and offered him one. He grinned, took a cigarette and welcomed me into his home.

"Come in and have some tea."

He took me into his house and his wife poured me a cup of yak butter tea. It was salty and despite its unusual taste, very refreshing. Even better was that when a Tibetan truck stopped for a few minutes, he convinced the driver that he should take me as far as the outskirts of Gala.

The driver was happy to take me further down the road towards Gala and helped me climb into the back of his truck. The narrow valley opened up into a plain surrounded by weather-beaten hills. After an hour or so, the driver pulled into a small compound and signalled me to get out.

At first, I was concerned that he had decided to hand me over to the Public Security Bureau, but I could not have been more wrong. Instead, he led me into a room where half a dozen men sat smoking and chatting as the women of the house prepared a meal. They asked me to join them and pressed a cup of yak butter tea into my hands. It was warm, salty and very much appreciated.

My hosts tried to teach me how to mix tsampa with yak butter tea to make patties. They passed me a dried lamb haunch and seemed pleased when I pulled out my knife to cut off some meat. Then the chang, a beer made with fermented barley, appeared. It tasted like some Belgian wheat beers, but did not seem quite as strong. The chang jug passed around the room several times and as we drank, the laughter and noise levels increased steadily.

As evening approached, it was time to get back on to the road. A mile out of Gala, the driver stopped and asked me to get out. He pointed to the distant town and told me that I would not be welcome at the army checkpoint.

"Better if you got out here."

With a wave, I headed out across Gala Tso as the truck continued down the road towards Gala, which was just visible in the distance. There was a moment of exhilaration as I left the road behind and headed west. Behind me lay the road to Lhasa, ahead of me was the route that I had pencilled on my map. The plan was straightforward: one day west, a couple of days heading more or less south through mountains and high passes and one day east would, in theory at least, bring me back on the road to the Chumbi valley. As night fell, I set up camp in the middle of an empty plain, a few miles away from the town of Gala.

Emotionally I was swamped with a combination of exhilaration and apprehension. Everything that I had ever learned about walking in mountains told me that I should not have been travelling on my own and that I needed better maps than the ones I was using. In theory, I was well enough equipped for the mountains and I knew that if I needed to, I could backtrack as far as Gala. A badly twisted ankle or a bad sprain would have been more of a challenge.

The question was whether the track marked on my chart actually existed. If it did, would it take me over a pass at around eighteen and a half thousand feet, across a wide valley and into a gorge that would take me into another valley that would lead me east towards the great plain of Tang La. Time alone would tell.

Morning came all too soon and as the sun rose, I headed west across the dried-pout bed of Gala Tso. Around me was a landscape teeming with wildlife: eagles; mallard ducks; bar-headed geese; marmots; mouse-hare and rare Black-necked cranes.

Halfway through the morning, I came across three herdsmen sitting around a yak dung fire. The youngest had a shock of black hair that reached skywards, shaggy eyebrows and a great beaming smile. His grandfather and older brother sat cross-legged beside him and made a place for me by the fire.

"Come and join us for some tea."

For half an hour or so, we drank mugs of yak butter tea sitting in the middle of a broad plain. I watched carefully as they tended their yak-dung fire. As wood on the high Tibetan plateau is hard to find, I realised that this was a craft worth learning. Eventually, then it was time for me to say good-bye and move on. I made good progress along the flat surface of the valley floor.

As evening approached, I set up camp by a stream and cooked dinner on a yak dung fire. Around me, there was nothing but the sound of the wind whispering in the sand. The light of the setting sun lit up the stream and in the distance, sheep shimmered in the haze. As I ate, the wind blew harder, stirring up dust angels that danced around me. I hoped that they were my guardian angels.

As darkness fell, the Milky Way appeared as a faint river of light across the night sky, crossed from time to time by satellites. Lying in my sleeping bag, I felt at ease and watched the sky fill with the light of billions of stars before closing the opening to my bivvy-bag. I shut my eyes and fell into a deep sleep.

As the sun rose, two passing Tibetans stopped by my camp and joined me for tea. They inspected my equipment with great interest and confirmed that I should turn south to find the pass that would take me to Tang La. There was no track to follow, so I climbed steadily from the level of Gala Tso at around 15,000 feet up to where the pass should have been, finally reaching an altitude of 18,500 feet. Looking back over the valley, I could see the village of Ge Dram and in the distance, what looked like great ruined towers scattered across the plain.

As I climbed, the good weather was pushed aside by a wall of grey, ominous cloud that engulfed me, creating a flattened, monochrome world of bare rock and drizzle. As the effect of altitude began to sap the strength from my legs, every step became an effort. The weight of my pack increased with every step and my lungs struggled to extract enough oxygen to keep my legs moving. The wind chilled the air and the rain turned to sleet, freezing on my clothes and face, making the going even more difficult. As I could not see where I was going, I had to turn back and set up camp in a hollow. The weather deteriorated and turned into a storm.

For an hour or so, I lay awake snug in my bivvy-bag listening to the sound of the freezing rain and howling wind. As my body warmth filled my down sleeping bag, I gradually fell asleep, lulled by the cacophony of the night.

After a chilly night at around 17,000 feet, I woke up to find my face inside a feathery mass of hoarfrost. My sleeping bag was covered with ice. Rather stupidly, I had left my boots outside and they were frozen solid. My sleeping bag and down-filled jacket had kept me warm but my camera had frozen and refused to work. The good news was that the storm had blown over, leaving a sky filled with scudding white clouds.

I climbed back up to what I thought was the pass and looked out across the valley on the other side. The view was stunning and made the pain of the previous day fade away into insignificance. The valley was vast and as far as I could tell, uninhabited. A few yaks grazed in the far distance, but there were no signs of human habitation. A river flowed carelessly across the valley floor, a winding ribbon of blue and green. The treeless valley floor itself stretched out to my left and right as far as I could see.

From my perch on the mountainside, I scanned the opposite side for the way south and saw it easily. It was a narrow cleft torn into the valley side and a good ten miles distant. The cleft matched the path shown on my map, giving me confidence that I was still heading in the right direction.

Standing on what I thought was the head of the pass, I watched a single cumulus cloud race towards me. In a few minutes, I was flying through a cloud six kilometres above the surface of the sea. It was exhilarating and despite the cold, I felt warmth spreading through my body. Was this my moment of enlightenment? For a few moments, I stood in the wind and looked out into a void that linked me with the distant mountains of the Himalaya. I felt very small before this grandeur and I understood how Buddhism thrived in these mountains.

"Om mani padme hum," whispered the mountain and the words were carried on by the passing wind. I shouldered my pack and descended to the valley floor, some three and a half thousand feet below me. As I made my way down, I found that I had just missed the pass and had climbed a thousand feet more than was necessary. Just as my spirits had been revived the sight of the great open valley, my camera eventually restarted having been revived by the warmth of my body. The valley floor was flat and featureless.

Slowed down by boggy conditions, I did not reach the cleft until two in the afternoon. Feeling tired after a restless night, I decided to stop and set up camp by the stream that flowed out of the cleft. Around me, fat marmots watched with interest, disappearing down their burrows whenever I looked in their direction. After the tribulations of the previous night, I felt that I needed a good night's sleep and crawled into my sleeping bag just as night fell. Above me, the great swathe of the Milky Way once again filled the night sky. A friendly satellite crossed the sky, sliding between the stars and planets, reminding me that I was not alone in the world.

Chapter 5

Once again, the night was bitterly cold and I awoke to find my bivvy-bag covered in frost. This time at least, I had remembered to bring my boots in with me and they were not frozen solid.

Feeling increasingly confident, I followed the cleft into the narrow gorge. After a couple of hours, I met a young herdsman keeping watch on a herd of grazing yak. He showed me how to use his yak-hair slingshot and in turn, I showed him how to use my binoculars. We shook hands and he returned to his herd.

Continuing down the gorge, I thought I heard something behind me. Turning, I saw two horsemen heading in my direction. As they got nearer, I saw that one had a Kalashnikov slung over his saddle. They were not in uniform and did not look like soldiers. A feeling of unease swept through me and the hairs on the back of my neck bristled alarmingly.

I need not have worried. The two horsemen trotted past me and waved. Had they been brigands, they could have robbed me and left me for dead. No one would have found me. The fact that they had overtaken me was a relief and I walked on feeling that I had had a narrow escape.

Chapter 6

After walking for another hour, my heart skipped a beat when I spotted two tethered horses in the middle of the track. As I drew nearer, I saw that they were grazing in a circular grassy area formed where the gorge opened out.

As I got closer, I could see that the two horsemen were waiting for me. As they watched me approach, one of them walked over to his horse and I could see that he was holding a Kalashnikov. The hairs on the back of my neck bristled again, my hands felt clammy and my heart began to pound. They had seen me, so there was no point in trying to go back. On horseback, they would have easily outrun me.

When I reached them, they asked me to sit with them and I soon discovered that they were in fact a two-man Chinese army medical team. They were both friendly and helpful. They were also keen to know where I was going.

I told them that I wanted to go to the village of Guru. This was the site of the Younghusband Mission's massacre of Tibetan troops, which I thought was about a day's walk to the east. With the aid of some small rocks, they made a three-dimensional map of the mountains around us and showed me the best way though the labyrinth of mountain passes to the village of Guru. I had two choices, to climb18,000 feet over a pass to the east or to continue south at a more comfortable 15,500 feet and then turn east along the same path at roughly the same altitude. Having already experienced life at 18,500 feet, I chose the latter because I did not really want to go to Guru at this stage. I still had my sights set on reaching the Chumbi valley, but thought that it would be more prudent to tell them I was heading somewhere a little nearer.

The older of the two men handed me what looked and tasted like blocks of dried yak cheese on a length of string. His colleague slung his AK47 over his shoulder and headed off into the mountains to shoot a marmot. I watched as my newfound friend picked up my pack and tied it to his horse. We walked together down the gorge. When we both heard the sound of a distant shot, my friend grinned and licked his lips. Ten kilometres later, the gorge opened up into another valley that ran east to west. He pointed to the east and told me that I would reach Guru by nightfall. I thanked him as he mounted his horse and trotted back to his dinner.

I continued until I was almost in sight of Guru and set up camp on a promontory overlooking the valley to the east. Sleep came easily and for once, I slept through until dawn. As my bivvy-bag was covered in ice, I crawled back into the warmth of my down jacket and ate breakfast in my sleeping bag as the sun began to lighten the sky to the east.

The darkness gave way to reveal a dull grey dome of steel that arched over the roof of the world. Twenty miles away, the faintest outline of the mountains could just be seen. The sky warmed and began to shift though shades of silver, yellow, straw, orange and finally to the blue of tempered steel. The Earth waited in silence as light flooded out between the peaks.

At first, all I could see was a jagged line of light that sliced into the darkness of the night. Then a river gleamed like quicksilver on the valley floor far below. The sun appeared from behind the Masang Kyungdu range and climbed into a clear blue sky, dominated by Gang Chhen, the Tiger Mountain. I watched in silence with the breath of the mountains brushing my lips. I felt alive and watched as the clouds to the east glowed with the promise of a new day.

I felt very much alone and my thoughts drifted back to times spent with the people I loved. What a pleasure it would have been to sit for a moment with each of them and share this view. I smiled at the memory of each one as the sun spread its Midas touch to the white peaks to the east forming a barrier between Tibet and Bhutan.

My thoughts drifted backwards and forwards in time and I became filled with the spirit of the mountains. I shivered to the glory of a perfect dawn. Below me, the villages were awaking, with families and monks rising from the death of sleep into the life of the new day. Plumes of smoke from yak dung fires in the village of Guru on the valley floor rose into the air, filling me with thoughts of families enjoying their breakfast of butter tea with *tsampa* in warm, dark rooms.

Finally, the sacred mountain of Chomolhari appeared, towering over the vast expanse of Tang La, marking the start of another day.

Chapter 7

Younghusband first passed through Guru in January 1904. The British Mission had advanced as far as Tuna and faced a Tibetan force that had set up a base in Guru, in an attempt to block the British advance on Lhasa. While Tibetans had visited his camp, they had steadfastly refused to let the British into their camp. The only message that they had for the British was that they should return to Yadong.

Frustrated by the delaying tactics employed by the Tibetans and aware of his lack of knowledge of the Tibetan force blocking his way, Younghusband decided on a course of action that would put him at great risk. Without informing General Macdonald, the military commander of the Mission, Younghusband decided that he needed to visit the Tibetan camp in Guru. His goal was to resolve the impasse by peaceful means.

On the morning of 13 January, Younghusband and two fellow officers, Captains O'Connor and Sawyer of the 23rd Pioneers set out on horseback towards Guru, some ten miles distant. They had no escort.

On the way, they met Tibetan messengers who had come to say that the Tibetan chiefs would not come to see Younghusband in Tuna. The sight of three unaccompanied officers on horseback, dwarfed by the enormity of the landscape, may have puzzled the Tibetans, who then watched as Younghusband and the other two officers continued towards Guru.

When they reached Guru, they found numbers of Tibetan soldiers out collecting yak dung in the surrounding plain and without any "military precaution" rode straight into the Tibetan camp. They found around six hundred soldiers huddled up in the cattle yards of the houses. They were armed with spears and matchlock rifles. Their response to Younghusband's arrival was laughter, rather than scowls. They found the sight of the three British officers on horseback very entertaining.

Younghusband asked to see the Tibetan general. They found him to be polite, well dressed and well-mannered. He smiled and introduced Younghusband to the other generals, who smiled and shook hands. Younghusband was then taken into another room and found three monks, who were seated. Their reaction was very different. They did not rise from their cushions and made only a minimal effort to greet Younghusband. The most senior Tibetan monk was from Lhasa. The other two were from Shigatse.

They settled down to drink tea and the Lhasa general explained that the Tibetans had a rule that no Europeans were to be allowed to enter the country. They explained that the reason for this rule was the need to preserve their religion. Younghusband explained that he had come unannounced in an attempt to resolve their differences by peaceful means. The Tibetans told him that the only way this aim could be achieved would be if the British Mission returned to Yadong. The scene for the coming violent confrontation had been set.

After a couple of hours walking, I found myself on the vast plain that leads to Tang La. In my mind's eye, I could see the British mission marching out from Tuna marching in columns, starkly outlined against the snow. It would have been bitterly cold and at 15,000 feet, hard work.

When the British approached Guru, the Tibetans did not open fire and it seemed that Younghusband's desire to avoid bloodshed would be achieved. The Tibetan general ordered his men to extinguish their fuses. In the calm that followed, the British and Tibetan forces came together. Photographs taken at the time show the British troops talking to the Tibetans and everyone seemed relaxed.

In a moment of confusion, a shot rang out and a Sepoy was shot in the jaw as he tried to disarm one of the Tibetan generals. Macdonald's troops responded with a hail of fire from bolt-action rifles and several Maxim machine guns. The charms worn by the Tibetans to protect them from bullets did not work and within a few moments somewhere between five hundred and a thousand Tibetans had been killed.

My journey south was made easier when I managed to hitch a ride with a couple of Tibetans on a pony cart. The road, lined by telegraph poles originally erected by the British Mission so that they could remain in contact with London by telegraph, was dwarfed by the looming splendour of Chomolhari, a jagged tooth of ice and rock that forms the cornerstone of the mountain range dividing Tibet from Bhutan and rises to more than 24,000 feet.

The cart tossed and bounced along the dirt road like a small boat in choppy waters. After an hour or so, we were passed by a thirty-truck army convey moving in the opposite direction. It was an uneasy time for me. At any moment, I expected to be stopped and questioned. I need not have worried, as they had more important matters on their minds. They drove past without stopping.

Two hours later, my driver took me into a compound where I met his family. His nine-year-old boy and teenage daughter hung back at first, but then came and sat next to me. Their mother, with her hair tied back in a braid poured me a cup of yak butter tea.

Soon afterwards, a battered truck pulled into the compound. Out jumped two Tibetans who told me that they lived in Yadong. When they heard that I wanted to go to Yadong, they offered me a ride.

They did not care a hoot about the regulation that banned them from giving foreigners a ride. The Tibetans sat in the cab and sang all the way across Tang La to Phari. I sat in the back of the truck with a sheep and a cockerel, who bickered incessantly.

Phari turned out to be a massive garrison town and was packed with Chinese soldiers. With a wicked grin, the driver asked me if I want to get out. I told him no and tried to flatten myself on the floor of the truck. The sheep looked at me with contempt and returned to its argument with the cockerel.

After what felt like an eternity, the engine coughed in the thin air and the driver eased the truck back onto the road. He stopped a little way outside Phari so that I could safely join him and his mate in the cab. They roared with laughter as I brushed the chicken shit from my jacket.

Behind us, the towering might of Chomolhari dominated the sky with its presence and as the sun sank towards Everest in the west, the air chilled noticeably.

The road began the steep twisting descent to the head of the Chumbi Valley, falling from 15,000 feet to 9,000 feet in a matter of an hour or two. Whenever we passed a set of prayer flags, my companions took off their hats and yelled something unintelligible in Tibetan. It would have been churlish not to join them. The truck carried us forward despite its obvious state of dilapidation. The driver chain-smoked and his mate entertained us with plaintive Tibetan love songs.

Finally, we reached the last checkpoint just below the head of the valley. Fearful of being caught, I tried to breathe in and become invisible. In fact, it was my lucky day. The check-post official was in the middle of his evening meal, so he waved us through without inspecting the cab. From that moment onwards, I knew that I would make it to Yadong. I had bypassed the checkpoint at Gala and slipped through the army checkpoint at Phari and eased my way past the last checkpoint at the entrance to the Chumbi valley, thanks to a bowl of noodles.

Moreover, I spent that night in the only hotel in Yadong. The hotel manager did not check my passport or ask to see my permit. I later discovered that the local chief of the local Public Security Bureau gave her a reprimand for not checking my papers more thoroughly. Later, I did what I could to apologise.

The hotel had several quaint features. The dining room was closed and room service non-existent. The bedrooms had attached bathrooms, but these were all locked, so guests had to either wash in the enamel bowl provided in their room or outside by the cold tap.

The only lavatories were outside and grim. As I squatted in the unlit interior, long-tailed maggots climbed up out of the hole and crawled out between my feet, leaving long trails of shining slime.

The light of day revealed thousands of them writhing about in the pool of decaying sewage at the end of the squatting slot. The sight and stench of the lavatory was so bad that the Chinese and Tibetans had given up and instead squatted on the path leading to the lavatory block. Night excursions to the lavatory required a torch and great care when walking in the shadows.

After a quick breakfast of rice porridge, green tea and pickled vegetables, I left the hotel and headed into the surrounding hills.

As quickly as I could, I left Yadong behind me and followed a goat track that led up the side of the valley towards the forested slopes. At first, the gradient was not too steep and I made good progress. Each step took me further away from the PSB and deeper into the sub-tropical vegetation that cloaked the hills around Yadong.

It did not take long to climb the first thousand feet, but then the combination of the steepness of the slope and the dense tangle of rhododendrons, bamboo and the rich variety of deciduous and coniferous saplings began to slow me down. At times, I was forced to crawl on all fours because of the steepness of the slope. My rucksack became entangled in the undergrowth more times than I could count. I reached the crest of the ridge by the middle of the afternoon. The views around me were of the deeply wooded valleys that swept over the southern slopes of the Tibetan Himalayas. I felt privileged to be there.

At the very top, I found a clearing and lay down for a rest. Overhead the sky was a deep blue dome speckled with tidy cotton wool clouds floating gently towards Chomolhari behind me. There was no sound and the thick, humid air coupled with the warmth of the sun, soon lulled me to sleep.

A strange rattling noise brought me to my senses with a start. With the hairs on the back of my neck prickling and a sinking feeling deep in the pit of my stomach, I opened my eyes and found myself looking straight into the dark, empty eyes of a Lammergeyer vulture circling some twenty feet above me. For a second or two, our eyes locked and in that instant I knew that he had hoped I was less alive. With what looked like a gesture of resignation, the great bird shrugged its broad shoulders and sloped off down into the valley in search of easier pickings.

It was time to move on, stumbling and crashing my way downhill, falling backwards several times as my feet slithered on rotting logs. Around me was a dense forest draped luxuriously with leaves and mosses.

The biggest obstacle turned out to be the litter of fallen trees, making movement difficult and at times, dangerous. It was impossible to find anywhere without a carpet of decaying branches and tree trunks half hidden under the dense vegetation. But the good news was that there were no leeches.

Strands of lichen hung from the trees like Christmas streamers and as dusk fell, clouds formed between the trees, creating a gloomy, mysterious world of dripping leaves and strange birdcalls.

When a seemingly solid log crumbled under my foot, I tripped forward and tumbled down the near vertical slope. After crashing through the undergrowth for what seemed like an age, I had a sense of falling through the air before being brought to an abrupt halt as my heavy backpack jammed in the branches of a fallen tree. It took me a few seconds to gather my senses enough to realise that I was hanging half-upside down over a rocky stream-bed some fifteen-foot below me.

I struggled to free myself. Whenever I tried too hard, my pack slipped a little, threatening to drop me head first into the stream. Eventually, I managed to almost dislocate one shoulder so I could release one of the shoulder straps and clamber up over the trunk to safety. For ten minutes or so, I sat perfectly still and considered what might have happened if I had not been so lucky.

When I started out again I was more careful and less trusting of anything that could have been rotten. It had been a tree-trunk about a foot thick crumbling under my weight that had hurled me down the slope in the first place.

To try and make my descent a little safer, I walked in the stream. Wet legs seemed better than a broken head. Finally, as evening approached, I could go no further. However, my luck had returned and I found myself on the only level surface in any direction. Some tree trunks had been washed down the stream and jammed across a narrow gully. Fragments of wood had been washed down and trapped behind the piled up logs making a tiny platform upon which I set up camp.

The stream was a good source of drinking water and the top layers of wood-chips were dry enough to make a fire. As the forest was engulfed by darkness, I made a small fire and cooked a hot meal. Just before I fell asleep, it occurred to me that if there was overnight rain, I would probably be washed away, but by then I was beyond caring.

Shortly after dawn, I broke camp and continued following the stream downhill. About fifty yards from my camp, the stream vanished over the edge of a 200 foot cliff face.

A shiver ran through me as I realised how close I had been to the precipice the night before. Feeling just a little queasy, I searched for a way down but it did not take me long to see that the edge of the rock face stretched into the forest as far as I could see in either direction. There was nothing to do but turn back. To make matters worse, I could see the line of a road along the valley floor below and what looked like military buildings in the distance. I then realised I risked blundering into a concealed military encampment and end up being arrested on espionage charges. Rather than run the risk of being arrested as a spy, armed with cameras, binoculars and detailed maps, in a sensitive border zone, I decided to abandon my plan to hike up to the Sikkim border. The risks involved were just too great. I had underestimated how much the Chinese had opened up the valleys around Yadong. With hindsight, I should have guessed, given that China had been fighting India in a border dispute in the nearby Arunachal Pradesh state earlier in the year.

With a deep feeling of disappointment, I climbed back up towards the top. On the way, I saw that a large animal had left an almost vertical trail through the vegetation, which I then followed. At one point, the animal had jumped over a pile of fallen tree-trunks stacked six feet high. On one trunk, I found claw-marks four to five inches across and realised that I had been trailing a large cat, possibly a snow leopard or even a tiger. Judging from the way undergrowth had been flattened, I guessed that the trail had been made early in the morning or during the night. The animal had been just a few metres away from my camp.

The Chumbi valley was reputed to be one of places where of the Abominable Snowman could be found. According to Chinese newspaper reports, several soldiers had been abducted by the female of the species in these woods. I decided to keep my eyes open.

The idea that a large animal such as the supposed yeti could survive on the high Tibetan plateau was hard to believe, as there is just not enough food. In the cloud forest, on the other hand, there was plenty of food: wild raspberries; strawberries; rose hips; nuts; and fungi of all kinds, not to mention the rest of the dense vegetation. Even I could have survived on the wild food growing in those hills.

Finally, what had started as a dull ache in my lower back became increasingly painful. I had sprained something when I had taken a tumble down the mountainside and had to accept that it would been unwise to continue. With a sense of disappointment, I gritted my teeth and headed back down the escarpment towards Yadong.

Chapter 8

Once back in Yadong, I returned to the hotel and faced a very hostile reception. The hotel staff had realised that I could not possibly have had a valid travel permit and told me in no uncertain terms that I was not welcome. I argued patiently for an hour or so and then suggested that they called the police.

The Tibetan manageress found a young army officer and asked him to call the PSB. He was not that keen to call them and in the end, they decided that I could stay there one night, but told me to leave first thing in the morning. This was not quite what I had hoped for, but it was a start and certainly better than nothing.

I was shown to a dormitory room occupied by three PLA officers. They had clearly been told to keep an eye on me and even followed me to the lavatories. Back in the room, we talked as well as we could and shared a bag of apples. They were very amiable and after a while, one of them popped out to get some beer. We drank together and despite the lack of a common language got on well together. When we finished the beer, I handed over some cash and one of them nipped out to get more. We all slept well.

For some reason, they left me in the middle of the night and I woke up alone. After breakfast, I packed and checked out as agreed. My next step was to find the Yadong police station and "turn myself in," as it was clear that the damage to my lower back was too painful for me to contemplate walking back the way I had come.

A brisk walk around the town failed to turn up anything looking remotely like a police station. I tried my limited Mandarin on a few Tibetans who looked at me blankly. I suppose it could have been my bad accent, but many Tibetans did not speak any Mandarin. Finally, I found the post office and an official who spoke English. He pointed out the way to the police station and carefully wrote "Yadong Public Security Bureau" in Chinese characters on the palm of my hand.

"*Yadong Gong-an-ju*," he said and I dutifully repeated his words.

"*Yadong Gong-an-ju.*"

I followed his directions and found two men waiting for me in the street in which the police station was located. When I approached them, I tried out my Mandarin and showed them the characters scrawled on my hand. They pointed to themselves and the man in charge asked me for my passport. I had found the right people.

Chapter 9

The officers escorted me to the PSB building and sat me down in an office in front of a large wooden desk. The youngest officer was in uniform. His colleague wore an officious-looking Mao suit and sat behind the desk. I guessed he was the more senior of the pair.

The discussions began. Their starting position was that I had to leave Yadong immediately. I countered by arguing that it would be better if I waited in Yadong for three days and then caught the bus to Lhasa. They told me that would be impossible and started asking me more questions in Mandarin. I answered as well as I could.

"Why are you here?"

"Because I am no good and Yadong is beautiful," I confessed in my miserable broken Mandarin.

"*Wǒ shi bou hao, Yadong shr hen hao.*"

They laughed at my wretched Mandarin and the atmosphere lightened a little. However, their position did not change. They peered intently at my passport and at my Alien Travel Permit (ATP) and shook their heads ominously.

"*Mei yuo Yadong?*" "You have no entry for Yadong?"

I confessed that I did not have an entry for Yadong, but they continued to scrutinise my permit. It occurred to me that it might help if I gave them another reason to let me wait for the bus and told them about my strained back. This moved them to fetch a more senior officer who in turn brought in his superior. Soon the room was filled with Public Security Officers playing pass-the-parcel with my travel documents. I sat on a couch and tried to smile serenely and not to appear too concerned by the whole business.

After a heated discussion between themselves, they came back to me and reminded me that I had been quite happily carrying my backpack when they found me. I realised that this angle of approach could get me into serious difficulties, so I told them the truth, that it was only after an hour or more that the discomfort in my back became unbearable.

All these negotiations were in Mandarin as the only English that they seemed to know was written on the back of the envelope that they showed me when they first found me:

"YOU ARE NOT PEMITED TO COME HERE. PLEAS GO AWAY."

The most senior officer then looked at my ATP for the hundredth time and asked me why I had an entry for Guangzhou (廣州), a city that was clearly *open*. That was an easy question to answer because the hand-written entry was for Korla (库尔勒市) not "Guangzhou". Given the differences between the Chinese characters for these places, I was confused and could not see where the conversation was going.

It occurred to me that this approach gave the PSB officials a line of argument that I had not considered. My ATP *might* have had an entry for the Chumbi valley(春丕河谷), but the Kashgar's PSB officer's handwriting was so bad that they could not tell. Rather than run the risk of punishing me for a committing a "non-existent crime", they decided to give me the benefit of the doubt and after a brief discussion, the entire assembly of PSB officers seemed to have agreed.

They could not let me off entirely, so they confined me to the central area of Yadong and told me very firmly not to leave except by bus to Lhasa. The only remaining problem was that of my accommodation. The PSB had told the hotel manager that I could not stay there. In addition, she had already refused to let me stay another night. Given the circumstances, I thought that the manager would be very unlikely to take me back.

As a final request, I asked the PSB either to let me stay with them or to phone the hotel and ask them to take me in. They readily agreed to the latter and clearly wanted to see the back of me as quickly as possible.

Somehow, I had managed to avoid being fined, deported or arrested. As I got ready to leave, the officer in the Mao suit asked me if I knew how to use a shovel. This was an interesting idea, perhaps he had some hard labour in mind.

But how could I? With a bad back?

He shrugged his shoulders and gave up.

Once the PSB agreed my fate, I was free to visit the nearest bar and ended up sharing bottles of cold beer with PLA soldiers and one of the friendlier PSB officers. When a bowl of steaming noodles arrived, I shovelled the food into my mouth and enjoyed the sensation of hot food slipping into my belly. As I gorged myself, an old man in a yellow sweater came up to me, stood to attention, saluted and bellowed "Atten-shun" with the ferocity of a seasoned army drill instructor. He then bowed his head to the back of my hand and gave me a toothless grin.

I could only assume that he was living proof of British influence in Tibet in the past. His shaven head and bright yellow pullover were to haunt me for the duration of my stay in Yadong. Whenever he saw me, he repeated the ritual. He was not quite old enough to have witnessed the Younghusband Mission to Lhasa, but he must have seen British troops drilling at some stage in his life.

The sight of Bhutanese traders in the centre of town wearing their traditional dress, woollen leggings, short skirts and wooden handled short-swords, was a reminder that Yadong had long been a trading post and that the border with Bhutan must have been at least partly open.

As the sun began its steady descent into the hills to the west, two journalists, one Chinese, the other Tibetan, sought me out, intrigued by my presence in a closed region.

"Would you like to come and eat with us? There is a canteen in one of the government buildings not far from here. We can walk."

Not knowing that they were inviting me to step outside the bounds of my supposed confinement, I accepted their offer. It was only as we walked away from the central area that I realised, but by then it was too late to go back. Nothing happened, confirming my suspicion that the PSB saw me more as a nuisance then a security threat.

In fact, our destination was not far from the central area. It was a squat, ugly building with an open door at the rear leading into a kitchen filled with vast cooking pots. It smelled like a charnel house. The sight of a severed black head told me that I had just missed the butchering of a yak. Apart from a large bloodstain on the paving stones outside the kitchen, the only sign of the slaughter remaining was the sagging loops of grey-pink entrails that had been hung out to dry on hooks around the kitchen.

The Chinese butcher joined us for a meal of fresh *momo dumplings* and buttermilk-tea. Two of the cooks appeared and watched me eat. After a few minutes, one of them pulled at the hairs on my arm and giggled. She said something in Tibetan and the others roared with laughter. Seeing my confusion, the Tibetan journalist asked her to explain.

She pointed to my feet and the fact that my size twelve boots were bigger than all the other boots around the table. Barely able to control her giggling, she pointed to my nose, which was clearly bigger than any of the other noses. Next, she showed everyone how large my hands were compared with all the other hands. And then she pointed to my groin with one hand and chortled into the other. I did not need a translator to understand the point of her joke, which reminded me of the soft drinks seller in Wuhan. I wondered whether the condemned man had already met his fate.

My cooks laughed and slapped me on the back. We celebrated with beers all round and eventually, staggered back to the hotel where I collapsed on to my bed.

The PSB made sure that I left on the next bus to Lhasa and were kind enough to give me a travelling companion. He told me that he had been told to make sure I went all the way to Lhasa. The bus climbed up and out of the Chumbi valley past Swiss-style chalet houses, rushing streams and luxuriant undergrowth. The narrow, twisting road eventually climbed up on to the wide expanse of Tang La, overshadowed by the broad shoulders of Chomolhari.

The bus carried me through the village of Guru and then to Gala Tso, where the guards at the checkpoint confiscated my passport and refused to let me pass. My travelling companion had to pull rank and calm them down. Reluctantly, they gave him my passport and allowed me to get back onto the bus. As we set off on the road to Gyantse, he grinned and gave me my passport back.

The bus stopped briefly in Gyantse and then pushed onwards towards the Karo-La glacier. We spent the night in a truck stop close to the Turquoise Lake and reached Lhasa in the middle of the following afternoon. I had been away for nearly four weeks and had not spoken to a single Westerner since the day I set out from Gyantse.

After a diet of rice, dried food and oatmeal, supplemented only by a few noodles in Yadong, I felt in need of some decent food. As the bus neared Lhasa, I dreamed about juicy Yak Burgers, a decent cup of coffee and perhaps a glass of wine.

Chapter 10

When the bus stopped on the outskirts of Lhasa, my companion got off to relieve himself. I decided to give him the slip and walk the last few miles to Lhasa. The prospect of further contact with the PSB at this stage was one that I was keen to avoid. I decided to head for the Lhasa Holiday Inn, rather than the centre of Lhasa. The clerk at the reception desk observed my rather unkempt appearance and checked me in with a smile.

The pleasure of lying in a bath of hot water was one that was hard to beat. The prospect of sleeping in a proper bed with clean sheets was even more appealing. For some reason I felt safe from the PSB in my room. Perhaps it was the sense of familiarity that comes with the trappings of Western living: the television, the fitted carpets, the minibar and the room service menu. The reality was that they were no longer interested in a mere trespasser.

Even as I lay soaking in my bath, murmurs of discontent were spreading through some of the younger monks in the great Drepung monastery to the west of Lhasa. The voices of dissent had always been there, but there was a new sense of frustration that was driving angry young men along a path of action that was about to change lives.

Part 5 - A time for tears

Chapter 1

During the early years of the Chinese occupation of Tibet, the People's Liberation Army systematically demolished thousands of monasteries and temples. These acts of vandalism were a crucial part of the Communist Party's plans for the "liberation" of the Tibetan people. The Party sought to smash the power of the lamas and replace what they saw as a medieval feudal system with a revolutionary Maoist regime controlled from Beijing.

Following a change in thinking towards Tibet in the 1980's, the Chinese employed workers and artisans in projects to rebuild some of the temples and monasteries flattened during the "liberation" of Tibet.

Deep within the corridors of power, influential thinkers had convinced others that wealthy foreign visitors would pay premium rates to see Tibetans practising Buddhism. Foreigners travelling in organised tour groups would not only bring in much needed hard currency but could also be kept under tight control. Senior officials also recognised that the Party could make use of the propaganda to be gained by opening up Tibet. They knew that any good news coming out of Tibet would help deflect international attention from any further human rights abuses. Much of Tibet remained closed to foreigners.

Built by the Party, the Lhasa Hotel first opened in 1985. A year later, the Party brought in the Holiday Inn chain to take-over the day-to-day management of the hotel. Designed to cater for tour groups at the upper end of the market, the Party built the hotel complex with several restaurants, bars, a disco and more than 1,300 beds. Located to the west of Lhasa next to Norbulinka, the Dalai Lama's old Summer Palace, the hotel was an island of modern living in what was still largely a medieval city.

Seeing me loitering with no intent in the lobby after a much-needed hot shower, the general manager of the Lhasa Hotel asked if I was enjoying my stay.

"I am having a very comfortable stay here, but there have been some odd encounters with some your staff. I asked a maid for a clean towel and was surprised when she told me that there were none left. I phoned through to reception and someone from Room Service delivered one to my room almost immediately. The maid either misunderstood me or just could not be bothered to help. This is just a very minor point, but if you have staff who act like that, other guests more needy than I could get pretty upset..."

As I spoke, I realised that I was coming across as someone who actually cared a great deal about clean towels. I should not have been concerned. Chris Schlittler smiled reassuringly, handed me one of his business cards and was unperturbed.

"One of my greatest challenges is that we cannot find experienced staff here in Lhasa. I had to bring in some European and Chinese managers, or this place would have fallen apart. We really have had to start from scratch."

More used to running luxury hotels in Europe, the general manager of the Lhasa Hotel was coming to terms with the joys of running the first international hotel on the Roof of the World.

"Most of my staff are local Chinese and Tibetans with little or no experience in the hotel trade. The concept of customer service in the Western sense is one that is almost alien to the local work ethic, but I am making progress to change all that!"

Chris grinned. "It is all about understanding their needs and giving them the right training."

A tour group began to assemble in the lobby. Chris watched them out of the corner of one eye. Nothing seemed to escape his attention.

"I can give you an example. Because no one thought of telling the cleaners that they have to empty the vacuum cleaners when the dust-bags are full, we have almost none here that work anymore. One by one, the dust-bags filled up and then the motors burned out. The problem was that it had not occurred to anyone that the cleaners had never used a vacuum cleaner before, so no one thought of giving them any training."

Sweeping his fingers through his hair, he smiled and shook his head. Perhaps a lesser being would have given up by now. I suspected that he was a man with a lot of patience and infinite belief in others, which helped him preserve his sanity.

"The majority of the people who work here have grown up in a society in which many things are not possible. The people who stay here come from societies in which most things are possible. This creates a big culture gap. Our guests get very upset when the staff will not make that extra special effort to satisfy their needs. I have to build a 'service' culture from nothing."

But some of the challenges he faced were even more fundamental. The infrastructure needed to support a large international hotel just did not exist in Lhasa.

"In most hotels, fresh meat is brought in by butchers in refrigerated vans. There are no refrigerated vans here, so when we need fresh meat, a yak is brought here and killed outside the kitchens."

This was one aspect of the hotel that management preferred to hide from most Western guests. The idea of a butcher killing animals on the premises could have upset some guests. At least I could be sure that the meat in the yak burgers served in the bar was fresh and that it was not bought from the fly-infested open-air meat market in Lhasa.

A tour-bus returning from a visit to the Potala Palace pulled into the forecourt and deposited a noisy party of wealthy old age pensioners into the lobby. Disturbed by the commotion, a small group of tousle-headed, bronzed mountaineers huddled over a map in the coffee bar made a conscious effort to ignore them. An anthropologist swept through the lobby with his head held high to indicate both the significance of his work and his disdain for the wrinkly sightseers.

Personally, I had nothing but admiration for the older guests. Apart from anything else, the effects of Lhasa's thin air must have really tested their stamina. For most of them, just being in Lhasa was the fulfilment of a lifelong dream, which was why their faces shone with excitement.

Chapter 2

After a good night's sleep, I woke up refreshed and hungry. I had a quick shower and strolled down for a lazy breakfast. The notice board in reception reminded me that the date was Sunday, 27 September 1987. The smell of fresh coffee, warm toast and fried eggs coming from the buffet was enough to make me think of faraway breakfasts with friends, family and loved ones.

One of the nicest aspects of eating alone is having the time to reflect on the past. Memories of perfect moments drifted before me like clouds on a summer's day. In one fragment of time, I was running naked, hand-in-hand with a blonde-haired angel along the deserted shore of a great ocean at the end of the world. The sky spun and we drifted into a frozen forest drenched with the scent of pine needles. Snug inside winter clothes, we were having a picnic in the snow, a real feast with slices of fresh bread, tranches of farmhouse ham and fine cheeses washed down with several glasses of champagne. The bottle was half-buried in an ice bucket made from crisp, white snow. From there I drifted into a cave filled with rustling leaves, where we kissed and made love. The west wind blew and I found myself floating into the warmth of a candlelit room filled with smiles and good food. I could almost taste the steaming bowl of homemade oyster soup. These were sweet memories of good times from another age.

As I soaked myself in a bath of nostalgic daydreams, a small group of young men in Lhasa were more concerned about the reality of the present. I had been asleep when twenty-one nervous young monks from Drepung monastery gathered to prepare themselves for an act of public protest against the authorities. As dawn broke, they set out in three separate jeeps for the centre of Lhasa in the knowledge that they were about to challenge a regime with a reputation for responding with force to any sign of public dissent.

As a waiter brought fresh coffee to my table in the Lhasa Hotel, the monks were coming together again in a teahouse on Barkhor Square. Several days later, I was able to talk to witnesses who helped me piece together an account of what they did next...

At around nine o'clock, they left the teahouse and set out on their first circuit of the Jokhang Temple carrying a homemade Tibetan flag. Each one of them was more than a little afraid, but they saw no other way of getting their message heard and with each step, they became more resolute.

The news that protestors were marching clockwise around the Jokhang Temple with a Tibetan flag generated a frisson of excitement that radiated out from the centre of Lhasa and nearly a hundred lay supporters soon joined them. Their demands were clear: the end of the Chinese occupation of Tibet; freedom; and independence for Tibet. The sight of the flag with its two Tibetan snow lions and snow-capped mountain representing Tibet carried by the protestors raised a glimmer of hope in the hearts of their followers and those who could do no more than stand and stare in astonishment.

As they processed around the holy circuit, the demonstrators passed pilgrims prostrating themselves full-length on the ground. These devotees had come from all over Tibet to pray in and around the Jokhang Temple and were determined not be distracted by anything as worldly as a mere demonstration. Many of them had walked hundreds of miles to make this their pilgrimage of a lifetime. Some were professional pilgrims paid to prostrate themselves by others who did not have the time to make the pilgrimage themselves.

As they heard the impassioned calls for Tibetan independence and saw the Tibet flag held on high, even the most devout of these pilgrims left their prayers and joined the marchers.

As the throng passed the incense burners in front of the Jokhang Temple, the women tending the fires laid down their bundles of juniper and stepped out through clouds of perfumed smoke to join them. Traders setting up stalls around the circuit stopped and stared at the marchers in disbelief. The last time there had been any significant public protest in Lhasa had been in 1959.

Four Westerners followed the demonstrators, taking photographs. After two full circuits, the demonstrators headed out across Barkhor Square. There was still no sign of a response from the authorities. The procession left Barkhor Square to the west and continued along Renmin Lu towards the offices of the Government of the Tibet Autonomous Region (TAR).

The lack of any reaction from the authorities gave the impression that the protestors had caught them off their guard. Only as they approached the TAR government compound was there any sign of a response. Police motorcycles with sidecars supported by a growing number of policemen in green uniforms with peaked caps appeared in front of the entrance to the TAR Government compound. At first, they did no more than stare at the marchers. Their faces were emotionless and this had the effect of making them look curiously inhuman. It was hard to believe that any of these men had girlfriends, wives or children.

As the protestors approached the entrance to the TAR Government compound, the senior officer ordered his men to break up the demonstration. With grim professionalism, the police charged with batons drawn. As they attacked one end of the demonstration, the motorcyclists accelerated and rammed the marchers at the other. A violent struggle between the police and the demonstrators ensued and after a minute or so, it was clear that there could only be one victor. Twenty-one monks from Drepung monastery were arrested, together with nine other demonstrators, seven men and two women. All too soon, the demonstration was over. As the dust settled, the only evidence that anything out of the ordinary had taken place was etched on the shocked faces of bystanders.

The arrested Tibetans were taken away in several vehicles to a police station to the west of Lhasa. Fifteen minutes later, they were put on a bus and taken to the Lhasa Gutsa detention centre.

The police also detained the four Westerners who photographed the incident. The police confiscated their passports and exposed films of the demonstration.

Blissfully unaware of any of these events, I finished off my breakfast and rented a bicycle. Being in no particular hurry, I headed into the centre of Lhasa at a steady pace and made no effort to keep up with the flow of traffic. Old men on battered bicycles left me standing. A bus rumbled past, kicking dust into my face. A Chinese butcher pushing a handcart piled high with the remains of a butchered yak was the only traffic moving in the other direction. When a young man with his girlfriend riding on the crossbar of his bicycle overtook me, I made a bit of an effort to pedal faster, but soon reverted to a more comfortable pace.

In Renmin Lu, a young tourist ran towards me waving his arms.

"Stop. I have to tell you what happened here a few minutes ago."

With emotion clogging his voice, he told me about the demonstration and the violence of the Chinese response. My first thought was to try to get a message to Reuters in Beijing. With as much haste as I could muster on my clapped-out Flying Pigeon bicycle, I rushed back to the hotel and found Stephen Nisbett's business card. It did not take me long to discover that the phone in my room no longer accepted calls to Beijing.

The Chinese receptionist told me that there was a "technical problem" with the line. One of the European hotel managers then explained that the Public Security Bureau had ordered the closure of all lines of communication out of the Lhasa Hotel.

Undeterred, I got back on my trusty Flying Pigeon bicycle and headed for the post office in the centre of Lhasa in the hope that the PSB had not closed down the telex machine there.

The clerk at the telex desk was very helpful. After watching me type the first few innocent lines, he even let me send the telex myself. As soon as he walked away, I added a couple of sentences describing the demonstration, the violent actions of the police and the arrest of the four foreign tourists.

Half expecting the PSB to arrive at any minute, I signed the telex using the pseudonym "Straw Hat" and hit the transmit key. There was a brief pause and for a moment, nothing happened. Nervously, I looked around to check that there was still no sign of the PSB. When the response code appeared in front of me telling me that Reuters in Beijing had successfully received the message, I breathed a sigh of relief and hoped that Stephen remembered the straw hat that I had sported in Beijing.

There was still no sign of the PSB and life continued as if nothing had happened out of the ordinary. With my heart pounding, I cycled away and only felt safe when well away from the building.

In Beijing, Stephen was eventually handed my telex and realised that he had a story that was worthy of further investigation. After some discussions within Reuters, Guy Dinmore, a colleague, was chosen to fly to Lhasa to do a follow up story. Jasper Becker, Beijing Correspondent of the Manchester Guardian agreed to come with him and they immediately booked themselves on the next flight to Chengdu.

Back in the Holiday Inn, I listened intently to news bulletins on the BBC World Service, but there was nothing about the demonstration, so I went to the bar for a beer.

News of a trial of eleven petty criminals to be held in Lhasa Stadium on Tuesday had reached the Lhasa Hotel and among the staff, there was talk of little else. Apparently, every work unit in Lhasa, including the Lhasa Hotel, was required to send one or two representatives. None of the European employees was keen to go.

Chapter 3

Monday passed without incident, but there was still nothing about the demonstration on the BBC World Service news. I began to wonder if Reuters had received my telex and even began considering whether the PSB could have faked the response code. More likely was the possibility that Reuters had decided that as they could not really verify the accuracy of my account, they could do nothing with the story.

I need not have worried. Reuters published their story of the demonstration on 28 September. The BBC broadcast the story later in the afternoon on the World Service. As soon as Reuters released the story, other members of the international press corps picked it up and booked flights to Lhasa via Chengdu. Some knew that Jasper and Guy had already arrived in Chengdu and had booked seats on the morning flight to Lhasa.

As soon as Guy and Jasper were safely on their way, Stephen had contacted the Foreign Affairs Office of the TAR Government to try to get an official to confirm that a demonstration had taken place. He tried an indirect question, knowing that a direct question would almost certainly get him nowhere.

"Can you confirm whether it was three or four Westerners that were arrested during the demonstration of monks in Lhasa?"

The official who answered the phone told him that it was not true that any Westerners had been arrested. He confirmed that there had been a disturbance, but denied that any Westerners had been arrested.

"...Four Westerners were detained, but released soon after. They were not arrested."

This was enough to confirm that there had been a demonstration and Reuters were eventually able to run the story.

In the end, the management of the Holiday Inn chose two Tibetans to represent the hotel at the trial and subsequent execution. In the evening of 29 September, news of the execution of one of the prisoners was the talk of the hotel. He was killed in the usual way with a single pistol shot in the back of the head. The authorities would eventually send his family a token bill for the bullet.

On the other hand, there were suggestions that the trial had been timed to coincide with the Dalai Lama's visit to the United States and that the execution was that of a political activist. During the visit, the Dalai Lama was due to meet several US Congressmen, including Jesse Helmes, Republican senator from North Carolina, an ardent right-winger, renowned for his anti-Communist views.

According to some observers, the purpose of the trial was to show the Tibetan people that the Party would punish criminals severely. Whatever the reason, most commentators saw the trial and execution as an overreaction.

During his visit to the United States, the Dalai Lama also addressed Congress. In an historic speech, he set out a five-point plan for peace. Details of his plan quickly became known in Lhasa. The Chinese government was furious that the Americans had given the Dalai Lama such an opportunity to state his views.

In his first point, the Dalai Lama proposed that the whole of Tibet, including the eastern provinces of Kham and Amdo, be transformed into a zone of "Ahimsa", a Hindi term used to mean a state of peace and non-violence.

"The establishment of such a peace zone would be in keeping with Tibet's historical role as a peaceful and neutral Buddhist nation and buffer state separating the continent's great powers. It would also be achieved. We must all exert ourselves to be reasonable and wise and to meet in a spirit of frankness and understanding."

The Dalai Lama could have been right in a moral sense, but the political reality was that there was no real support for an independent Tibet. Few countries had demonstrated any appetite for a serious battle with China over Tibet. Instead, Tibet served as a vehicle for putting moral pressure on China to improve its record on human rights.

There had been persistent rumours over the years that the CIA had been involved in some covert support of Tibetan rebels, but their efforts seemed to have been on a small scale. Whether there was any appetite for any more tangible support for the Dalai Lama in the United States was doubtful. China was just too big for anyone to want to upset. The best that Tibetans could hope for was that China could be encouraged to be more sensitive.

Back in the bar of the Lhasa Hotel, a middle-aged American filmmaker who had just travelled overland to Lhasa from Chengdu in a four-wheel drive Landcruiser was keen to talk about his journey over a beer.

"It was one hell of a drive. I have never seen roads like that anywhere in the world."

He paused to wipe a bead of sweat off his brow.

"I'll tell you something else, miles from anywhere we were 'held up' by a gang of Tibetans armed with AK47's. When I saw the weapons pointing at us, I was sure we were going to die. I nearly crapped myself."

I had an idea how he had felt. He sipped his beer and took a deep breath.

"My Chinese driver was terrified. He was sure that they were going to shoot him. But they did not even rob us. In fact, the incident ended peacefully with a photo call in front of the Land Cruiser. They looked like Khampa tribesmen to me, because they all had red braids tied into their hair. Whoever they were, they looked pretty wild."

His story appeared to tie in with rumours that small mobile groups of armed Khampa tribesmen funded by the CIA were still operating in Eastern Tibet and even in the area north of Mustang in Nepal.

By the evening of 29 September, all of the Westerners who had been detained had been released and given their passports back. Life in Lhasa seemed to be returning to normal.

The next day, I decided to move into a more traditional Tibetan hotel right in the centre of Lhasa, a short distance from Barkhor Square. The only available room was basic with a concrete floor, a bare light bulb and two single beds. There was a backpack by one of the beds. When a bearded Australian eventually turned up and found me installed in his room, he was polite, but distant.

The hotel manager had promised to let me know as soon as a single room became available. He was also keen for me to see the festivities in Barkhor Square.

"There is a festival today in Barkhor Square for the coming Asian Games. You should go there and see."

Chapter 4

Barkhor Square was packed with farmers, shop assistants, schoolchildren, students, monks, nuns, Chinese workers and men in uniform, but I managed to find a good viewpoint from the Barkhor Café. From there, I watched as the Chinese athletics team appeared and jogged around the square to polite applause. I suspected that their coaches had brought them up onto the high Tibetan plateau for some high altitude training to boost their red blood cell count, which would certainly enhance their performance.

The parade of athletes was followed by a display of traditional Tibetan dancing. The atmosphere seemed relaxed and even monks from Drepung monastery joined in with the festivities. They played welcoming fanfares on Tibetan drums and twelve feet long Tibetan horns. There were many uniformed personnel in the crowd, but there was no sign that any of them was armed. The authorities seemed to have successfully prevented demonstrators from disrupting a very carefully stage-managed event.

Visiting nomads continued praying in front of the Jokhang Temple, despite the noise of the crowd. The day ended without incident and life in the square returned to normal.

This was the calm before the coming storm.

As I sat in a teahouse in Lhasa, I caught sight of several of the monks who had been arrested by the People's Military Police (PMP) on television addressing a crowd of soldiers in green "army-style uniforms." The event served only to trigger a reaction that the Chinese had not anticipated. For some, the night was spent praying in preparation for the coming day. Tension was mounting as discontent wound its way along alleyways and down smoking chimneys.

The calm of the evening belied a growing feeling of anger that was sweeping across Lhasa.

Chapter 5

The first of October was also Chinese National Day. Just after nine in the morning, twenty-three monks from Sera monastery set out along the Jokhang Temple circuit walking in a clockwise direction. They were joined by eight monks from the Jokhang and three from Nechung monastery. Once again, lay Tibetan sympathisers joined them. They began to march around the Temple in a group, calling for independence for Tibet.

This time, the police were better prepared and responded more quickly. On the fifth circuit, the marchers found their way blocked by around one hundred police officers supported by jeeps and motorcycles with sidecars.

Again, the police broke up the march with a baton charge supported by motorcyclists with sidecars who drove into the demonstrators. This time, they also wielded electric cattle prods. Around fifty people, including monks from Sera monastery were arrested and taken to the two storey, flat-roofed police station facing the south-westerly corner of the Jokhang Temple. Among them were three Westerners who had been photographing the march.

As news of the arrests spread through Lhasa, a crowd of nearly three thousand Tibetans assembled in front of the police station.

High-ranking TAR Government officials arrived at the police station and spent thirty minutes trying to convince the detainees that these political activities should be brought to an end.

As the police dragged the three Westerners through the police station, they saw the monks squatting in the courtyard being beaten with shovels by men in uniform.

Meanwhile, in Barkhor Square, the mood of the crowd became increasingly agitated as news of the beatings spread. Some of the demonstrators broke up paving stones, while others collected rocks from building sites in the streets around the Square. They began to bombard the watching police and a Chinese TV crew, who retreated into the police station, leaving their vehicles unattended.

Groups of women and children overturned their abandoned vehicles and set them on fire. The tally of burning vehicles soon mounted. Before long, eight jeeps, three motorcycles with sidecars and a truck close to the TAR Government Offices in Renmin Lu were ablaze. Years of repressed anger were released in a frenzy of destruction.

As I made my way towards the main body of the demonstrators, I walked too close to one of the burning jeeps as its fuel tank exploded with a dull thud. The heat of the explosion seared my face, forcing me to break into a belated jog.

At the other end of the square, demonstrators had piled blankets and towels around a motorcycle with sidecar that had been dragged against the main entrance to the police station. Fuel leaking from the motorcycle had soaked into the fabric and had been set on fire in an attempt to force the release of the arrested monks.

The fire quickly took hold of the building and dark clouds of smoke billowed up into the sky. In the resulting confusion, most of the arrested demonstrators escaped into the alley between the police building and the school. A monk from the Jokhang, Champa Tenzin, tried to help the escapees out of the burning police station, but was forced back into Barkhor Square with the skin on his forearms burning. He was later paraded on shoulders of the crowd round Barkhor Square.

A surge of the crowd carried me forward to a position opposite the north-facing side of the police station. A dozen or so Tibetans gathered around me to shield me from flying rocks and the attentions of the police. They pointed to my camera and made it clear to me that they wanted me to take pictures of the riot and the police response. I was happy to oblige.

Fire engines and reinforcements arrived. Some were armed. The crowd fought them off with a barrage of stones. They were not equipped with riot gear. The reinforcements retreated to a safe distance along Renmin Lu and hung around in aimless groups. They seemed to be waiting for someone to make a decision.

Video cameramen supported by armed police officers appeared on the roof of the now burning police building. The intelligence arm of the PSB, or perhaps the People's Military Police (PMP), was keen to film the demonstrators, presumably so that they could track them down at a later stage. They were greeted with a hail of stones. At first, the police officers' only response was to throw stones and rocks back at the crowd. It was not long before they started shooting.

At around eleven o'clock, the sound of single shots and automatic fire echoed across the square. The distinctive sound of a Kalashnikov being fired in semi-automatic mode brought back memories of time spent with the Mujahideen in the Chitral valley.

However, it turned out that the first shots were fired inside the police station. A twenty-five year old monk from Sera monastery was killed instantly. Two lay Tibetans were wounded, one in the shoulder and the other in the leg.

The first sound of gunfire did not give me much cause for concern. At first, I assumed, wrongly, that the soldiers were aiming their shots over the heads of the demonstrators to try to get them to disperse. At worst, I supposed that they could have been firing rubber bullets or tear gas canisters. After all that was what had usually happened in Northern Ireland. It was not conceivable to me that the authorities would have sanctioned the killing of unarmed demonstrators. I had forgotten Bloody Sunday.

When the crowd did not disperse, police gunmen aimed at the demonstrators' feet. Ricochets danced across the surface of Barkhor Square; some crashed through doors; some slammed into walls; some buried themselves in calves and thighs. Then, without warning, a marksman armed with a high-velocity rifle raised his sights and fired with deadly intent.

Making good use of the chaos caused by the fire, three of the arrested monks escaped from police building, only to be mown down by very accurate fire from the marksman.

The unseen marksman killed several people in the crowd immediately and badly wounded others. With the encouragement of the Tibetans around me, I tried to capture as much as I could of what was happening on film. Through the camera viewfinder, the riot seemed very unreal. I felt no sense of danger and could not consider the possibility that I was putting myself at risk. The excitement of the moment was intense and a surge of adrenaline made sure that I felt no fear.

Throughout my teens, I lived with images of the violence of the Vietnam War, in newspapers, magazines and on the television. The horrors of warfare that accompanied many evening meals became commonplace and to an extent, lost their impact. Through the viewfinder of my camera, the sight of young men in uniform shooting into the crowd did not seem to be very much different.

A young man standing in the crowd with one fist raised in defiance was shot about twenty metres from me. The high velocity bullet entered the front of his head and passed into the shoulder of the man standing behind him. Killed in an instant, he stood very still for a second and then crumpled to the ground. The remains of the back of his skull and bits of brain were splashed over his wounded friend.

His death finally alerted me to the very real danger that the marksmen could have shot me, especially as I was so much taller than the average Tibetan. In fact, I must have stood out like a sore thumb and would have made an easy target if anyone had chosen to aim at me. Turning away from the police station, I made a hasty exit from the square and found refuge behind a thick stone wall. Using the buildings around the north of Barkhor Square as cover, I worked my way round to the front of the Jokhang Temple. To my surprise, I found that I was shivering with excitement; the reality of the killings had still not really registered.

Chapter 6

Meanwhile, Jasper Becker and Guy Dinmore arrived at the Lhasa Hotel, having flown in on the morning flight from Chengdu. As they checked in, their eyes were drawn to a hand-written message scrawled on a blackboard set up in the lobby:

DUE TO TRAFFIC PROBLEMS

THE REGULAR SHUTTLE BUS

TO THE BARKHOR SQUARE

HAS BEEN CANCELLED.

WE APOLOGISE FOR ANY

INCONVENIENCE

They were both keen to make the most of their time in Tibet and looked for a taxi to take them to the centre of Lhasa. The problem was that there were no taxis to be seen around the hotel and no one was able to say when a taxi might turn up. Being intelligent and resourceful journalists, they decided instead to rent bicycles from the hotel.

As they prepared to get on their bicycles, the sound of gunfire coming from the centre of Lhasa caught their attention. Jasper recognised the sound and frowned.

"That sounds like a Kalashnikov being fired in semi-automatic mode. What the hell is going on?"

camera to appear. In the silence, the whining noise of the flash slowly charging itself was almost deafening. Eventually, the green light appeared and I finally managed to photograph the wound in his leg.

Then we approached the wound itself. In reality, there was little more that we could do. We tried to tell his family that he had to be taken to a doctor. The trouble was that they knew that if he went to a doctor, he would be arrested. If he did not go to a doctor, the wound would probably become infected and there was always a risk that he would lose his leg. He could also have died of shock.

As the house had no electric lights, we worked in almost total darkness, aided only by the light from a torch. The family watched as we cleaned and dressed the wound, filling the silence with their whispers. Afterwards, the man's wife placed cups of lukewarm yak-butter tea before us and smiled.

The door to the courtyard opened and a man slipped in with the news that police patrols were in the vicinity looking for wounded Tibetans. We could not leave until they were certain that the police were not outside. The prospect of the police finding us giving first aid to a wounded Tibetan and misunderstanding our motives was not appealing. As we waited silently for the patrols to move away, the riot rumbled on in Barkhor Square.

As soon as the Tibetan lookout gave the "all clear" signal, we made our escape and headed back towards the scene of the riot.

A hundred yards from the bloodbath in Barkhor Square, a Uygur black marketeer stopped me to ask if I wanted to change any money. In the midst of all this unrest, there were still people trying to make a profit as if this were any ordinary day. The smell of burning vehicles hung uneasily in the air as a reminder that this anything but an ordinary day.

Chapter 8

With great care, I moved around the southern side of the Jokhang Temple to try to see what was happening in Barkhor Square. The way was blocked by market stalls that had been turned on their sides by the rioters to make barricades. As I got nearer, I could just make out the remains of the still-burning motorcycle and sidecar jammed against the main entrance of the burning police station. Dense clouds of smoke billowing out of the front of the police station provided evidence of the intensity of the fire within.

Caught up in the excitement of the moment, three Americans and a Britain were seen throwing rocks at the Chinese during the riot by other foreigners. This could have been a problem for all foreigners in Lhasa, because the Chinese would have liked nothing better than to have had the opportunity to suggest that external agitators had triggered the riot. There was a rumour that a few days before the main riot, the police had caught two of them posting anti-Chinese propaganda in and around Lhasa. Apparently, they had even put up one pro-Tibet poster in the main police station.

The shooting continued and then almost stopped, leaving behind an uneasy calm. From time-to-time, the occasional sound of gunshots clattered around Barkhor Square. Some of the gunfire was clearly from at least one automatic weapon.

At approximately twelve-thirty, about five hundred police reinforcements arrived in Barkhor Square. They immediately set about clearing the area in front of the police station and the surrounding alleyways. Then they fired automatic weapons over the heads of the demonstrators.

As rioting Tibetans fled from the gunfire, I noticed that many of them were laughing and giggling. I could only assume that they had been infected by the madness that had swept through Lhasa.

Despite being outnumbered by the crowd, the reinforcements remained outside the police station, facing the rioting Tibetans. They had not been equipped with riot gear, nor did they have shields with which to protect themselves from the barrage of rocks hurled at them. Their injuries were very real.

Around this time, the police arrested twenty more demonstrators and held them in the school opposite the burning police building. The police beat them with rifle butts and rocks. Later, foreigners reported that they saw monks standing with the rioters taking off their robes to avoid being arrested.

Visiting nomads prostrated themselves in front of the Jokhang Temple as the rioting continued. They had travelled a long way to carry out this important ritual and saw no reason to let the disturbances get in their way.

Two boys aged about ten moved out in front of the crowd and stood facing the police station. Using slingshots woven from yak-hair, they hurled rocks into the police station with great accuracy. As one boy's slingshot snapped and the stone shot off at an angle, he caught me watching him from behind the barricades and grinned.

A movement caught my eye. Looking up, I could see a uniformed officer who appeared halfway along the roof of the burning police building. He pulled out his pistol and fired into the crowd. The crowd responded with a hail of well-aimed stones. When a stone knocked off his peaked cap, he bent down, picked it up, dusted it down and put it back on his head. He then continued firing shots into the crowd. He was very composed and very focused. As he looked down onto the crowd with a look of contempt on his face, it seemed clear to me that this was not a controlled response, it looked like an act of vengeance.

Demonstrators, including small boys, crouched behind barricades in front of the police station and continued to sling stones through the smoke-filled windows. The fire moved swiftly from room to room devouring anything in its way. Only when purple plumes of smoke poured out of shattered windows, did the barrage of stones stop. There was nothing to be gained by stoning clouds of smoke.

Unseen by the demonstrators, a young German, one of the Westerners taken to the police station, had been there for nearly three hours and was getting increasingly worried. As the fire took hold, the police moved him deeper into the building in an attempt to escape the choking smoke and the heat of the flames.

Despite the very evident danger to themselves from flying rocks and stones, his captors gave him their only enamelled washing bowl and told him to use it to protect his head. The young German eventually escaped from the burning police station with the help of Tibetan police officers. They had to break a hole through a wall to the roof of the building next door to escape the fire. Later, he told me that throughout his time in the police station, the police officers were generally friendly towards him and he was adamant that they had done everything they could to make sure that he was not harmed.

At around two in the afternoon, an eight-year-old boy was shot and killed in Barkhor Square. The bullet entered his back and exited leaving a fist-sized hole in his chest. A section of the crowd carried his pathetic little body on a plank down Renmin Lu towards the TAR Government compound. Leading the throng was another eight-year-old boy. As they passed, a few of the marchers threw stones at the windows of Chinese shops and restaurants, but this was more like a funeral procession than a demonstration.

The procession stopped in front of the TAR Government compound. As a line of police moved to block the Fugate entrance to the compound, the sombre mood changed and gave way to anger. The mourners started tearing up paving stones to throw at the guards standing in front of Fugate. A handful of men attacked a passing truck and set it on fire. A few moments later, they attacked a jeep and set it on fire. The boy's limp body was left on a raised traffic island in front of the TAR Government compound.

Back at the barricades, I bumped into Guy Dinmore of Reuters who introduced me to his companions, Jasper Becker and Scott Douglas-Bellard, the new US Consul in Chengdu, in Lhasa on his inaugural visit to Tibet.

Around three o'clock in the afternoon, the police moved away from Barkhor Square and left the police station to burn itself out. Shortly afterwards, the crowd melted away, leaving behind only bloodstains, burned-out vehicles, empty shell cases, scattered piles of stones and rising columns of smoke.

There were around two hundred foreign tourists in Lhasa on the morning of the riot, but only about fifty of them were in or around Barkhor Square. Chinese press reports of the riot would eventually describe them as 'foreigners posing as tourists.'

Chapter 9

In the evening, many of the fifty or so foreigners who witnessed the riot met up in one of the Tibetan hotels in the centre of Lhasa. They swapped stories and shared their feelings of revulsion for what they had seen. They also discussed how to get the news of the riot and the deaths of the demonstrators to the outside world. No one had planned the gathering, it was a spontaneous reaction to a terrible event.

When I suggested that if the authorities found us meeting together, they would probably conclude that we were a group of organised agitators, there was a general agreement that any future meetings should be smaller and less noisy.

In the end, there was consensus that individuals in each hotel would meet in their hotels and that any information shared during those meetings would be pooled before being passed to the outside world. After the meeting, I cycled back to the Holiday Inn with Scott, Guy and Jasper. We ended up in the bar.

By the end of the day, most of the organised tour groups had left by plane for the safety of Chengdu. Because the telephone and telex lines out of Lhasa were closed, neither Jasper nor Guy was able to file their eyewitness accounts of the riot. Their frustration was very evident. They did not know that members of the international press corps had already met and interviewed some of the tourists who had escaped to Chengdu, having flown there from Beijing. Ironically, it was journalists who had not witnessed the riots who filed the first stories.

On my way back from the Lhasa Hotel to the Banak Shol Hotel at one in the morning, a pack of wild dogs stopped fighting and fornicating long enough to charge out to attack me. Two of them were still locked together. As the bitch ran out at me, the dog was forced to follow and was dragged along by his penis. The sound of his yelping was enough to wake the dead. I kicked out, pedalled away from them and continued past a smouldering motorcycle left in the middle of the road.

According to Tibetan folklore, these dogs were all reincarnated monks, which was why they were tolerated in the centre of Lhasa. Although the streets were deserted, the atmosphere was electric and I felt as though I could almost have been the last human on earth.

As the new day dawned, it seemed that the authorities had not yet come to terms with the situation. The police were noticeable only by their absence. Even the traffic police were absent. There was a real sense that the authorities had decided it would be best to keep a low profile in the centre of Lhasa. The lack of any sign of action also led me to wonder if there was a lack of effective leadership at TAR Government level. Could they really have they decided to do nothing?

Scott and I met up for breakfast at the Lhasa Hotel and returned to the scene of the riot to find a hive of activity in the burned-out police station. In those parts of the building that had been burned-out, looters had moved in and were busy salvaging any timbers that survived the fire. Equipped with sledgehammers and pickaxes, they were busily demolishing internal walls to extract door-frames, joists and window frames.

A few of the looters were sifting through the scores of charred police files that lay scattered over the floor in the hope of finding something of interest. There was little that was not mundane: registration forms, applications for residency permits, census forms and the charred remains of a propaganda film about coal mining in Tibet. There were no criminal or arrest records to be found.

As the looters knocked down one internal wall too many, part of the building collapsed forcing Scott and me to make a hasty retreat to the alley between the police station and the schoolhouse. As one of the first floor rooms finally caved in, our attention was drawn to a small boy trapped on a first floor window ledge. The room behind him had collapsed and he was screaming for help. I called up to him in English.

"Jump, I'll catch you!"

I think that he understood me, but he was too scared to move. Hearing more masonry falling behind him, he turned to see a rising cloud of dust filling the window frame that threatened to engulf him.

A passing Tibetan finally convinced him that he should jump and watched as the boy leapt out through the dust cloud into space. As I held out both arms to catch him, another small child appeared from behind me and ran off with my camera bag. With him went my camera, passport, cash and most of my photographs of the riot. So it goes. In a flurry of arms and legs, the falling boy landed in my arms, slithered to the ground and ran off unharmed, leaving me to discover my loss.

For a while, I searched the streets and alleys around the Jokhang in the vain hope of finding someone who could help me find the thief and get my bag back. Disbelief turned to resignation and finally to acceptance. The loss of my camera and most of the film of the riot left me with a sickening feeling in the pit of my stomach.

Scott and Guy Dinmore bought me a beer and lent me enough money to last me until I could get some funds transferred to Lhasa from my bank account in the UK.

Small children were still combing Barkhor Square and the surrounding alleyways for spent shell cases that they kept in cloth hats. It did not take them long to collect several hundred shell cases from a variety of weapons: 7 mm and 9 mm automatic pistols; Uzi-type low-velocity machine pistols; and high velocity Kalashnikov rifles. Some were already playing games of fives with the shell cases.

The Sera, Draping and Garden monasteries were closed to the outside world and roadblocks were set up, isolating Lhasa from the rest of Tibet. Only the road to the airport remained open, allowing those who could to escape.

In Renmin Lu, I bumped into the Tibetan journalist that I met in Yadong. He looked miserable.

"My Chinese colleague was very badly beaten up by the rioters yesterday. This was a very bad thing. He was just trying to do his job."

The news of the beating saddened me, because they had been very kind to me when I was under house arrest in the Chumbi valley.

One of the first signs of a response from the authorities was the appearance of a convoy of trucks filled with armed militia, led by jeeps with sirens wailing careering through the streets. The convoys first appeared in the late afternoon and continued through the night.

All over Lhasa, selected Tibetans were beaten and dragged from their homes in the middle of the night by teams of plain-clothed PSB officials. Many of them ended up in solitary confinement at Drapchi prison near Lhasa. Propaganda posters appeared everywhere. Public announcements were broadcast in Tibetan, Chinese and English, warning people not to get involved with "*SPLITTISTS*" [sic]. The atmosphere became tense and wild rumours swept across Lhasa.

"A monk from Jokhang monastery, shot through upper arm into his chest. He died in a Chinese hospital on/about 6 October."

"In addition to the dead that we examined, we treated twenty-three individuals who had been wounded. We treated sixteen people with bullet wounds. Four had leg wounds; one woman was shot in the breast; two had grazes, one of these was a monk from the Jokhang; one woman was shot in the buttock and had an exit wound in her shoulder. There were eight other people with lesser wounds in their arms, chests and so on."

"We treated two monks with burns and five people with contusions caused by beatings with rifle butts, stones, belts, shovels, etc."

Reports of the death of a second monk from Sera monastery remained unconfirmed. Several Tibetans claimed to have seen his body being loaded onto a truck and taken away by the police. At least one Chinese man was seen being beaten to death by the rioters. Several people described having conversations with Tibetans who claimed that they had seen a dead Westerner being loaded into the back of a truck. Again, this rumour could not be confirmed. The meeting broke up and we moved off in different directions.

When I knocked on the hotel door just before midnight because it was locked, the manager told me that all hotels had been told to "lock their doors at ten in the evening". However, as no official curfew had been announced he let me in anyway with a grin.

On my way to my room, a noise in the street below caught my attention. From a staircase window, I witnessed a man being dragged down the street by a group of plain-clothed PSB officers. They were accompanied by a small group of uniformed policemen. The man looked as if he had been beaten and slumped as if he was only semiconscious. They moved off and were consumed by the darkness.

The Barkhor Cafe in Barkhor Square became the focal point for the international press corps. Business was good for the café. All day long, they did a brisk trade selling countless cups of coffee and slices of chocolate cake. Loud speakers installed on telegraph polls broadcast warning messages from the government.

Day and night, convoys of armed troops careered though the city, led by PMP jeeps with sirens blaring. Lhasa began to feel like a city under siege. The atmosphere was electric and as each day dawned, it seemed that we were slipping ever closer to another moment of madness.

At around quarter to four in the afternoon of 6 October, fifty to sixty monks from Drepung monastery walked to Lhasa and marched towards the TAR Government offices in Renmin Lu. At first, the police let them march through several checkpoints. They called for the release of the monks arrested on 27 September, for independence and freedom for Tibet.

On the road opposite the Potala palace, the police finally moved in and arrested twenty to thirty demonstrators. Some were beaten as they were arrested and were thrown into the PMP trucks like so many sacks of potatoes. As the demonstration continued, more Tibetans joined in, bringing the number of marchers back to approximately sixty. The demonstrators halted in front of the TAR Government compound. At all times, the demonstrators were peaceful. They carried no weapons and marched with great dignity.

Ten minutes later about two hundred and fifty armed police arrived in trucks. Electric stun guns were used against the demonstrators for the first time. All the demonstrators were arrested and some were beaten with wooden batons. This time, they were all released before nightfall.

As rumours of further demonstrations abounded, the authorities moved a squad of plain-clothed policemen into Barkhor Square.

Another squad in riot gear marched across the square and eventually, marksmen appeared on the roof of the Tibetan hospital overlooking it.

Frustrated by the clampdown on communication lines out of Lhasa, Jasper flew back to Chengdu to file his stories, leaving Guy to cover events in Lhasa.

A Chinese newspaper article reported that Tibetan activists had taken pistols and rifles from armed policemen during the riot on National Day and had then used them to kill their fellow countrymen.

Senior officials in the TAR Government continued to offer conflicting accounts of events and even junior officials contradicted statements made by their superiors. There were several different sets of statistics for the number of killed and wounded Chinese troops and police officers issued by the Foreign Affairs Office. While they all contradicted each other at some level of detail, the most commonly issued statistics were six dead and nineteen wounded PSB officers.

News reached the hotel that the dead monk from Sera monastery was to be given a traditional sky burial. One of the journalists told me that Agence France-Presse had paid a young American to photograph the sky burial.

The American slipped out of Lhasa in the dead of night and evaded the police checkpoints. Later, he photographed the ceremony and watched as the monk's body was hacked into pieces with an axe so that the flesh could be stripped and fed to vultures. The bones were then ground up with *tsampa* and the vultures finished off the resulting mixture.

I heard that the police had re-arrested one of the doctors who had been arrested before the riots for carrying "Tibetan flags" and that they had given him ten days to leave Lhasa. This was probably for the best, as the secret police, normally dressed in black leather jackets with a peaked cap and dark glasses, were everywhere and would have tried to use him to lead them to the homes of wounded Tibetans. He left Lhasa on the tenth day.

Several young Westerners became embroiled in arguments with journalists over fees for photographs. Tensions mounted. One foreigner tried to sell a hand-written Tibetan statement that he had been given to take out of Tibet.

The journalists divided themselves into two groups. One centred on AFP and the other around Reuters. There seemed to have been some animosity towards AFP, seen as the least reputable of the press agencies.

The authorities then asked the journalists to leave Lhasa on a technicality. The letter of the law stated that they should have asked permission to visit Lhasa. In reality, permission to travel to open areas outside Lhasa was not normally required.

Ed Garden of the New York Times threw a party for the journalists on their last night in the Lhasa Hotel. He got very drunk and the party ended with Ed chasing security policemen around the corridors of the hotel with a camera. He became involved in a struggle and very nearly ended his career in China.

The following morning the journalists were driven to the airport and as they waited on the apron to board the Chengdu flight, they watched Jasper Becker coming down the gangway with another journalist. Guy Dinmore called out to him and advised him to talk to me before checking into the Lhasa Hotel.

Jasper found me and I helped him find a room in a suitable hotel. We then visited Lhasa Stadium, the site of the show trial and execution before the riot and saw the platform on which the prisoner had been shot. Next stop was Lhasa University. Based on what he had seen while covering the Seoul student riots in June, Jasper was convinced that we would find signs of student unrest on the campus. We found nothing. We discovered that only two percent of the students were Chinese and that the Tibetan language was being taught for the first time in a long while. As the students seemed to be very uncomfortable about being seen talking with us, we left.

The decision makers could not make up their minds. The bus services out of Lhasa were regularly shut down and reopened. The PSB opened and closed telex and telephone lines on a regular basis. Telephone conversations were monitored and lines cut if there was any mention of the riots. When one Danish woman tried to call home, her call was interrupted and she was told to talk only in English. PSB officials vetted all telex messages out of the Lhasa Hotel and blocked any telexes that referred to riots and those that were not in English or Mandarin.

I met young Nepal-based Tibetans in cafes who dropped hints of an armed anti-Chinese movement. They claimed that they did not want to rely on peaceful means to remove the Chinese from Tibet. Many had been in the Indian army. Several claimed to have volunteered for postings in the paratroopers and in the special forces. They said they also volunteered for postings to the Indian-Tibetan border. The Chinese supposedly retaliated by posting Tibetan conscripts to face them on the same border.

The madness continued, with odd incidents taking place nearly every day. Thierry, the gay French aristocrat and a smack user, who I had first met in Pakistan, attacked three PSB officers in a bar and put one in hospital. He was let off with a warning, after breaking down in court. The PSB officers had been drunk and had been trying to take his jewellery.

Scott and I appeared to have been assigned PSB minders. They spoke Mandarin with strong Chengdu accents and had not had enough time to adjust to the altitude. Scott suggested that we slowed down so that they could keep up. They were very embarrassed when he approached them to tell them of our decision. They did a lot of souvenir hunting as they followed us. I suppose that their wives and girlfriends expected something when they eventually got home.

Seven days after the riot, foreigners were warned that they must not photograph, watch or take part in disturbances. The authorities also warned both Tibetans and foreigners of the dangers of any involvement with "*splittists*". Simultaneously, friendly Tibetans warned us that there were more plain-clothed police on the streets than normal.

A spokesman at the Foreign Affairs Office told Jasper that three of Lhasa's top officials were absent on the day of the riot. One was in Boulder, Colorado; one in Beijing for the National Party Congress; and one was reported to have been on leave 'somewhere' for six weeks and no one knew when he was due back.

Journalists reported a general breakdown of leadership as officials gave conflicting accounts of what happened. Junior staff were happy to contradict senior staff behind their backs. The incoming journalists told me that there were a number of armed troops and high-ranking officers with 'Beijing accents' on their flight. They also told of military flights being brought in from Chengdu with at least a thousand new troops. Tibetans told me that the troops that had been stationed in Lhasa, about five thousand in total, were being replaced by troops from Chengdu. The Lhasa troops were being sent to the Sino-Indian border. This was not seen as a positive move for them. They left behind some very distraught girlfriends.

Policemen wearing riot gear were seen for the first time, but only a few were fully equipped.

Rumours abounded. On my way into Lhasa after a visit to one of the monasteries, Scott and I were flagged down by a distraught Westerner.

"I have just been told that fifty monks were machine-gunned to death behind the Potala at eleven this morning. Apparently they carted the bodies away, but there are still hundreds of shell cases everywhere."

We cycled to the Potala and found nothing but peace and serenity. Almost every day, someone had been told that something was about to happen. "There will be another riot tomorrow" or "monks from Drepung will march at six in the morning" or "the day after tomorrow" or "in a fortnight," etc. But nothing happened. Little by little, Lhasa returned to some semblance of normality, at least outwardly.

In the weeks that followed the riot, Scot and I visited each of the great monasteries in Lhasa: Drepung, Sera, Nechung and the Jokhang Temple and interviewed monks in a mixture of Chinese, English and some very basic Tibetan. We met monks who had been shot and monks who had friends who had been shot. We compiled statistics on the reported numbers of dead and wounded and counted the trucks in the convoys that tore through the streets of Lhasa, day and night. One convoy had fourteen trucks and around thirty-five soldiers in each, all wearing helmets and carrying Kalashnikovs. The convoy was led by motor cycles with sidecars carrying soldiers armed with heavy machine guns.

In a deserted enclave at the back of Sera monastery, Scott and I ended up sitting cross-legged on a wooden floor in a carpenter's workshop, drinking yak-butter tea with two shaven-headed Tibetan monks.

The monks tried to explain the complexities of the organisational structure of Tibetan monasteries under the Chinese. Since the arrival of the Red Army, each monastery had been organised as a work unit and the monks described as the `workers'. A two-tiered monastic and political organisational structure was put in place and the power of the state used to control the lives of Tibetan holy men and women.

The traditional monastic hierarchy continued, largely apart from the political order imposed by the state. As the bottom of the hierarchy were the Rapjung, novice monks, distinguishable by the brown robes they wore. Next in the pecking order were the Getsul, with a minimum age of twenty, but more usually between twenty-five and thirty.

The Gelong were of the same age, but were students studying for the equivalent of a degree. The general curriculum consisted of five basic courses, including dialectics, disciplinary rules and principal doctrines. It used to take a Gelong about twenty years to finish the course and qualify to sit for the examination for the degree of Geshe.

Above these was the Lama and finally the Abbot or Khanpo. The Khanpo was head of the very nucleus of the organisation, the Tatshang.

The Tatshang or 'Theological College' was responsible for everything pertaining to the monastery, but also had a say in certain important political decisions. Political guidance was provided by the Chinese Religious Bureau with thirty-five representatives, of whom seven were Chinese.

There were two groups of monks at most of the monasteries: 'official' monks, who were paid by the state and approved by the CRB under a quota system; and 'unofficial' monks, who were supported by the families, waiting for CRB approval. In 1987, the quotas for Drepung and Sera had been slashed. In previous years, the monasteries had a quota of ten each.

In 1987, Drepung was allowed no new monks and Sera only two. Perhaps this change had fuelled some of the anger that had sparked off the demonstrations. The fact that those monasteries linked to the Panchen Lama were significantly better funded that those traditionally linked directly to the Dalai Lama was another source of discontent.

The history of the Panchen Lama is one of a man torn between ideologies. In 1959, he supported the Communist takeover of Tibet and called for Tibetans to support the Chinese government. His views changed over the years. In 1964, he was arrested for criticising the Communist rule of Tibet. He was reinstated in his official positions in 1978 and made several appeals to the Dalai Lama, imploring him to return from exile in India.

The monks also told us that all the monks from Drepung who had been arrested were Gelong, studying for their Geshe. This may have been true, as none of the reports in the official newspapers had described any of the arrested monks as being novices, manual labourers or kitchen staff.

A chance encounter with an American scholar gave me a different perspective on events in Tibet. In his view, the Chinese had liberated the Tibetans from what was essentially a medieval feudal system controlled by the Lamas.

"These riots will not help the Tibetans. In fact, they could reverse the progress that had been made over the past ten years. The Chinese have been modernising the country and investing millions of dollars in infrastructure including roads, schools and hospitals. In the old days, most Tibetans were illiterate peasants. All these attempts to roll back the clock and create an independent Tibet can only make matters worse."

"Too many foreigners come here with a romantic view of the past who just do not understand the harshness of life here before the Chinese took over."

Posters proclaiming Public Announcement No. 3 were posted all over Lhasa in Tibetan, Chinese and English. Tibetans were warned that the authorities would mete out punishment to the troublemakers who "stir up support and participate in the disturbances manipulated by a few splittists".

Tourists were told, "foreigners are not allowed to crowd around watching and photographing the disturbances manipulated by a few splittists and they should not do any distorted propaganda concerning disturbances, which is not in agreement with the facts."

The poster also stated that the city authorities wished to "extende (sic) welcome to friends from the different countries in the World who come to our region for sightseeing, tour, visit, work, trade discussion and economic cooperation."

The TAR issued a statement "advising" all foreigners to leave Lhasa by 16 October. As the notice had not been posted in a public place, no one took any notice of it, but the PSB had stopped extending entry visas in Lhasa, leaving quite a few Westerners without valid travel documents.

The Nepalese border was still "open" but in reality, no more Westerners were being allowed into Tibet. They refused to extend my temporary travel document and would not let me call my bank in England to get funds transferred to me in Lhasa.

The TAR authorities acted as if they were becoming increasingly paranoid and eventually Lhasa's foreign workers found themselves facing accusations that they had helped ferment discontent.

"I don't know. He was like this when I came back from having a few drinks with my friends."

"Wake him up."

"I don't want to touch him. I might get sick myself."

I slumped back on my bed and took a large swig of beer.

"If I drink enough of this, I will not get sick. Do you want some?"

The PSB officer ignored me and tried to wake the Australian, but made little progress. He had not spent years studying at the military academy just to end up having to touch dirty, sick foreigners in a cheap hotel in Lhasa. In the end, he gave up and they all left.

The Chinese-controlled Tibetan Television News Service interviewed a Tibetan woman. She confirmed that she had witnessed Chinese troops firing at the rioters. When the footage was aired, she was shocked to see someone had edited her statement. In the edited version, she was seen saying that the troops had not fired. She was very upset.

When it was finally clear that my stolen possessions were not going to turn up and the international telephone lines were re-opened, I called my parents in England to ask them to arrange for some funds to be transferred from my bank account to the Lhasa branch of the Bank of China.

"Chris! Where are you?"

After the events of the past couple of months, it was strange to hear my mother's voice at the other end of the line.

"Lhasa, in Tibet."

"Goodness, what are you doing there? I thought that you would have been in Kathmandu by now."

"It is a long story."

"I know. I heard that you have been robbed and lost your passport, money and a camera."

For a second or two, I was taken aback, as I had not been in contact with my family since Chengdu.

"Yes, but how on earth did you know about this?"

She had answered as only a mother could.

"I am your mother. It is my job to know these things!"

Jasper later explained that he managed to file a story about me rescuing the boy from the burned-out PSB building and that the story had been published in the Guardian. Somehow, news of this had been picked up by my long-suffering parents. My mother had also asked a family friend to ask his son, who worked for Reuters, to see if he could get any news about me, which all helped my mother know where I was and what I had been doing.

Three days after speaking to my parents, the funds had been transferred from my bank account in England to the Lhasa branch of the Bank of China. The bank even called my hotel to let me know that the funds had arrived.

With the funds needed to travel to Kathmandu safely in my pocket, I realised that the time had come for me to leave Tibet. All that remained was find a way to the Nepalese border before the winter snows made the route impassable. I had to hope that I could find transport and that the PSB would open the Lhasa-Nyalam route long enough for me to make it to the Friendship Bridge. On the other side of the bridge was the town of Kodari, the gateway to the outside world.

Chapter 10

As I started to plan my departure, the Tibetan television station broadcast statements by some of the monks arrested on 27 September. The monks were seen stating that the Chinese had done good things in Tibet and for the Tibetan people. The announcer stated that nine of the twenty-one arrested monks had been released. He then introduced a film showing them being greeted by the abbot in front of an audience of several hundred men in uniform.

Scott and I decided to try to talk to some of the released monks in the morning to find out more about what had happened to them in Drapchi prison and why they had demonstrated in the first place.

On what I thought was to have been my last full day in Lhasa, Scott and I cycled the five miles from the centre of Lhasa to Drepung monastery and were taken by an old monk into the Great Debating area.

Shaded by leafy willow trees, the open-air area was filled with monks sitting in groups debating Buddhist doctrine with great energy. Some sat cross-legged on the ground and others stood, occasionally slapping their hands in sweeping, dramatic motions to try to distract their debating protagonists.

The old monk introduced us to three of the nine released monks and who told us that they had been freed on 28 October. The monks told us that they had only been beaten on the first day and that they had been held in solitary confinement except for daily three-hour "re-education" sessions.

They were fed twice a day with simple *momo* dumplings and water. They had been threatened with more beatings if they refused to appear on television giving pro-Chinese statements. They told us that the Chinese had also asked them to speak out against the Dalai Lama and that they had refused.

This appeared to suggest that the Chinese had dedicated a team of around 11 re-educators to this task, assuming that each re-educator processed two monks a day. On the day of the monks' release, one more monk had been arrested. There was no news of the monks remaining in prison.

On their return to Drepung, the released monks had been treated as heroes, at least by some of the younger monks. The monks we met were between twenty and twenty-five and did not look like well-educated scholars. It did not seem possible that they were all Gelong. I could not see any outward signs of either maltreatment or malnutrition. All three monks were very reluctant to talk with us, but their brother monks were very keen.

At night, we listened to Jasper's short-wave radio to see if any of our reports had made it through the Chinese news blockade. Journalists from Beijing and even Hong Kong called the Banak Shol Hotel to get updates on the situation, using the prearranged name 'Bill Ellis' to avoid problems with authorities. The PSB listened in and occasionally cut the line.

Several Tibetans insisted that a dead Western male had been seen being bundled into a PMP truck. This story was never confirmed. No Westerners were reported missing, but a search of the hotels revealed that the PMP had removed luggage from one room, under what seemed suspicious circumstances. The move was initially seen as confirmation that a Westerner's death was being covered up by the authorities. However, the owner of the luggage turned up four days after the riot and confessed that he had been hiding from the PMP for an unrelated reason. His luggage was eventually returned and he left Tibet.

Little by little, life in Lhasa returned to some degree of normality. The shops and markets re-opened and for the time being, the protests stopped. While little had been accomplished in the short term, the world had been reminded of the Tibetans' desperate desire to be freed from what they believed to be the occupation by the Chinese of their homeland.

As I watched the sun setting to the west of the massive bulk of the Potala for the last time, I was alone with my thoughts and at peace. The events of the past two months had left me with very mixed feelings about China and Tibet. On one hand, I felt a profound sense of sadness and had memories of a violent riot that would haunt me for the rest of my life. On the other hand, I had seen great beauty in my travels to the Chumbi valley and had even been forgiven for trespassing by the officers of the PSB. I knew that I would always remain deeply affected by the desperate plight of a forgotten people and their struggle for freedom.

Leaving Lhasa by bus seemed the easiest way out and the good news was that the bus service to the Nepalese border was running. With the funds sent to me by my father, I bought a ticket and all too soon found myself back on the road to Gyantse. The bus was packed with Chinese workers, Tibetans and a few foreigners.

Once again, I faced the long climb over the high passes and the bruising effect of the unmade road on my aching joints. The still, turquoise waters of Yamdrok Lake were as peaceful and calm as Lhasa was not. After another 90 kilometres of bone-crunching unmetalled road, the bus arrived in Gyantse.

There was just time in the late afternoon for me to explore Gyantse one more time. On one of the main streets, I came across a small boy sitting in an old packing crate that served as his playpen. He looked up at me with soulful eyes, resigned to a long wait for his mother. Around the crate were signs of the treats that he had been given to keep him amused: a single sweet wrapper and an empty carton of fruit juice. A small dog peered into the box, keeping an eye on the boy while his mother was occupied elsewhere.

Perhaps this small boy, hemmed in on all sides, kept amused with some token treats and watched over by a guard dog, symbolised the future of Tibet. My hope was that as time passed, the parents of the boy would no longer believe that they needed the services of the guard dog.

After a night in a dormitory, I climbed back onto the bus which clattered out of Gyantse in a cloud of dust and headed west. To the south lay the Himalayas, stretching from East to West as far as the eye could see. Their presence was almost oppressive and it seemed almost impossible that there could be a way through these endless folds of rock, snow and ice.

The first rest stop was in Shigatse, the second largest city in the Tibet Autonomous Region. Dominating the city, the Tashilhunpo monastery was in pristine condition and looked as though it had escaped the predations of the Cultural Revolution.

In fact, during the Cultural Revolution, the homes of around four thousand monks had been destroyed. The monastery itself was not damaged as much as any of the other monasteries in Tibet. This had a lot to do with the Panchen Lama, who unlike the Dalai Lama had remained in Chinese-controlled territory.

It is perhaps an irony that in 1980, the Chinese government admitted that mistakes had been made in Tibet and set about trying to implement a number of reforms designed to improve the lives of Tibetans. The reforms were seen by many as being too little, too late.

At the same time, the migration of Han Chinese into the region was accelerated. Most stayed in the larger towns where they set up businesses and opened hotels. Many Tibetans thought that they had little say in the changes that were taking place. Resentment against Chinese rule grew and the bitterness that came from feeling something precious had been taken from them erupted into the violence seen in Lhasa on 1 October 1987.

Turning south east off the main road between Nyalam and Shigatse, we drove down a deep valley to drop off some monks. While the driver went off to find some food, I took the time to visit the Sakya monastery and its great library, a survivor of the worst ravages of the Cultural Revolution. Home to the Sakya School, one of the four major Schools of Tibetan Buddhism, the monastery is a solid structure set in a grey landscape, dominating all in sight with its presence. Completed in 1073 AD, the monastery was built in the same era as the cathedrals that dominate many cities in England.

The great library was a long, dark and narrow corridor, lined with shelves full of ancient texts in Tibetan, Chinese, Mongolian and Sanskrit, some of which are believed to have been written for Kublai Khan. There were over 84,000 scrolls and texts, making this one of the greatest libraries of the ancient world.

Despite being isolated in a remote corner of the Tibetan plateau, Sakya has been a centre for learning and teaching for centuries. Central to many Asian religions and philosophy is the idea that when we die, our spirit begins life in a new body. Depending on the moral quality of the previous life, the new body could be an animal or human. The ideas and holy learnings of the Sakya messages flowed out from Tibet, to be carried deep into China, Mongolia and more recently, to India and the United States, changing the lives of countless people over the ages.

In Buddhism, the idea of reincarnation is that the death of one personality leads to the creation of a new personality. The teachings of Sakya tell us that the only way to break out of this cycle of repeated reincarnation is to meditate, which frees the mind from the obstructions that obscure the path to Nirvana.

My path took me though fertile valleys with fields of ripe barley, to the village of Tingri. The road was unmetalled and in places heavily damaged by floodwaters. Despite the poor condition of the road, nothing stopped our progress and the bus battled on over potholes and boulders.

As the bus approached Tingri, drivers heading towards Lhasa signalled our driver to stop and told him that the road to Nyalam was blocked by an unseasonal early snowstorm. He was not impressed and continued, giving me hope that the road would have been cleared enough that we could get through. Everest to the south was hidden in dense cloud.

At Tingri, the police had blocked the road and the driver decided that we should return to Lhasa, which we had left five days before.

Seven days travelling in a bus along unpaved roads is an exhausting experience, but I had to find a way back to the Nepalese border, which meant retracing my steps and facing the 700 kilometre journey back to Lhasa.

Four days later, I found myself back in Lhasa, which gave me the chance to see old friends again. My main goal though, was to find a way of getting through the snow that blocked the route beyond Tingri.

With the help of a couple from Tasmania, I found a driver with a four-wheel drive Toyota Landcruiser who was willing to take a chance, as well as our money and drive us to the Nepalese border.

Once again, I set out on the road to Gyantse, this time with travelling companions and in some comfort. The Landcruiser ate up the miles and made good progress. After just two days, we reached Nyalam, only to discover that we could go no further in the Landcruiser as most of the road ahead of us had been washed away.

Our driver collected his dues in the knowledge that he faced the 830 kilometre return trip to Lhasa in the morning. He also knew that as the Chinese had closed the border to people travelling from Nepal into Tibet, there were no passengers to help fund his return trip. He shook our hands and bade us farewell. He left behind our memories of his good nature and broad Tibetan smile.

After a night in a truck stop dorm, we set out together for the border. The 30 kilometre walk to the border town of Zhangmu took the best part of a day. Starting at 13,000 feet, we descended to around 7,500 feet above sea level. The route followed the remains of the road, which traced twisting hairpin bends down the face of a steep-sided valley.

Where the road had been destroyed by landslides, the route took us along makeshift paths that skirted unstable fields of debris. As we descended, the climate changed becoming milder, more humid and almost subtropical. The harsh scenery of the high Tibetan plateau gave way to cloud forests that draped themselves across the lower slopes of the Himalayas like a blanket. As in the Chitral valley, the silence of the forests was broken only by the sound of water rushing down narrow channels to the river in the valley.

Arriving in the border town of Zhangmu just before sunset, there was little to do other than find a room, eat and sleep, as the border crossing to Nepal had closed already. After spending a day on my feet, I slept well and woke up feeling ready for the last stage of my journey out of China. All that remained was to clamber down the steep track from Zhangmu to the Friendship Bridge across the Bhote Koshi River.

The last hour or so of walking in silence through the dense vegetation that hemmed in the track was a time to reflect on a journey across a great country emerging from so many years of turmoil and on the cusp of becoming a modern industrialised nation.

legs were little more than skin and bone, held together by straining strands of rope-like muscle. Rickshaws carrying entire families competed for space with bicycles piled high with household goods, women, children, goats and trinkets. Cows wandered aimlessly through the melee. Some lay sleeping by the side of the road. Some slept on the road.

When the bus finally stopped, I discovered that I could barely walk. My knee and hip joints were frozen with pain. Running down the mountainside, with a heavy pack on my back, had bruised my joints so badly that I needed help getting off the bus.

Finding a hotel in Kathmandu was easy enough. For a couple of days I rested and little by little, my battered joints recovered enough for me to be able to explore this great city of the Emerald Valley.

Chapter 2

After two months in Tibet, the wealth of different cuisines to be found in Kathmandu set my taste buds on fire and overwhelmed my digestive system, which had grown accustomed to a simple diet. Nepalese restaurants selling dhal bhat stood shoulder to shoulder with European cafes set up to cater for tourists with more international tastes: coffee from Colombia; apple strudel from Germany; crepes from France; and delicate pastries from Vienna. Except of course, it was all actually made in Nepal with local ingredients.

Eager Patagucci tourists milled around looking for bargains in the many shops selling fake antique necklaces and bracelets made of silver inlaid with lumps of polished turquoise. Travel agents offered cheap flights and every kind of Nepalese adventure from treks around the Annapurna Circuit to white-water rafting on the Trishuli River. Running between the tourists small children held out their hands to beg for loose change, sweets or pens.

A chance encounter with Nitza, a tall, dark-haired Californian drew me away from the ordered chaos of Kathmandu to Nagarkot, a small village famous for its sunrise view of the Himalayas. It was a pleasure for me to have a travelling companion after so many months of being on my own. It was also a relief for me to escape the noise and bustle of Kathmandu for the calm and beauty of this perfect place.

The hotel staff woke us up just before dawn and we sat outside on our veranda wrapped in blankets to watch the rising of the sun light up the distant Himalaya. A cheerful member of the hotel's staff served us breakfast, a delight of sweet milk-tea and porridge, which helped keep the chill at bay. Sitting on rattan chairs, we waited in the darkness for the first sign of dawn. A sense of anticipation fell upon us and we waited in silence as the Earth turned slowly to face the sun.

As the day dawned, the hulking shadows of the distant Himalaya became alive, with the highest peaks glistening against the background of a silver sky. The valley slopes beneath the hotel appeared, revealing neat rows of emerald-coloured terraced fields and a simple farmhouse overlooking the void to the west. To the farmer and his family, the daily awakening of the distant peaks was part of the routine of their daily lives. For me, it was a precious gift.

From there, my journey carried me gently back to my family. After Nepal, came a few weeks in Thailand. The days passed in a blur; a week living in a beach hut on Phi Phi Island; Christmas Day in Chang Rai; and New Year's Day in Bangkok. Leaving Thailand behind, I flew to Hong Kong for a brief sojourn to see old friends and prepare for my departure to the States.

On the long flight from Hong Kong to San Francisco, I had time to reflect on the Day of Tears in Lhasa and the few messages from family and friends that had found me as I travelled across the face of Asia.

The deaths in Lhasa seemed so pointless. While they had raised international awareness of the problems faced by Tibetans, no nation was likely to do anything to make their lives any better, because doing so would have been seen as a challenge by the Chinese state. The growing economic power of the Chinese dragon was something that no foreign government could ignore.

The reality of their situation was that only the Chinese state had the ability to make their lives any better. Attempts by the outside world to try to tell China what it should do seemed likely to make matters only worse. The Chinese state had to choose to do what was right for the Tibetans. Perhaps they could learn from the Americans and their attempts to improve the lives of native Americans. Given the long-term impact of white settlers on native American peoples, I could only hope that the Chinese would do better.

The biggest irony of the events of the Day of Tears was that the Chinese state had already set out along this road and had recognised that mistakes had been made in the past. The protests had given the more conservative elements of the Chinese state an excuse to reverse some of the reforms that the more liberal elements had been implementing.

Who could feel anything but sadness for yet another ancient culture facing an uncertain future? Tibetan Buddhism has fascinated and inspired people around the world for centuries, but it is a belief system that is out of step with the beliefs of people living in a modern, materialistic world.

Time alone will tell if the Tibetans will be able stay to true to their ancient system of beliefs in the face of a changing world. So far at least, Tibetans in and outside of Tibet have mostly preserved their Tibetan culture and remain fiercely protective of their beliefs. More than most people with a culture under threat from the modern world, the Tibetans have succeeded in getting support for their cause from around the world. Perhaps, the Tibetan system of beliefs will survive because it offers a very different perspective to those seeking a way of escaping from trials of life in a material world.

When my thoughts turned to my family and friends, I knew that I had to pick up from where we had left off and knew that for some friends, this would not be easy. Being away for more than a year creates a certain distance that is sometimes too great a bridge to cross.

At least I knew that I was going back to see my father, who had been seriously ill for many years. He had become frail, but had found the strength to write to me as I travelled. His letters came with news of the family, but also served to inspire me to continue when times had been hard.

He understood the joy that comes from opening a letter from friends or family when you are far away from home. He never normally wrote letters, least of all lengthy letters, but he managed to write to me regularly. I still treasure those letters above all.

My good Californian friend, Nitza, found me somewhere to rest and recover in a small "garage" apartment in La Jolla within earshot of the breakers of the Pacific Ocean. Southern California was Paradise on Earth, but I had to get home.

Before I left, I tried to call the Zephyr one last time, only to find that I was too late. Her mother told me that she had left Wisconsin again and was working as a nurse in Guatemala. Any chance of meeting up with her in Madison had gone.

A few days later, I boarded a plane that carried me back to England.

Chapter 3

Back in London, I found employment and soon life returned to some semblance of normality. There were no mountains, no riots and no open skies. The routine of commuting and earning a living took over. Instead of living on the open road, I found myself installed in a rented room in a house in Tulse Hill, south London.

Despite the underlying restlessness that had driven me on my travels, I tried hard to settle into the daily grind of urban life. My dreams, on the other hand, taunted me with memories of the open road, vast landscapes and the freedom to travel as my mood suited me.

Being back in my own world helped me reflect again on the sights and experiences of a journey that had absorbed a year of my life. The transition from a nomadic to a settled way of life was not easy at first, but as once new experiences like commuting became routine, little by little I settled down.

As I travelled to and from work in London on the train, I would sometimes day-dream, lulled by the rocking motion of the carriage and imagine that I was standing on a high mountain on the roof of the world with nothing but the wind in my face between me and the deep blue sky. I also thought about the suffering of those families who had lost relatives in the Lhasa riots and those brave souls who had been injured.

Fleeting images of Afghan refugees trying to survive in their camp along the banks of the raging Kunar River trickled into my mind as I tried to concentrate on my work.

It was sobering to think that as I enjoyed the freedom of the London, young monks were still being arrested in Tibet and imprisoned in the Drapchi Prison near Lhasa. From time to time, I would come across new accounts of brutality against the Tibetans in the press and stories about the continuing inward migration of Han Chinese. From what could I see from afar, the Tibetans somehow had managed to rise above these challenges and continued to struggle to retain much of their way of life and identity.

In one respect, the erosion of their ancient way of life continues and there is a risk that it will only be a matter of time before their culture is preserved only as a tourist attraction. On the other hand, there are signs that in China, a religious reawakening is taking place and that Buddhism is once again finding a home in the hearts of the Chinese people.

Outside of Tibet, exiles have established colonies in which they try to live their lives in the Tibetan way, but will even those havens survive the all-pervasive onslaught on ancient cultures that is endemic in the modern world? Perhaps the strength of Tibetan Buddhism and the Tibetan way of life will keep the forces of change at bay. Time alone will tell.

Pressure groups in the West continued to publicise the problems faced by Tibetans, but their efforts did little more than strengthen the case for those in the Chinese state who fear foreign interference in their affairs. The more liberal thinkers in the Chinese state found that their efforts were undermined by the efforts of these protesters.

One day, after a hard day's work, the phone rang as I was changing into jeans and a t-shirt. The call was answered by Gavin Gray, the journalist who shared the house with me.

"Chris, it's for you."

I picked up the phone. As I had only just moved to into the house, I had not given my phone number to any of my friends, so I could not think who might have called. It was a mystery.

Puzzled, I picked up the phone. "Hello?"

"Hi Chris, it's me. How are you?"

It was the Zephyr. Her voice was as sweet as ever, reminding me of a line in a poem by Alexander Pope: "Soft is the strain when Zephyr gently blows."

The Zephyr had phoned my mother, who had given her my Tulse Hill telephone number. Our conversation flowed like honey, as we shared memories of our time together and talked as old friends about the past times and the present.

A letter followed, opening with the news that the Zephyr was moving to California to live with a carpenter. After her call and the warmth of our conversation after so many months of silence, those words came as a shock and echoed like the dull thud of a closing door in an empty house. I could not face reading the rest of the Zephyr's letter. With great sadness, I put the letter back in its envelope and tucked it away in a drawer with all the others.

Although I had settled down to life in England, I did not give up searching for the next journey. Whenever possible, I found opportunities to travel, mostly on business. To meet the demands of my job, I found myself traveling to the United States, South America, the Middle East and every now and again to the Far East. On one such trip, I circumnavigated the world in nine days. I also moved to west London, married and became a father of two beautiful children.

One day, eleven years after my last conversation with the Zephyr, I found myself sorting through a pile of old papers. Half-hidden in a pile of letters from my father, the Zephyr's letter slipped out and fell to the floor. Picking up the scattered pages, I started to read the letter again and this time I read every word.

On the very last page, she told me that she wanted to continue our relationship and that she looked forward to hearing from me. She wanted to get to know me again.

The words rose from the paper and were as fresh as on the day on which they had been written. The trouble was that I had waited eleven years too long to read the whole letter and had closed a door that could have stayed open. The Zephyr had reached out to me with words written from the heart and I had not listened.

This moment of realisation was broken when my six-year-old daughter appeared in a rush of excitement.

"Hurry up Dad, we need to go or we will be late."

She stood in the doorway, her blond hair shining in the glow of the morning sun and looked at me with her mother's eyes.

I put the letter back into its envelope, pausing for a moment to reflect on what might have been and what had been.

"Let's go!"

A small hand grasped my finger and pulled me towards the study door.

My son and wife were waiting for us at the bottom of the stairs, their smiles lighting up the gloom of our hallway. Outside, the sun shone and the sound of songbirds filled the air.

The warmth of the Zephyr had once breathed new life into a long dormant dream of a journey, but as that journey ended, this gentlest of breezes had passed on, as is the way of the wind from the west. When the Zephyr's words finally tumbled into the light, they found themselves alone in a world that had changed. They had arrived too late.

One day perhaps, in a quiet moment, the wind from the west will blow once more and I will catch the faintest breath of the song that once stirred me to travel along the Divine Highways.

be in keeping with Nepal's proposal to proclaim Nepal a peace zone and with China's declared support for such a proclamation. The peace zone proposed by Nepal would have a much greater impact if it were to include Tibet and neighbouring areas."

Warming to his audience, the Dalai Lama continued.

"The establishing of a peace zone in Tibet would require withdrawal of Chinese troops and military installations from the country, which would enable India also to withdraw troops and military installations from the Himalayan regions bordering Tibet. This would be achieved under an international agreement that would satisfy China's legitimate security needs and build trust among the Tibetan, Indian, Chinese and other peoples of the region. This was in everyone's best interests, particularly those of China and India, as it would enhance their security, while reducing the economic burden of maintaining high troop concentrations on the disputed Himalayan border."

This was a point that was bound to irritate the Chinese. Too much had already been invested in Tibet to make any wholesale withdrawal possible. The loss of face would have been too great.

In his second point, he demanded that the population transfer of Chinese into Tibet, pursued by the government in Peking in order to force a "final solution" to the Tibetan problem by reducing the Tibetan population to an insignificant and disenfranchised minority, be stopped.

The Dalai Lama described an on-going process of ethnic cleansing that threatened the survival of the Tibetan people. Given that he was addressing representatives of a nation that had already completed a similar process with the indigenous tribes of American Indians, he at least had an audience that understood the subject.

"The massive transfer of Chinese civilians into Tibet in violation of the Fourth Geneva Convention (1949) threatens the very existence of the Tibetans as a distinct people. In the eastern parts of Tibet, the Chinese now greatly outnumber Tibetans. In Amdo province, for example, where I was born, there are, according to Chinese statistics, 2.5 million Chinese and only 750,000 Tibetans. Even in so-called Tibet Autonomous Region (i.e., central and western Tibet), Chinese government sources now confirm that Chinese outnumber Tibetans."

The Dalai Lama told congress that the Chinese population transfer policy was not new. It had been systematically applied to other areas before. Earlier in this century, the Manchurians were a distinct race with their own culture and traditions. Today only two to three million Manchurians were left in Manchuria, where 75 million Chinese had settled. In Eastern Turkestan, which the Chinese now call Xinkiang, the Chinese population had grown from 200,000 in 1949 to 7 million, more than half the total population of 13 million. In the wake of the Chinese colonisation of Inner Mongolia, Chinese numbered 8.5 million, Mongols 2.5 million.

Congressmen heard that in the whole of Tibet in 1987, the 7.5 million Chinese settlers outnumbered the Tibetan population of 6 million. In central and western Tibet, now referred to by the Chinese as the "Tibet Autonomous Region", Chinese sources admitted the 1.9 million Tibetans already constituted a minority of the region's population. These numbers did not take into account the estimated 300,000 - 500,000 Chinese troops in Tibet, 250,000 of them in the Tibet Autonomous Region.

The Dalai Lama made it clear that for the Tibetans to survive as a people, it would be imperative that the population transfer was stopped and Chinese settlers return to China. Otherwise, he said, Tibetans would soon be no more than a tourist attraction and relic of a noble past.

In his third point, he declared that fundamental human rights and democratic freedoms must be respected in Tibet. The Tibetan people must once again be free to develop culturally, intellectually, economically and spiritually and to exercise basic democratic freedoms. The latter point seemed to have overlooked the lack of any democratic process in the feudal system overthrown by the Communist Party when China occupied Tibet.

Congressmen listened intently as he drew their attention to human rights violations in Tibet.

"Human rights violations in Tibet are among the most serious in the world. Discrimination is practised in Tibet under a policy of "apartheid" which the Chinese call "segregation and assimilation". Tibetans are, at best, second-class citizens in their own country. Deprived of all basic democratic rights and freedoms, they exist under a colonial administration in which all real power is wielded by Chinese officials of the Communist Party and the army."

He acknowledged that the Chinese government had allowed Tibetans to rebuild some Buddhist monasteries and to worship in them, but then reminded Congress that serious study and teaching of religion was still forbidden. He told them that only a small number of people, approved by the Communist Party, were permitted to join the monasteries.

"While Tibetans in exile exercise their democratic rights under a constitution promulgated by me in 1963, thousands of our countrymen suffer in prisons and labour camps in Tibet for their religious or political convictions."

In his fourth point, the Dalai Lama stated that serious efforts must be made to restore the natural environment in Tibet. Tibet should not be used for the production of nuclear weapons and the dumping of nuclear waste.

"Tibetans have a great respect for all forms of life. The Buddhist faith, which prohibits the harming of all sentient beings, whether human or animal, enhances this inherent feeling. Prior to the Chinese invasion, Tibet was an unspoiled wilderness sanctuary in a unique natural environment. Sadly, in the past decades, much of the wildlife and the forests of Tibet have been destroyed by the Chinese. The effects on Tibet's delicate environment have been devastating. What little is left in Tibet must be protected and efforts must be made to restore the environment to its balanced state."

"China uses Tibet for the production of nuclear weapons and may also have started dumping nuclear waste in Tibet. Not only does China plan to dispose of its own nuclear waste but also that of other countries, who had already agreed to pay Peking (sic) to dispose of their toxic materials. The dangers this presents are obvious. Not only living generations, but future generations are threatened by China's lack of concern for Tibet's unique and delicate environment."

In his fifth and final point, the Dalai Lama said that negotiations on the future status of Tibet and the relationship between the Tibetan and Chinese peoples should be started in earnest.

His words were heard in Lhasa as a message of hope.

"We wish to approach this subject in a reasonable and realistic way, in a spirit of frankness and conciliation and with a view to finding a solution that is in the long term interest of all: the Tibetans, the Chinese and all other peoples concerned. Tibetans and Chinese are distinct peoples, each with their own country, history, culture, language and way of life. Differences among peoples must be recognised and respected. They need not, however, form obstacles to genuine co-operation where this is in the mutual benefit of both peoples. It is my sincere belief that if the concerned parties were to meet and discuss their future with an open mind and a sincere desire to find a satisfactory and just solution, a breakthrough could

With as much speed as they could muster given the effect of Lhasa's thin air, they both pedalled towards the centre of Lhasa. As they got closer to the sound of the shooting, they encountered hundreds of panicking Tibetans running in the opposite direction, away from Barkhor Square.

At the crossroads by the Friendship Store, they passed hundreds of armed soldiers standing around, apparently waiting for orders. Every journalistic instinct must have told them to keep going. Gradually, they realised that they were about to bear witness to an important moment in Tibetan history. They pedalled on to Barkhor Square and found several thousand angry Tibetans besieging a burning police station.

Chapter 7

After a breathless dash, I finally reached the entrance to the Jokhang Temple and met an elderly British couple in a hurry to leave. They paused for a moment to tell me about their experiences on the roof of the temple. Despite the continuing riot behind us, they did not seem concerned for their own safety, but they were very upset.

"We were on the roof of the temple when the shooting started and witnessed the reaction of the monks around us."

The woman was calm, but very angry. Her husband stood by her and stared at me with sadness in his eyes.

"We saw monks taking a weapon from an armed policeman on the roof of the Jokhang Temple. They did not try to use it. Instead they tried their best to smash it to pieces."

Clearly moved by what she had seen, the woman glowered in the direction of the police station.

"This was all so terrible, dreadfully terrible and so unnecessary. The Tibetans are a peaceful people."

Later, a Tibetan told me that a group of angry demonstrators had stoned the policeman to death.

The police killed at least seven Tibetans in the space of a couple of hours. Sixteen more were shot and wounded. Nine had been beaten by police officers wielding rifle butts, belts and shovels. A couple of monks were burned, one very badly.

A few minutes later, a diminutive Englishman clutching a first aid kit followed by a very agitated Tibetan approached me.

"Do you know anything about first aid?"

He had a very direct manner and was clearly in a hurry. Peering at me from behind his glasses, he seemed anxious for me to offer to help.

My first aid training had usually been good enough in the past, but had always been basic. I nodded and tried to explain that my knowledge of first aid was limited.

"Any first aid knowledge would help. Please can you come with us?"

The Tibetan led us into the maze of narrow alleys behind the Jokhang and through a gateway into an open courtyard. He closed the ancient outer door behind us and then took us across the courtyard into an unlit room. At first, I could make out nothing in the darkness, but as my eyes adjusted to the gloom, I saw a man in his thirties sitting in a chair.

As I got nearer, I could see that he had a bullet hole in his leg, just above his ankle. The wound was not bleeding much and there was no sign of an exit wound. The entry point was rectangular, with one end slightly rounded. Judging from the size of the hole and my limited knowledge of firearms, I guessed that he had been shot with a low-velocity 9mm weapon, possible a pistol. It looked as if the bullet had entered lengthways. I was no expert, but it could have been a ricochet or perhaps the bullet had been tumbling when it hit. A round from a high-velocity weapon would probably have taken half of his lower leg away.

This not the first time that I had been faced with injuries that I did not know how to treat. When I was only seventeen, I bunked off school with two friends and tried to hitchhike to the nearest cinema. After failing dismally to get a ride, it became clear to us that we were going to miss the film. To make matters worse, the skies opened up, drenching us with freezing rain.

When the rain turned into hail, we began to wonder if we would have been better off catching a bus. At that moment, a truck coming towards us jack-knifed and careered into a mini-van that had just passed us. The remains of the mini-van spun across the road and came to a stop on the verge some fifty yards away from us. The truck ended up embedded in a house.

We ran to the mini-van to find that the engine been ripped off its mountings and had been driven through the bulkhead into the space occupied by the driver. Despite horrific injuries, the driver was still alive. His head had been split open revealing part of his brain; one of his legs had been severed above the knee by the engine block; and the steering column had penetrated his ribcage on impact. As the mini-van came to a halt, he had been thrown backwards, which tore him off the steering column, pulling a section of lung out of his ribcage onto his waistcoat.

Not knowing what else to do, I covered him with my coat in an attempt to keep him warm and took his pulse. I was just in time to feel him die.

The feeling of helplessness that overwhelmed me then, returned as I saw the hole in the poor man's leg. The wounded Tibetan shivered as the combination of shock, pain and terror worked its way throughout his body. After a brief discussion about how best to help him, we made a start. Our first action was to ask his wife for a blanket to keep him warm.

At the request of the family, I tried to photograph the Englishman cleaning and dressing the wound. As the batteries in my camera were close to the end of their life, they took an age to charge up the flash. Everyone waited in the gloom for the green light on my

The main body of the international press corps arrived from Beijing on the morning flight from Chengdu. It was a good turnout, with photographers and correspondents from the New York Times, Agence France-Presse, United Press International, the Washington Post, the Christian Science Monitor, the London Times and the Paris Tribune. Representatives of the Japanese press were noticeable only by their absence. The journalists brought with them some of the spirit of the foreign correspondents sent cover a crisis in a fictional African state in Evelyn Waugh's satirical novel "Scoop".

Eventually, Scott and I paid a visit to the main PSB offices in the outskirts of Lhasa to report the loss of my passport. As expected, no-one had handed in my passport or my traveller's cheques. The interviewing PSB officer, Mr Cheng, issued me with a temporary travel document and told me to report to him every day in the unlikely event that something *"turned up"*.

Scott told me that he had seen Cheng at the Foreign Affairs Office and that he thought that Cheng was a senior PSB officer.

Propaganda loud speakers were installed in a building under construction facing Barkhor Square. Announcements were broadcast in English, Tibetan and Chinese telling people of the new regulations. Everyone was warned against getting involved with "*splittists*".

Journalists attending briefings in the TAR compound were convinced that they had picked up a strong sense that individuals in authority were frantically trying to blame each other, suggesting that the leaders of the central Tibetan Government really had lost control of the situation. The civilian leadership seemed to have fallen apart and in the vacuum that followed, Lhasa waited uneasily as the military stepped in and gradually took control.

The madness and paranoia that had spawned the riots remained as a miasma that seeped under doorways and into hearts. At one of the nightly meetings in a Tibetan hotel, I found myself confronted by a small group of earnest, but misguided young men. They had convinced themselves that I was a British Intelligence officer and were keen to exclude me from the nightly meetings. The atmosphere was unpleasant and the evidence against me was set out before the assembled backpackers. One by one, my accusers addressed the assembled backpackers. Their words tumbled out like wasps on a summer's day.

"He told me that he used to work for NATO. But he never told me what he did."

"I have seen his maps. They looked like military maps to me."

"I happen to know that he has two passports. I have seen them."

Even my roommate had decided to speak against me. As a lawyer, he really should have known better. The tirade continued anyway.

"How come he just happens to have bumped into an American diplomat? It must be more than just a coincidence."

And so on. My short hair must have been the real give-away.

To them it all seemed so black and white. I could have told them that my role in NATO was as an international civil servant in the Administration Office of a NATO agency and that my ex-colleagues would have laughed at the very idea of me being thought of as any kind of spy. I could have told them that my "military" maps were no more than Operational Navigation Charts available from any decent map shop. I could have told them that I had a second passport as the result of a failed attempt to get a visa from the Sudan. The trouble was that all attempts by me to deny their accusations were taken as further proof of the fact that I was indeed a spy. Only a real spy could have come up with a cover story as good as mine.

I could only hope that these rumours did not reach Cheng in the Public Security Bureau. He was certainly looking for spies.

As paranoia set in the mood of the group darkened and the meeting started to feel like a witch-hunt, with me as the main suspect.

Moving on from the espionage debate, a young American doctor informed everyone that my suggestions for treating the Tibetan with a bullet wound in his leg were completely wrong and that I had put the man's life at risk. He did not offer a better course of action, nor did he mention the involvement of the other Englishman, who had actually cleaned the wound and stood shoulder-to-shoulder with my accusers.

There were a number of individuals who spoke out in my "defence" and in the end, no conclusion was reached. Nevertheless, I left the meeting feeling sadder and a little wiser.

Later, a Vietnam veteran told me not to worry.

"In Vietnam, soldiers wounded in a fire-fight were initially treated with field dressings and morphine. Then they were packed off to a field hospital for surgery. From what I heard, you guys at least cleaned and dressed the wound and you did your best to keep the man warm. There is not much more that you could have done, as you are not a doctor. I guess taking him to a Chinese hospital was not really an option in the circumstances."

The Western doctors reported that they had treated the Tibetans who had escaped from the police station. They had to deal with deep head wounds and confirmed that the wounds were consistent with the kind of wounds caused by shovel blows.

Afterwards, one of the doctors told me "a lot of stitching was needed."

One of the doctors then read out a summary of the injuries they had treated since the riot.

"I am going to start with the dead that we examined."

The doctor continued in a curiously detached voice, reading aloud from a small notebook.

"Boy, aged sixteen to eighteen, killed by a blow by a blunt instrument to right-hand side of head sometime between one and two o'clock."

"Boy, aged sixteen to eighteen, shot in head and killed between one and two o'clock in front of burners outside the Jokhang. The bullet continued through his head and into the shoulder of the man standing behind him."

More than one witness stated that they had seen bits of the dead man's cranium and brain sprayed over the wounded man's face.

"Boy, seven to eight, shot in back from window of police station."

The sight of his tiny body being carried by the crowd of mourners was among the most poignant sights that day.

"Man, age thirty plus, shot in thoracic cavity through his heart. The shot had been fired from above and had left an entry wound in his shoulder and a large exit hole in his groin."

"A monk from Nechung monastery, shot in head while escaping from police station. The shot must have been fired from roof of the police station. The damage to the skull indicated that the shot was from a high-velocity rifle."

"A monk from Sera monastery, shot in head and abdomen as he escaped from the Police station."

They expelled the three British language teachers that they had employed to teach English. One was forced to pay a large fine for running an illegal library of novels and travel books in one of the Tibetan hotels and for possessing photographs of the Dalai Lama. The library had been running for sixteen months and was subject to regular police inspections. Another had his passport confiscated and was questioned occasionally by the PSB. His attitude was more belligerent and he refused to pay his fine. Eventually, the PSB allowed him to leave.

The teachers were not the only foreigners that the authorities wanted out of Lhasa. As the PSB had stopped issuing Alien Travel Permits, the flight to Chengdu remained as the only legal way out of Lhasa.

One afternoon, I met two Tibetans who claimed to have come from India. They were well-educated and spoke very good English without any trace of an accent. I was sure that they were both monks. They wore secular clothing and vanished when I told them that the PSB had followed me when I was with Scott.

The Chinese-controlled Tibetan language newspapers reported that an amnesty would be granted to any demonstrators who gave themselves up before 19 October. The article also stated that films confiscated from Westerners were being developed and used to identify the people who had been demonstrating.

On one of my many visits to the PSB to ask if my passport had turned up, the Head of the Foreign Section, Mr Cheng, asked me if ILFORD HP5 film should be developed as a colour or a black and white film. The roll was clearly marked 'MADE IN ENGLAND.' I had no idea how the film should have been developed. I just knew that it was not my film.

One hot afternoon after a long cycle ride, Scott and I ended up in a bar run by a Chinese man with a great sense of humour. A German sitting near the bar joined us. As the barman poured our beer, Scott informed the German that I was half-Chinese. Surprisingly, he was not convinced.

Turning to the German, Scott continued. "He has a Chinese passport because his mother was Chinese."

The German was still not convinced.

"Chris, show him your passport."

I pulled out my temporary Chinese travel permit and showed it to the German, who was thoroughly confused and asked the barman to translate for him. The barman took my travel permit and read it carefully.

"Does that say that he is really Chinese?"

The barman kept a perfectly straight face and joined the joke.

"Oh yes. It says his mother was Chinese."

The barman handed back my travel permit and served another customer. He had spotted that we were having fun and saw no reason why he should get in the way. The German was dumbfounded and still very suspicious.

"You do not look very Chinese to me...how was it that you speak English so good?"

"I am only half Chinese and half Russian. My mother came from Xinkiang province. I was orphaned and ended up being adopted by an English family."

The German left believing that I was half-Chinese. The barman roared with laughter and then said something to Scott in Mandarin. Scott's reply had them both doubled up with laughter.

"What did he say? What did you say?"

"He wanted to know why my Mandarin is so good given that I am not Chinese and why your Mandarin is so bad given that you are Chinese."

"What did you tell him?"

"I told him that your mind is too slow to speak Mandarin properly."

More beers followed. Scott was also keen to point out that I was not always dressed with the greatest degree of sartorial elegance. He had a point. In an attempt to maximise the amount of space in my bags for the supplies needed for my trek down to the Chumbi valley, I had packed only one pair of trousers. On the days when these were being laundered, I wore fluorescent pink Chinese leggings, with sporty white stripes down both sides. They did look ridiculous on me, but at least they fitted, which was more than could be said of leggings in any other colour on sale in the market.

Scott was keen to point out that the fashionable Chinese male tended to wear such leggings under their trousers.

"They do not wear leggings as a replacement for their trousers!"

Those Westerners who had stayed were showing no sign of leaving. Many of them had decided to stay to be witnesses to any further events. This was not quite what the authorities wanted.

One night, around midnight, word spread though the hotel that PSB officers were moving from room to room, checking passports, visas and travel permits. This alarmed my Australian roommate, whose visa had expired. He asked for my help.

As the sound of their room checks drew closer, my Australian roommate curled up in his bed and started to whimper as if in pain. I emptied out my backpack on to the floor and scattered empty beer bottles around me. There was a rap on the door, quickly followed by the sight of four uniformed PSB officers crowding into the room. One of them spoke good English. He was terse, but polite.

"May I see your passports?"

Feigning drunkenness, I staggered across the room and pulled out my temporary travel permit.

"This is all I have. A boy stole my passport outside that burned-out building in Jokhang Square."

The PSB officer frowned and peered at my permit.

"When are you going to leave Lhasa?"

"When I can get some money. The boy took my travellers' cheques as well. I need to call England to get some more money, but the phones here don't work."

He was clearly appalled at my drunken state and the squalor of our room. On cue, the Australian moaned and doubled up as if in pain.

"What is the matter with him?"

"He is sick."

"Has he seen a doctor?"

For the most part, the Chinese people I had encountered were warm, good-natured and had welcomed me into their lives. They worked hard and received precious little back for their efforts. Their world was structured by a State that was learning to cope with the scale of the challenge of running a country as immense as China.

Most people lived simple lives, without the luxury of the amenities considered essential in the West. In the summer, the heat and lack of power for air-conditioning forced people to leave their homes and live in the streets. In the depth of winter, they shivered because of the lack of heating.

Many people had endured a lifetime of turmoil and were only just getting used to a more settled way of life. The older generation had lived through wars, revolutions and the days of the warlords. Many of them still lived in fear of the Chinese State, which in turn feared the people.

Progress had been made, as I could see that the doors that had kept foreigners out of China were beginning to open, letting in outsiders and new ideas. I had seen that the Chinese state was still wary of foreigners, understandably so given their past and recent history.

Perhaps someone had realised that the new ideas would have travelled to China anyway, flowing in along the once dead trade routes that marked out the Silk Road.

The state also seemed to want visiting foreigners to see only those parts of China in which they had the greatest pride. Many of the other, more mundane tracts of the Middle Kingdom were still closed to foreigners. Throughout my travels across China, I sensed a tension between those who wanted to see a more liberal and more open China and those who feared the consequences of change.

The official face of the Middle Kingdom revealed a character that was complicated. At times friendly and helpful, but with a darker side that growled when threatened. One day, it would be good to go back and see how this great nation had developed.

At passport control, my temporary travel papers were taken from me by a sour-faced man in a green uniform and high-heeled shoes. There was then no turning back and as soon as I could, I walked towards the border and Nepal.

Crossing the Friendship Bridge, I was swamped by mixed emotions. On one hand, I felt that the bridge was there to help me escape from what seemed to be a brutal, uncaring regime. At the same time, I was leaving behind a people who had welcomed me into their lives with open arms. The border crossing also marked a mental end to a journey that had started many years before in a ploughed field in rural England. There would be more journeys in the future, but this one had ended.

With a dark, heavy feeling in my heart, I crossed over to Nepal and found myself in the frontier town of Kodari.

Part 6 - A time for reflection

Chapter 1

As several kilometres of the road to Kathmandu had been washed away by floodwaters, the only way out of Kodari was by foot. At first, the prospect of yet another day of walking filled me with a sense of desperation.

Shouldering my pack, I set off along a rough track that ran alongside the river and as my mood lightened, started an adrenaline-charged downhill race with a Nepali porter. At first, we walked, then jogged and finally started to run. The effect of two months at high altitude gave me a level of stamina that carried me downhill as if I was floating on air. I hopped over boulders; skipped over streams and kept pace with my running mate as we sped down the valley. I felt exhilarated and ran even faster, barely stopping to rest.

Eight kilometres later, a makeshift bus stop marked the end of the race and I was soon heading south towards Kathmandu in a battered Nepalese bus.

As we neared Kathmandu district, the volume of traffic on the road increased and the driver was forced to overtake slow-moving traffic, always waiting until the last minute to avoid the incoming traffic. It was too much for me, so I tried to sleep. As the bus slowed down in the outskirts of Kathmandu itself, I woke up and peered out of a grimy window into a crowded street.

My first impression was of the energy of the place, with roads and pavements teeming with vehicles and people bustling through their lives. The bus filled with the scent of burning incense rising from roadside shrines and the heady aroma of exhaust fumes from thousands of two-stroke engines. Motor cycles jostled with heavily-laden handcarts pushed by painfully thin men. Their bodies told of a lifetime of physical labour spent living in poverty. Their arms and

© 2016 by Chris Frost

All rights reserved. No part of this document may be reproduced or transmitted in any form or by any means, electronic, mechanical, photocopying, recording, or otherwise, without prior written permission of Chris Frost, 26 Bolton Road, Chiswick, London W4 3TB.

Printed in Great Britain
by Amazon